PRINCIPLES OF ORGANIZATION

Under the General Editorship of
ROBERT K. MERTON
Columbia University

THEODORE CAPLOW
Columbia University

Principles of Organization

Harcourt, Brace & World, Inc.
New York / Chicago / Burlingame

Library of Congress Catalog Card Number 64–25626

Printed in the United States of America

ACKNOWLEDGMENTS   The author wishes to thank the following for permission
to reproduce materials in this book:

American Sociological Association: For the table on page 197 from Robert
K. Merton, "Social Structure and Anomie," *American Sociological Review,*
Vol. III, No. 5 (October, 1938).

Free Press of Glencoe: For the table on page 98, reprinted with permission of
the publisher from *Working Papers in the Theory of Action* by R. F. Bales
and E. A. Shils. Copyright 1953 by The Free Press, a corporation. For
quotations on page 358 from *Community Conflict* by James Coleman. For
quotations on pages 320–22, reprinted with permission of the publisher
from *The Functions of Social Conflict* by Lewis A. Coser. Copyright 1956
by The Free Press, a corporation. For the table on pages 46–47, reprinted
with permission of the publisher from *A Comparative Analysis of Complex
Organizations* by Amitai Etzioni. Copyright © 1961 by The Free Press of
Glencoe, Inc.

Harcourt, Brace & World, Inc.: For quotations on pages 92–97 from *The Human
Group* by George C. Homans. Copyright, 1950, by Harcourt, Brace &
World, Inc.

Harvard University Graduate School of Business Administration: For quotations on pages 255–56 from *Administering Changes: A Case Study of
Human Relations in a Factory* by Harriet D. Ronken and Paul R. Lawrence.

Robert K. Merton: For the table on page 197 from Robert K. Merton, "Social
Structure and Anomie," *American Sociological Review,* Vol. III, No. 5
(October, 1938).

Prentice-Hall, Inc.: For Figure 2–2 on page 55 from Raymond Villers, *Dynamic
Management in Industry.* © 1960, Prentice-Hall, Inc.

Princeton University Press: For quotations on pages 128–29 from *The Society
of Captives* by G. M. Sykes. Copyright 1958, Princeton University Press.

Routledge & Kegan Paul, Ltd.: For quotations on pages 320–22 from *The Functions of Social Conflict* by Lewis A. Coser.

University of Chicago Press: For Figure 2–3 on page 57, reprinted from *The
Folk Culture of Yucatán* by Robert Redfield by permission of The University of Chicago Press. Copyright 1941 by the University of Chicago Press.

University of Minnesota: For Figure 2–6 on page 73 from the University of
Minnesota Organizational Chart, Institute of Technology, 1953. (The university is now revising the arrangement shown.)

Preface

The argument of this book is that human organizations are a class of natural phenomena the attributes of which are not time bound or culture bound, and the workings of which are orderly, so that the sociology of organization is more susceptible to development as a science than other branches of sociology. This thesis grows less contentious year by year. It is not yet accepted by all students of society, but among those involved in the empirical study of organizations it is nearly taken for granted.

This volume is an effort to demonstrate that a single theoretical model, although rough and incomplete, can be used to analyze organizations of any type or size, regardless of their cultural or historical location, and to generate useful predictions. The effort is small, but the need for such knowledge is overwhelming. The major threats to civilization's survival are undoubtedly products of the organizational environment, as are our small, real hopes of universal felicity.

The manuscript was expertly scanned at various stages for sociological errors by Robert K. Merton, Raymond W. Mack, Clifford Kirkpatrick, Robert Dubin, and Reece J. McGee; for lapses of judgment and historical perspective by Jacques Barzun; and for mistakes in usage and sense by Elaine Binno, Violeta Mitinas, Harriet Caplow, and my amiable and literate daughters, Deborah and Ann. Despite these multiple precautions the initial stock of faults was large enough to provide the reader with as many as he has patience to notice, and for these I must claim sole credit.

Englewood, New Jersey   T. C.
July 14, 1964

v

Contents

PRINCIPLES OF ORGANIZATION

Introduction

WHAT IS AN ORGANIZATION?

We begin with definition: an organization is a *social system* that has an *unequivocal collective identity,* an *exact roster of members,* a *program of activity,* and *procedures for replacing members.*

Not all sociologists will agree entirely with this definition, but it does not diverge sharply from prevailing usage. We know the following about the minimum elements by which we recognize an organization:

1. A *social system* is a set of persons with an identifying characteristic plus a set of relationships established among these persons by interaction. As in other fields of analysis, in order to describe a system we must be able to identify all the elements that belong in the system and exclude all those that do not belong. We must be able to use consistent criteria to do this. In a social system, we must be able to identify the persons involved—which means that they must have at least one distinctive characteristic in common—and must also be able to show that these people are related by interaction.

2. The *unequivocal collective identity* is the organization name, which is recognized by all of its members and by many outsiders as well. The name often conveys a good deal of information about the organization's purposes, location, and

1

affiliations, and it enables collective action to be taken without confusion. In the felicitous language of the old law books, "though it is the will of the King that erects the corporation yet the name is the knot of its combination, without which it could not perform its corporate functions." [1]

3. The *exact roster of members* enables an organization to identify its members, and at any given moment, to divide the human race into members and nonmembers of the organization.

4. The *program of activity* may be very extensive or very brief, but in every instance at least some definite goals are specified, and activities that are intended to achieve these goals follow some sort of calendar and are arranged in advance.

5. *Procedures for replacing members* cover the recruitment of new members and the transfer of old members from one position to another.[2]

As we proceed through our discussion, the reader—if our joint enterprise is successful—will come to recognize the characteristics of organizations at a glance. We hope to demonstrate that human organizations comprise a single natural class with many distinctive features.

By the definition given at the outset, a family, a political party, a work crew, a criminal gang, a platoon or regiment or army, a bank, a board of commissioners, a government department, a neighborhood church, a labor management council would all be specimens of organization, as would a baseball team, an order of knighthood, a steel company, a bridge club, a government, a symphony orchestra, a college sorority, and a band of terrorists. If our assumptions about social organizations are valid, these very diverse entities will resemble each other in certain significant ways—for example, they will initially respond to an outside threat by increased solidarity and they will overestimate their own prestige compared to that of nearby organizations of the same type.

[1] Sir William Blackstone, *Commentaries on the Law of England*, ed. W. D. Lewis (Philadelphia: Rees, Welsh, 1902), Book I, Chapter 18, p. 475.

[2] In a few special cases, outside recruiting is discontinued at some point in the life of an organization: for example, a college class when it passes into the alumni stage or the Shakers when they took their momentous decision to initiate no more outsiders. This has the effect of extinguishing the organization within a predictable time.

It is also necessary for the purposes of this discussion to identify social systems that are *not* organizations. Many of these are enormously important, but they lack an organization's capacity for unified purposive activity. Among the more conspicuous "non-organizations" are races and ethnic groups (they have no programs), social classes (their collective identities are not unequivocal and their rosters not exact), cliques and play groups (they lack a collective identity), interest groups such as "liberals" or "old-fashioned conservatives" (they have no rosters). Solitary individuals and pairs are not considered to be organizations, since they do not display a network of interaction.

The modern *nation* is not an organization, but the *state* is. The professions and the skilled trades differ from other occupations in being organized. A clique or a crowd may transform itself into an organization by adopting a collective identity and setting up a program. It also happens, although rarely, that an organization dissolves but leaves an informal group as its successor.

These distinctions are not made for the pleasure of making distinctions. There are great and demonstrable differences between a group of people who interact with each other and have common interests and the same group of people welded into an organization. An angry mob is not an army. A widespread grievance is not equivalent to a *coup d'état*.

WHAT THIS BOOK IS ABOUT

Although the sociology of organization still stands somewhere between folklore and science, with each passing year the likelihood becomes greater that this area of social inquiry can be described by linked propositions, analytical models, and statements carrying high probabilities. The field of organization appears more orderly than most other branches of social science, but there are major obstacles to its development.

Organizations are complex creatures. The gross description of specimens requires nearly endless toil and time. Fine dissection of even the smallest organization is a *tour de force*.

Other obstacles to this emergent science are created by its students. The language used by sociologists to describe collective behavior is highly impressionistic, evocative, and intellectually stimulating, but it is often imprecise. For example, definitions of the group—the simplest of all social systems—often fail to specify whether groups are composed of *people* or of *behavior* or of *relationships*. The study of organizations is sometimes restricted to large organizations without any attempt to specify the minimum size of a large organization. Only by close attention to the niceties of definition will it be possible to make clear statements about our subject matter.

Another kind of problem carries over from fields of sociological inquiry that make use of categories created by the observer for analytical purposes. These categories refer to verifiable events, but the classification is subjective—or at least nonverifiable. We can never be certain that two observers will use these analytical categories in exactly the same way. Is Moravian pietism an embodiment of the Protestant Ethic or a denial of it? Is suburban "togetherness" favorable to anomie (because it attenuates the citizen's relationship to the larger community) or the opposite of anomie (because it stresses intimate relationships and primary group controls)? In such sociological studies—as in literary criticism or theology—the observer has a wide choice of frames of reference. The sociology of organization, however, appears to be closer to botany or to qualitative chemistry in that the choice of observational categories is rather narrow and becomes narrower as observations accumulate.

Even with our present limitations, it is notable that students who start with the most dissimilar assumptions are forced to take account of certain phenomena—*status consistency* and *boundary maintenance,* for example. The slow, steady convergence of viewpoints is the most striking impression one gains by reading such recent collections of papers as Mason Haire's *Modern Organization Theory,* Albert H. Rubenstein and Chadwick J. Haberstroh's *Some Theories of Organization,* Charles P. Loomis' *Social Systems,* and Amitai Etzioni's *Complex Organizations,* or research summaries such as Allen Barton's *Organizational Measurement.*

The purpose of the present volume is to systematize some of what is known about organizations in general, even at the cost of ignoring much that is known about particular organizations.

ORDER OF TREATMENT

Chapter One, "The Nature of Organizations," begins with the problem caused by the lack of a common language and tries to show how fundamental terms can be unequivocally defined. This is followed by a catalog of the possible modes of relationship between organizations and of organizations with their own components. The chapter covers the special case of the community and the implications of size for organizational analysis. It concludes with a review of other approaches to organizational taxonomy.

Chapter Two, "Organizational Structure," is an essay in anatomy. Beginning with the table of organization, which records positions, statuses, interactions, and activities, it goes on to other structural features, such as procedures, norms, roles, symbols, and artifacts, and it tries to explain how they fit together and why they are mutually essential.

Chapter Three, "The Organization in Motion," introduces an analytical model based on the four variables of status, interaction, valence, and activity. The model is applicable to any organization at any time or place. The relationships introduced are only sketched in this chapter. They will be taken up and reconsidered in different lights in the later chapters.

Chapter Four, "Organizational Effectiveness," wrestles with the bête noire of organizational analysis—the intractable and inescapable problem of evaluating achievement. The implications of organizational rationality are considered at length, and the variables by which organizational effectiveness can be measured are introduced as stratification, integration, voluntarism, and achievement. The chapter investigates their interrelationships and then moves on to problems of stability and points-of-stress. The question of perfectibility, the extensive empirical evidence on factors related to effectiveness and productivity, and the paradox of authority versus democracy are explored.

Chapter Five, "Making the Organization Man," describes the socialization process through which new members of an organization or new incumbents of a position acquire the appropriate self-images, involvements, values, and accomplishments. The primary modes of socialization are described: schooling, training, apprenticeship, mortification, trial and error, assimilation, co-option, conversion, and anticipatory socialization. Five case studies are examined in detail to show the effects of different modes of socialization. The chapter concludes with an analysis of deviant adaptation.

Chapter Six, "Organizational Sets," contains the first extensive discussion of these sets and their structural parts, with special attention to prestige orders and their social functions and to the diffusion of institutional patterns. The phenomena of status exchange, self-aggrandizement, and status consistency are described in some detail.

Chapter Seven, "Organizational Improvement," considers the multiple efforts of the modern industrial corporation to raise its own effectiveness and tries to evaluate the sociological discoveries to which this effort has led. The topics surveyed include scientific management, the human-relations approach, field theory and group dynamics, Theory Y, integration problems, marginality, rule-making and rule evasion, communication networks, individual adjustment and maladjustment, the design of incentives, the planning of emotions, personnel selection, job enlargement, status schisms, and bureaucratization.

Chapter Eight, "The Utopian Formula," examines the old formulas for conflict-free organizations, drawing on the literature of imaginary utopias and on four well-documented historical experiments: a Benedictine convent, the Oneida Community, an Israeli kibbutz, and the Hutterite Brotherhood. The pros and cons of utopian organization are considered at some length.

The final chapter, "Organized Conflict," considers conflicts in which the protagonists are organizations. These are divided into three major types—episodic, continuous, or terminal—which are shown to differ with respect to their sequences, strategies, and modes of resolution. Another variant of the analytical model is proposed—based on the variables of subjugation, insulation, violence, and attrition—and used to examine the empirical evidence. The chapter closes with an application of organizational theory to international conflict.

PRIMARY ASSUMPTIONS

Our entire discussion of organizations will be based on certain primary assumptions.

1. *All human organizations, regardless of the time, place, or cul-*

tural setting in which they occur, belong to a single class of a natural kind.[3] There are two reasons why scientific specimens of any kind —butterflies, mountains, molecules, or social groups—need to be classified. The first purpose of classifying a specimen is to make it possible to talk or write about it without creating unnecessary confusion. Scientific taxonomies assure a degree of agreement among observers. Perfect agreement would mean that every butterfly, mountain, molecule, or social group could be given exactly the same label by every scientifically trained observer. This objective is approached, if not fully achieved, in some of the natural sciences.

The other reason for classifying specimens is quite different. It often happens that all the butterflies or mountains or molecules or social groups that are grouped together under a class label have many more features in common than are necessary to identify a specimen of the class and affix the label. The label may then provide a high *yield of information.* That is, the observer who gathers a small amount of information about the specimen—just sufficient to affix the label—is rewarded by a vast amount of surplus information—everything that is known about the class to which the specimen belongs.

The great social anthropologist Radcliffe-Brown describes such high-yield classes as "classes of a natural kind."

> If you group together two or more things by reason of the fact that they have certain elements in common, and you find you have a class about which nothing is true except one common property *X*, then it isn't of much use to you. If, however, every member of the class has also characteristic *Y*, and nothing else has it, you have then *a relationship between X and Y*, and a class which becomes significant. Then, if you find you have made a class such that you can discover properties *V, W, Z*, etc., all of which are characteristic of this class and of no other, then you obviously have a class of very considerable importance, particularly if you have reason to suspect that you can prolong the list indefinitely. When you establish a class of that kind in phenomenal reality, then you can say you have a class of a natural kind.[4]

[3] As previously defined, an organization is a social system having an unequivocal collective identity, an exact roster of members, a program of activity, and procedures for replacing members.

[4] A. R. Radcliffe-Brown, "The Nature of a Theoretical Natural Science of Society" (Chicago: University of Chicago Press, 1948) (mimeographed).

It is surprising, gratifying, and not altogether explicable that social organizations—identified and labeled by means of the four criteria given above—seem to comprise a class of a natural kind. In other words, there are a great many things we can say about *any* social organization as soon as we have labeled it—for example, that its members overestimate its importance for outsiders.

2. *Organizations have certain features that do not occur at all in other collectivities.* For example, although the status order of an organization *resembles* a system of social classes, the most superficial inquiry reveals essential differences. The status of an individual in an organizational position is more definitive. The organization explicitly prescribes whether his position is superior, equal, or inferior to those other positions with whose incumbents he is required to interact. There is always an ascertainable status difference between a given organizational position and the highest position in the same organization. Small gains and losses in status are followed by immediate modifications in the activity and the interaction pattern of the people involved. None of this is true for social stratification in the general society. A subject's social class may not be described in the same way by any two observers and sometimes cannot be objectively determined at all.

3. *Organizational events are orderly and regular in the sense that certain antecedents always lead to certain consequents, regardless of place, time, cultural setting, or the personalities of the participants.* The detailed exposition of this assumption must wait for later sections (especially Chapter Three), where it is explained, for example, how an increase in interaction between unequals, when the amount of joint activity remains unchanged, leads to a decrease of the superior's power. If this principle is valid, it will hold as well in a Polynesian burial society as in a team of brain surgeons or in a nursery school.

4. *Organizations are subject to a double principle of limited possibilities.* First, there are only a few ways an organization can be structured to accomplish a given purpose. Second, once provided with a structure, an organization can perform only a limited number of functions and these in a somewhat circumscribed way. The limitation of possibilities is both gross and subtle. It is easy to see that there are only a limited number of possible family forms (nuclear, patriarchal, extended) or of marriage arrangements (monogamy,

polyandry, polygyny).[5] It is not so easy to trace the complex linkage between despotic leadership and the formation of peer groups.

It is an interesting experiment to look for new forms of polity beyond the six types described by Aristotle in the *Politics* as monarchy, aristocracy, constitutionalism, tyranny, oligarchy, and democracy. Remarkable ingenuity is required to find a seventh type in the real world, although fictional alternatives such as anarchy or juvenocracy are easy to construct.

The limitation of possibilities is inherent in the mutual dependence of organizational form and function. Among the signs of this dependence are the development of very similar institutions without historical contact, for example feudalism in Europe and in Japan, and the predictable appearance of characteristic problems in certain organizations, such as red tape in a bureaucracy. Many of Machiavelli's remarks about power in Cesare Borgia's Romagna are equally applicable to machine politics in Chicago. The broker's role in the pricing mechanism in a Malay fishery [6] is duplicated on the floor of any stock exchange. Indeed, the mutual dependence of form and function in organization is so familiar that we take it for granted. We ordinarily expect that an organization the form of which is held constant, such as a legislature, will continue to show certain continuities of activity and interaction even when the society around it has been transformed beyond recognition.

THE SIVA VARIABLES

At various points in the following pages, the significant situations of organizational life will be described by means of four variables denoted by the letters S, I, V, A. They appear first in Chapter Three with reference to the pair relationship between any two positions in an organization and are there called status, interaction, valence, activity. They appear again in Chapter Four in connection with the organization's effectiveness in coping with its environment, under the names of stability, integration, voluntarism, and achievement.

---

[5] ". . . or rules of descent, residence or mate selection. Murdock is able to demonstrate a whole system of linkages among these elements with the use of cross-cultural data." See especially the theorems in Chapter 7, "Determinants of Kinship Terminology," George P. Murdock, *Social Structure* (New York: Macmillan, 1949).

[6] Raymond W. Firth, *Malay Fishermen* (London: Trench, Trubner, 1946).

In Chapter Five, the socialization process is visualized as the acquisition of self-images, involvements, values, and accomplishments. In the final chapter, situations of conflict are described in terms of variables that resemble the measures of cooperation with signs reversed: subjugation, insulation, violence, and attrition. These several sets of terms with the same initial letters are only a mnemonic device. They are to remind the reader that a single analytical model is proposed for the description of situations that differ greatly in scale and outward appearance but are thought to have the same basic pattern.

This pattern is activated whenever two or more individuals, having some common goals and some disparate goals, engage in joint action. In each of these situations, the S variable refers to some aspect of the relative *strength* of the parties, the I variable refers to the degree of their mutual *influence* within the relevant action system, the V variable refers to the *volitional* component of the situation, and the A variable measures the results of the joint *action* of the parties within the relevant context.

There are many different ways of expressing this fundamental insight, some of them much simpler than others. The very simplest formulation is that when individuals or groups act together over some period of time their relationship can be usefully described by measuring the stability of their joint behavior, their sharing of information and attitudes, the feelings they develop in connection with each other, and their joint impact on the environment. (The reader versed in Parsonian theory will note that the four variables correspond to his "actor's orientations to objects," which are, respectively, responsible, intellectual, expressive, and instrumental.) When we come to the intricate but apparently regular interdependences of the four variables, it is plain that these ought to be expressed in mathematical formulas. Just as plainly, we lack appropriate mathematical formulations for these matrices, the variables of which are quantitative but cannot be calibrated. Small changes in status or interaction can be detected and verified; but no one has yet devised a way of comparing numerical measurements of status or interaction in one situation with the corresponding measurements in another situation. The implications of this problem will be pursued through later chapters. For the moment, we turn aside to consider some other features of organizations.

CHAPTER ONE

The Nature of Organizations

THE PROBLEM OF TERMINOLOGY

The modern literature on social organization shows impressive agreement about such matters as the importance of interaction and the universality of group norms. If we turn to psychology, social psychology, and anthropology for information on the behavior of organized groups, we will find these subjects discussed in much the same vocabulary. The difficulties begin when we try to use this language for analytical purposes. Nuances that were almost imperceptible become flat contradictions when the terms are applied to data. Thus, an organization is sometimes defined as a "set of related individuals" and sometimes as a "pattern of relationships." These two statements look enough alike to pass muster on a casual reading, but when the term *organization* is used in statements describing actual situations the two meanings turn out to be irreconcilable. A set of live people is by no means the same as a set of relationships.

It is conceivable that a body of knowledge might develop without an adequate terminology. Indeed, it seems to have happened in this field. When the research results of different investigations are reformulated in a common language,[1] they often show more agreement than their authors originally recognized. When the language of one theorist is laboriously translated into the vocabulary of an-

---

[1] For example the studies described in George C. Homans, *Social Behavior: Its Elementary Forms* (New York: Harcourt, Brace & World, 1961).

other, many apparent differences disappear. Nevertheless, it cannot be denied that scientific progress has been impeded by the Tower of Babel in which the organizational sociologist works,[2] and the following attempt to clarify the distinctions among *groups, organized groups,* and *organizations* should be viewed in relation to this perennial problem.

GROUPS AND ORGANIZATIONS

A *group* is composed of three or more people, all having a common identifying characteristic and each interacting with some or all of the others.

The *organized group* is a particular variety of social group. It is based on the repetition of interaction among members, and the resulting relationships have some degree of permanence. The organized group is a continuous group. It can disperse, reassemble with the same membership, and repeat the relationships established between pairs of positions. Unorganized social groups can also disperse and reassemble, but the correspondence of the new group with the old remains in doubt because of changes in membership or relationships.

In very small groups, particularly those consisting of three or four persons, the repetition of a social situation may occur by chance, as in the case of people who meet at the same corner every morning to take the same bus. As the number of persons increases, it becomes less probable that the same situations can recur by chance. A point is quickly reached at which the repetition of situations involving the same persons and the same relationships among them must be arranged by specific mechanisms.

The first requirement for the repetition of situations is an *un-*

---

[2] "We live by being ambiguous," writes J. Robert Oppenheimer, "by not settling things because they do not have to be settled, by suggesting more than one thing because their co-presence in the mind may be a source of beauty. But in talking about science one may be as ambiguous as ever until we come to the heart of it. Then we tell a fellow just what we did in terms that are intelligible to him, because he has been schooled to understand them, and we tell him just what we found and just how we did it. If he does not understand us, we go to visit him and help him; and if he still does not understand us, we go back home and do it over again. This is the way in which the firmness and solidity of science is established." *Encounter,* October, 1962, p. 6.

equivocal roster of membership. At an absolute minimum, members must be identifiable to each other. As a practical matter, they are usually also recognized by nonmembers and may go to considerable pains to exhibit their membership by symbols and insignia. It is virtually impossible to identify membership except by reference to an entity with a name. While it is possible to imagine exceptional circumstances—such as a criminal conspiracy—in which members might be identified without the naming of the group, this occurs very rarely, if at all. Cliques, gangs, and casual groups of all kinds acquire names when their membership becomes definite. In doubtful cases, one of the simplest ways for an outside observer to distinguish an organization is to inquire whether it has an "official" name.

The second requirement for the repetition of situations is calendarity. If members of the group are to come into contact, and to interact on different occasions, there must be a schedule according to which they plan their activities. The simplest form of organizational program is the daily routine of a family or workshop, modified by seasonal and annual variations. Associations with written rules usually incorporate a schedule of the time, place, and order of meetings in their documents.

If an organization continues, it is certain to lose members through death, incapacitation, absence, expulsion, resignation, and so forth. The overwhelming majority of organizations provide orderly procedures for the removal and admission of members. The most elementary membership procedures are death and birth, but there are always others as well.[3] In large organizations, the adherence of new recruits and the loss of old members are matters of daily occurrence.

Changes in the membership *group* may or may not affect the collective identity of the *organization*. Large churches have preserved the same identity for many centuries, with all the marks of real continuity. In some other cases, small changes in membership have a cumulative effect, so that without any definite moment of transition, a change of identity is finally observed. This is a quite typical line of development for political parties, whose names (Liberal,

[3] A large portion of *La Cité Antique* is devoted to the subject of adoption in the classic family, which Fustel de Coulanges regarded as the fundamental device for the eventual formation of clans and states. See *The Ancient City* (Anchor ed.; Garden City, N.Y.: Doubleday, 1962).

Radical-Socialist) often survive the change in orientation and eventually stand in contrast to the party's actual platform. In still other cases, continuity is interrupted at a definite point. In the middle-class family system a new conjugal family is begun at each marriage and appears to retain its identity through births, deaths, adoptions, and absences until the time when neither member of the original pair heads a family household. Finally, there are a good many instances in which there is no clear-cut solution to the question of whether organization X is a continuation of organization Y. Is there continuity, for example, between a blacksmith shop and the manufacturing corporation that emerges from it a century later?

To return to the distinction between group continuity and organizational continuity, we can describe the United States Senate. The Senate is a group of one hundred persons performing specified individual and collective functions. It undergoes a slight change every seven months on the average, when a member dies or resigns. Every two years, the group undergoes a major change when the terms of a third of its members expire simultaneously. However, at each election a good many of the incumbents are returned to office and there are always a few Senators with very long terms of service. As an organized group the Senate at any given moment shares some members with all the Senates of the past thirty years and presumably has some members in common with the Senate of thirty years hence. There is no definite point at which it ceases to be the same group. For certain purposes, we may speak of a new group each time a new member is elected or appointed to fill a vacancy. For other purposes, we might regard the group as continuing until a majority of the original members had been replaced, or all of them. In any case, it is quite certain that the Senators of 1962 are not the same group as the Senators of 1862.

Organizational continuity is another matter entirely. The Senators occupy *positions* that can be described without reference to a particular incumbent, and they participate in prescribed events the occurrence of which is not affected by changes in the membership group. Legally, senatorial positions may exist without any incumbent at all, as in the case of an unfilled vacancy, and there is certainly legal continuity between the Senate of 1862 and the Senate of 1962, although the method of selecting Senators has been changed in the intervening period, and the number of Senators has been increased by the admission of new states. Furthermore, the Senate can be discussed as a system of interacting positions and as a group with a calendar of prescribed events without *any* references to particular Senators or to particular dates.

Taking a given organization at a given moment in time, we can study it either as a set of persons (the group) or as a set of positions (the institution) or as both together (the organization).[4] Taking it in the longer run, there are several different possibilities:

1. Some organizations lose their identity when all or most of their original members have been replaced. In other words, the set of positions is coterminous with the membership roster. The conjugal family is an outstanding example.
2. Some organizations do not lose their identity when all of the original members have been replaced, so long as there is no break in the continuity of membership. The Senate may continue to serve as an example.
3. Some organizations do not depend upon a particular set of members for their continuity, and can be repopulated an indefinite number of times. The carnival queen and her court are an example.[5]

This last case—the *recurrent organization*—should not be confused with the set of empty positions called an *institution*. The positions which constitute a football team or a symphony orchestra can be considered abstractly, without reference to the membership of any particular team or orchestra, and their relationships can be described without reference to individual personalities or historic events. This abstract entity—for example the football team described in a rule book—is not an organization but an institution or

---

[4] The intellectual genealogy of this problem goes back to the thirteenth century and beyond. It was traced by Frederic William Maitland in his long Introduction to the English translation of Otto von Gierke's *Political Theories of the Middle Age* (Cambridge, Eng.: Cambridge University Press, 1913). Maitland's own view of the question, close to that taken here, is that ". . . there seems to be a genus of which State and Corporation are species. They seem to be permanently organized groups of men; they seem to be group-units; we seem to attribute acts and intents, rights and wrongs to these groups, to these units," p. ix.

[5] Leopold von Wiese and Howard Becker describe this phenomenon in detail as "temporary plurality patterns" in their *Systematic Sociology* (New York: Wiley, 1932).

institutional pattern, a blueprint furnished by the larger society to new groups who want to organize for a particular purpose.

THE MULTIPLICITY OF ORGANIZATIONS

We have described the organization as a social system, a *system* being a set of elements and the relationships among them. To describe a system, we must be able to identify all of the elements that belong to the set and to exclude all of those that do not. We must also be able to express all the relationships relevant to the system in terms of measurable amounts or definable states.[6] Within any system there may be sets of elements that have special characteristics not shared by other elements in the system. If each of these specially labeled elements is functionally related to all of the other elements with the same characteristics, then they constitute a subsystem. The process of subdivision may be repeated almost indefinitely as sub-subsystems are identified within the subsystems and so forth.

Any organization we study is likely to be related to other organizations in one of the following ways:

1. *As a component of another organization.* Infantry Company B and Regiment A may serve as examples. All members of B are members of A, but not all members of A are members of B. B is just as much an organization as A. It has its own mission, its own name, its own program, and its own procedures for replacement. But all of these are derived in one way or another from A. The

---

[6] Cf. Everett E. Hagen, "Analytical Models in the Study of Social Systems," *American Journal of Sociology,* Vol. LXVII, No. 2 (September, 1962), 145:

> An analytical model is defined by defining the elements and their interrelations. The relationships among the elements of a system are statements of the alternative values (magnitudes) or states of one of the elements associated with alternative values or states of one or more of the other elements. Because the elements are assumed to vary in magnitude or state, they are termed variable—which, broadly, includes constants—that is, the variation in some may be zero. If two variables are related in this way, each is said to be a function of the other without regard to the direction of causation between them. While the flow of causation between any two elements may be in one direction and not in the other, among all of the elements taken as a group, apart from the impact of forces from outside the system, all depend on all. Let it be noted clearly that this concept of mutual interdependence or interaction does not involve circular reasoning or indeterminacy.

program of B is only understandable as part of the program of A. Even B's collective identity carries a notation of its inclusion in A. The dissolution of A as an organization would ordinarily imply the termination of B's collective identity and the interruption of its activities. B may have its own components (platoons in our example), which will necessarily be components of A also.

2. *As a faction of another organization.* All its members are members of A, but its program of activity is not part of the program of organization A. A fraternity in a school that forbids its students to join fraternities is an example of a factional organization.

3. *As congruent with another organization.* We speak of congruence when the membership roster of one organization is identical with the membership roster of another but the organizations have separate purposes and identities. This situation occurs when a legislature adjourns and reconvenes as a Committee of the Whole, or when two separate corporations have the same board of directors.

4. *As linked to another organization.* In this condition, some of the members of A are members of B but they are not congruent and neither is a component or segment of the other. A factory has a seven-man board of directors and a nine-man executive committee of divisional managers. Five men serve simultaneously on both bodies, leaving two directors who are not divisional managers and four divisional managers who are not directors.[7] Another familiar type of linkage occurs when organizations are represented by delegates to another organization. Thus, for example, the labor unions who send delegates to a local labor council are linked to it by their representatives. Linkages of this kind are found very frequently in hierarchies, when successive levels are tied together by granting high-status members of each component organization membership in the next higher component. The national committee of an American political party is composed of delegates from state committees, which is in turn composed of delegates from county committees, themselves composed of delegates from district and precinct committees. Almost all military and bureaucratic organizations follow this principle to some extent by assembling the heads of subordinate departments as a council of advisors under certain circumstances.

[7] The example is from Elliott Jaques, *The Changing Culture of a Factory* (New York: Dryden, 1952).

ORGANIZATIONAL COMPONENTS

The *primary group* may be defined as a group in which each member interacts directly and regularly with every other member, often in the presence of all members. A *secondary group* is any group that does not meet these conditions.

Both primary and secondary groups may be either organized or unorganized. A nuclear family is an organized primary group. A clique is an unorganized primary group. A political party is an organized secondary group. A crowd of demonstrators is an unorganized secondary group.

The term *primary group* was first introduced by Cooley about fifty years ago. His description has been quoted as much as any paragraph in the sociological literature:

> By primary groups I mean those characterized by intimate face-to-face association and co-operation. They are primary in several senses, but chiefly in that they are fundamental in forming the social nature and ideals of the individual. The result of intimate association, psychologically, is a certain fusion of individualities in a common whole, so that one's very self, for many purposes at least, is the common life and purpose of the group.[8]

Cooley himself did not speak of the secondary group, but it follows so naturally as a label for nonprimary groups that he is usually given credit for the term.

The characteristics of the primary group are described by later writers as face-to-face association, temporal priority (primary groups are first met in childhood), intimacy, involvement of the total personality, and identification with the group as a whole.[9]

Compared to a secondary group with similar functions, a primary group is not only smaller but more cohesive, less durable, and less formal. Participation in any primary group implies some degree of emotional involvement. There is considerable evidence that an individual's adjustment or maladjustment in a given social environment usually depends upon his acceptance in an appropriate primary

[8] Charles Horton Cooley, *Social Organization: A Study of the Larger Mind* (New York: Scribner, 1909). The quotation is from page 23 of the 1927 edition.

[9] Ellsworth Faris, "The Primary Group: Essence and Accident," *American Journal of Sociology*, Vol. XXXVIII, No. 1 (September, 1932).

group.[10] Indeed, a fairly good case can be made for linking total life-time adjustment with experience in primary groups and explaining psychiatric disorders as the outcome of unsuccessful experience in primary groups.

It would be absurd, of course, to think of primary and secondary groups as competing types of organization. All organized secondary groups are built up out of primary groups. As MacIver and Page point out:

> The face-to-face group is the nucleus of all organization, and, as we shall see, is found in some form within the most complex systems—it is the unit cell of the social structure.[11]

The *peer group* [12] is an organized (but unofficial) primary group; its program includes the protection of its members from the rules and requirements of the larger organization in which it appears. Peer groups are necessarily factional. The larger organization often attempts to suppress them or denies their existence. Although the peer group is as old as human society, it was not much analyzed until about thirty years ago, when studies of factories [13] revealed the existence of peer groups that regulated the daily output of workers. They were at first regarded as perverse and pathological; however, as further studies demonstrated their functions, it was gradually perceived that peer groups do not represent a breakdown of the larger organization, but are essential components of it.[14]

[10] See Chapter Seven below.

[11] Robert MacIver and Charles Page, *Society: An Introductory Analysis* (New York: Rinehart, 1949), p. 219.

[12] The peer group, of course, is only one kind of primary group. There are many others. For example, the face-to-face working team which includes superiors and subordinates is a primary group that invites extensive study, although it is not a peer group.

[13] For a summary and critique of studies reporting the activities of peer groups in industrial organization, see Morris Viteles, *Motivation and Morale in Industry* (New York: Norton, 1953).

[14] For example, Shils, reviewing Samuel A. Stouffer et al., *The American Soldier* (Princeton, N.J.: Princeton University Press, 1949), concludes that ". . . these data support the more complex hypothesis that primary group solidarity functions in the corporate body to strengthen the motivation for the fulfillment of substantive prescriptions and commands issued by the official agents of the corporate body. . . ." Edward A. Shils, "Primary groups in the American Army," in Robert K. Merton and Paul F. Lazarsfeld (eds.), *Continuities in Social Research* (Glencoe, Ill.: Free Press, 1951). Very similar results emerged from my comparison of three unrelated studies of naval or-

The functions performed by the peer group may be briefly summarized:

1. It provides certain satisfactions to its members which they require for the effective performance of their tasks but which the larger organization itself is unable to supply. For example, peer groups in military units supply the emotional support that civilians ordinarily find in the family.

2. It provides channels for horizontal communication and monitors them. Most organizational charts are markedly defective in regard to horizontal communication—necessarily so, because interactions that are not regulated by a status mechanism are difficult to arrange by authority. The peer group, although composed of equals from the organizational viewpoint, develops enough of an internal status order to channel local communications effectively. Witness the following description of a high school clique by Hollingshead:

> Membership is voluntary and informal. Members are admitted gradually to a pre-existing clique and dropped by the mutual consent of its participants. Although there are no explicit rules for membership, the clique has a more or less common set of values which determines who will be admitted, what it does, how it will censure some member who does not abide by its values. . . . Its members frequently identify their interests with the group in contrast to the interests of the family, other cliques, the school, and society. . . . Each member has a group status derived from his ability to achieve something or to contribute something to the well-being of the clique.[15]

3. By standardizing the rate and quality of performance for similar or identical tasks, the peer group at once protects its members from arbitrary evaluation and increases the predictability of achievement for the larger organization. This often involves a larger price—in output limitation—than the larger organization wishes to pay, but it is in some measure functional.

4. The peer group provides "engineering from below." In large

ganization published by Davis, Page, and Turner. See Theodore Caplow, "The Criteria of Organizational Success," *Social Forces,* Vol. XXXII, No. 1 (October, 1953).

[15] August B. Hollingshead, *Elmtown's Youth* (New York: Wiley, 1949), pp. 205–06.

organizations, especially, planning activities are centered near the top in order to maintain coordination. This means that many tasks and sequences are undertaken with inadequate information and are badly planned. The peer group may introduce the necessary corrections. Blau gives an example from the federal agency he studied:

> In this group of officials, the practice of consulting one another was supported by norms; an agent was expected to help a colleague who asked for advice and was stigmatized if he refused. Conversely, the norm prohibiting the reporting of bribes corresponded to the practice of not making such reports, although official rules prescribed that they be made. These unofficial patterns arose in response to implicit needs of the organization. Effective determination of violations required that anxiety which interfered with making accurate decisions be relieved. Effective negotiation with employers required that offers of bribes be used to extract concessions from them and not to antagonize them without furthering the objectives of the agency. The practice of consulting colleagues and the taboo on reporting bribes met these requirements. They were new elements of the bureaucratic organization.[16]

The idea of the primary group is intertwined with the concept of *informal* organization. Long ago, Giddings drew a distinction between *authorized* organizations—those established by adequate and rightful authority—and *unauthorized* organizations.[17] Somewhat later, Eubank distinguished between groups that are *spontaneous,* "formed as a natural growth by persons who do not deliberately plan the organization in advance"; and groups that are *predetermined,* "deliberately formed with some defined purpose . . . ." [18] The terms *formal* and *informal* organization derive from the Western Electric study. The formal organization, according to Roethlisberger and Dickson,[19]

---

[16] Peter M. Blau, *The Dynamics of Bureaucracy* (Chicago: University of Chicago Press, 1955), p. 159.

[17] Franklin Henry Giddings, *Readings in Descriptive and Historical Sociology* (New York: Macmillan, 1906), p. 431.

[18] Earle Edward Eubank, *The Concepts of Sociology* (Boston: Heath, 1932), p. 150.

[19] Fritz J. Roethlisberger and William J. Dickson, *Management and the Worker* (Cambridge, Mass.: Harvard University Press, 1939). The quotations are from pages 558–59.

. . . is composed of a number of strata or levels which differentiate the benchworker from the skilled mechanic, the group chief from the department chief, and so on. These levels are well defined, and all the formal orders, instructions and compensations are addressed to them. All such factors taken together make up the formal organization of the plant. It includes the systems, policies, rules and regulations of the plant which express what the relations of one person to another are supposed to be in order to achieve effectively the task of technical production.

The informal organization includes:

Distinctions of social distance, movement, or equilibrium . . . the hierarchy of prestige values which tends to make the work of men more important than the work of women . . . the primary groups, that is, those groups enjoying daily face-to-face relations . . . actually existing patterns of interaction between people in different social places . . . sentiments and values residing in the social organization by means of which individuals or groups of individuals are informally differentiated, ordered and integrated . . . personal relations . . . informal groups, in terms of which each person achieves a certain position or status.

By these definitions (note their partial circularity), there is no such thing as *a* formal organization or *an* informal organization. All living organizations are both formal and informal at the same time. In short, every organization exhibits some formal elements—those that are explicitly prescribed—and some informal elements—those that are not explicitly prescribed.

Other writers, however, have described what appear to be separable types of organizations—formal and informal. Dubin writes:

The independent informal association is usually grounded in the common interests of its members. Members can come into and move out of such association as needs, interests and compatibility dictate. To some extent the informal group within a formal organization shares these characteristics. The notable addition to the situation is that the informal group in a formal organization has meaning and significance primarily in relation to the formal organization of which it is a part.[20]

[20] Robert Dubin, *Human Relations in Administration* (New York: Prentice-Hall, 1951), p. 57.

We shall follow the original usage whereby formal and informal refer to elements of an organization and never to the whole. There is something essentially incongruous about the notion of an informal organization. Even the most furtive organizations are capable of exhibiting formality on suitable occasions. It is more convenient to distinguish between the *formal elements* of an organization (elements that are explicitly prescribed) and its *informal elements* (those not explicitly prescribed) and to recognize that we must look for both in every organization we study.

There are differences, however, between legitimate and illegitimate, recognized and unrecognized, official and unofficial organizations. Official organizations are sponsored or recognized by a "parent" organization. Unofficial organizations are sponsored only by their own members. A peer group, a street-corner gang, a drinking club, or a political conspiracy is an unofficial organization. A family, a college, a political party, or a corporation is official.

In modern society, almost all official organizations turn out, on close inspection, to be ultimately authorized by the state, which licenses marriages, charters corporations, and registers voluntary associations. There appear to be two reasons for this phenomenon. First, property cannot be securely held without the sanction of the state. Since official organizations of any consequence have collective property, it is evident why they require authorization. Second, any organization that wields substantial power must occasionally resort to violence. In modern society, in which the state's monopoly of violence is nearly unquestioned, the state must usually provide the means of coercion for private organizations, although there are exceptions, such as criminal syndicates.

The phenomenon of authorization is often overlooked. It may seem implausible that the memorandum establishing a new janitor crew in a branch factory of a manufacturing corporation is authorized ultimately by the state, but the state *does* confer the corporate charter from which the company's board of directors derives its right to appoint the executives who are entitled to do such things as hiring a new janitor crew.

This chain of authorization is more than theoretical. The legitimacy of each link can be subject to challenge and test. The consequences are sometimes curious, as when an American court was called upon to decide which of two archbishops in the Russian Orthodox Church had been properly called to the episcopal succession.

THE SPECIAL CASE OF THE COMMUNITY

Almost all human beings belong to communities, groups composed of those who reside within a bounded territory. The smallest community is a household. The largest is a nation.

The community has some but not all of the attributes of an organization. There is a collective identity—ordinarily the name of the place—but that identity need not imply the possibility of collective action. There is something that resembles a roster of membership. Residents identify themselves and are identified by others as living inside the territory, but most communities cannot furnish an accurate list of residents. There is no program of activity, but there is considerable regularity in daily and seasonal behavior.[21] The replacement of members is accomplished by birth, death, and migration, although these are not organizational procedures in the usual sense.

Some—but not all—communities are congruent with organizations. Peasant villages throughout the world are likely to be organizations as well as communities. Towns, cities, and districts usually have organized governments that are closely identified with the community, although by no means the same thing. Nations, which are communities, are partly congruent with organizations called states, which are composed of officials and citizens. A state has a name, a roster, a program, and procedures of replacement.

Communities generate organizations very easily, and vice versa. Diamond describes the conversion of the Virginia Company into a community in the early part of the seventeenth century. Originally, every settler was an employee of the company, under its control, subject to its discipline, and engaged primarily in company work. The difficulties of recruitment and the failure of the enterprise to bring in the expected profits made it necessary for the London

---

[21] The limitations of the community with respect to collective action are brilliantly analyzed in James D. Thompson and Robert W. Hawkes, "Disaster, Community Organization, and Administrative Process," in George W. Baker and Dwight W. Chapman (eds.), *Man and Society in Disaster* (New York: Basic Books, 1962).

managers to offer such inducements as land ownership, exemptions from duty, and the importation of wives, which soon transformed the organization into a community:

> At one time in Virginia, the single relationship that existed between persons rested upon the positions they occupied in the Company's table of organization. As a result of the efforts made by the Company to get persons to accept that relationship, however, each person in Virginia had become the occupant of several statuses, for now there were rich and poor in Virginia, landowners and renters, masters and servants, old residents and newcomers, married and single, men and women, and the simultaneous possession of these statuses involved the holder in a network of relationships, some congruent and some incompatible with his organizational relationship.[22]

Some authors suggest that situations of this kind can best be analyzed by taking organization as a variable. They would prefer to describe a group as *more* or *less* organized, taking account of the vast differences among groups in cohesiveness and complexity.

The question of when a group becomes an organization cannot be finally resolved here, but we shall take the position that discussing groups as more or less organized is like describing organisms as more or less alive. In both cases, there are transitional states between the two conditions, but these do not count for very much in relation to the overwhelming distinction between life and death in the organism and between the possibility and impossibility of sustained collective action in the group.

ORGANIZATIONAL SIZE

Not only does the size of an organization affect all phases of its activity, but changes of size at certain points along the scale are more important than at other points. A four-man committee is quite different from a three-man committee—for example, with respect to the formation of coalitions—but the difference between nine and ten members is barely perceptible. If a work crew is increased in size from fifteen to thirty, its entire social structure is certain to change because the pattern of primary group interaction cannot be

[22] Sigmund Diamond, "From Organization to Society: Virginia in the Seventeenth Century," *American Journal of Sociology*, Vol. LXIII, No. 5 (March, 1958).

continued intact. A work crew of two hundred men, however, might be doubled in size without any drastic change in structure.

Some organizations, such as string quartets, have a fixed size and can function only with the right number of members. Others, such as symphony orchestras, are more variable and can function satisfactorily within a range of membership size.

By convention, the smallest organized groups have three members, this being the least number able to replace themselves without a break in group continuity. However, the limitation seems arbitrary in the case of certain dyads—such as partnerships and childless marriages—which are intended to serve as the nuclei of organizations and which resemble organizations in many respects. It is also possible to discover freak organizations with a membership of one. These usually involve the simultaneous appearance of an individual in more than one position, like the last survivor of a military outpost who assumes command of himself.

Although the measurement of membership populations is more accurate and satisfactory than mere classification, classification by size cannot be entirely avoided. It is unrealistic, for example, to discuss manufacturing establishments without making a classificatory distinction between small workshops and giant factories.

Any classification of organizations by membership size must be somewhat arbitrary. The classification used here is based on the criterion of interaction possibilities. It reflects the restrictions imposed on the interaction network by the sheer number of participants. These restrictions are nearly independent of other organizational characteristics.

The membership sizes proposed in the following scheme should be taken as approximations only. The *small* organization is small enough for its members to form a primary group—whether or not they actually do so. Small organizations range from three to about thirty members. The nuclear family is a small organization.

The *medium-size* organization is too large to permit the development of all possible pair relationships among members. But it is small enough so that one or more members, including a leader or leaders, can interact directly with all of the others. The medium-size organization ranges from a minimum membership of about thirty to a maximum of about a thousand.

The *large* organization is too large for any member to know each of the others but not too large for one or more leaders to be recognized by all of the others. These key members will be recognized by many more people than they are able to recognize. The large organization ranges from a lower limit of about one thousand members to an upper limit in the neighborhood of fifty thousand, but this upper limit is especially variable. Most universities are large organizations.

The *giant* organization has too many members too widely dispersed to permit the direct interaction of any individual with all of the others. Key members may be recognized by most other members, through mass communication. A lower limit of fifty thousand may be set for the giant organization and there is no upper limit. Political parties are usually giant organizations.

The overwhelming majority of organizations in any society are small, since this category includes the basic units of larger organizations. Most small organizations are easily assembled. Indeed, it is difficult to find an example of a small organization that does not assemble its members face-to-face at regular intervals. It appears that only a small organization can provide sustained emotional support for its members and that only a small organization can exercise power without delegation. Executive committees, administrative commissions, councils of war, courts of justice, examination boards, juntas, and juries seldom have more than fifteen or twenty members. Medium-size organizations concerned with power, such as legislatures, are always found on closer inspection to be controlled by an organized inner circle.

The inimitable Professor Parkinson has documented the tendency of executive councils to increase in size until they become too unwieldy for decision-making, whereupon an inner council is formed to assume power. In the fullness of time, this overexpands in turn and develops an inner circle of its own to take over the succession.[23]

There has been comparatively little discussion of the medium-size organization. It has neither the emotional significance of the primary group nor the fascinating complexity of the giant organization. The category includes a large proportion of the world's extended families, voluntary associations, representative assemblies, religious congregations, schools and academies, factories and mines, prisons

[23] C. Northcote Parkinson, *Parkinson's Law and Other Studies in Administration* (Boston: Houghton Mifflin, 1957).

and hospitals. The medium-size organization is large enough to require rationalized procedures and formal specifications but small enough to be easily controlled or modified by an influential individual.

In the large organization it is no longer possible for any member to know all of the others, but it is still possible for a number of leaders to be known to all other members. The situation of this central cadre is exceptionally favorable because the leaders' unique personal influence may be used to reinforce their formal authority and vice versa. A large organization must have an administrative apparatus, but it need not develop the massive inertia that opposes any change of course in a giant organization. One of the most important characteristics of the large organization is the members' illusion of full acquaintance with each other. The employee in a large factory who is familiar with the physical plant, the names and personalities of the department heads, and the location and purposes of the principal cliques is often quite unaware that his knowledge fails to circumscribe the entire organization.

The line between large and giant is difficult to draw. Some widely dispersed organizations with only a few hundred members behave very much like giants. Some voluntary associations with millions of members do not. The giant organization is usually pyramidal. A broad rank and file is topped by many levels of specialists and officials. The social distance between the bottom and the top of the pyramid is too great to allow easy interaction even when interaction is mechanically possible. The integrity of the giant organization must be maintained by mass communications—standardized messages broadcast to the membership at large. Formal devices must be developed for recognizing the individual and recording his organizational experience in standardized form. These make it possible to move him from one component to another as an interchangeable unit.

Social interaction takes place at all levels of the giant organization. Indeed, it can be viewed as a great cluster of component organizations, ranging from triads to giant organizations in their own right. But the interaction of any single member no longer involves a large proportion of the total membership. In the nature of things it is impossible for anyone to have a detailed knowledge of the entire structure. Familiarity with a few elements of the structure and personal interaction within a local sector provide sufficient orientation for ordinary activity.

RELATIONAL COMPLEXITY

The relational complexity of small groups increases rapidly with small increases, in size. This phenomenon, the philosophical implications of which were discussed long ago by Herbert Spencer and Georg Simmel, was first quantified by Bossard, who developed a "Law of Family Interaction" as follows:

> With the addition of each person to a family or primary group, the number of persons increases in the simplest arithmetical progression in whole numbers, while the number of personal relationships within the group increases in the order of triangular numbers.[24]

This analysis eventually led to a more extensive treatment by Kephart, who studied the implications of group size for three types of relationship: between persons, between persons and combinations, and between combinations. The following discussion is based on Kephart's formulas.[25] Four interactive types are distinguished:

Interactive type number 1 concerns pair relationships between individual persons in a group. Each member has a potential relationship with every other. The number of possible relationships for any member is equal to the size N of the group minus one. The total number of relationships possible for the entire group of N members will be $N \times (N - 1)$ divided by 2, since each possible relationship is counted by two participants. The number of potential relationships (PR) for any single member increases at the same rate as the size of the group: $(PR = N - 1)$

$$N = 2 \quad 3 \quad 4 \quad 5 \quad 6 \quad 7 \quad \cdots$$
$$PR = 1 \quad 2 \quad 3 \quad 4 \quad 5 \quad 6 \quad \cdots$$

The number of potential relationships in the whole group increases much faster than group size. It is given by the formula $PR = \dfrac{N(N - 1)}{2}$, which produces the following series:

$$N = 2 \quad 3 \quad 4 \quad 5 \quad 6 \quad 7 \quad \cdots$$
$$PR = 1 \quad 3 \quad 6 \quad 10 \quad 15 \quad 21 \quad \cdots$$

[24] J. H. S. Bossard, "The Law of Family Interaction," *American Journal of Sociology,* Vol. L, No. 3 (November, 1945), 292.
[25] William M. Kephart, "A Quantitative Analysis of Intragroup Relationships," *American Journal of Sociology,* Vol. LV, No. 6 (May, 1950), 544–49.

It may be easier to visualize what is involved if we consider an example. In a four-person family composed of father, mother, son and daughter, there are six possible pair relationships: [26]

1. father — mother
2. father — son
3. father — daughter

4. mother — son
5. mother — daughter
6. son — daughter

Interactive type number 2 includes all of the pair relationships plus all relationships between an individual and a combination. In the small primary group each member has to deal not only with his fellow members individually but on occasion with each possible pair, each possible triad, and so on up to the total of other members. The formula for the total of these relationships is:

$$PR = 2^{(n-1)} - 1,$$

which produces the following series of potential relationships for each member as the group size increases:

$$N = 2 \quad 3 \quad 4 \quad 5 \quad 6 \quad 7 \quad \cdots$$
$$PR = 1 \quad 3 \quad 7 \quad 15 \quad 31 \quad 63 \quad \cdots$$

This is a rapid increase, indeed, but it is almost insignificant compared to the mushrooming total of relationships for the group as a whole. The number of potential relationships for the group as a whole is given by the formula:

$$PR = \frac{N}{2} \times (2^n - N - 1),$$

and this series grows as follows:

$$N = 2 \quad 3 \quad 4 \quad 5 \quad 6 \quad 7 \quad \cdots$$
$$PR = 1 \quad 6 \quad 22 \quad 65 \quad 171 \quad 420 \quad \cdots$$

The previous illustration may be continued. There are twenty-two possible relationships of individuals with individuals and of individuals with groups in our four-person family: [27]

[26] There are three pair relationships for each family member.
[27] There are seven such relationships for each family member.

1. father — mother
2. father — son
3. father — daughter
4. father — children
5. father — women
6. father — mother and son
7. father — all others
8. mother — son
9. mother — daughter
10. mother — children
11. mother — men
12. mother — father and daughter
13. mother — all others
14. son — daughter
15. son — parents
16. son — women
17. son — father and sister
18. son — all others
19. daughter — parents
20. daughter — men
21. daughter — mother and son
22. daughter — all others

Interactive type number 3 includes all those relationships in a group that involve a combination or subgroup. Such relationships are of two kinds, of course—relationships between an individual member and a combination and relationships between combinations. The formula for computing the number of such relationships involves certain complexities that cannot be treated here but which are described in Kephart's original paper. The series obtained for combinations (or subgroups) of two members looks like this:

$$N = 2 \quad 3 \quad 4 \quad 5 \quad 6 \quad 7 \cdots$$
$$PR = 0 \quad 3 \quad 15 \quad 55 \quad 180 \quad 546 \cdots$$

Returning to our family illustration, the fifteen relationships that fall into this category are as follows:

1. father — children
2. father — women
3. father — mother and son

4. mother	—	children
5. mother	—	men
6. mother	—	father and daughter
7. son	—	parents
8. son	—	women
9. son	—	father and sister
10. daughter	—	parents
11. daughter	—	men
12. daughter	—	mother and brother
13. parents	—	children
14. men	—	women
15. father and daughter	—	mother and son

Interactive type number 4 is the sum of all the relationships involved in the three interactive types just discussed; it can be obtained by a single formula:

$$PR = \frac{3^n - 2^{(n+1)} + 1}{2}$$

This important formula takes account of *all* the interpersonal relationships that can occur in a group of given size. As the following series shows, the increase in the number of relationships accelerates with small increases in group size, and a point is very soon reached at which it is impossible for all the potential relationships to be realized. The following is the series for the sum of pair and combination relationships:

$$N = 2 \quad 3 \quad 4 \quad 5 \quad 6 \quad 7 \cdots$$
$$PR = 1 \quad 6 \quad 25 \quad 90 \quad 301 \quad 966 \cdots$$

Returning to our illustration, there are twenty-five possible relationships, of all types, in the four-person family:

1. father	—	mother
2. father	—	son
3. father	—	daughter
4. father	—	women
5. father	—	children
6. father	—	all others
7. father	—	mother and son
8. mother	—	son

9.	mother	—	daughter
10.	mother	—	men
11.	mother	—	children
12.	mother	—	father and daughter
13.	mother	—	all others
14.	son	—	daughter
15.	son	—	women
16.	son	—	parents
17.	son	—	father and daughter
18.	son	—	all others
19.	daughter	—	men
20.	daughter	—	parents
21.	daughter	—	mother and son
22.	daughter	—	all others
23.	parents	—	children
24.	men	—	women
25.	father and daughter	—	mother and son

As we move to larger groups it becomes virtually impossible to visualize all of the possible relationships. Many of them cease to be meaningful in medium or large groups because it is extremely unlikely that any member of a large organization will confront certain possible combinations of other members. Even in groups that do not much exceed the size of an average household, the number of potential relationships is staggeringly high. Under the formula for interactive type number 4, the total of possible relationships reaches the fantastic figure of 29,268 for a ten-member organization. In medium-size, large, and giant organizations, of course, the number of *potential* relationships is astronomical, and even the *realized* relationships defy enumeration.

There is reason to believe that larger organizations are proportionately less affected by variations in size than are smaller organizations. The national governments of nations such as Switzerland and Denmark have much the same features that appear in the governments of the United States and India. Armies, business enterprises, and religious denominations with fifty thousand members seem to show most of the same elements as those which are ten or a hundred times as large. It is likely that larger organizations are more successful in maintaining themselves than are smaller organizations of the same type. It has repeatedly been shown that a business enterprise's chances of survival increase directly with its size.[28] Although the evidence is incomplete, there are good theoretical reasons for supposing that the stability and size of organized groups must always be correlated. Since the number of relationships in an organization increases much faster than membership size, larger organizations have a much denser network of relationships than have smaller organizations of the same general type. In addition, the largest organizations in a particular environment tend to be mutually supportive— if only because the collapse of one, like the fall of a great tree, threatens those around it. Finally, large organizations, being dispersed over wider territories, are less at the mercy of local accidents than are small organizations.

The growth of organizations has scarcely begun to be studied quantitatively, but Haire's classic paper [29] on the growth of four industrial firms suggests a host of orderly relationships. In each case, the over-all growth fits a smooth logistic curve reasonably well. When employees are divided into "inside" and "outside" categories, analogous to the surface and mass of a physical body, there is some tendency for the outside category to increase by a square function and the inside by a cube. Haire is also able to show that—contrary to accepted myth—the proportion of staff employees to supervisors stabilizes at a fairly early point in the growth curve, but the ratio of supervisors to employees declines sharply with increases in size.[30]

The absolute size of organizations has been increasing rapidly in

[28] See, for example, F. Stuart Chapin, *Contemporary American Institutions: A Sociological Analysis* (New York: Harper, 1935), p. 68; Seymour M. Lipset and Reinhard Bendix, "Social Mobility and Occupational Career Patterns," *American Journal of Sociology,* Vol. LVII, No. 5 (March, 1952); and A. J. Jaffe, "The Calculation of Death Rates for Establishments with Supplementary Notes on the Calculation of Birth Rates," *Journal of the Inter-American Statistical Institute,* September, 1961.

[29] Mason Haire, "Biological Models and Empirical Histories of the Growth of Organizations," in his *Modern Organization Theory* (New York: Wiley, 1959). Haire's use of biological models for the growth of organizations has been sharply challenged—using Haire's own data—by Jean Draper and George B. Strother, "Testing a Model for Organizational Growth," *Human Organization,* Vol. XXII, No. 3 (Fall, 1963).

[30] Confirmatory evidence is presented in Theodore R. Anderson and Seymour Warkov, "Organizational Size and Functional Complexity," *American Sociological Review,* Vol. XXVI, No. 1 (February, 1961), and in Otis Dudley Duncan, "Size and Structure of Organizations" (Chicago: University of Chicago, 1961) (mimeographed).

the modern world under the combined influence of population growth, urbanization, and the refinement of communication and record-keeping. Until well into the nineteenth century, the largest factories had only a few hundred employees because it was difficult to coordinate the work of greater numbers. Several factories in the United States now employ more than twenty-five thousand people each. Some of them are so large that motorized vehicles are used to go from one end of the shop to the other. Above the level of the single establishment are manufacturing companies with hundreds of thousands of employees and government agencies:

> The Defense Department . . . already employs 1,175,915 civilians (not to speak of soldiers, sailors, airmen, and marines) and uses nearly 10 percent of our gross national product. It spends more than the whole national product of Canada, Japan, India, or Communist China, more than all states and local governments in the United States, including all public education for 40,000,000 people from kindergarten to state universities. . . . Defense assets are greater than the combined wealth of the 100 largest corporations in America. (Indeed, some of their wealth depends largely on their ability to get contracts from the Defense Department.) Some individual defense installations have a greater worth than does the Ford Motor Company. The annual purchases of the Air Force alone are larger in volume than the output of America's greatest industrial producer— General Motors. The array of items purchased, distributed and used for defense is forty times as numerous as those marketed by Sears, Roebuck and Company.[31]

In every type of economic, political, military, educational, religious, scientific, even artistic and literary endeavor, the fundamental framework of the giant organization appears, with its impersonal posts and positions, its inflexible definitions of behavior, its filing systems, its internal web of communication, its formalized public relations. The most interesting feature of mass organization is that it tends always toward a standard form. In a folk society, there is little resemblance between the blacksmith shop, the church, the school, and the poorhouse; but these institutions, when expanded to giant scale, all look very much alike. They all have a personnel system and a budget. They all use similar rules of accounting, they have similar

---

[31] Harlan Cleveland, "Dinosaurs and Personal Freedom," *Saturday Review,* February 28, 1959, pp. 13–14.

provisions for transportation, retirement, sick leave, policy-making, record-keeping, and research. This does not mean that giant organizations designed for different functions have identical forms. They never do, but with each increase in scale the visible similarities increase also.

ORGANIZATIONAL TAXONOMY

The first systematic classification of organizations appears in Aristotle's *Politics*. This famous treatise might well be considered as the earliest study of the sociology of organization. The classification is detailed, functional, and supported by numerous examples.

Six forms of government are described. Authority may be exercised by the one, by the few, or by the many. It may be exercised either for the common good or for the benefit of the rulers. The good forms are called monarchy, aristocracy, and constitutionalism. The perverted forms, in which power is selfish, are tyranny, oligarchy, and democracy. (The word *democracy* is used pejoratively by Aristotle, although, as the discussion proceeds, the distinction between good and bad forms of government turns out to be less absolute than first appears.) There are five subtypes of monarchy: the Spartan, the barbarian, the elective dictatorship, the heroic, and the absolute. Each category is furnished with illustrations, and marginal specimens are carefully noted. There is only one form of aristocracy; it is presented as a conceptual ideal and cannot be completely attained. But there are three varieties of tyranny: despotism, elective dictatorship, and what we would call gangsterism. There are four kinds of democracy, four kinds of oligarchy, and an important mixed form— the polity—which is a compromise between the two. All in all, this ancient set of lecture notes provides one of the best examples of an organizational classification founded on empirical data.

Lawyers, from ancient times, have been at the game of defining and distinguishing different kinds of organization. The laws of Solon permitted the free establishment of private corporations, and occupational corporations, called universities, played an important part in ancient Rome. It was the Roman lawyers who formulated the maxim *"tres faciunt collegium,"* which may be freely translated as "an organized group must have at least three members."

The English common law distinguished a considerable variety of organizational types, and Blackstone [32] provides a classification of "corporations aggregate," which "consist of many persons united together into one society, and are kept up by a perpetual succession of members, so as to continue forever."

Corporations aggregate may be divided into ecclesiastical and lay corporations. Ecclesiastical corporations are created for the furtherance of religion and are composed of clerics. Lay corporations may be civil or eleemosynary. As examples of the civil corporation, Blackstone mentions municipal governments, the trading companies of London, church wardens, the college of physicians and surgeons, the Royal Society, the Society of Antiquaries, and Oxford and Cambridge universities. The eleemosynary category includes hospitals, almshouses, and asylums. It is interesting to note that this classification combines organizations (government bureaus, welfare agencies, business firms, professional societies, and universities) which are now legally dissimilar.

The development of organizational taxonomies has been a favorite sport of sociologists almost from the beginnings of the discipline. In *Concepts of Sociology,* published in 1932, Eubank lists more than three dozen systems of group classifications, proposed by as many writers.[33] Many of these were really pseudoclassifications, designed not to be used in the collection, labeling, and analysis of data, but only to support theoretical assertions. The principal usefulness of such schemes is to call attention to dimensions that might otherwise be overlooked. However, the three dozen systems contain references to size, integration, authority, autonomy, permanence, insulation, voluntarism, achievement, homogenity, and most of the other measurable characteristics of organizations, even when no measurement is contemplated.

The first sociological classification of organizations intended for

[32] Sir William Blackstone, *Commentaries on the Law of England,* ed. W. D. Lewis (Philadelphia: Rees, Welsh, 1902), p. 469.

[33] Eubank, *op. cit.,* especially Chapter 8. The authors whose classifications are described include Spencer, Ward, Ross, Tonnies, Hobhouse, LeBon, Sumner, Cooley, and Giddings. A later but less inclusive treatment of the history of organizational taxonomy is Logan Wilson, "Sociography of Groups," Chapter 7 in Georges Gurvitch and Wilbert E. Moore (eds.), *Twentieth Century Sociology* (New York: Philosophical Library, 1945).

use rather than show appears in Park and Burgess' *Introduction to the Science of Society,*[34] and runs as follows:

A. The family
B. Language (racial) groups
C. Local and territorial communities:
    I. Neighborhoods
    II. Rural communities
    III. Urban communities
D. Conflict groups:
    I. Nationalities
    II. Parties
    III. Sects
    IV. Labor organizations
    V. Gangs, etc.
E. Accommodation groups:
    I. Classes
    II. Castes
    III. Vocational groups
    IV. Denominational groups

As the authors themselves remark, "The foregoing classification is not quite adequate nor wholly logical."

According to Park and Burgess, social groups are primarily task groups, oriented to external goals. Even the most ephemeral social groups exhibit a range of task functions. The wishes that are satisfied by an organization are believed to precede its formation. They consist essentially of "appetites and natural desires" that are modified in the process of becoming organized, but there is no suggestion that new motives arise out of the organization itself. The incompatibility of the individual and the group is stressed, and W. I. Thomas and Florian Znaniecki are quoted by Park and Burgess with approval: "Personal evolution is always a struggle between the individual and society—a struggle for self-expression on the part of the individual, for his subjection on the part of society."

Many kinds of organization are omitted entirely from this classification. Labor organizations are included but business enterprises are not. Nationalities are counted, but governments and all the or-

[34] Robert E. Park and Ernest W. Burgess, *Introduction to the Science of Society* (2d ed.; Chicago: University of Chicago Press, 1924). The quotations are from pages 45–50.

ganized components of the state are left out. There is no place for schools, legislatures, or country clubs. The Boy Scouts and the League of Women Voters are excluded, along with prisons, hospitals, polar expeditions, and courts of law.

The reason for these omissions seems to be that Park and Burgess recognized only the family, the tribe, and the city as organizational types having internal structures. They viewed all other collectivities in terms of conflict and accommodation, so that organizations—such as the Boy Scouts—not conspicuously involved in external struggles are omitted, together with others—such as business enterprises—the external relations of which cannot be reduced to a single theme.

The next important contributor to organizational taxonomy was Chapin. In his *Contemporary American Institutions*,[35] he classified what he called the *nucleated social institution* into its component parts in order to permit quantitative analysis.

At first sight, Chapin's *nucleated social institutions* appear identical with what are now called *organizations.* "It will be useful," he writes, "to differentiate local government, local political organization, local business enterprise, the family, the school, the church, and welfare agencies as specific or nucleated institutions, to be contrasted with art, mythology, language, law, ethics, science, etc., which are general or diffused symbolic institutions."

The component parts of every *nucleated institution* are: (a) common reciprocating attitudes of individuals and their conventionalized behavior patterns; (b) cultural objects of symbolic value (that is, objects charged with sentimental meaning to which human behavior has been conditioned); (c) cultural objects possessing utilitarian value, material objects that satisfy creature wants, objects called property; (d) oral or written language symbols that preserve the descriptions and specifications of the patterns of interrelationship among the other three parts. When the formulation is compactly organized it is called a code.

Each of these parts can be objectively observed, and the observations can be verified. "Attitudes may be measured by scales of opinion. Symbolic culture traits may be enumerated and otherwise described. Utilitarian or material culture traits have weight, volume and value in the price system. Codes are susceptible of legal analysis and interpretation."

[35] Chapin, *op. cit.* The quotations are from pages 13–18.

This is the first and last group classification in which we shall find material artifacts emphasized:

> A well-founded description of a nucleated institution involves more than behavior patterns; it necessitates description of the cultural objects to which this behavior is conditioned, cultural objects of symbolic and of utilitarian value, and the recorded specifications of their interrelationships embodied in a code that can be transmitted from one generation to another.

Nevertheless, "attitudes and behavior patterns are the very essence of the institutional structure," and it is "the configuration of relationships that is the real core of the social institution."

Although the nucleated social institutions that Chapin *denotes* are the same as the organizations we have been discussing, his *definition* of them is totally different. Nucleated social institutions are not made up of people and the relationships between them. Chapin chose to study the culture—rather than the social structure—of organizations. There is nothing unreasonable about this approach. Organizations do have cultures—objects, symbols, and practices attached to membership positions. The transmission of culture traits is not equivalent to interaction. It is often a one-way process and it may take place across great distances.

Another approach to the problem of classification is the systematic sociology of Von Wiese, edited and amplified by Becker. In their *Systematic Sociology* [36] all of the key problems of organizational taxonomy are clearly raised, although the strain of transformation from German phenomenology to American pragmatism sometimes obscures the answers.

Von Wiese and Becker identify three types of *plurality patterns* or *interhuman structures:* crowds, groups, and abstract collectivities, distinguished from each other by duration and by degrees of abstractness. One of the first questions raised is whether a plurality pattern is made up of people or relationships. The authors decide that it must involve both.

There are two important kinds of crowd: concrete and abstract. Concrete crowds are pretty much the same as the crowds and mobs described in textbooks of social psychology—transitory and amorphous, with some elements of common purpose. Abstract crowds are

[36] Von Wiese and Becker, *op. cit.*

dispersed populations, with a degree of self-identification. The "masses" are the abstract crowd par excellence.

The group is defined as an "interhuman plurality pattern of such relatively long duration and relative solidarity that the persons therein affiliated come to be regarded as a relatively homogeneous unit." It is distinguished from the crowd by its duration and solidarity, and from the abstract collectivity by the "definite, empirical human beings" of which it is composed. The group, as an ideal type, is characterized by continuity, division of function among members, common attitudes, the growth of traditions and customs over time, and interaction with other groups.[37]

The abstract collectivity is the most difficult plurality pattern to understand. Some abstract collectivities are true abstractions, others are large-scale organizations, ambiences, or personifications of statistical data.

At one point in *Systematic Sociology,* the triple classification is temporarily abandoned and plurality patterns are arranged in a number of dichotomous categories. A plurality pattern may be either *amorphous* or *organized*. It is amorphous when the network of relationships does not show any clear-cut division of functions. A plurality pattern may be *temporary* or *permanent*. The authors are particularly fascinated by a special variety of plurality pattern in which a set of activities is repeated at set times, without any continuity in the intervals; for example, the annual employees' picnic, the Saturday-night dance, or a carnival. Plurality patterns may be *regulated* or *elective*. Regulated patterns are created by some authoritative power and depend upon some larger or higher social system. Elective patterns are voluntary and spontaneous, without fixed obligations. Plurality patterns may be *natural* or *artificial*. The natural patterns are the family, the clan, the sib, the male sex, the female sex, and any other pattern based on sex or age.

Plurality patterns conditioned by geography are called locality patterns. The most important types are the village, the city, and the region. Ideological plurality patterns are based on religious, mystical,

---

[37] Von Wiese and Becker are particularly interested in the smaller groups. They present a systematic classification of dyads and discuss the dynamics of triadic and tetradic (four-member) groups at some length. In fact, they distinguish rather sharply between dyads and triads—"groups in which the personal element predominates"—and all groups having more than three members.

and utopian fantasies. They range from pure myths, such as Valhalla, to practically oriented utopias, such as the ultimate Marxist society in which the state has withered away.

Another interesting concept is the negative plurality pattern—the members of which are primarily conditioned by the fact that they do *not* belong to a particular organization. Renegades, outlaws, and "cads" form amorphous groups with the common characteristic of *non*-belongingness.

Sanderson's "outline for the description of groups," [38] published in 1938, was the first working taxonomy in the style of the biological sciences:

> Until we take the trouble to describe different kinds of groups with the same care that a biologist describes a species, genus, or family of plant or animal life, we shall fail to have any adequate understanding of the nature of the group. How far would zoology advance if its students merely talked about sparrows, bugs, or squirrels, with no exact description? The first duty of the zoologist is to describe exactly a new species or to determine whether the specimen in hand has the characteristics of any species already described. [39]

The Sanderson classification, presented as incomplete, covers not only organizations but also unorganized groups and aggregates. Each category is explicitly described in such a way as to permit labeling.

The three major categories are based on the manner of selecting members: involuntary groups, voluntary groups, delegate groups. Involuntary groups are subdivided by their membership criteria, that is, location, common culture, or contiguity. Voluntary groups are divided into organized and unorganized. An organized group has a single leader. Organized groups are further subdivided according to whether the leader is dominant, and then successively according to the form of choosing the leader, the form of choosing the membership, and other characteristics. Thus Type II, 2A, b.2 denotes nonsecret fraternal orders. Delegate groups are bodies composed of delegates of their respective groups, such as conventions or congresses.

Unlike botanical taxonomies, this classification scheme does not clarify the relationships of similar forms, nor does it throw any

---

[38] Dwight Sanderson, "A Preliminary Group Classification Based on Structure," *Social Forces,* Vol. XVII, No. 2 (December, 1938), 196–201.

[39] Dwight Sanderson, "Group Description," *Social Forces,* Vol. XVI, No. 3 (March, 1938). The quotation is from page 311.

light on the origin of complex forms. On the other hand, any observed group can be unequivocally labeled, and entities with similar structures are necessarily placed together, regardless of their superficial differences. These are the essentials of a useable taxonomy.

One of the simplest and most useful arrangements is that of MacIver and Page's *Society: An Introductory Analysis,*[40] which contains three major categories: the community, the unorganized group, and the organization. Here, for the first time in the long history of group classification, organizations and unorganized groups are clearly separated, and a plain distinction can be made between the community and its government.

The defect of this system is that it is too simple. It does not distinguish systematically between the tribe and the village, the family and the club, the state and a learned society. However, MacIver and Page suggest that additional subtypes might be developed and even propose criteria: size of membership, some quality of interaction (or of group interest), the degree of formal recognition, and the type of interest pursued.

LaPiere[41] distinguishes between the group—any number of human beings who interact with one another in any manner—and the status group, which grants significant, specific status to its members. Status groups may be large or small, temporary or enduring, with continuous or sporadic interaction, highly or slightly structured. These distinctions are expressed as gradations, not as attributes, and LaPiere relates each of them to social control. The control exercised by the group over the individual member is inversely correlated with membership size and directly correlated with the age of the structure, the frequency of interaction, and the degree of structuring. The important varieties of status groups are work groups, community groups, recreational coteries and clubs, peer groups, and the family.

The most curious feature of this classification system is the complete separation of large-scale from small-scale groups. If a status group is large enough, it ceases to be a status group and becomes an *institutional organization.*

> There are, however, many forms of associations which in all dimensions except that of size cannot be categorically distinguished from status groups. These are the formal organizations, such as primitive

[40] MacIver and Page, *op. cit.*
[41] Richard LaPiere, *A Theory of Social Control* (New York: McGraw-Hill, 1954). The quotation is from page 110.

tribes, peasant villages, and modern corporations, that are usually designated by sociologists as "institutions." Institutional forms of organization are many and varied, but they all have in common durability, frequency of association, elaborate structures and relatively large size. In the first three dimensions they are status groups in character; but their relatively large size means that the kind of status accorded the individual member is more generic than specific.

Krech and Crutchfield define the *psychological group* as "two or more people who bear an explicit psychological relationship to one another." [42] The term is explicitly limited to groups (a) whose members interact, (b) whose members perceive all their fellow-members, and (c) that are "relatively small, of relatively short duration and relatively informal." A *social organization,* for them, is a specific grouping of actual people characterized by (a) cultural products, (b) a collective name or symbol, (c) distinctive action patterns, (d) a common belief system, and (e) enforcing agents or techniques.

Although the authors are not entirely consistent in their terminology, psychological groups and social organizations seem to be the principal subclasses of a larger category of *social groups.* A given collectivity can be both a psychological group and a social organization at the same time, but there are no intermediate terms.

A number of recent taxonomies take the distinction between organizations and unorganized groups for granted and concentrate on the distinctions *among* organizations, especially those of large scale. Most of the classifications are focused on differences in goals and modes of goal achievement. One of the most interesting of these is Hughes' [43] almost casual classification of five dominant organizational models in modern society: the voluntary association, the military model, the philanthropic model, the corporation model, the family business model.

Parsons [44] classifies organizations in keeping with his theoretical model of the pattern variables, that is by the social need to which the organization is oriented. He divides them into those: (a) oriented

[42] David Krech and Richard S. Crutchfield, *Theory and Problems of Social Pyschology* (New York: McGraw-Hill, 1948), p. 18.

[43] Everett C. Hughes, "Memorandum on Going Concerns" (Society for Applied Anthropology, 1952) (unpublished paper).

[44] Talcott Parsons, "Suggestions for a Sociological Approach to the Theory of Organizations," *Administrative Science Quarterly,* Vol. I (1956), and *Structure and Process in Modern Societies* (Glencoe, Ill.: Free Press, 1960).

to economic production, (b) oriented to political goals, (c) concerned with social integration, and (d) concerned with pattern maintenance.

In its original form, this classification is perhaps too abstract to be directly applicable, but it has been adapted and elaborated by other scholars.[45] Parsons has also developed the useful concept of the three major hierarchical levels in a large-scale organization. At the technical level the productive activity of the organization is carried on. The managerial level is primarily concerned with mediation between components of the organization and with coordination of their activities. The institutional level connects the organization with other organizations and with the general society.

Blau and Scott have worked out an interesting classification based on the *cui-bono,* or "prime beneficiary," principle.[46] They note that four populations can be distinguished in relation to any given large-scale organization—the members or rank-and-file participants, the owners or managers, the clients, and the public at large—and they propose to classify organizations as to which of these populations is their prime beneficiary. The application of this criterion leads them to four types of organization:

1. Mutual benefit associations, such as unions, professional associations, and political parties, in which the prime beneficiary is the membership.
2. Business concerns, such as industrial firms, banks, and retail stores, in which the owners are the prime beneficiary.
3. Service organizations, such as social agencies, hospitals, and schools, in which the clients are the prime beneficiary.
4. Commonweal organizations, such as armies and police departments, in which the public at large is the prime beneficiary.

The principal use to which they put this classification is to distinguish different modes of participation and different points of stress,

[45] Including Samuel N. Eisenstadt, "Bureaucracy and Bureaucratization," *Current Sociology,* Vol. VII (1958), Frances G. Scott, "Action Theory and Research in Social Organization," *American Journal of Sociology,* Vol. LXIV, No. 4 (January, 1959), C. Wayne Gordon and Nicholas Babchuk, "A Typology of Voluntary Associations," *American Sociological Review,* Vol. XXIV, No. 1 (February, 1959).

[46] Peter M. Blau and W. Richard Scott, *Formal Organizations: A Comparative Approach* (San Francisco: Chandler, 1962), pp. 42–45.

integration being the salient problem of mutual benefit associations, efficiency, of business concerns, goal conflict, of service organizations, internal control, of commonweal organizations.

A somewhat similar taxonomy based on another criterion is proposed by Etzioni,[47] who classifies organizations according to whether their predominant pattern of *compliance* is coercive, utilitarian, or normative, and according to the relative salience of the predominant pattern. Coercive organizations include concentration camps, prisons, and custodial mental hospitals. Factories, mines, and offices are usually utilitarian organizations. Churches, hospitals, and schools are normative organizations. Since all three modes of compliance are recognized to occur to some extent within each category, the scheme relies rather heavily on thirteen common-sense categories that appear as subdivisions of the three main classes. These common types (the existence of uncommon types is recognized) are as follows:

1. *Predominantly coercive*
   Concentration camps
   Prisons (most)
   Correctional "institutions" (large majority)
   Custodial mental hospitals
   Prisoner-of-war camps
   Relocation centers
   Coercive unions
   Place in category undetermined: Forced-labor camps

2. *Predominantly utilitarian*
   Blue-collar industries and blue-collar divisions in other industries
   White-collar industries and white-collar divisons in other industries
      (normative compliance is a secondary pattern)
   Business unions (normative compliance is a secondary pattern)
   Farmers' organizations (normative compliance is a secondary pattern)
   Peacetime military organizations (coercive compliance is a secondary pattern)

3. *Predominantly normative*
   Religious organizations (including churches, orders, monasteries, convents)

[47] Amitai Etzioni, *A Comparative Analysis of Complex Organizations* (New York: Free Press, 1961). The classification table is from pages 66–67.

Ideological political organizations
General hospitals
Colleges and universities
Social unions
Voluntary associations
  a. fraternal associations (high social compliance)
  b. fund-raising and action associations (high social plus secondary emphasis on pure normative compliance)
Schools (coercion in varying degrees is the secondary pattern)
Therapeutic mental hospitals (coercion is the secondary pattern)
Professional organizations (including research organizations, law firms, newspapers, planning firms, etc.; utilitarian compliance is the secondary pattern)

Place in category undetermined: "Core" organizations of social movements

4. *Dual structures*
Normative-coercive: Combat units
Utilitarian-normative: Majority of unions
Utilitarian-coercive: Some early industries, some farms, company towns, and ships

Quite another approach to taxonomy is the attempt of Haas and his associates [48] to derive an organizational taxonomy empirically, by drawing large samples of heterogeneous organizations from the great pool of American society and grouping them by the presence or absence of selected organizational characteristics. Initial lists of possibly significant characteristics contained 210 items. These were later reduced to ninety-nine "researchable dimensions," and further reduction is anticipated. The items range from such simple facts as the organization's age to rather difficult measures, such as an index of vertical and horizontal complexity. For sampling purposes, the investigators make use of the following headings, among others:

Government agencies
Business firms
Educational institutions
Religious organizations

[48] Eugene Haas, Richard H. Hall, and Norman J. Johnson, "Towards an Empirically Derived Taxonomy of Organizations" (Columbus, Ohio: Department of Sociology and Anthropology, Ohio State University, 1963) (unpublished paper).

Fraternal and service organizations
Labor unions
Occupational and professional organizations
Social and recreational organizations
Welfare agencies and civic associations
Political and lobbying organizations
Mass communication organizations
Ethnic associations

Certain common features of these newer taxonomies deserve notice. First, all of them are highly aware of large, official, urban organizations and relatively indifferent to specialized organizations of smaller scale. Second, when these taxonomies are applied to large-scale organizations, many of their components cannot be forced into the same category as the parent organization. Third, no structural or functional classification of organizations devised so far enables us to displace the labels of ordinary usage. Finally, the number of organizational types, even in a complex modern society, is rather small. The following list, which is neither exhaustive nor orderly, can be shown to cover—with reasonable specificity—most of the identifiable organizations in the United States in the twentieth century. For the time being, at least, the recognition of species and genera in this field does not enable us to dispense with the kitchen names of the specimens.

Social Organizations
COMMON-SENSE CATEGORIES

Adolescent gangs
Athletic leagues
Athletic teams
Brothels
Churches
Colleges
Consumer cooperatives
Corporate enterprises
Country clubs
Courts
Criminal syndicates
Denominations

Examining boards
Exchanges
Expeditions
Extended families
Fraternities and sororities
Gambling houses
Genealogical societies
Governing boards
Government bureaus
Honorary societies
Hospitals
Hotels and resorts

Interest associations
Juries
Labor federations
Labor unions
Learned societies
Legislatures
Lodges and brotherhoods
Merchant and naval ships
Military commands
Missions and settlement
houses
Monasteries and convents
Museums and libraries
Newspaper staffs
Nuclear families
Orchestras and bands
Plantations
Police and fire departments
Political parties

Prisons and jails
Private schools
Producer cooperatives
Professional associations
Professional offices
Public schools
Research laboratories and
institutes
Residential clubs
Restaurants
Retail stores
Sects
Social agencies
Summer camps
Taverns and nightclubs
Theatrical companies
Universities
Veterans' organizations
Workshops

These commonplace designations are still indispensable for describing and circumscribing the organizational field.

CHAPTER TWO

Organizational Structure

THE TABLE OF ORGANIZATION

A table of organization is a chart that shows the positions in an organization and the prescribed interaction between those positions. Each little box on such a chart represents a position or a category of positions. Height on the page is a measure of status. Vertical lines represent the interaction of superiors and subordinates. Horizontal lines represent the interaction of equals.

As a two-dimensional chart with little boxes connected by lines, the table of organization seems to be a modern device, but the concept it represents is very ancient. A famous example is Exodus xviii: 14–22:

> And when Moses' father in law saw all that he did to the people, he said, What is this thing that thou doest to the people? why sittest thou thyself alone, and all the people stand by thee from morning unto even? And Moses said unto his father in law, Because the people come unto me to enquire of God: When they have a matter, they come unto me; and I judge between one and another, and I do make them know the statutes of God, and his laws. And Moses' father in law said unto him, The thing that thou doest is not good. Thou wilt surely wear away, both thou, and this people that is with thee: for this thing is too heavy for thee; thou art not able to perform it thyself alone. Hearken now unto my voice, I will give thee counsel and God shall be with thee: Be thou for the people to God-ward, that thou

mayest bring the causes unto God: And thou shalt teach them ordinances and laws, and shalt shew them the way wherein they must walk, and the work that they must do. Moreover thou shalt provide out of all the people able men, such as fear God, men of truth, hating covetousness; and place such over them, to be rulers of thousands, and rulers of hundreds, rulers of fifties, and rulers of tens. And let them judge the people at all seasons: and it shall be, that every great matter they bring unto thee, but every small matter they shall judge.

The tables of organization of the ancient Chinese empire under the Ts'in and Han dynasties can be fully reconstructed from the records of positions and their relationships that have come down to us, including such details as salaries and the courtesy titles of wives.[1] The Mu-che-yuan ling, for example, was a functionary responsible for supplying horses from the capital to one of the six frontier commanderies. He had three assistants, each with special duties, and he himself reported to one of the assistants of the imperial T'ai-pu, who was in charge of all official transportation.

The elaborate table of organization of the Roman republic, with its consuls, censors, tribunes, aediles, quaestors, and prefects, has influenced all subsequent public administration in the Western world.[2] Each of these officials had very precise duties. The aediles, subordinate to the consuls, were charged, for example, with the maintenance of roads, walls, and bridges, the management of the public baths, the public markets, poor relief, supervision of the theater, and the inspection of weights and measures. The qualifications for the office were explicit, including prior experience as quaestor and the posting of a bond.

It is feasible to reconstruct tables of organization for the towns and city states of medieval and early modern times (Figure 2–1), or of early navies and banking houses.[3] With the development of large-scale government in early modern times, bureaucratic elaboration went to lengths unknown before or since. By the middle of the

[1] Edouard Chavannes, *Les Mémoires Historiques de Se-Ma T'sien* (Paris: Ernest Lerouz, 1897), Vol. II, 513–33.

[2] Joachim Marquardt, *Roemische Staatsverwaltung* (2d ed.; Leipzig: S. Hirzel, 1881); J. H. Madvig, *Die Verfassung und Verwaltung des Roemischen Staates* (Leipzig: Teubner, 1881), Vol. I.

[3] S. Isaacsohn, *Geschichte des Preussischen Beamtenthums* (Berlin: Puttkammer and Muehlbrecht, 1874).

Figure 2–1

FIFTEENTH-CENTURY TOWN ADMINISTRATION IN PRUSSIA

Stadtrath (Town Council)

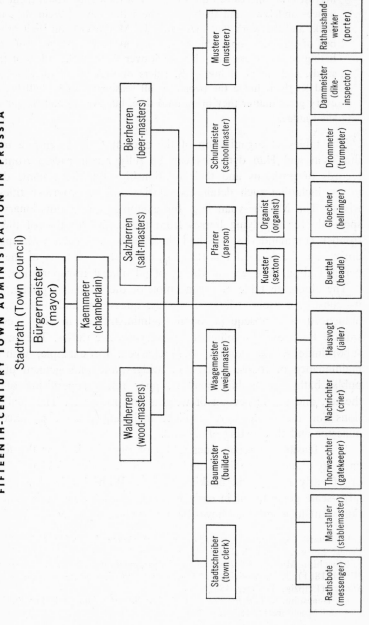

eighteenth century, the Prussian civil service under Frederick William I included 143 consecutive and clearly defined ranks, from field marshal down to cellar clerk.[4] Some of the forms of military organization devised by Frederick William were eventually adopted in all other Western armies and remain unchanged to the present day. It was this same Prussian bureaucracy that later furnished the background for Max Weber's great theory. In the middle of the eighteenth century, it was said to produce a public revenue greater than that of the Russian empire and to have a lower per capita burden of taxation than any of its neighbors. Key positions were filled by boards or "colleges," and the individual bureaucrat was subject to peer-group discipline and collective responsibility. The rules were unusually explicit. Most government business was conducted in writing and the king rarely saw his ministers face to face. The civil service was linked on the one hand to the army, from which all its lower officials were drawn, and on the other hand to the universities, which trained candidates for the higher posts in cameralism and jurisprudence. Its distinctive features included formal in-service training, central auditing, and a system of promotional examinations.[5]

The Venetian constitution, with its curious system of indirect elections and its specification of committees of different sizes for different purposes, was perhaps the most intricate table of organization ever developed. The supreme judicial function, for example, was divided among a Council of Forty, the Panel of Twenty (*Zonta*), the Council of Ten, the Council of Six (*Signoria*), the Committee of Three (*Capi*), and the Committee of Four (*Collegia Criminale*).[6] To anyone who supposes that organizational complexity is a modern invention, the Venetian state must be a surprise.

[4] Albert Lotz, *Geschichte des Deutschen Beamtenstaates* (Berlin: Von Decker, 1914).

[5] Walter L. Dorn, "The Prussian Bureaucracy in the Eighteenth Century," *Political Science Quarterly,* Vol. XLVI (1931), 403–23 and Vol. XLVII (1932), 75–94 and 259–73, Gustav Schmoller, "Der Deutsche Beamtenstaat vom 16–18 Jahrhundert," in *Jahrbuch Fuer Gestzgebung, Verwaltung und Volkswirtschaft im Deutschen Reich* (Leipzig: Von Duncker & Humblot, 1894), and Carl J. Friedrich, *Constitutional Government and Democracy: Theory and Practice in Europe and America* (rev. ed.; Boston: Ginn, 1950).

[6] See, among others, W. Carew Hazlitt, *The Venetian Republic: Its Rise, Its Growth and Its Fall* (London: Black, 1900). See also P. G. Smolenti, *La Vie Privée à Venise* (Venice: Ferdinand Ongania, 1882), pp. 32–38, and L. M. Ragg, *Crises in Venetian History* (New York: Dutton, 1928), pp. 78–82.

Tables of organization have also come down to us from less imposing establishments. Toward the end of the eighteenth century, a London newspaper described the "list of officers" in a gambling house. There were:

A Director who superintends the room.

An Operator who deals the cards at a cheating game called faro.

Two Crowpees who watch the cards and gather the money for the bank.

Two Puffs who have money given to them to decoy others to pay.

A Clerk who is a check upon the puffs to see that they sink none of the money given them to play with.

A Sprit who is a puff of lower rank, who serves at half salary while he is learning to deal.

A Flasher to swear how often the bank has been stripped.

A Dunner who goes about to recover the money lost at play.

The Waiter to fill out wine, snuff candles, and attend in the gaming room.

An Attorney, a Newgate Solicitor.

A Captain who is to fight any gentleman who is peevish for losing his money.

An Usher, who lights gentlemen up and down stairs, and gives the word to the porter.

A Porter who is generally a soldier of the foot guards.

An Orderly Man who walks up and down the outside of the door, to give notice to the porter, and alarm the house at the approach of the constables; and

A Runner who is to get intelligence of the justices' meetings. Link boys, watchmen, chairmen, drawers . . . affidavit men, ruffians, bailees, cum multis aliis.[7]

Tables of organization are discussed in the very earliest writings on industrial management. Babbage, in 1832, worked out improvements in factory tables of organization (Figure 2–2) that anticipated the principles of "scientific management." [8] The practice has continued down to the present day, and the preparation, analysis, and revision of tables of organization has become a continuous activity in modern management. The use of such tables for management pur-

[7] *St. James's Evening Post,* quoted in Christopher Hibbert, *The Road to Tyburn: The Story of Jack Sheppard and the Eighteenth-Century London Underworld* (New York: World, 1957).

[8] Charles Babbage, *On the Economy of Machinery and Manufactures* (London: C. Knight, 1832).

Figure 2–2

A MINING ENTERPRISE IN THE 1880'S

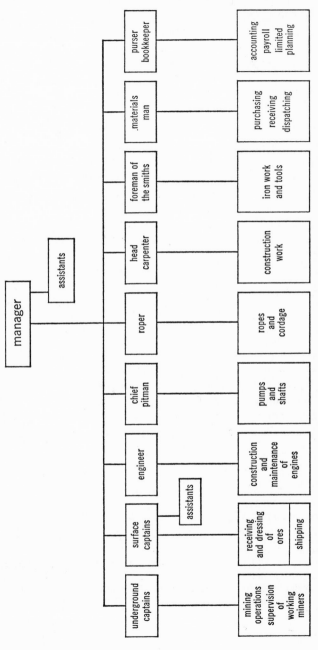

FROM Raymond Villers, *Dynamic Management in Industry* (Englewood Cliffs, N.J.: Prentice-Hall, 1960), p. 20.

poses can be studied in any large corporation. Their use as analytic devices is illustrated in dozens of studies.[9]

Although the table of organization developed originally as a method of mapping large-scale organizations, it appears to be equally useful in the description of organized primary groups. The anthropological literature on kinship leans heavily on this device to describe family structure (Figure 2–3).[10] Many studies of gangs and peer groups show that they can be analyzed by the same means.[11]

Any table of organization resembles any other in representing the structure of the organization to consist of positions and interactions. Positions are identified by activity and status. The title of the position on the chart ordinarily identifies its activity. Its distance from the bottom or the top of the chart measures its status. The lines that are drawn between positions indicate prescribed (or occasionally observed) interaction with other positions. Most tables of organization emphasize interaction between superiors and direct subordinates. They minimize or omit interaction between equals and between widely separated positions. Villers,[12] whose book on management contains what is probably the best discussion of industrial tables of organization, has analyzed such special relations as advice, service, and mutual guidance. Many writers distinguish among line organization, in which all formally prescribed communications are between unequals, line-staff organization, in which staff specialists (having superiors and equals but no subordinates) are added to the line, and functional or horizontal organization, in which authority is divided among specialists and different channels of vertical interaction are prescribed for different problems.[13] Dubin presents a

[9] For example, Conrad M. Arensberg and D. McGregor, "Determinants of Morale in an Industrial Economy," *Applied Anthropology*, Vol. I (1942), and Harriet O. Ronken and Paul R. Lawrence, *Administering Change: A Case Study of Human Relations in a Factory* (Boston: Harvard University, Division of Research, 1952).

[10] For example, Claude Levi-Strauss, *Les structures élémentaires de la parenté* (Paris: Presses Universitaires de Frances, 1949).

[11] For example, William F. Whyte, *Street Corner Society* (Chicago: University of Chicago Press, 1955).

[12] Raymond Villers, *Dynamic Management in Industry* (Englewood Cliffs, N.J.: Prentice-Hall, 1960).

[13] For an authoritative treatment of this question, see Wilbert E. Moore, *Industrial Relations and the Social Order* (New York: Macmillan, 1946), Chapter 6.

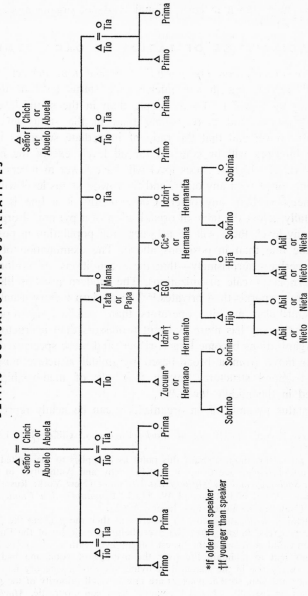

Figure 2-3

DZITAS—CONSANGUINEOUS RELATIVES

*If older than speaker
†If younger than speaker

FROM Robert Redfield, *The Folk Culture of Yucatan* (Chicago: University of Chicago Press, 1941), p. 202.

graphic classification of "unit linkage systems," some of which are not adequately shown in conventional tables of organization.[14]

CHARACTERISTICS OF TABLES OF ORGANIZATION

Tables of organization are pyramidal at the top. Perfect "pyramidicity" means that in any intermediate status level of the organization there will be fewer people than in the status level immediately below and more people than in the status level immediately above, and that the ratio of immediate superiors to immediate inferiors will be constant for all levels except the highest and lowest. The highest status level will have fewer members (ordinarily only one) than any other, and the lowest status level will have more members than any other. Consequently, if a line is drawn horizontally across the table of organization of a pyramidal organization at any level, there will be a larger total population in positions below the line than in positions above. The examination of cases shows—perhaps surprisingly—that these conditions are seldom met in modern large-scale organizations. The modern army is likely to have more corporals than privates.[15] The modern factory usually has more semiskilled machine operators than unskilled laborers. The modern university has more assistant professors than instructors. As these organizations become larger, richer, and more specialized, they seem to move from a broad-based pyramidal structure toward a diamond-shaped structure, having the bulk of membership concentrated in the middle levels.[16]

The status pyramid of an organization can be neatly represented

[14] Robert Dubin, *The World of Work* (Englewood Cliffs, N.J.: Prentice-Hall, 1958).

[15] For interesting discussions of this point as it applies to the United States military establishment, see Chapter 2, "Hierarchy and Authority," in Morris Janowitz, *Sociology and the Military Establishment* (New York: Russell Sage Foundation, 1959), and Raymond W. Mack, *Communication Challenges in the 60's* (New York: Bozell and Jacobs, 1962).

[16] Something analogous occurs in societies as they move along the path of economic progress. Before 1700, the overwhelming majority of the European population could be found at the lowest budget level, with a subsistence income barely sufficient to maintain life over the average of good and bad years. With the steady rise in the standard of living, the modal category has moved steadily upward also, so that paupers are now a small minority of the population in any industrially advanced country. See Jean Fourastié, *Machinisme et Bien-Etre* (Paris: Les Editions de Minuit, 1951).

by a diagram like a population pyramid, but in which the vertical scale represents status while the horizontal scale represents the population at each status level. Diagrams of this kind are very useful in showing us the general shape of an organization and providing a graphic impression of its status order, but they are conceptually inferior to population pyramids in one important respect. There is no way of calibrating the vertical scale so that it represents *equal* intervals of status (the vertical scale of a population pyramid *does* represent equal increments of age).

A high pyramid with a steep slope does not necessarily indicate a great concentration of power. It may reveal the contrary. There is some evidence that organizations with despotic leaders have flatter pyramids with fewer levels than those in which personal power is limited and widely diffused,[17] since despotism is antithetical to the autonomy of subordinates.

Even though few organizations are perfectly pyramidal and many approach the diamond shape, we can expect to find an almost perfect pyramidal segment at the top of any sizeable organization. The reasons are inherent in the function of coordination of information and activity. The pyramidal shape corresponds to the condensation and generalization of information as it moves upward through channels of communication and to the expansion and particularization of directives as they move down through the same channels.

The distribution of components itself (as distinct from the distribution of membership) tends to be consistently pyramidal, since the component organizations on each level are usually subdivisions of the components on the next higher level and therefore more numerous. In a university, for example, there are necessarily several faculties, more departments than faculties, and more classes than departments.

Some other curious features of a table of organization were pointed out by Roethlisberger. His hypothetical naive observer observes a factory organization chart and sees that

> (1) The people at the top of the organization, including the person to whom he is talking, appear to be separated by many steps from the people at the bottom of the organization. (2) Although every place in the organization chart has a label attached to it, the labels

[17] Stanislaw Andrzejewski, *Military Organization and Society* (London: Routledge & Kegan Paul, 1954).

at the top and middle of the chart refer to single persons, whereas the labels at the bottom, such as "workers," "clerks," etc., refer to groups of persons. These observations raise three questions in the observer's mind, so he asks the general manager: (a) Do the people at the bottom of the organization have any difficulty in understanding the economic and logical objectives of the people at the top? (b) Do the people at the top have difficulty in understanding the way the people at the bottom feel? (c) Although this chart shows how management is organized, how are all the people labeled "workers" (who, he understands, constitute two-thirds of the population) organized? [18]

STATUS SCHISMS

In a great many organizations, the pyramid is divided in two by a status schism, which establishes a formal discontinuity between the upper and lower segments. A status schism appears to increase the total amount of authority in the organization by giving all members of the upper segment some control over all members of the lower segment, regardless of whether their positions are connected in the table of organization. The increments of reward provided by the organization to members in the upper segment are greater than those conferred in the lower segment.

Armies divide their personnel into officers and enlisted men. Banks make a similar division between officers and employees. Corporations invent and multiply distinctions between executives and workers. Many churches have a status schism between clergy and laity. Hospitals have a dramatic status schism between doctors and nurses. The enhancement of power and disproportionate reward seem always to be associated with a status schism, but there are many other effects as well, such as the inhibition of informal interaction across the status gap—the prohibition of "fraternization"— and the almost invariable stereotypes whereby members of the lower segment are perceived by the upper as childlike and irresponsible, while members of the upper segment are perceived by the lower as incompetent and corrupt.

We are shockingly ignorant about the real implications of status schisms and cannot yet determine whether they are essential in

[18] Fritz J. Roethlisberger, *Management and Morale* (Cambridge, Mass.: Harvard University Press, 1941), p. 74.

military organizations or elsewhere, nor can we determine what their balancing utilities and costs may be, considered from the standpoint of the organization as a whole.

SIMPLE AND COMPOUND ORGANIZATIONS

Another inescapable problem of analysis is that while the membership of some organizations can be arrayed on a single vertical scale of status, a good many others exhibit two or more status scales, the positions of which are incommensurate. We shall define *simple* organizations as those having a single status order and *compound* organizations as those having several. The distinction may be a little hard to grasp, but it is essential to any systematic analysis of tables of organization.

We have noted that all the members of organized groups occupy positions. Some positions, such as chairman of the board, can have only a single incumbent at a given time. Others, such as member of the association, are as inclusive as the organization itself.

In some organizations—large and small—there are certain activities performed by *all* members of the organization. In other words, all members share a common position, in addition to whatever specialized positions they may occupy, and the organization is thus compound. All the members of the Roman Catholic Church share a common membership position and have the same duties, for example, regarding confession and communion. The Pope is no less and no more a Catholic than an infant baptized yesterday.

But not all organizations are like this. A modern university has a student body, a faculty, a board of regents or trustees, a president and some other general officers, hundreds of clerical and maintenance employees, and a large roster of alumni. All of these people, taken together, constitute the university, but they do not usually describe themselves as its *members* because—strictly speaking—there is no such position as member of the university. That is to say, there are no activities performed by students, professors, trustees, janitors, and alumni indifferently.

Simple and compound organizations with similar functions often look very much alike. The British Cabinet is a simple organization (although with a rather complicated status order) the Prime Minister being himself a Cabinet minister and *primus inter pares*. The United States Cabinet is a compound organization, President and Cabinet.

The differences are significant. The British Cabinet must stand and fall as a body, is primarily responsible to its parliamentary backers, and can act to some extent without the Prime Minister. The U.S. Cabinet consists of individuals responsible to the President. They can be replaced one by one and cannot act collectively without a presidential directive.

All of the members of simple organizations are linked in a single network of communications. By contrast, communication between the separate status orders of a compound organization is usually quite restricted. There is no routine channel for professors to communicate with alumni about educational affairs, or for corporate employees to discuss policy with stockholders. The long-range goals of the major sectors in a compound organization are assumed to be separate at best, and are often flatly opposed.

ANALYSIS OF TABLES

It is sometimes objected that the table of organization does not tell us how an organization works, only how it is *supposed* to work. Informal interaction accounts for part of the discrepancy, but there are other reasons too, such as the tendency for information to lag behind the small social changes that occur continuously and the tendency for desirable conditions to be hopefully included as facts.

Nonetheless, the table of organization always tells us a great deal, and it is doubtful whether we can talk sensibly about a particular organization without it. Consideration of organization *structure* must begin with the elements found in the table (Figures 2–4 and 2–5).

POSITIONS

Some of the most difficult problems in the analysis of organizations develop when we attempt to distinguish clearly between people and positions, office-holders and offices, actors and roles. Many sociologists regard social interaction as a process in which the participants are not people in the usual sense but segments of behavior. Barnard, for example, defines the formal organization as a system of consciously coordinated activities or forces of two or more persons.[19]

---

[19] Chester I. Barnard, *The Functions of the Executive* (Cambridge, Mass.: Harvard University Press, 1938), especially Chapter 6.

Figure 2–4

A LARGE ORGANIZATION
(PUBLIC SCHOOL SYSTEM)

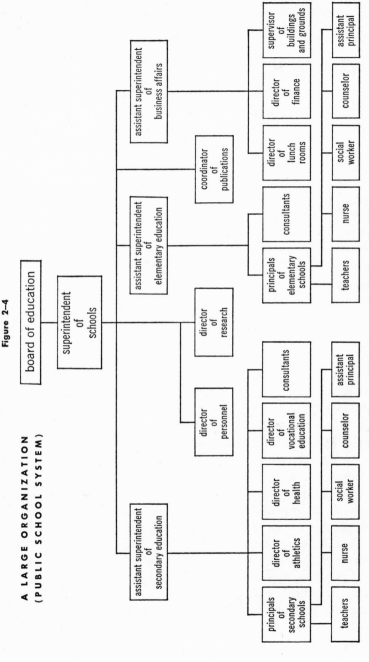

FROM an unpublished paper by Richard S. Zeglen.

Figure 2–5

A SMALL ORGANIZATION (SEWER CONSTRUCTION CREW)

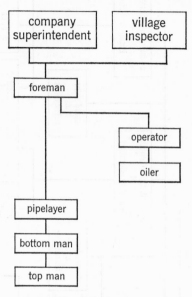

FROM a student paper.

This is a tenable assumption, but it is very difficult to work with. We shall make the simpler assumption (which has the incidental advantage of being closer to the common-sense view) that an organization includes the *persons* who are its members. The members of any organization can be placed in categories called positions.

An organizational position is a category of membership whose incumbents are expected to act and interact in explicitly prescribed ways peculiar to that category. It probably makes sense to talk about positions in unorganized groups also, but in that case it falls to the observer to determine which positions he will recognize. Organizational positions, by contrast, are defined by the organization itself—usually in meticulous detail.

Because positions are categories, they can be combined and divided in various meaningful ways. Almost all organizations exhibit certain dichotomous categories of special importance. Thus, in some

of our specimen organizations, we observe that the entire membership can be divided *for some purposes* into two positions: parents
and children, clergy and laity, management and labor. *For other
purposes,* however, these same organizations recognize more differentiation. Thus, within the general categories of officers and men,
the United States Army classifies its personnel as general officers,
field officers, company officers, warrant officers, noncommissioned
officers, and privates. Another subdivision distinguishes a score or
so of branches: Infantry, Engineer, Artillery, Armored, Medical
Corps, Quartermaster Corps, Signal Corps, and so forth. There are
five grades of general officer, three of field officer, three of company
officer, four of warrant officer, six of noncommissioned officer and
specialist, and three of private, making twenty-four ranks in all.[20]
Cutting across this whole set of positions is a system of several hundred job and specialty classifications. Each soldier has two different classification numbers. One stands for the job for which he
is best qualified. The other stands for the job to which he is currently
assigned. Military positions are further identified by unit assignment and by such other divisions as line and staff, headquarters
and field, regular and reserve, domestic and overseas. If we continue
this process long enough, we finally arrive at the position of John
Jones, sergeant first class, regular enlistment, infantry platoon sergeant
in Platoon X, Company Y, Z Battalion, 000 Regiment, 00 Division,
0 Corps, job classification 123, military assignment 321. Since this
position has only a single incumbent, subdivision can proceed no
further.

A full description of Sergeant Jones' position makes it clear that
there are certain prescriptions of activity and interaction that apply
to him alone. Only Jones is responsible for drawing up the morning
report of Platoon X and reporting unexplained absences. Other
prescriptions of activity and interaction apply to all members of the
00 Division. We can find some of them by casual inspection of bulletin
boards in the divisional area. Still other prescriptions apply to all
sergeants, others to all infantrymen, to all enlisted men, and so
forth. They can be found in field manuals, general orders, directive
circulars, the Articles of War, and military customs. Many of the
prescriptions are highly detailed. We know a great deal about the

[20] Army Regulations 600–15, *Rank and Precedence* (Washington, D.C.:
Department of the Army, August, 1955).

patterns of activity and interaction of an infantry sergeant as soon as we know the position he occupies.

We can say that a person *occupies* a position, or that he is the *incumbent* of a position and designate any of the categories of membership to which he belongs, so long as there are prescribed activities and interactions that are peculiar to people in that category. When the requirements of the position are known to the observer, this is a straightforward procedure. When they are not, errors are likely to occur. The most common error is to explain the behavior required in a position by the personal traits of the incumbent.

Positions are usually named and identified by means of three elements, which may be thought of, somewhat metaphorically, as coordinates. These are activity, status, and location.

The *activity* of an organizational position is the incumbent's share of the organization's total program for manipulating the environment and achieving its goals. It is roughly equivalent to what a particular organization defines as useful work. The activity of a position does not include all of the incumbent's behavior, or even all of the work he performs, but only what he does in his "official" capacity as part of the larger program. Attached to most organizational positions is some kind of label summarizing the principal activity of incumbents. Such labels are secretary, teacher, priest, janitor.

The *status* of an organizational position is its location in the rank order of relative influence prescribed by the organization. When persons holding positions of unequal status interact in an organizational context, the higher-ranking member ordinarily exercises the greater influence and modifies the behavior of the other more than his own is modified. Most organizations take pains to make status as definite as possible. The label attached to an organizational position often specifies its status, for example senior secretary, substitute teacher, bishop, janitor foreman.

The third coordinate of an organizational position is its *location* in the geography of the organization. This label tells us in which part of what organization the position functions. Continuing with the same examples, the full labels might read: senior secretary, legal department, General Electric Company, or substitute teacher, junior high school, Elmtown, or Anglican Bishop of London, or night janitor foreman, Municipal Hospital.

These simple coordinates of an organizational position are the most important for outsiders and strangers to know and the easiest to convey by shorthand designations. They are fixed attributes and do not usually change without a definite procedure of promotion, demotion, reclassification, or transfer.

Studies of social mobility often use a three-dimensional model based on three coordinates. On the vertical axis of the model, mobility is a change in status, either upward (promotion) or downward (demotion). Horizontal mobility is measured on one horizontal axis as a change from one activity to another, as when a punch-press operator is reassigned as a lathe operator in the same shop. Migration is represented on the other horizontal axis as a change from one location to another in an organization. It may involve spatial displacement but need not do so.

STATUS

Like most of the other terms introduced in these chapters, the term *status* shows a common core of meaning on which most social scientists can be brought to agree. Status is visualized as higher or lower; it compels such figures of speech as "status ladder," "social climbing," and "vertical mobility." The association of status with a vertical scale is a metaphor that seems to occur in all cultures, traceable perhaps to children's sense of the superior height and power of adults. The metaphor is so ingrained that human interaction can scarcely be discussed without it.

Status may refer to three related but quite different phenomena. First, it may be an observer's estimate of a subject's social-class affiliation in an open society. This is the status sought by "status-seekers." The heart of the whole arrangement is its indeterminacy. Although individuals and families are arrayed from high to low in an open society, there is no way of determining the exact position of any individual relative to any other, and no way of dividing the continuum into classes or strata which do not overlap. In addition, the norms governing the interaction of unequals in an open society are rather indefinite, so that it is uncertain how much power will be attached to higher social status in a particular situation.

Status may also refer to an attribute we would prefer to call prestige, namely the consensus of an informed audience concerning the rank order of preferability of competing individuals, organizations, or products. It is in this sense that professional baseball players have more status than professional football players, or the Ivy League more than the Big Ten, or Episcopal ministers more than Baptist ministers. The concept obviously overlaps with the preceding one, but it is based on a consensus that can be objectively verified. It becomes extremely important in studying sets of organizations.

The *organizational* status order differs from these other systems of social ranking in being unequivocal, transitive, and inclusive.

The status order is unequivocal. Every position in an organization has a definite place in the rank order of relative mutual influence. (The term *rank* is freely used in military forces and some other large-scale organizations, although it may sound absurd when applied to the family or the juvenile gang.) Rank or status is an ascertainable fact, commanding a high degree of consensus. It does not depend on the observer, and objective procedures are usually provided for its verification. Any change in the status of a position must be sanctioned by the organization and involves corresponding changes in other positions.

The status order is transitive. If A has higher status than B and B has higher status than C, then A has higher status than C. Moreover, such scales are partly calibrated, so that the status difference between A and C in the foregoing example will be recognized as roughly equivalent to the sum of the status differences between A and B and B and C.

The status order is inclusive. Every member of an organization has a place in its status order; there are no statusless positions. People occupying the same or similar positions ordinarily have the same or similar status. Any two members interacting within the context of the organization are usually able to identify themselves as equals or unequals, and if unequal to determine who is superior.

If we examine pairs of "higher" and "lower" positions in *any* social system whatever, we find a number of systematic differences, for example that the higher initiates activity for the lower more frequently than the lower for the higher, that the higher enjoys a larger share of available rewards than the lower, that the activity of the lower is modified to a greater extent by the presence of the higher than vice versa, that the higher has a greater power to injure and benefit the lower than the lower has with the higher, and so forth. The common element in all these situations is that if the members of a group are arrayed by their ability to modify each other's behavior, the resulting distribution will be closely related to the distributions of goods, privileges, reputation, and self-esteem and to the assignment of tasks. The problem in applying this definition is that it is not always possible to measure directly an ability to modify behavior. We must often have recourse to some other scale; we can estimate status from the distribution of goods (income statistics) or of reputation (an occupational-prestige scale) or of activities (job analysis). Sometimes we must proceed even more indirectly, and estimate status from the fact of association with persons of known status. Since these scales are not perfectly correlated with each other, there will sometimes appear to be several different status orders in an unorganized group.

In an organization, however, there is a powerful strain toward consistency of status indicators. Since a difference of status is a difference in ability to influence organizational decisions, any large discrepancy between the influence exerted by a given position and the rewards allocated to that position will tend to be self-correcting in the long run.

For similar reasons, discrepancies in the rank order of influence also tend to be self-correcting. Let us suppose that A is entitled to give orders to B, that B is entitled to give orders to C, and that C is entitled to give orders to A. Either A will be able to control C through B and prevent C from giving orders to A, or C will be able to control B through A, and prevent B from giving orders to C. In either case, the discrepancy disappears.

Nevertheless, discrepancies do exist and new ones are likely to appear as old ones are corrected. The problems then erected will be discussed later. For the moment, it is sufficient to note that in every large-scale organization where identical status differences are prescribed between many different pairs of positions, personalities, historical accidents, and experience in interaction are likely to modify the prescribed status difference between adjacent and unequal positions, so that the status difference between foremen and assistant foremen, for example, will seldom be exactly the same from one department to the next, even though the prescribed status difference is uniform throughout the factory.

The foregoing assumptions appear to be workable in the empirical description and in the analysis of organizations if certain qualifications are taken into account. The most important are the following:

1. The status order is an array of positions, not of people. It sometimes happens that a strategically placed individual is able to exert an influence out of all proportion to the position he occupies, either because he serves as alter ego to an organizational superior or because he acquires an unexpected popularity among equals and inferiors. History is full of notable cases: Savonarola, Colonel House, Madame Pompadour, Peter the Hermit, Rasputin, Buckingham, Harry Hopkins—a fascinating company. Such situations are inherently unstable. Sometimes they have ended with an execution and sometimes with conferment of the appropriate status, as Savonarola was burned and Hopkins was made a Cabinet member.

2. The idea of a status order that includes all the members of an organized group does not preclude the possibility that two positions will have equal or substantially equal status. Indeed, it strongly suggests that the incumbents of the same position will be treated as equals. The study of interaction patterns among equals, especially in peer groups, is one of the crucial topics in the study of status orders.

3. Compound organizations, such as business corporations or universities, may exhibit separate status orders in their major components. Stockholders, for example, can be easily arrayed by the amount of their stock ownership, while the status of executives is clearly denoted by their titles and salaries. But there is no very good way to compare the statuses of a minor stockholder and a junior executive. In legal theory all stockholders are superior to all officers and employees, but in practice the two orders are incommensurate. This is another way of saying that interaction between minor stockholders and junior executives is not anticipated as part of the program of the corporation.

4. There is often some degree of inconsistency between the status

order of an organization and the status order of one of its components or segments. This inconsistency is especially likely to appear in giant organizations. The lieutenant assigned to command a small warship finds a lieutenant commander on his staff as surgeon or meteorologist. The foreman of an important shop in a manufacturing company may be paid more than a plant manager elsewhere in the company. Even these minor inconsistencies are troublesome to all concerned and are usually removed as soon as convenient.

5. In both large and small organizations, conflicts over status are frequent and often bitter. People who disagree about their relative status cannot easily work together. During the time that a struggle for status between connected positions is actually in progress, it may be impossible to determine which is higher. The activity of the two positions will not be coordinated, and part of the interaction network will either be inactive or operating on a makeshift basis.

6. In special cases, the status order of an organized group may change from one situation to another. This phenomenon must be confined to narrow limits if the organization is to maintain its identity. Situational shifts in the status order are most likely to be observed in organized primary groups, in which many different functions are distributed among a small number of members.[21]

The activities to be undertaken by an organization in the accomplishment of its tasks are always differentially distributed among the members. Some degree of specialization may be found in any organizational position. The division of labor is not an incidental property of organization but its very essence. Organizations come into being to enable men to accomplish tasks that cannot be accomplished without specialization and coordination.

Specialization is ordinarily carried further in a large organization

---

[21] Paterson, studying cliques of officer pilots in the Royal Air Force, observed as many as three leaders, whom he called respectively the ex-dominus, the in-dominus, and the exemplar. The ex-dominus assumes the leading role in the clique's external activities, while the in-dominus has the preeminent place in internal interaction. The exemplar best embodies the group's values in his behavior and is imitated by the others. Thomas T. Paterson, *Morale in War and Work* (London: Parrish, 1955).

than in a small organization of the same type, and it is more marked in organizations subject to strict discipline than in those that invite voluntary participation.

Any organizational activity requires resources of some kind—time, labor, energy, tools, materials, and the sacrifice of alternative activities. It is often necessary to distinguish between the activities, which are easy to describe, and the goals they serve, which may be hard to ascertain.

Sometimes it is desirable to distinguish between *external activities,* by means of which the organization modifies its environment, and *internal activities,* by means of which it assures the maintenance of its own structure. In any organization certain activities are essential in the sense that the organization cannot survive unless they are satisfactorily performed. The family that is incapable of maintaining a household dissolves. The political party that ceases to attract adherents disappears from the scene. The factory that cannot produce a useable product or cannot dispose of it profitably shuts down. The pressure group whose objective has been achieved must either disappear or discover a new program.[22]

Activities of organizations are not all essential. Because of their flexibility, small-scale organizations such as families and gangs are able to engage in a great variety of projects. Because of their complexity, large-scale organizations, such as armies and universities, develop a multitude of auxiliary goals. Thus, the program of one state university[23] includes—besides a vast amount of teaching and research—the operation of a broadcasting station, an airfield, a chemical storehouse, a daily newspaper, a fruit orchard, archaeological excavations, a symphony orchestra, a theater, an iron mine, forests, a kindergarten, many libraries, many farms, art galleries, a carnival, a hospital, a morgue, a fleet of trucks, a power station, museums, an armory, an ice-skating rink, a police force, restaurants

[22] The frantic efforts of the Townsend movement to find new goals after the original purposes of the organization had been superseded are described in Sheldon L. Messinger, "Organizational Transformation: A Case Study of a Declining Social Movement," *American Sociological Review,* Vol. XX, No. 1 (February, 1955). See David L. Sills, *The Volunteers* (Glencoe, Ill.: Free Press, 1957), for a more general discussion of goal replacement in voluntary associations.

[23] The University of Minnesota, as of 1959. Figure 2–6 shows the range of activities within a single one of its institutes.

Figure 2-6

COMPONENTS OF AN
ENGINEERING FACULTY

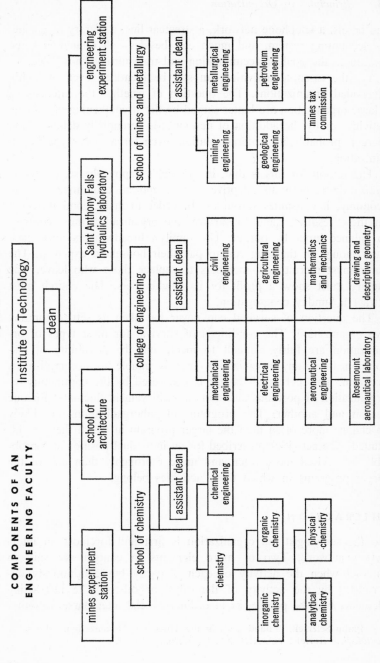

FROM the University of Minnesota Institute of Technology Organizational Chart, 1953. (This arrangement is now being revised.)

and hotels, a telephone network, a streetcar line, a literary magazine, an accounting system, and much else besides—all related in some fashion to the goal of accumulating and transmitting knowledge. Yet the essential activities can still be identified even in highly diversified organizations. The question of whether the interests of a large organization are better served by the strengthening of existing activities or by the addition of new ones is perennially debated, and there is probably no general solution, even for a given type of organization.

The reason for this is that, in Selznick's happy phrase, every organization is both an adaptive system and an economy.[24] As an economy, it consumes resources. In order to make good its claim on these resources and to survive, the organization must contrive to balance input by output. The family's breadwinners must each earn enough in the long run to pay their household expenses. The party must recruit new members to replace those who leave. The factory must show a profit for its stockholders. The church must attract a Sunday congregation.

The question of survival can never be taken as settled for any live organization. The conditions of survival for most types of organization are fairly difficult to meet, and the possibility of dissolution faces any organization that is unable to accomplish its program. This perennial danger is countered by the continuous reorganization of positions and units as achievement fluctuates for one reason and another. The programs of suborganizations are likely to change more often than the larger program in which they are included. The activities prescribed for an individual position will probably be revised more often and more thoroughly than any of the larger programs in which these activities belong.

INTERACTION

To the sociologist, an organization is first and foremost an interaction network. Two or more elements in contact are said to interact when the activity of each is partly but continuously determined by the activity of the other or others. The interacting elements may be people, as in ordinary social intercourse, or other

[24] Philip Selznick, "Foundations of the Theory of Organization," *American Sociological Review,* Vol. XIII, No. 1 (February, 1948).

organisms, as in a bee colony, or things, such as the pistons and flywheel of a motor. They may also be abstractions. The interaction of thesis and antithesis composes the Hegelian synthesis. The interaction of constitution and environment determines the character of a man or a chrysanthemum.

A process of interaction may endure for centuries or for only a fraction of a second. In either case, it must be long enough for the influence of A on B to be incorporated in B's activity and to influence A's own activity in turn. Human interaction is *social* if it involves symbolic communication. A symbol is a sign that has common denotation for persons who interact with each other. Many symbols are words, but gestures, acts, and objects may also be symbols.[25]

Let us look at some of the more obvious implications of the statement that an organization is an interaction network. First, every position must be in direct or indirect contact with all other positions.

[25] Interaction by means of significant symbols was first explained by Mead: The gesture is that phase of the individual act to which adjustment takes place on the part of other individuals in the social process of behavior. The vocal gesture becomes a significant symbol . . . when it has the same effect on the individual making it that it has on the individual to whom it is addressed. . . . The gesture in general and the vocal gesture in particular, indicates some object or other within the field of social behavior. . . . The function of the gesture is to make adjustment possible among the individuals implicated in any given social act with reference to the object or objects with which that act is concerned, and the significant gesture or significant symbol affords far greater facilities for such adjustment and readjustment than does the non-significant gesture, because it calls out in the individuals making it the same attitude toward it (or toward its meaning) that it calls out in the other individuals participating with him in the given social act, and thus makes him conscious of their attitude toward it (as a component of his behavior) and enables him to adjust his subsequent behavior to theirs in the light of that attitude. George H. Mead, *Mind, Self and Society,* ed. Charles W. Morris (Chicago: University of Chicago Press, 1934), p. 46.

Mead also introduced the concept of the "generalized other," pointing out that everyone is aware of general attitudes that are typical of a social group to which he belongs, over and beyond the attitudes of individuals encountered in specific situations. These attitudes, organized into a pattern of encouragements and prohibitions, are incorporated into the self, so that the actor is able to observe his own actions and to react toward them in much the same way that he reacts to the actions of other people. This self-consciousness is the basic mechanism of social control. It enables us to respond consistently to the expectations developed in a social system.

If we describe the organization by a sociogram, in which circles represent positions and lines represent interaction between positions, the minimum requirement is that every circle must be connected directly (by a single line) to at least one other circle and indirectly (by a chain of lines leading through other positions) to every other circle in the diagram.

If the functions of the organization are to be accomplished, it must be possible for those in charge of coordinating the program of activity to communicate with all positions, and for each position to communicate with them. It follows from the foregoing requirement that almost all positions in an organization will be in a relationship of direct interaction with at least one status superior. The occasional exceptions—when orders, instruction, and directive cues are received through a peer rather than a superior—are inherently unstable because the peer's ability to control the situation by minor modifications of the messages or by timing their delivery tends to convert him into a superior.

If the organization as a whole is to function in a predictable way, the form and content of interaction between any pair of positions must be partly prescribed and to that extent predictable. Since indirect interaction consists of a chain of direct interactions it, too, is predictable when the relationships between direct interactors are specified. However, since some degree of uncertainty and unpredictability is introduced by each intermediary, it is likely that roles will need to be more exactly prescribed in indirect than in direct interactions. For this reason, large organizations, which necessarily have a larger proportion of indirect interactions, usually prescribe roles in greater detail than small organizations of similar type.

We shall use the term *role* for all the behavior of the incumbent (or incumbents) of an organizational position that interacts with the incumbent (or incumbents) of another organizational position. Any position will therefore include a separate role for every position with which it is directly connected on a sociogram.

The reader is warned that this definition cannot be presented as authoritative. There is probably less agreement among authorities about roles than about any other topic in organization theory. One textbook defines *role* as actual performance as distinct from expected performance.[26] Another defines it as the expected behavior in a posi-

[26] Kingsley Davis, *Human Society* (New York: Macmillan, 1950), p. 90.

tion in contrast to the actual behavior.[27] One sociologist requires roles to be internally consistent.[28] Others describe a role as composed of *variable* behaviors. Neiman and Hughes, after reviewing the treatment of the term by more than eighty writers, decided that the concept was "vague, nebulous and non-definitive." [29] Yet there does appear to be a common core of meaning in the literature, containing three elements:

1. Roles are associated with organizational positions.
2. Roles have something to do with the tension between expected and observed behavior.
3. Roles are involved in interaction.

Although obscure, the term is somehow indispensable. The usage proposed here attempts to simplify this disorderly tangle of meanings. When we say that A's position includes a role for the relationship AB, we imply that B's position also includes a role for the same relationship. In other words, A cannot be said to interact with B unless B also interacts with A, and the existence of a role A_b implies and requires that there will be a discoverable role B_a. Interaction, because of this element of mutuality, differs from the mere communication of information. Interaction always involves a pair of positions but not necessarily a pair of persons. The incumbent of one or both positions may be a group. The teacher addressing a large class is involved in interaction because his behavior is modified by the reciprocal behavior of the class taken as a whole, and their behavior is modified by his. The broadcaster addressing a message to an unseen audience is involved in communication but not necessarily in interaction with that audience.

Some sociologists would prefer to think of A as having a multiplicity of roles toward B. Like the theory that groups are composed of segments of behavior, this viewpoint is reasonable but operationally awkward. We shall take the simpler position here that A—the incumbent of an organizational position—has only one role toward B, a member of the same organization, although there may be a

[27] Victor A. Thompson, *Modern Organization* (New York: Knopf, 1961), p. 59.
[28] Leonard S. Cottrell, "Adjustment of the Individual to His Age and Sex Roles," *American Sociological Review,* Vol. VII, No. 5 (October, 1942).
[29] L. H. Neiman and J. W. Hughes, "The Problem of the Concept of Role —a Resurvey of the Literature," *Social Forces,* Vol. XXX (1951).

great many distinguishable elements in the role and although the pattern of interaction may change from one situation to another. Of course, A and B *as individuals* may participate together in more than one organization and so develop more than one pair of reciprocating roles.

It should never be forgotten that organizational behavior does not include all of social life. People also interact in unorganized groups and independent dyads. To the extent that consistent mutual orientations are developed in these situations, it is possible to speak of nonorganizational roles. However, these lie outside our present inquiry.

SEPARATING ACTIVITIES AND ROLES

The analytical separation of activities and roles is not always easy. Activities always involve a contact with the environment. Roles always involve a contact with other persons. The difference between them is that an activity consists of certain prescribed manipulations of the environment, but a role consists of certain prescribed ways of communicating with others about the environment. The difficulty arises because the environment to be manipulated often consists of other people, and one of the modes of manipulating them is to engage in interaction. The analytical problem is slight when the task is hewing wood or drawing water. It is serious when the task consists of supervision or psychoanalysis. For example, here is Firth's description of an activity performed by the leader of a Malay fishing crew: [30]

> One of the most important elements of the craft is the technique of submerging oneself in the water and "listening" for fish. The expert holds on to the boat with one hand and keeps his head and body below the surface, listening for the noises which the fish make. His first task is to locate the fish in the vicinity, identify what kind they are and form an opinion as to their quantity. . . . These sounds are said to be due to pelagic fish swimming through the water in shoals or to demersal fish feeding at the bottom; some are due to fin and tail movements of large fish. . . . Much of the technical information which an expert accumulates is shared by the more skilled fisherman—knowledge of winds and currents, fishing banks, the

[30] Raymond W. Firth, *Malay Fishermen* (London: Trench, Trubner, 1946). The quotations are from pages 101–04.

ways of different kinds of fish and the depths at which they are mostly to be found, identification of positions by shore bearings or by the nature of the bottom, the efficient handling of boats and gear, etc. But the identification of fish noises is acknowledged to be acquired only by training and to demand a "flair."

Here is a description of the corresponding role:

> The relation between the expert and his crew is one of free association, either party being at liberty to break the bond at any time. He is the leader and commander of the crew . . . but they are not simply wage-earners and they are not bound to obey him. While he leads them, and sometimes drives them in matters of technique and organization, he shows what, to the outsider, is often a surprising readiness to consult them on matters of policy. Their mutual relations are governed not by any set formula of rights and duties, but by a number of practical assumptions about what is reasonable in the circumstances of their work.

COMPLEMENTARITY

No role can occur alone.[31] Many roles occur only in complementary pairs, such as husband and wife, leader and follower, pastor and flock, teacher and pupil, seller and buyer, employer and employee. Neither role can be enacted unless the other is enacted also. There can be no husband without a wife, no leader without followers, no employer without employees. The husband whose wife dies, the leader whose followers desert him, and the employer who dismisses all of his employees are no longer husband, leader, or employer.

At first glance, this rule does not seem to apply to all of the roles mentioned above. We can think of a teacher without pupils or a pastor without a flock. The explanation is that the same word is commonly used for an occupation and for the role that it implies. Someone who has the necessary certificates and diplomas and has been certified for employment in the public schools may be de-

---

[31] Throughout this discussion, only pair relationships are considered, since the introduction of multiple relationships creates formidable problems of description and analysis. Inasmuch as any group can be described as a matrix of pair relationships, this is a workable assumption, from which it follows, for example, that there appear to be two and only two positions in each complementary relationship. However, it would be easy enough to find instances of complementarity in larger groups (the role of second baseman might be said to require eight other roles) if the arbitrary restriction to pair relationships were removed.

scribed as a teacher, but he does not assume the teacher's *role* until the day he meets his first class. Any ordained minister of religion may be described as a pastor, but his *role* as a pastor must refer to a particular congregation.

Needless to say, similar roles may be attached to many different positions in an organization and, conversely, a given position may have a wide assortment of different roles. In an army, for example, each rank is expected to have a leader role in relation to the rank below, and a follower role to the ranks above. In a family, a man may have clearly separable roles as son, father, husband, nephew, uncle, father-in-law, and brother—and he may lose any one of these roles because of the death or departure of his role partner without losing the others. The complementarity of roles involves the coordination of activities that are mutually supportive but not identical and the development of reciprocal rights and duties in connection with these activities. Thus, A leads B; B follows A. A teaches B; B learns from A. A assigns work to B; B performs the work assigned by A. The necessity for coordination is fundamental; it rests upon the fact that the organization's goals, whatever they are, cannot be achieved by a solitary individual but require the efforts of a group of persons performing specialized activities in a coordinated program. The program—communicated through interaction—sets a positive, negative, or zero value on each activity in terms of its estimated contribution to the common goal. When A and B interact in an organizational context, A is aware of certain acts which B expects him to perform, of other acts which B expects him to avoid, and of many possible acts which are indifferent to the purpose in hand. B has a complementary set of expectations for A. When we talk about the organization abstractly, we naturally emphasize the expectations built into each role. When we study it in operation, we stress the observed behavior. Yet the two categories are inseparable, because the overt behavior in an organizational role is structured by expectation at every moment, while the expectations in a role relationship are continuously amplified, and frequently revised, by innovations in overt behavior.[32]

[32] For further discussion of complementarity, see Alvin W. Gouldner, "The Norm of Reciprocity," *American Sociological Review*, Vol. XXV, No. 2 (April, 1960).

THE NORMATIVE SYSTEM

As we examine organizational positions in detail, we discover that each position consists of an entire pattern of expectations. These expectations cover more than the roles of the position. There are also expectations about the activities to be performed, about the feelings to be developed toward the incumbents of related positions, and about perceptions and beliefs. Some of these expectations are improvised for particular occasions—either by the incumbent or his friends. Other expectations are vague, ambiguous, or contradictory. There remains, however, for any position in any organization a core of expectations that command consensus, either because they are shared by all members or because they are explicitly promulgated.

An organizational norm is a statement supported by the organization describing the behavior expected from the incumbent or incumbents of a given position in a given set of circumstances. No two positions will be governed by the same set of norms but, as we have already seen, the analyst has some choice between a broad or narrow grouping of positions. In simple organizations it is possible to identify a membership category shared by all members and therefore to treat all members—for some purposes—as occupying the same position. By subdividing broad categories, we reduce in each case the scope of the norms but increase their number. This is a complicated way of saying that the program of any organization requires the standardization of behavior in some respects and the differentiation of behavior in other respects.

All norms are supported by sanctions. There is always some means of punishing nonconformity. Sanctions vary from definite —in most modern armies the penalty for deserting in the face of the enemy is "death by shooting"—to indefinite—if a Tikopian chief divides the food at a feast unfairly, his reputation may suffer. Sanctions vary enormously in severity. Most organizations recognize a scale of norm violations from trivial to very serious, and the corresponding sanctions are graded in accordance with this scale, although usually imperfectly.

One of the important discoveries of small-group experimentation has been that even unorganized laboratory groups develop norms and sanctions and expel or isolate members. On the other hand, offenses against organizational norms sometimes go unpunished, even when they are flagrant and recognized. Crime does pay, from time to time and for various reasons, in every social system. Perfect conformity with any set of norms is unlikely. In stable situations, each operative norm evokes a predictable and stable level of conformity. Enforcement is successful when other members react to a member's departure from his earlier degree of conformity in such a way as to bring him back to that degree of conformity.[33] Norm enforcement is not a separate compartment of organizational life. It is inherent in the concept of an interaction network composed of positions having prescribed statuses, interactions, valences, and activities.

Emotions, beliefs, and sentiments are prescribed for the incumbents of organizational positions just as routinely as activities. The failure to perceive this can lead to considerable haziness about "social values." Organizations are distinguished from other social systems by their instrumental and formally rational character. Long ago, William Graham Sumner, contemplating the range of custom in primitive societies, observed that the mores can make anything right or wrong. In organizations, this aphorism must be nearly reversed. Although organizations vary ad infinitum in their goals, many of the virtues they prize in their members are unaffected by the cultural surroundings. Every organization evaluates favorably conformity to its own norms. All organizations everywhere desire their members to be loyal, obedient, trustworthy, zealous, skilled, and sound in judgment. All organizations are sensitive to treason, rebellion, disloyalty, and irresponsibility among their members and attach importance to emotional and ideological conformity as well as to prescribed activities.[34]

Despite sanctions and penalties at critical points, almost every organization depends more upon consent than force to accomplish its objectives. To operate any organizational system by coercion alone would require enormous energy. Even in prisons, guards and inmates modify the organizational structure to substitute reciprocity for coercion at many points.

[33] Cf. George C. Homans, *The Human Group* (New York: Harcourt, Brace & World, 1950), especially p. 301.

[34] For a corresponding attempt to establish universal private values in the esthetic domain, see Leonard B. Meyer, "Some Remarks on Value and Greatness in Music," in Morris Philipson (ed.), *Aesthetics Today* (Cleveland: World, 1961).

On the other hand, every organization but the smallest is made up of components and factions that are organizations in their own right, having their own norms and sanctions. As some of the norms of any organization concern its protection against the surrounding environment, and as the surrounding environment of a component or faction includes the larger organization, some conflict of norms will be observed in every organization except the smallest.

An organizational ideology has a double function. On the one hand, it rallies members in a common cause, reinforces their commitment, and creates psychological barriers against desertion by tying their affiliation to organizational loyalties and values. At the same time, by linking the organization's practical goals to wider purposes shared with outsiders, an ideology provides ways of wooing allies and isolating enemies.

NORM ENFORCEMENT

Expectations and rules interlock to such an extent that they are almost indistinguishable. For some purposes, however, it may be helpful to think of an expectation as a shared belief about what the behavior of an organizational member should be and to think of a rule as a definite statement of what that behavior should be.

Some rules are internalized and others are not. Some rules are self-enforcing and others are not. A self-enforcing rule is not necessarily internalized, but an internalized rule is largely self-enforcing. There are several major categories with regard to the probability of enforcement:

1. Some rules are enforced easily and painlessly. These command complete agreement—such as a rule against smoking in a powder magazine—or complete indifference—such as a rule specifying the format of official communications.
2. Some rules are well enforced because their violation is interpreted as an attack on the organization resulting in automatic expulsion—for example, the rule in a political party against supporting opposition candidates.
3. Many rules are enforced by organizations as the agents of outside organizations, without any particular commitment. The "No Smoking" rule may be imposed by an insurance company.
4. Some rules evoke real conflicts of interest and are fundamentally

unenforceable—for example, factory rules against output limitation.

5. Some rules are meant to be *partly* enforced. Partial enforcement is thought to be essential, and complete enforcement impossible, as in the case of the rules promulgated by American parents against demonstrations of sibling rivalry.

Another kind of variability in norm enforcement is analyzed by Merton [35] in his discussion of three major types of conformity. Persons subject to norms may conform *behaviorally*, by following the norm in their overt behavior, or *attitudinally*, by communicating their acceptance of norms and their associated values, or *doctrinally* by stating the norms to others and repeating their ideological justification.

Each of these types of conformity may occur with or without the others. As Coser [36] points out:

> . . . selection between these types of conformity is often socially prescribed. Some status holders may expect that a person show mainly attitudinal conformity ("it's not that I mind the way he acts, it's his attitude"); others congratulate him for his doctrinal conformity ("he's sure good to have around when it comes to whipping up enthusiasm"); still others demand behavioral conformity only ("why doesn't he just do his job, who cares about what he thinks?").

Zetterberg [37] explains norm compliance as the product of a fundamental human desire to be favorably evaluated by others, and the tendency of these others to assign favorable evaluations to attitudes and actions resembling their own. He proposes that "an actor's actions have a tendency to become dispositions that are related to the occurrence of favorable self-evaluation. . . ." and that "in an action system any actor has a tendency to develop attitudes that are synonymous with uniform evaluations (attitudes and/or social values) in the system. . . ."; that "in an action system any action has a tend-

[35] Robert K. Merton, "Conformity Deviation and Opportunity Structure," *American Sociological Review*, Vol. XXIV, No. 2 (April, 1959).

[36] Rose Laub Coser, "Insulation from Observability and Types of Social Conformity," *American Sociological Review*, Vol. XXVI, No. 1 (February, 1961).

[37] Hans L. Zetterberg, "Compliant Actions," *Acta Sociologica*, Vol. II (1957), 184, 186.

ency to develop cognitions that are synonymous with uniform descriptions in the system. . . ." and that "in any action system any actor has a tendency to develop self-cognitions that are synonymous with the uniform descriptions of him that are in the system."

These verbal formulas, and a number of further statements that Zetterberg derives from them, are useful in understanding the perpetual dialogue between the individual and the organization. They show why there is always an impulse toward conformity. They do not, however, explain why there is always a countervailing (but not necessarily equal) impulse toward nonconformity. Presumably, the tendency of an actor to develop attitudes that are synonymous with evaluations in one system is checked by the inconsistency of such attitudes with the dominant evaluations in another. His craving to develop self-attitudes that conform to the image held by others in one system is frustrated by the need to take account of inconsistent evaluations developed in other systems. These clamorous and irreconcilable demands arise out of simultaneous membership in successive levels of the same organization and simultaneous membership in different types of organizations, out of prior organizational experience, and even out of reference groups to which the subject does not belong. These groups may be imaginary; they may be situated in the past or in the future. Their norms are not enforceable in any external way, but they are enforced nevertheless. The real individual in a real organization always conforms to the norms imperfectly and somewhat after his own fashion.

CONTINUITY AND REPLACEMENT

If we observe a large organization over a period of time, we note that its roster of membership changes almost continuously, yet the organization remains the same. We take this interesting process for granted. But it deserves closer analysis.

In order for organizational continuity to be achieved, it must be possible to: (a) distinguish each individual member from all other members; (b) distinguish each position from all other positions; (c) determine which members occupy which positions at any given moment; (d) add or subtract members; (e) add or subtract positions; (f) move members from one position to another.

The identification of persons is relatively simple. Under ordinary circumstances, no problem arises about the continuity of member A over a period of time. He remains the same person, even though his behavior may change. If A is replaced by B, there is no overlap between them and no question of whether B is different enough from A to be considered a separate person.

The identification of positions is much less certain. There is often some difficulty in determining whether a position has remained the same, been modified, or been replaced—whether, for example, the new position of vice president in charge of sales is the same as the old position of sales manager.

The problem of organizational continuity has many practical consequences. Property and privileges are often vested in the organization—as a more or less immortal collectivity—rather than in the membership group. Political and spiritual authority are usually attached to organizational positions rather than to individuals. The power to rule, in any social system, is based on the right of certain individuals to occupy certain positions.

The matters affected by continuity are too crucial to be left to chance. All organizations include replacement procedures, by means of which they are able to add or subtract members, add or subtract positions, and determine who occupies a position at any given moment. We may define a *replacement procedure* as a predetermined sequence of social interactions undertaken deliberately for the purpose of accomplishing a modification of social relationships. The common use of the term in bureaucratic administration accords with this sociological definition. There are procedures for appointment, promotion, contracting, budget-making, and the like. The term has a similar meaning in law, in which there are procedures of arrest, indictment, conviction, and parole. There is a procedure for empaneling and discharging a jury, for suing and for defending a suit, for contracting marriage, for adopting a child, for seeking a divorce, or for claiming an inheritance. In religious organizations, there are procedures for baptism, confirmation, marriage, divorce, and burial. Formal education may be analyzed as a series of specific procedures for matriculation, examination, promotion, and graduation.

The key elements of any replacement procedure are these:

1. The identity of the actors is established.
2. There is a review of evidence, according to established rules.

3. A decision is made.
4. The decision takes effect at a particular moment of time.

The last step in important replacement procedures—the moment when the decision takes effect—is often marked by a *ceremony* that includes:

1. a convocation
2. an exhortation
3. the taking of an oath
4. the presentation of insignia
5. the preservation of an official record.

All of these elements, in the order just described, may be found in such procedures as marriage, inauguration, apprenticing, enlistment, and graduation.

It is common to all of the replacement procedures that great importance is attached to the moment of entry into the new position and to the verification of the event by written records and crowds of witnesses. The incumbency of a position, these precautions seem to say, has great value and must be protected against usurpation. Unlike membership in an unorganized group, which is a matter of opinion, membership in an organization is made an objective fact by proof of membership. This is often intangible—a name or a password —but it is usually supported by tangible signs: a paper, a badge, a robe, a scar.

THINGS AND SYMBOLS

Organizations *always* specify the relationship of membership positions to three kinds of objects: (a) identifying symbols, (b) status symbols, and (c) material property.[38] The importance of *identifying symbols* varies from one organization to another, but they are always to be found. An identifying symbol is a sign or thing or person that symbolizes the organization to its members. It may be a flag, a cross, a ring, a ceremony, an ancient building, a totemic animal, a tree, a song, a costume, a typographic design, a season of the

[38] The visible paraphernalia of organizations have often been ignored in sociological analysis. The classification used here derives partly from that given in F. Stuart Chapin, *Contemporary American Institutions: A Sociological Analysis* (New York: Harper, 1935).

year, or a gesture. The name or nickname of the organization is inherently symbolic. Its chief may easily become a symbol (the king, the Pope, the mikado, an orchestra conductor, a ship's captain). Honor to the symbol is honor to the organization. An attack on it is an attack on the organization. The identifying symbol often comes to be treated as sacred. It is then felt to have a power in itself, somewhat independent of what it symbolizes, so that it must be approached with circumspection.

The distribution of identifying symbols presents a peculiar problem for the differentiated large-scale organization. The factory as a whole may have its symbolic culture traits, but Department 36 can operate nicely without them. Even in military organizations, in which symbolism is emphasized and in which unit identifications are reinforced by flags, emblems, and insignia, these refer to certain designated suborganizations, such as regiments and companies, and not to others, such as army groups and platoons, although the latter organizations are quite as real as regiments or companies. In large organizations, the number of subdivisions multiplies almost indefinitely as growth and specialization proceed. The emotional response to organizational symbols cannot be correspondingly subdivided. Each organizational loyalty competes with every other, and the intensity of response to symbols tends to be decreased by their subdivision.

The study of *status symbols* is a fascinating minor branch of sociology. Working with limited materials, so that stars, crowns, and crosses appear in dozens of different societies, human ingenuity has labored on status insignia, language, furniture, and forms of address. Space does not permit a full exploration of this chamber of curiosities, but note, for example, that head gear are disproportionately important as status insignia—from crowns and halos to shakos and school caps. Of all types of furniture, the chair is the most adaptable as a status symbol. Note such diverse examples as the king's throne, the chairman's chair, the professor's chair, the bishop's cathedra, the African chief's stool, and the father's chair at the head of the table.

The primitive and unavoidable devices for indicating successive steps in rank are: increasing the size of the insignia, increasing the number of insignia, constructing the insignia out of more valuable material. Note the regular progressions from the thin gold stripe of the naval cadet to the multiple, massive stripes of admirals or the steady increase of desk size from junior executives to senior vice presidents, or the improvement from the plain broadcloth of parish priests to the velvet and satin of cardinals. There is no standard form of the salute, but the taking of a fixed posture by the inferior followed by the negligent acknowledgment or nonacknowledgment by the superior is a very widespread phenomenon.

All of the major European languages and many non-European ones have evolved cautious grammatical forms for addressing status superiors. The curious convention of third person address is recurrent, together with flattering titles such as Your Honor, Your Excellency, Your Grace, and Your Magnificence.[39]

[39] "Farr's Law of Mean Familiarity . . . can be expressed by a curve, but is much clearer set down as follows: The Guv'nor addresses:
    Co-director Michael Yates as MIKE
    Assistant director Michael Yates as MICHAEL
    Sectional manager Michael Yates as MR. YATES
    Sectional assistant Michael Yates as YATES
    Apprentice Michael Yates as MICHAEL
    Night-watchman Michael Yates as MIKE"
From Stephen Potter, *One-upmanship* (New York: Holt, 1952), p. 44.

CHAPTER THREE

The Organization in Motion

THE ANALYTICAL MODEL

This chapter introduces an analytical model describing the adaptation of an organization to the continuous small changes in its environment.[1] The model is based on four variables, each of which is a regular function of every other. It is conceived to be culture-free—that is, applicable to organizations regardless of time or place—and it has "stability in the small." This means that when an external influence causes a slight change in the magnitude of one variable, the sequence of changes evoked in the other variables because of their functional interrelationship tends to restore all of the initial values. It does not have "stability in the large." When a large change in any of the variables is induced by an external force, the functional interdependence of the four variables persists, but the original values are never restored.

The study of a model should not be confused with the study of the real world. Predictions derived from the study of the real world are more or less *probable,* but predictions derived from analysis of the model are either *correct* or *incorrect.* The model contains only what we put into it. The real world contains more than we can ever

---

[1] "An analytical model is a mental construct consisting of a set of elements in interrelation, the elements and their interrelations being precisely defined." For a brief and elegant description of how such models are intended to work, see Everett E. Hagen, "Analytical Models in the Study of Social Systems," *American Journal of Sociology,* Vol. LXVII, No. 2 (September, 1961). The quotation is from page 144.

get out of it. No model is an exact replica of its subject, but a useful model identifies and simplifies strategic variables so as to produce a fairly good—never a perfect—fit between effects in the arena of observation and effects obtained by manipulating symbols. The tests of an analytical model are its internal consistency, the amount of simplification achieved, and whether it can be used to predict real events. Prediction is accomplished by a kind of stylized analogy: terms describing real events are translated into the terms of the model, manipulated symbolically, observed for outcome, and then translated back into the original in order to predict the real outcome.

The most obvious difference between a model and the real world, aside from complexity, is that the model must be treated as closed in order to function at all. After the initial push that sets it in motion, it is insulated from any further contact with the environment for the duration of the problem. Events in the model always take place under the condition of "other things being equal." This enables us to trace separate threads of causation through the tangled skein of reality.

A single model of organizational function is applicable to any tribe of men at any time in their history. This assertion is a corollary of our thesis that organizations constitute a species of a natural kind. The model is extraordinarily crude and clumsy; but if its general applicability can be demonstrated, refinement will follow as a matter of course.

EQUILIBRIUM MODELS

We shall begin with the work of George Caspar Homans, who in a major work that was published in 1950 [2] developed a model of group

[2] *The Human Group* (New York: Harcourt, Brace & World, 1950). His more recent work, notably *Social Behavior: Its Elementary Forms* (New York: Harcourt, Brace & World, 1961), is less directly related to the problem considered here. See also the collection of papers in *Sentiments and Activities* (New York: The Free Press of Glencoe, 1962). Extensive use has also been made of two papers that take *The Human Group* as a point of departure, Herbert A. Simon, "A Formal Theory of Interaction in Social Groups," *American Sociological Review*, Vol. XVII, No. 2 (April, 1952), and H. W. Riecken and George C. Homans, "Psychological Aspects of Social Structure," Chapter 22 in Gardner Lindzey (ed.), *Handbook of Social Psychology*, Vol. II, *Special Fields and Applications* (Cambridge, Mass.: Addison-Wesley, 1954).

behavior. Homans' model is based on four variables: activity, inter-action, sentiment, and norms.

After a preliminary discussion of groups and their component parts, Homans summarizes and analyzes five case studies by other investigators in terms of these variables. The cases are: the Bank Wiring Observation Room, originally investigated by Roethlisberger and Dickson as part of the Western Electric study; the Norton Street Gang, which Whyte studied by participant observation and described in *Street Corner Society;* the family in Tikopia, based on Firth's works on that idyllic coral island; Hilltown, a New England commu-nity described in a thesis by Hatch; and an organizational problem in a small manufacturing company, reported by Arensberg and McGregor. All of these cases refer to organizations. The gang, the family, and the workshop are small organizations; the company is a large organization; the community contains organizations.

The relationship between interaction and sentiment is the pivotal idea around which the discussion revolves. Homans begins his analy-sis of the Bank Wiremen by describing their two cliques. Those who worked together or at adjacent stations engaged in congenial inter-action and friendliness. The fundamental hypothesis is developed very carefully. First, it is noted that ". . . persons who interact frequently with one another tend to like one another" (p. 111).[3] But liking and disliking are relative terms. There are many degrees of liking, and it is difficult to find a zero point on the scale. The difficulties are met by restating the original hypothesis in differential terms: "If the frequency of interaction between two or more persons increases, the degree of their liking for one another will increase, and vice versa" (p. 112).

This formulation, too, is put aside as incomplete, since it neglects the group context in which the relationship occurs. Another restate-

[3] The page numbers in parentheses here and throughout this section refer to *The Human Group.* The original studies to which Homans refers are Fritz J. Roethlisberger and William J. Dickson, *Management and the Worker* (Cam-bridge, Mass.: Harvard University Press, 1939); William F. Whyte, *Street Corner Society* (Chicago: University of Chicago Press, 1943); Raymond Firth, *We, The Tikopia* (London: Allen & Unwin, 1936) and *Primitive Polynesian Economy* (London: Routledge & Kegan Paul, 1939); D. L. Hatch, "Changes in the Structure and Function of a Rural New England Community Since 1900" (unpublished dissertation, Harvard University, 1948); Conrad Arensberg and Douglas McGregor, "Determination of Morale in an Industrial Company," *Applied Anthropology,* Vol. I (1942).

ment follows: "If the interactions between the members of a group are frequent in the external system, sentiments of liking will grow up between them, and these sentiments will lead in turn to further interactions over and above the interactions of the external system" (p. 112). The external system includes those relationships that are imposed on the bank wiremen as part of their jobs. This statement proposes that voluntary interaction will evolve out of any system of compulsory interaction and that the interactors will develop positive sentiments toward each other.

Other aspects of the dependence between sentiment and activity are expressed by such statements as: "The more frequently persons interact with one another, the stronger their sentiments of friendship for one another are apt to be" (p. 133), ". . . persons who feel sentiments of liking for one another will express those sentiments in activities over and above the activities of the external system" (p. 134), and ". . . a decrease in the frequency of interaction between the members of a group and outsiders, accompanied by an increase in the strength of their negative sentiments toward outsiders, will increase the frequency of interaction and the strength of positive sentiments among the members of the group, and vice versa" (p. 113).

Observing similarities in output within the two cliques of bank wiremen, Homans proposes the mutual dependence of activity and interaction: ". . . persons who interact with one another frequently are more like one another in their activities than they are like other persons with whom they interact less frequently" (p. 135).

The hypotheses that have been quoted so far represent the exposition of a single major theorem: that in a group situation in which we can distinguish activities, interactions, and sentiments (imposed from outside and generated from within), these elements will be interrelated in such a way that a change in one of them will be followed by a change in the others. This is a fundamental theorem. It is applicable to innumerable empirical situations, and it is not self-evident.

The hypotheses we have quoted form a set of verbal equations. They are stated with sufficient precision to be translated into mathematical form. However, as Homans points out, the fundamental proposition does not apply to all possible situations. The intercorrelation among the six variables (activity, interaction, and sentiment in the internal system and activity, interaction, and sentiment in the external system) seems to be highest in peer groups where every member has approximately the same status.

Another major topic in *The Human Group* is the influence of social ranking upon the activity–interaction–sentiment system. Social ranking is defined as the evaluation of an individual by other members of his group. Evaluation is identified as a sentiment based on the comparison of each member's activities with those of the others. The standard of comparison is said to be provided by group norms.

In this connection the case of the Bank Wiremen is pursued further. Noting that the clique of connector wiremen maintained a certain social superiority over that of the selector wiremen and also came closer to the output standard of the entire crew, Homans hypothesizes that: ". . . the higher the rank of a person within a group, the more nearly his activities conform to the norms of the group" (p. 141). This is said to apply to subgroups as well as individual members. Noting that members of the higher-ranking clique felt free to exchange jobs with outsiders, he hypothesizes that ". . . the higher a person's social rank, the wider will be the range of his interactions" (p. 145) and that ". . . a person of higher social rank than another originates interaction for the latter more often than the latter originates interaction for him" (p. 145). The observation that the social ranking of the two cliques arises out of the arrangement of the bank wiremen's jobs but carries over into spontaneous sociability leads to the suggestion that ". . . a person who originates interaction for another in the external system will also tend to do so in the internal" (p. 146).

The next case discussed is the Norton Street Gang. Examining their sociometric distribution, Homans concludes that the "sentiments of the leaders of a group carry greater weight than those of the followers in establishing a social ranking" (p. 181). This is clearly related to the previous statement that high ranking members of the group come closer to realizing its norms.

Again matching a previous statement about the bank wiremen, it is proposed that ". . . the higher a man's social rank, the larger will be the number of persons that originate interaction for him, either directly or through intermediaries" (p. 182). The converse is that ". . . the higher a man's social rank, the larger the number of persons for whom he originates interaction, either directly or through intermediaries" (p. 182). A number of corollaries are inferred from the same evidence. First, "the more nearly equal in social rank a number of men are, the more frequently they will interact with one another" (p. 184). Second, "if a person does originate interaction for a person of higher rank, a tendency will exist for him to do so with the member of his own subgroup who is nearest him in rank" (p. 184). Third, "the higher a man's social rank, the more frequently he interacts with persons outside his own group" (pp. 185–86).

Homans then turns to Tikopia and summarizes Firth's description of the family in that tiny, isolated society, showing how pair relationships are affected by contiguous relationships. The father in Tikopia supervises the work of his sons, and the mother supervises the work of her daughters. The discipline of a parent over children of the same sex is much more severe than over children of the opposite sex. The father–daughter and mother–son relationships are more affectionate than the father–son relationship, which is marked by constraint, or the mother–daughter relationship, which is rather routinized. Homans suggests that: "The higher becomes A's frequency of originating interaction for B compared with his frequency of originating interaction for C, the stronger becomes his feeling of affection for C compared with his feeling of affection for B" (p. 249).

This seems to contradict what has been previously said about interaction and friendliness and also implies the odd principle that the lack of authority over another person is gratifying.

In the Tikopian family, the father favors the younger son and the elder son has some authority over his brothers. Homans proposes that: "So far as A and B both originate interaction for C, the relationship between them is one of constraint, and interaction between them tends to be kept at a minimum" (p. 250). The hypothesis is indefensible in this form. It would lead us to predict that the relationship between mother and father in any family system would be one of "constraint" because they both originate interaction for their children or that the relationships among the members of an oligarchy would be constrained because they originate interaction for the same subjects.

A simpler explanation seems to account for this and several other Tikopian situations, including the alliance of grandfathers and grandchildren against the man in the middle, the constraint between husband and wife in public, and the warm affection between the child and his maternal uncle. It appears that when a number of pair relationships in the same system have approximately equal interaction, the relationships with the most authority develop the most constraint.

The case material from the Tikopian family all suggests that the effect of a status difference in a pair relationship is to reduce the total amount of interaction that accompanies a given amount of activity. Status lessens the need for *voluntary* coordination. The inferior has a motive to avoid interaction: it may lead to undesired compulsions for himself. The superior has a motive to reduce "unnecessary" interaction: it increases the inferior's influence and decreases his own authority. The normal effect of an increase of status difference in an interacting pair is an increase of activity. Overt disagreement about goals is reduced and the status difference allows a quicker and easier, if not more efficient, selection of means.

If the introduction of a status difference in a pair relationship reduces interaction and increases activity, it should also reduce the dependence of sentiment on interaction, partly because fluctuations of interaction will be reduced and partly because sentiments have an involuntary component. The use of authority to maintain or modify sentiments is a universal feature of human organizations.

The effect of status on the interaction–activity–sentiment system has another aspect. Respect and constraint appear to be inherent in organizational relationships involving substantial status differences. In such situations, an increase of interaction or activity may result in an increase of either positive or negative sentiments, or both. Equals become more friendly as they work together and communicate more. The sentiments of unequals in the same circumstances are much more difficult to predict.

Homans introduces certain new combinations of the fundamental variables in discussing the topic of *social control,* for example that: "A decrease in the frequency of interaction between the members of a group and in the number of activities they participate in together entails a decline in the extent to which norms are common and clear" (p. 362). This is followed by the more inclusive hypothesis that: "A decrease in the frequency of interaction will bring about a decrease in the strength of interpersonal sentiments" (p. 361). He seems to regard equilibrium and organizational discipline as virtually synonymous, stating that: "A social system is in equilibrium and control is effective when the state of the elements that enter the system and of the mutual relationships between them is such that any small change in one of the elements will be followed by changes in the other elements tending to reduce the amount of that change" (pp. 303–04).

STATUS AND INTERACTION

In one place in *The Human Group* it is said that the higher a man's social rank, the larger will be the number of persons that originate interaction for him and the larger will be the number for whom he originates interaction. Elsewhere it is stated that communication flows toward the leader in both general and private conversations. Riecken and Homans in their later paper explain that: "The higher a member's rank, the more interactions he will receive from other members. . . . Interaction tends to flow from low rank people to high rank people." [4] However, in Homans' discussion of the father–son relationship in Tikopia, the father is said to originate interaction for the son, and this is made the basis of the important theoretical statement that: ". . . when two persons interact with one another, the more frequently one of the two originates interaction for the other, the stronger will be the latter's sentiment of respect (or hostility) toward him" (p. 247).

A classic series of experiments by Bales [5] illustrates the arithmetic of this ambiguity. If we take an individual's position in the rank order of communication in Bales' experimental group as analogous to status, the remarkable pattern in Table 3–1 appears.

The *total amount* of communication is greater for the leader than for the second-ranking man, and so on down the list. The *total amount* of interaction *initiated* is also greater. Nevertheless, if we examine the pair relationships one by one—as shown by the cells in the table—we discover that with minor exceptions the *lower*-ranking

---

[4] Riecken and Homans, *op. cit.,* p. 170.

[5] Robert F. Bales, "The Equilibrium Problem in Small Groups," in Paul Hare, Edgar F. Borgatta, and Robert F. Bales (eds.), *Small Groups: Studies in Social Interaction* (New York: Knopf, 1955). For comparable data on established, organized groups see K. A. Gidwani et al., "Leader Behavior in Elected and Non-elected Groups," *Human Organization,* Vol. XXI, No. 1 (Spring, 1962).

Table 3-1

RANK ORDER OF COMMUNICATION*

RANK ORDER OF PERSON ORIGINATING ACT	SPEAKING TO INDIVIDUALS OF EACH RANK:						TOTAL TO INDIVIDUALS	TO GROUP AS A WHOLE	TOTAL INITIATED
	1	2	3	4	5	6			
1	—	1238	961	545	445	317	3506	5661	9167
2	1748	—	443	310	175	102	2778	1211	3989
3	1371	415	—	305	125	69	2285	742	3027
4	952	310	282	—	83	49	1676	676	2352
5	662	224	144	83	—	28	1141	443	1584
6	470	126	114	65	44	—	819	373	1192
TOTAL COMMUNICATIONS RECEIVED	5203	2313	1944	1308	872	565	12,205	9106	21,311

* Aggregate who-to-whom matrix for eighteen sessions of six-man groups, all types of activity.

FROM Robert F. Bales and Edward A. Shils, Working Papers in the Theory of Action (Glencoe, Ill.: Free Press, 1953), p. 129.

member of each pair initiates most of the interaction. Moreover, the differences are roughly proportional to differences in rank.

The remainder of the ambiguity disappears as soon as we distinguish between the initiation [6] of *interaction* and the initiation of *activity*. The clue is found in the commonplace language of administrative practice, in which orders "flow down" the chain of command and reports "flow up." Although it is customary [7] to speak of the leader initiating interaction for the followers in such set events as the changing of the guard, observation of such events usually discovers a tendency for followers to initiate *interaction* and for leaders to initiate *activity*.[8] It is the sentry who reports to the officer of the guard, and thus originates interaction between them, even though he acts under control of the officer. Several empirical studies support the view that inferiors usually seek out superiors to initiate interaction with them, although there is some contradictory evidence also.[9]

[6] *Initiation* and *origination* are used interchangeably in the literature.

[7] Eliot D. Chapple and Carleton S. Coon, *Principles of Anthropology* (New York: Holt, 1942).

[8] Similar observations about these two processes have been made by William F. Whyte, *Man and Organization: Three Problems in Human Relations in Industry* (Homewood, Ill.: Irwin, 1959), and Peter M. Blau, "Social Integration, Social Rank, and Process of Interaction," *Human Organization,* Vol. XVIII, No. 4 (Winter, 1959–60), 152–53. Blau explains the matter very neatly:

A crucial concept in the systematic study of social interaction is that of origination of action. But this concept has been used to refer to two distinct social processes, which has resulted in much confusion. Some investigators have employed the term to refer to the tendency of one individual to originate the *interaction* of social contacts between himself and others, whereas other investigators referred by it to the tendency of one individual to originate *activities* for others. This distinction can be easily illustrated. If A goes up to B and asks him, 'What shall I do now?' and B tells him and A does it, then A has originated the interaction with B, but B has originated an activity for A. These are clearly two entirely different phenomena. The frequency of origination of interaction indicates the extent to which a member of a group takes the initiative in bringing about social contacts. The frequency of origination of activities for others, in contrast, indicates the degree of influence a member exercises over the rest of the group. The latter measure, but not the former, distinguishes leaders from followers. Whether the individuals who often initiate social contacts also tend to exert a disproportionate influence over the activities of others is, of course, an empirical question and not one which can be decided on logical grounds or by definition.

[9] Harold H. Kelley, "Communication in Experimentally Created Hierarchies," *Human Relations,* Vol. IV (1948), 39–56; Bobbie Norfleet, "Interpersonal Relations and Group Productivity," *Journal of Social Issues,* Vol. IV

Dubin [10] presents evidence to show that the proportion of time spent with superiors, and incidentally the initiation of interaction upward, is greater in the lower status levels of an industrial organization; it declines toward the upper levels. By a sort of perspective effect, those of low status spend more time looking upward than downward in the status order; those of high status have their eyes fixed mainly on the panorama below.

If it is sometimes optional who shall initiate *interaction,* the initiation of *activity* is the essential attribute of higher status. Indeed, status may be operationally defined as position in a rank order of activity initiation. The father in the Irish farm family routinely initiates activity for his son. The son very seldom initiates activity for the father, although he often initiates interaction.

It is easy to understand why superiors initiate more activity than inferiors. All initiation of activity faces the possibility of resistance. Activity is oriented to goals, and the inferior is sought out by the superior as a means to specific ends. The lower the inferior's status, the less his ability to resist the proposed activity. The higher his status, the greater his ability to offer effective support. The selection of persons for whom activity will be initiated always presents a tactical problem for the initiator.

Similar reasoning explains why interaction tends to be initiated from low to high. Control involves feedback, and if A is to control B's activity, information about B's activity must be continuously provided—ordinarily by B—so that A will have a basis for decision. Similarly, if B cannot make decisions without A's approval, he is forced to initiate interaction whenever a need for decision exists.

(1948), 66–69; Josephine F. H. Klein, "The Development of Relationships in Small Groups" (unpublished dissertation, University of Birmingham, Eng., 1952); Robert F. Bales, *Interaction Process Analysis: A Method for the Study of Small Groups* (Cambridge, Mass.: Addison-Wesley, 1950); F. F. Stephan and E. G. Mishler, "The Distribution of Participation," *American Sociological Review,* Vol. XVII, No. 5 (October, 1952), 598–608; Norman H. Berkowitz and Warren G. Bennis, "Interaction Patterns in Formal Service Oriented Organizations," *Administrative Science Quarterly,* Vol. VI, No. 1 (June, 1961). Although in complex working situations, such as the outpatient clinics described by Berkowitz and Bennis, it may sometimes be the case that superiors initiate more interaction than inferiors.

[10] Robert Dubin, "Business Behavior *Behaviorally* Viewed," in George B. Strother (ed.), *Social Science Approaches to Business Behavior* (Homewood, Ill.: Dorsey-Irwin, 1962).

SIMON'S EQUILIBRIUM MODEL

Homans' model of social interaction was elaborated by Simon,[11] who showed that a social system might have *two* points of equilibrium—a *stable* equilibrium at a rather high level of activity and solidarity and an *unstable* equilibrium at a low level. In the stable equilibrium, any path close to the equilibrium point leads toward it. In the unstable equilibrium, any close path leads away.

Simon uses four, instead of six or eight, variables. These are:

I   the intensity of interaction among the members;

F   the level of friendliness among the members;

A   the amount of activity carried on by members within the group;

E   the amount of activity imposed on the group by the external environment.

I, F, and A are treated as dependent variables. The independent variable is E, the activity imposed by the external environment. With these variables, Simon is able to make certain additions to the concept of equilibrium. He suggests that "the level of group friendliness will increase if the actual level of interaction is higher than that 'appropriate' to the existing level of friendliness. That is, if a group of persons with a little friendliness are induced to interact a great deal, the friendliness will grow; while, if a group with a great deal of friendliness interacts seldom, the friendliness will weaken." Similarly, "the amount of activity carried on by the group will tend to increase if the actual level of friendliness is higher than that 'appropriate' to the existing amount of activity, and if the amount of activity imposed externally on the group is higher than the existing amount of activity."

The relationships between the variables are assumed to be linear and are then generalized to a nonlinear system. In discussing the

[11] Herbert A. Simon, "A Formal Theory of Interaction in Social Groups," *American Sociological Review,* Vol. XVII, No. 2 (April, 1952). The quotations are from pp. 202 et seq. See also James G. March and Herbert A. Simon, *Organizations* (New York: Wiley, 1958), pp. 84–90, 109, for supplementary comments.

conditions for a stable equilibrium, Simon finds by manipulation that the amount of interaction must exceed that which would be generated by an equilibrium level of friendliness in the absence of any group activity. In other words, the amount of interaction that corresponds to the equilibrium level of friendliness in an organized group must exceed the amount that might occur in an unorganized congeniality group made up of the same members. If this were not so, an initial level of friendliness would induce enough interaction to increase the level of friendliness and would generate an ascending spiral in which both friendliness and interaction would increase without limit. A similar restriction is required to prevent an ascending spiral between activity and friendliness.

A NEW ANALYTICAL MODEL

We begin with the definition of terms. The *status* of an organizational position is its place in the prescribed rank order of influence in the organization. By *status* we mean the quantitative difference—however measured—between A's ability to modify B's behavior and B's ability to modify A's behavior, when A and B interact.

The status of a member of an organized group, at a particular moment of time, is his place in the actual rank order of influence. It is a commonplace observation that there are differences between the status order of positions, as prescribed by the organization, and the status order of people occupying those positions. These are sometimes called "formal" and "informal" statuses. The commonplace observation has probably been made too often. It obscures the more important fact that the correlation between prescribed and observed status orders is very close. Accidents of personality and circumstances introduce status differences among people in nominally equal positions or reduce status differences between adjacent, unequal positions, but major inequalities are seldom removed—let alone reversed—in this way. A general may be influenced by his chauffeur more than the regulations anticipate, but it is very unlikely that he will take direct orders from the chauffeur. Small children may rebel against parental authority, but they never take over the household budget. Management may complain of dictation by labor, but executives do not seek election as shop stewards. In the following pages, we shall assume that the status difference between two members of an organization is the same as the expected status difference between the positions they occupy, unless otherwise stated.

Interaction, as a variable, represents the mutual influence resulting from symbolic communication between a pair of organizational positions. Operationally, it is a composite measure; both the volume of interaction and its intensity need to be taken into account. The immediate product of interaction is a consensus between the members of the interacting pair about somebody or something in their behavioral field. In close interaction, the development of consensus tends to follow a typical sequence with respect to an object, somewhat as follows: whether to notice it, how to perceive it, what to do about it, how to evaluate what was done.

Valence, as a variable, is a measure of the desire of the members of an interacting pair to interact with each other. It is roughly synonymous with mutual attractiveness or interpersonal affect. It is used rather than *sentiment,* which is too broad a concept for our purpose, or *friendliness,* which is too narrow.

Since valences are emotions or feelings, they cannot be directly observed. The information an observer obtains about the valences of a subject must be based on the subject's own report or inferred from his overt behavior. Since people often express attitudes they inwardly deny, the subjective nature of valence poses a problem of measurement that is unsolvable in theory. It is less forbidding in practice. The attitudes that are concealed in one organizational situation, such as the resentment of a subordinate toward his supervisor, will be freely expressed in another situation, as when the resentful subordinate explains matters to his peer group. By taking account of such discrepancies in overt attitudes, we are able to recover much of the information that is lost by our inability to observe emotions directly. Many valences—likes, dislikes, loves, hates, loyalties, jealousies—are specific requirements of a position, and the organization takes cognizance of them in many ways, insisting on certain feelings, permitting others, prohibiting some.

Activity is always rationally conceived, since the organizational tasks performed by any interacting pair are part of the organization's program for achieving collective goals, and whatever behavior is not part of that program cannot properly be described as organizational activity. However, positions in overlapping organizations may be held simultaneously and their activities interwoven. For example, two lumbermen may saw down a tree as part of the work program of the logging company but do it slowly as part of the output restriction program of their peer group. Such complications can usually be resolved by careful measurement and by a clear perception that activity is a measure of progress and *not* effort, of output and *not* input.

CONSTRUCTING THE MODEL

We are now ready to construct a model of the organization in action, based on the four variables of status, interaction, valence, and activity. The purpose of the model is to predict the changes that will occur in the entire system composed of these variables, when a change in any variable is imposed from outside.

We want to be able to answer such questions as: What will be the effect of increasing the number of committees in a voluntary association? How will the efficiency of a work crew be affected when the schedule of their foreman is changed so that he can communicate with them only occasionally? Which relationships in a middle-class family will be marked by constraint? What will be the effect of appointing two life-long enemies as president and board chairman of the same company? What will happen to the status order of a ship's crew marooned on a desert island?

The scope of this model is sufficiently wide to cover many different problems. Its validity remains to be determined. We shall assume that the model is in stable equilibrium for small increments, so that a minor change in status, interaction, valence, or activity imposed by an outside force tends to be followed by a series of successive changes the ultimate effect of which is to restore the initial values of the variables. The model is assumed to be in unstable equilibrium for large changes. The effect of a large change in one variable imposed by an outside force is to set up a series of successive changes in the other variables and to move them cumulatively further from the initial equilibrium. In both cases, the fundamental and essential assumption is that any change in one variable imposed from outside the system must be followed by changes in all the other variables that in turn affect the first variable.

It is possible to measure status, interaction, valence, and activity in the pair relationships of individuals, or in the relationship between the whole organization and an individual member, and to estimate average values for all of the relationships included in an organization. In the following pages we shall first examine relationships between pairs of positions and then go on to consider how far the same model may be applicable to entire organizations.

OPERATION OF THE MODEL

The twenty-four cells in Table 3–2 present the fundamental relationships of the SIVA model in crude form. There are four basic assumptions:

1. Changes in interaction are proportional to changes in activity, taking into account that more interaction is normally developed for a given amount of activity than is absolutely required.
2. The interaction between an unequal pair is proportional to the amount of their joint activity and inversely proportional to the status difference between them.
3. The valence between a pair of interacting peers fluctuates proportionately with their interaction.

Table 3–2

A MODEL OF THE PAIR RELATIONSHIP
IN AN ORGANIZATION

DIRECTION OF CHANGE	RESULTING TENDENCY *			
	STATUS	INTERACTION	VALENCE	ACTIVITY
Status plus	—	minus	indeterm.	plus
Status minus	—	plus	indeterm.	minus
Interaction plus	minus	—	plus	plus
Interaction minus	plus	—	minus	minus
Valence plus	indeterm.	plus	—	plus
Valence minus	indeterm.	minus	—	minus
Activity plus	plus	plus	plus	—
Activity minus	minus	minus	minus	—

* In one variable at a time, holding the others constant.

4. The valence between a pair of unequals fluctuates *unpredictably* as their interaction changes.

The *raison d'être* of human organization appears in the second of these assumptions. The larger a status difference, the less the interaction needed to sustain a given amount of coordinated activity.

Table 3–2 asserts that a slight increase of activity between equal positions in an organization will be followed by slight increases of interaction and valence; that a slight increase of interaction will be followed by slight increases of activity and valence; that a slight increase of valence will be followed by slight increases of activity and interaction; and that a decrease of one of these variables will have the opposite result. When status differences are introduced, the functions remain, but their proportionality is changed. The greater the status difference in an interacting pair, the less the interaction that will accompany a given amount of joint activity, and the less the change in the volume of interaction that will follow a given change in activity. Viewed another way, if the status difference is increased, a greater increment of activity will follow a given increment of interaction.

These statements are essentially tautological. The denotation of a status difference between A and B is only another way of expressing the observable fact that A and B can arrive at a common line of activity with less interaction than would be necessary between equals. This restriction of communication is the essential feature of organized activity. When the interaction that accompanies a given amount of activity increases, the power of the superior is automatically reduced, since the surplus interaction allows the inferior to exercise an unforeseen and unscheduled influence. If the amount of activity is observed to increase without any corresponding increase of interaction, it must be presumed that the ability of the superior to limit debate—so to speak—has increased, and this is an increase of status difference. Such changes may be very small, so that the status of either position relative to other positions is not much affected; but even minute status changes are usually perceptible to the persons involved, since changes require immediate modifications of behavior.

The mechanism whereby a status difference reduces the volume of interaction necessary to sustain a given volume of activity is reversible. The ancient proverb that familiarity breeds contempt may be translated to say that an increase of interaction between unequals without an accompanying increase in their activity decreases the effective status difference between them. Superiors can make friends of their subordinates only by sacrificing some of their authority.

In relationships between equals, valence can be treated as a linear, or nearly linear, function of interaction. This simple principle explains the nearly spontaneous formation of peer groups in all the nooks and crannies of large-scale organizations. Moreover, valence seems to respond indifferently to interaction involving work or play, so long as there is no status difference between the interactors. The immediate effect of introducing a status difference is to qualify the dependence of interaction on valence in two ways. First, as the status difference increases, the amount of interaction is determined less by the wishes of the participants and more by organizational requirements. The tendency for valence to vary with activity persists, regardless of status difference, while the variation of valence in response to small increases or decreases of interaction is subject to a multiplier effect as the status difference increases. This part of the picture is incomplete. It represents the positive side of authoritarianism, but interaction between unequals also stimulates negative valences, which we have not yet mentioned.

An important implication of the model, one not apparent at first glance, is that when one of the variables cannot change in the expected direction, another variable must change by a greater than expected amount to maintain the equilibrium. Thus, in a situation in which the amount of interaction is not allowed to vary (as in a prison) an increase of activity will be followed by a much sharper increase of valence than would be expected if interaction were free to vary also. In relations between unequals in which other multipliers are at work, a very small increase in interaction may be followed by an enormous increase in either valence or activity if only one of them is free to vary. In any case, variation can occur only over a narrow range. Each of our four variables has definite upper and lower limits in most organizational relationships.

LIMITS ON VARIATION

The limits of status variation in an unequal relationship are set by the table of organization. In the usual case, the power of a superior over an inferior cannot vary above the power of his own superiors, nor below the power of intervening inferiors. If variations should occur beyond these limits, the status order would become unstable, and the situation no longer be in equilibrium.

It may seem strange that such intensely subjective phenomena as love or hate have quantitative limits. Yet, with respect to any pair relationship in an organization, there is an upper limit above which positive valence may not rise, and a lower limit below which it may not fall, without destroying the relationship or transforming its character.

Lower limits are found in situations involving authority and dependency. In most forms of the family, positive valences are prescribed between parents and children. When the minimum positive valence is not maintained, the mores or the laws define the situation as intolerable and prescribe remedial action, as when children are neglected. Most hierarchies specify the minimum valences between certain inferiors and superiors—priests and bishops, for example. A definite lower limit of valence is established for such relationships; any decline below this limit is officially defined as a crisis.

Upper limits seem to be set for nearly all pair relationships in organizations. The development of positive valence across a status gap is always subject to *some* restriction. A positive valence that exceeds these limits is regarded as a threat to the status order, and punitive measures are commonly taken to repress unsuitable attachments.

All such limits are special cases of a very general phenomenon, the tendency for valence in a pair relationship to be limited by obligations to third parties. The valence of a married woman toward other men is limited by obligations to her husband. The valence of an adult toward a child unrelated to him is limited by the double expectation that he will have a greater valence for his own children and a lesser valence than the unrelated child's parents have toward their child. The valence of a leader to one of his subordinates is limited by his obligation to maintain roughly equal valences to all subordinates on the same level. The valence of a subordinate to his leader is limited by his obligation to maintain solidarity with his peers.

Similarly, a man's valence to his mother-in-law has a lower limit below which he violates an obligation to his wife. The leader, even in authoritarian hierarchies, must show some minimum positive valence to each member of a group of subordinates or risk losing the support of the others. Two subordinates whose superiors are close friends must preserve at least the appearance of amicable relations.

The lower limits on activity in pair relationships in the organized group are generally defined by the tasks to be performed. Some degree of successful achievement is a prerequisite for the continued existence of the organization. The factory must produce goods and produce them at a reasonable cost if it is to stay in existence. The household must provide its members with something to eat and a place to sleep, or there will be no household. The voluntary association must be able to muster a quorum for its meetings or cease to meet. The upper limits to activity in the pair relationship are usually set by resource limitations. The time, effort, and materials expended in one kind of activity must be withheld from other activities. Since every organization competes for resources with other organizations of the same society, and every activity competes for resources with other activities of the same organization, the upper limits of activity in a pair relationship can usually be determined with fair accuracy.

Interaction, too, has upper limits—fixed by time, opportunity, and other role-demands—and lower limits, determined by the organizational program.

STATUS DIFFERENCE AND VALENCE

The indeterminate relationship. Table 3–1 proposes that a small increase or decrease in status is followed by an indeterminate change in valence and, conversely, that a small change in valence is followed by an indeterminate change in the status difference of a pair relationship. This indeterminacy may be read directly from the model, in the sense that an increase in status is followed by a decrease in interaction, which tends to decrease valence, but also by an increase of activity, which tends to increase valence.

We know from organizational case studies that changes in status are likely to be followed by changes in valence and that these may be either positive or negative. We can only surmise in the present state of knowledge whether there is no direct dependence between status and valence, the effects observed being indirect, or whether there is an orderly dependence we do not yet understand. It may be hypothesized that:

1. Relationships between unequals usually show more emotional affect than relationships between equals at the same interaction rate in the same context.

2. The valences of the inferior show more fluctuation in response to a given stimulus than those of the superior.

3. The reciprocity between a pair of interactors, with respect both to perceptions and sentiments, decreases with increasing status difference.

4. Valences between unequals are subject to limits set by the respective peers.

5. Relationships with large status differences are often marked by ambivalence.

Status and ambivalence. The analysis of ambivalence appears to be crucial for the understanding of interaction between unequals in organizations. Although the concept has a long history in psychology and psychiatry,[12] a paper dealing explicitly and systematically with sociological ambivalence did not appear until 1963.[13] The authors remark in passing that "However great its legitimacy, authority is known to have a high potential for creating ambivalence among those subject to it. Authority generates a mixture of respect, love and admiration and of fear, hatred and contempt." In his original formulation Bleuler identified three types of ambivalence: the emotional–affective, the voluntary–conative, and the intellectual–cognitive. The ambivalence generated in interaction between unequals is emotional–affective, involving the simultaneous appearance of positive and negative valences in the same relationship, but it may easily be shown to have voluntary–conative implications, in the form of conflicting wishes to cooperate and not to cooperate, and an intellectual–cognitive element as well, since unequal relationships often involve a mixture of consensus and dissensus.

As a first attempt to include ambivalence in the analytical model, we might suppose that an increase of status difference in a pair relationship, with interaction and activity held constant, is followed by

[12] It was introduced by Eugen Bleuler in 1910.

[13] Robert K. Merton and Elinor Barber, "Sociological Ambivalence," in Edward A. Tiryakian (ed.), *Sociological Theory, Values, and Sociological Change: Essays in Honor of Pitirim A. Sorokin* (New York: Free Press, 1963). The quotation is from page 111.

an increase in ambivalence. This is plausible, but not very useful, since no one has yet devised a satisfactory way of measuring ambivalence.

There is a special problem in coping with ambivalence in an equilibrium model. Such models assume a steady state of the variables, modified by small positive or negative increments, while ambivalence is accompanied by what Merton and Barber call "the oscillation of behaviors."

Hostile sentiments play such an important part in the ordinary affairs of organizations that it is difficult to see how we can describe interaction networks without introducing negative values of valence. The question immediately arises whether the other variables of status, interaction, and activity, can also be shown to have meaningful negative values. Negative status differences turn out to be interchangeable with positive status differences, since a positive difference viewed from the position of the superior becomes a negative difference from the position of the inferior in the same relationship. The advantage of one participant is numerically equivalent to the disadvantage of the other.

The concept of negative interaction or *insulation* implies the deliberate resistance of the parties to each other's influence and it is quite meaningful, although it should be kept in mind that some degree of positive interaction will probably be observed at the same time.

It is very easy to assign a meaning to negative values of activity. Activity, it will be remembered, is a measure of the useful joint effort directed by an interacting pair toward a common goal. Negative activity or *attrition* is a measure of regression from a common goal and can be measured by the cost of mutual frustration. It is one dimension of conflict. Conflict, like other kinds of organization behavior, has costs that must be met and consequences that are evaluated by definite criteria. We shall not be surprised to find that positive and negative activity can coexist in a situation at the same time and may turn out to be mutually dependent. Conflict and cooperation are *expected* to occur simultaneously whenever unequals interact.

A tentative statement of the interdependence of the negative variables in a pair relationship can be derived by merely changing all of the signs in Table 3–2. This version of the analytical model will be discussed at greater length in the chapter on organized conflict.

CATALYTIC EFFECTS IN ORGANIZATIONAL PAIRS

The third person as catalyst. For convenience, we shall assume that A, B, and C occupy contiguous positions in an organization, that the analysis starts with a situation in equilibrium, and that it deals with relatively small increments of change. We note first that the mere presence of a superior or inferior on the scene modifies a pair relationship in predictable ways. Table 3–3 shows this catalytic

Table 3–3

CATALYTIC EFFECTS IN PAIR RELATIONSHIPS

STATUS OF THIRD PARTY RELATIVE TO PAIR	RESULTING TENDENCY WITHIN RELATIONSHIP			
	STATUS	INTERACTION	VALENCE	ACTIVITY
Common superior	minus	minus	indeterm.	plus
Common inferior	minus	minus	indeterm.	plus
Superior's peer	plus	minus	minus	plus
Inferior's peer	plus	minus	minus	plus
Superior to one inferior to other	plus	minus	minus	minus

effect in five possible situations: an interacting pair [14] in the presence of a common superior, a common inferior, the superior's peer, the inferior's peer, and a third party of intermediate status, respectively. Needless to say, this simple arrangement does not take care of more complicated cases involving a greater number of interactors, nor does it take into account the situational factors that may limit the movement of the variables in the predicted directions. It *is* hypothesized that despite such complications, the forces represented will have a discernible effect in any situation conforming to the model.

The table asserts that the effect of status difference within an inter-

[14] The pair in question are assumed to occupy contiguous positions in an organization.

acting pair of unequals will decrease in the presence of their common superior, together with the amount of their interaction, while their activity and valence will increase. When two members of an organization find themselves in the presence of a common superior, their ability to influence each other is superseded by the ability of the superior to influence both of them and his ability to rearrange the relationship between them. Since such rearrangement represents a loss of autonomy for them, they are strongly motivated not to display all their relationship. There is both a real decline in the ability of A to influence B and an apparent decline, based upon reluctance to expose their interaction to observation. Activity increases through the usual workings of authority, and valence increases as a response to the "threat" posed by the common superior.

The effects are similar, although much weaker, in the presence of a common inferior. Here the ability of the interacting pair to influence each other is attenuated by their more or less equal ability to influence the inferior. The uncertainty of C's behavior and his ability to assume a balancing role in any conflict between A and B limits the ability of A and B to influence each other. The effect, of course, becomes much more marked when C is a whole group of inferiors.[15] As in the previous case, A and B are likely to attempt to conceal their relationship from C but are less able to do so than when C is an individual.[16]

The table indicates that the interaction of a superior A with his inferior B is reduced when A's peer C is present. The valence of the pair also declines, while the status difference between them and their joint activity increases. The authority of the superior is reinforced. At the same time, his obligations to his own peer group require him to minimize his solidarity with B. The presence of A's peer exposes the relationship AB to observation from above and

---

[15] The convention that forbids an admiral to interfere with the navigation of his flagship is designed to protect both the flagship captain, whose control of his ship is reduced by the presence of a superior on board, and the admiral, whose superior rank might be undermined by the habitual obedience of the crew to the captain.

[16] A fuller explanation of why inferiors can obtain more information about the interaction of superiors than superiors can obtain about the interaction of inferiors is found in Reece J. McGee, *Social Disorganization in America* (San Francisco: Chandler, 1962), pp. 124–28.

reinforces organizational requirements at the expense of whatever private adaptations have been worked out between A and B. For the same reasons, conflict and hostility between A and B are also reduced in this situation.

Similar effects are observed when the superior A interacts with the inferior B in the presence of B's peer C, but this situation is more variable and the effect is less certain. The organization anticipates that A's control over C will reinforce his control over B, but whether this actually occurs depends somewhat on the resistance to A's authority offered by B and C when reinforced by each other's presence. The description of the third party as a catalyst oversimplifies the processes actually at work. As the foregoing analysis suggests, changes in the relationship AB are also accompanied by simultaneous changes in the relationships AB and BC; B cannot be viewed as inert. It is interesting to examine the effect of changes in the relationship of both members of the interacting pair to the third party, holding status constant.

The transitivity of valence. We have seen that organizational status is transitive, so that if A outranks B and B outranks C, A will outrank C. The analysis of communication networks shows interaction to be transitive also. If A interacts with B and B interacts with C, it is almost always possible to observe the reciprocal influence of A and C on each other's behavior even when they have no direct contact. The transitivity of valence is a little more complicated. Among peers, transitivity can be summarized by four statements known to every small child the world over. (a) My friends' friends are my friends. (b) My friends' enemies are my enemies. (c) My enemies' friends are my enemies. (d) My enemies' enemies are my friends.

Figure 3–1 shows these diagramatically. The two stable triads of peer relationships are those having three positive relationships, or two negative relationships and one positive. The point has been noted before. Heider,[17] presenting his theory of structural balance, remarks that, "In the case of three entities, a balance state exists if all three relations are positive in all respects, or if two are negative

[17] Fritz Heider, "Attitudes and Cognitive Organization," *Journal of Psychology*, Vol. XXI (1946), and *The Psychology of Interpersonal Relations* (New York: Wiley, 1958).

Figure 3–1

TRANSITIVITY OF VALENCES IN THE TIKOPIAN FAMILY

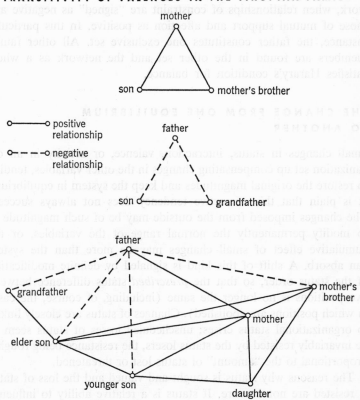

and one positive." The principle has been generalized for any number of participants, in an interaction network, considered as points in a signed graph by Harary.[18] "A signed graph is balanced if and only if its points can be separated into mutually exclusive sets S1 and S2 in such a way that each positive line joins points of the same sets while each negative line joins two points from different sets."

[18] Frank Harary, "A Structural Analysis of the Situation in the Middle East in 1956," *Journal of Conflict Resolution,* Vol. V, No. 2 (June, 1961). The quotation is from page 170. See also (with Dorwin Cartwright) "Structural Balance: A Generalization of Heider's Theory," *Psychological Review,* Vol. LXIII (September, 1956), and James A. Davis, "Structural Balance, Mechanical Solidarity, and Interpersonal Relations," *American Journal of Sociology,* Vol. LXVIII, No. 4 (January, 1963).

Taking the extended family in Tikopia as example, Figure 3–1 shows the application of this principle to the whole interaction network, when relationships of constraint are "signed" as negative and those of mutual support and affection as positive. In this particular instance, the father constitutes one exclusive set. All other family members are found in the other set and the network as a whole satisfies Harary's condition for balance.

THE CHANGE FROM ONE EQUILIBRIUM TO ANOTHER

Small changes in status, interaction, valence, or activity in an organization set up compensating changes in the other variables, tending to restore the original magnitudes and keep the system in equilibrium. It is plain that this corrective tendency does not always succeed. The changes imposed from the outside may be of such magnitude as to modify permanently the normal range of the variables, or the cumulative effect of small changes may be more than the system can absorb. A shift of this kind is signaled by definite modification of the status order, so that the *prescribed* status difference between two positions is no longer the same (including, of course, the cases in which positions are abolished). Changes of status are closely linked to organizational status crises; unscheduled losses of status seem to be invariably resisted by the status losers, the resistance being roughly proportional to the "amount" of status lost or threatened.

The reasons why status is sought and valued and the loss of status is resisted are not obscure. If status is a relative ability to influence others, it is necessarily a relative ability to satisfy wants. Decline in the status of the position implies a decline in the ability of the incumbent to procure satisfactions through the organization and, on the minimum assumption that some of his behavior is directed toward the achievement of satisfactions and the avoidance of frustration, we may infer not only that status loss will be resisted but that the resistance will be roughly proportionate to the threatened frustration.

By the familiar principle of relative deprivation, which proposes that status changes [19] are evaluated in relation to the distribution of statuses in the subjects' reference groups, the status of a position may

[19] As Merton points out, ". . . 'deprivation' is the incidental and particularized component of the concept of relative deprivation, whereas the more

be sensed by its incumbent to be drastically reduced when the status of adjacent positions is increased. One device for persuading officials with tenure to resign is to promote their colleagues while leaving their positions unchanged.

Some apparent exceptions need to be explained. Demotions may occur as predictable events in a career. High officials are often limited in the number of terms of office they may serve. A demotion is not ordinarily resisted as a loss of status if it is built into the position and its occurrence has been anticipated. It may well be experienced as a deprivation, but the characteristic response is regret or some other private sentiment, not the violent alienation from the organization which is characteristic of status loss. On the other hand, a nonpromotion is often experienced as a status loss, and as particularly unpleasant when the expectation of promotion is built into a position. Positions have a time dimension for their incumbents, and the attributes of a position include past and future, as well as present, statuses.

Gains of status are not sought as uniformly as losses are resisted. Promotion is sometimes refused and sometimes accepted with indifference or bad grace. If we examine specific cases in which promotion is refused, for example workers who refuse promotion to foreman or foremen who do not wish to be executives,[20] there appear to be a number of mutually reinforcing explanations.

First, promotion, like demotion, means disruption of established habits and established relationships. The gain of status in a large organization may require the abandonment of positions in peer groups and suborganizations, and since these positions are also valued, promotion may be experienced as a net loss of status. (These same risks are associated with demotion, *without* offsetting benefits.) Second, promotion usually involves new activities and new measures

significant nucleus of the concept is its stress upon social and psychological experience as 'relative.' " Robert K. Merton, *Social Theory and Social Structure* (Glencoe, Ill.: Free Press, 1957), p. 235.

[20] An example of the first is found in the study of a Belgian foundry by Frans van Mechelen, *Arbeider, Loon en Ondernemings-Gemeenschap* (Antwerp: 'T Groeit, about 1954). An example of the second is the study of "Executives and Supervisors: Contrasting Self-conceptions and Conceptions of Each Other," by Charles H. Coates and Roland J. Pellegrin, *American Sociological Review,* Vol. XXII, No. 2 (April, 1957). When asked "If you could start all over again, would you like to become a top-level executive?" the great majority of supervisors stated emphatically that they would not.

of accomplishment and is refused by people who "do not want the extra responsibility." The candidate may be uncertain about his capability in the higher position, while secure about his present performance. Note that in those status orders in which promotion does not involve any change of duties, it seems to be always accepted when offered. Associate professors never refuse promotion to full professor. Third, promotion often entails additional participation in organizational activities, in accordance with the correlation between status and participation. Whether a member is willing to increase his participation in a given organization at a given moment is always a moot question.

CHAPTER FOUR

Organizational Effectiveness

As we have seen, organizations are devices for accomplishing definite purposes. The concepts of success or failure follow inevitably from this view of the organization as a device or mechanism or means to particular ends. In this chapter, we shall consider how organizational effectiveness can be defined and measured.

The mechanism is established in the first place for getting things done that require the coordination of individual efforts. Many projects of human importance, ranging from procreation to the orbiting of artificial satellites, cannot be accomplished at all by a solitary individual. Other projects, such as agriculture or the building of boats, can be accomplished much more easily with a division of labor than without it. Every organization, even the most rudimentary, involves the consumption of energy and other resources, and every organization is formed for definite purposes, although these may be modified in the course of its history. It may occasionally happen that an organization develops without a reason, or loses its original purpose and does not find another, but it is difficult to imagine what motives would then lead to its continued operation.[1]

---

[1] The great Georg Simmel presented this account of a marginal case:
. . . not long ago, there came the news from a city in Northern France, regarding a strange "Association of the Broken Dish." Years ago, some industrialists met for dinner. During the meal, a dish fell on the floor and broke. One of the diners noticed that the number of pieces was identical with that of those present. One of them considered this an omen, and

119

When we say that organizations are purposive, we mean:

1. Every organization is founded for a definite purpose or a set of related purposes.
2. Every organization requires an input of resources and must show an output sufficient to balance in whatever system of measurement is appropriate.
3. The activities and interactions prescribed for the incumbent of an organizational position are functionally related to some collective purpose.
4. Yardsticks or criteria of some kind for evaluating organizational effectiveness are culturally provided for every organization and its members.

The remainder of this chapter deals with the criteria of organizational effectiveness.

It may be useful at this point to review the description of a functioning organization that emerges from our discussion thus far. Statically viewed, an organization consists of people, positions, and goals. Each position includes norms that prescribe the activities, the roles, and the sentiments by means of which these people are to pursue these goals, plus a set of norms for filling the positions. Viewed dynamically, the organization is a network of relationships between pairs of positions. Each of these relationships can be described by the four interdependent variables of status, interaction, valence, and activity, and each is influenced in various ways by contiguous relationships. It is evident that there must be descriptive variables for the entire organization corresponding in some way to those for the pair relationship, since a rise or fall in the average activity or valence

---

in consequence, they founded a society of friends who owed one another service and help. Each of them took a part of the dish home with him. If one of them dies, his piece is sent to the president, who glues the fragments he receives together. The last survivor will fit the last piece, whereupon the reconstituted dish is to be interred. The "Society of the Broken Dish" will thus dissolve and disappear.
Georg Simmel, *The Sociology of Georg Simmel,* trans. and ed. Kurt H. Wolff (Glencoe, Ill.: Free Press, 1950), pp. 124–25.
Simmel himself furnishes the commentary:
The feeling within that society, as well as the feeling of others in regard to it, would no doubt be different if new members were admitted and the life of the group thereby perpetuated indefinitely. The fact that from the beginning, it is defined as one that will die gives it a particular stamp. . . .

of pair relationships, for example, is certainly a meaningful phenomenon for the organization as a whole. Then, too, although it is sometimes useful to restrict analysis to internal relationships, we cannot indefinitely ignore the relationships of an organization with its external environment and especially with other organizations and their members.

Continuing the development of the analytical model explored in the previous chapter, we shall start by proposing four variables for comparing the effectiveness of any two organizations of similar type or of the same organization at different times.[2]

THE CRITERIA OF ORGANIZATIONAL EFFECTIVENESS

Organizational effectiveness can be measured by the following variables:

S	*Stability*	(maintenance of status differences)
I	*Integration*	(maintenance of interaction)
V	*Voluntarism*	(maintenance of valences)
A	*Achievement*	(maintenance of activities)

These new measures have a strong resemblance to the SIVA variables for the pair relationship, and it is hypothesized that they are interdependent in the same way (Table 4–1). Let us look a little more closely at each of these terms.

STABILITY

Stability is a measure of the organization's ability to conserve or increase the status of its positions, or, in other words, to maintain its own structure.[3] By maintaining status differences, the organization

[2] Whether it is theoretically possible to develop standard measures for comparing the effectiveness of organizations of different types (for example the integration of an army vs. that of a nuclear family) is still an unresolved question.

[3] The term *maintenance* is borrowed from Parsons and is taken to mean that the magnitudes of the variable do not fall below their starting values or some other stated minimum. In the long run, the fundamental organizational problem is to maintain *or increase* stability, integration, voluntarism, and achievement.

Table 4–1

A MODEL OF ORGANIZATIONAL EFFECTIVENESS

DIRECTION OF CHANGE	RESULTING TENDENCY *			
	STABILITY	INTEGRA- TION	VOLUN- TARISM	ACHIEVE- MENT
Stability plus	—	minus	indeterm.	plus
Stability minus	—	plus	indeterm.	minus
Integration plus	minus	—	plus	plus
Integration minus	plus	—	minus	minus
Voluntarism plus	indeterm.	plus	—	plus
Voluntarism minus	indeterm.	minus	—	minus
Achievement plus	plus	plus	plus	—
Achievement minus	minus	minus	minus	—

* In one variable at a time, holding the others constant.

controls the behavior of its members and some aspects of the external environment. The abilities to continue existing programs, to initiate new programs, to manipulate goals, to resolve problems of recruitment and succession, and to enforce norms are all included. A highly stable organization, such as a naval unit, can even reverse its goals (that is, change sides) without interrupting its activity or modifying its interaction network. An increase in stability can be achieved by an increase in authority (increasing the average status difference between positions) or by an increase in the number of differentiated positions (increasing the total amount of status difference) or by a growth in membership (increasing the number of status differences). All of these have the same effect. They increase the amount of social control and—if other variables remain unchanged—the ability of the organization to carry out its program.

INTEGRATION

Integration is a measure of the organization's ability to maintain or increase the total volume of interaction among its positions or, negatively, to control internal conflict. More interaction implies better mutual adjustment, less factionalism, more communication about problems and procedures, and greater consensus among members about the organizational program. The integration of an organization may be increased by an improvement in the means of communication or the opportunities for communication. The integration of an organization rises when its members are assembled in one place, and it declines when they are dispersed. An increase of membership size can increase integration if the average interaction in pair relationships holds constant, but more often it has the effect of decreasing integration by decreasing the opportunities for interaction between positions.

VOLUNTARISM

Voluntarism is a measure of the organization's ability to maintain the valences between its positions and among its component individuals and groups without coercion. Roughly equivalent to morale, it measures the organization's ability to provide satisfaction for individuals and the desire of members to continue their participation. The higher the voluntarism, the less the coercion needed to hold participants and to enforce organizational norms. The assumptions behind this concept may be summed up as follows:

1. Participation in high valence relationships is gratifying, that is, people like to be liked.
2. The desire to continue participation in an organization is a function of the gratifications it provides.
3. An individual's desire to continue his participation in a large organization depends on the satisfaction he obtains in his organizational relationships.

Few organizations, of course, depend entirely on voluntarism for their continuity. The continued participation of dissatisfied members may be assured by force, as in armies or prisons, or by the cost of leaving,[4] as in families and business firms. But involuntary participation always creates problems of integration and achievement.

ACHIEVEMENT

Achievement is the net result of the organization's activity. It is always subject to evaluation in the organization's own environment and is usually measurable with some degree of objectivity. The appropriate units of measurement vary from one type of organization to another. An input–output ratio, either in dollars or in other quantities, is appropriate for a factory or a farm. It is not applicable to a political party, for example, in which the votes obtained may be the appropriate measure, irrespective of the time and money expended to obtain them. Many types of organization, ranging from mountain-climbing expeditions to wartime armies, are subject to a simple binary standard of success *or* failure. Others, such as private schools and symphony orchestras, are evaluated only by the quality of their output, quantity being irrelevant. The achievement of multiple-purpose organizations, such as families and states, is represented by several kinds of output, which need to be measured separately.

Nevertheless, the yardsticks are always there; they are provided by the institutional pattern and are familiar to the participants in an organization and to their neighbors. Organizations are usually rational in intention, if not in fact. The rational intention requires some appraisal of the success of the common effort, either by comparison with the achievement of similar organizations or by means of a model.

OTHER FORMULATIONS

Other sociologists, studying organizational effectiveness from different standpoints, have arrived at very similar formulations. Parsons' paradigm of the social act [5] is succinctly summarized as follows by Scott:

[4] For an admirable summary of the motives affecting participation in industrial organizations, see James G. March and Herbert A. Simon, *Organizations* (New York: Wiley, 1958), Chapter 4, "Motivational Constraints: The Decision to Participate," especially pp. 93–105.

[5] It has taken various related forms; see especially Talcott Parsons, *The Social System* (Glencoe, Ill.: Free Press, 1951), (with Neil J. Smelser) *Econ-*

An "action system" is composed of a number of units (which are observable role behaviors in a social system); this action system is confronted with a series of basic problems which must be solved if it is to continue operating as a system. These are: (1) *adaptive problems,* the adapting of behavior to the physical and social environment of the system and the manipulation of objects, including persons, so as to make for more favorable relations; (2) *gratificatory problems,* activity connected with the attainment and enjoyment of the goals of the system; (3) *integrative problems,* activity directed to the "adjustment" of the relations of systems' members to each other; and (4) *pattern-maintenance problems,* activity directed toward the maintenance of the identity of the system as a system, renewal and reaffirmation of its own values and existence.[6]

Parsons' *integrative problems* appear to correspond to the definition of *integration* we proposed above. It appears, although more uncertainly, that *gratificatory problems* are approximately equivalent to *voluntarism,* that *adaptive problems* have to do with *achievement,* and that *pattern-maintenance problems* are related to *stability.*

In an empirical study of organizational effectiveness, Georgopoulos and Tannenbaum define organizational effectiveness as

> the extent to which an organization as a social system, given certain resources and means, fulfills its objectives without incapacitating its means and resources and without placing undue strain upon its members. This conception of effectiveness assumes the following criteria: (1) organizational productivity; (2) organizational flexibility in the form of successful adjustment to internal organizational changes and successful adaptation to externally induced change; and (3) absence of intraorganizational strain, or tension, and of conflict between organizational subgroups. These three criteria both relate to the means–ends dimension of organizations and, potentially, apply to nearly all organizations. The first relates to the movement of the organization towards its goals (locomotion); the others relate to the

omy and Society (Glencoe, Ill.: Free Press, 1956), and the two-part article "Suggestions for a Sociological Approach to the Theory of Organizations," *Administrative Science Quarterly,* Vol. I (June, 1956) and Vol. I (September, 1956).

[6] Frances Gillespie Scott, "Action Theory and Research in Social Organization," *American Journal of Sociology,* Vol. LXIV, No. 4 (January, 1959), 386–87. For specific discussion of the four system problems see also Robert Dubin, "Parsons' Actor: Continuities in Social Theory," *American Sociological Review,* Vol. XXV, No. 4 (August, 1960), and Talcott Parsons, "Pattern Variables Revisited: A Response to Robert Dubin," *American Sociological Review,* Vol. XXV, No. 4 (August, 1960).

requirements or organizational survival in the face of external and internal variability, and to the dimension of preservation (or incapacitation) of organizational means.[7]

Clearly, this notion of productivity is equivalent to *achievement;* flexibility is a way of describing *stability* over a period of time, and the absence of intraorganizational strain is a measure of *integration.* Since the study focuses on the relation of the organization to its external environment, the omission of *voluntarism* is understandable.

In his classic paper "Social Structure and Anomie," [8] Merton discusses four models of deviant adaptation: *innovation, ritualism, retreatism,* and *rebellion.* They may be considered as negative descriptions of the criteria of organizational effectiveness. Rebellion is a breakdown of stability, retreatism signifies a failure of integration, and ritualism is the opposite of voluntarism. The relationship of innovation to achievement is a little more complex. Innovation, as Merton explains in several places, is the substitution of new, unsanctioned purposes for those originally held by the organization. Innovation rather than nonachievement appears in this list because Merton's discussion concerns modes of individual resistance to organizational requirements rather than organizational failure. The symptoms of organizational failure are instability, disintegration, nonparticipation, and nonachievement. The inability to satisfy any *one* of the criteria of organizational effectiveness—stability, integration, voluntarism, and achievement—ordinarily destroys the organization and brings the story to a close.

FINDING THE POINTS-OF-STRESS

The four criteria are in a sense tautological. It is self-evident that no organization can continue to exist unless it maintains its structure

[7] Basil S. Georgopoulos and Arnold S. Tannenbaum, "A Study of Organizational Effectiveness," *American Sociological Review,* Vol. XXII, No. 5 (October, 1957). The quotation is from pages 535–36. See also the discussion of organizational effectiveness in R. L. Thorndike, *Personnel Selection: Test and Measurement Techniques* (New York: Wiley, 1949), pp. 129–44, and in Morris Viteles, *Motivation and Morale in Industry* (New York: Norton, 1953), especially Chapter 8, "Supervision, Productivity, and Morale."

[8] Robert K. Merton, "Social Structure and Anomie," in *Social Theory and Social Structure* (Glencoe, Ill.: Free Press, 1949).

in the face of changing circumstances, holds dissension and misunderstanding in check, provides enough satisfaction to individual members so that they are willing to continue, and is able to accomplish the essential tasks in its program. The determination of whether each criterion has been satisfied in the given case is not as difficult as we might suppose, nor is it left to the sociological analyst. The standards for determining how well an organization satisfies each of the fundamental criteria are built into the institutional pattern. The blueprint for constructing an organization specifies a set of meters and gauges for checking its operation. Purposeful activity, by its nature, requires some feedback of results so that errors can be corrected and output improved.

However, when we examine empirical cases, we discover that only a few organizations attach equal importance to all of the criteria. This comes about not because any of the requirements can be disregarded but because, in a given type of organization at a particular time and place, some criteria may be much easier to satisfy than others.

When one of the criteria is especially difficult for the organization to satisfy, it becomes the subject of constant concern by members. When the satisfaction of the other three criteria is taken for granted or is thought to depend on the satisfaction of the difficult criterion, we may speak of a point-of-stress.[9]

Stability is the point-of-stress in such widely different organizations as the prison studied by Sykes,[10] Whyte's street-corner gang, and the Malay fishing crews described by Firth.[11]

Integration as a point-of-stress is particularly easy for academic observers to understand since it is characteristic of a number of the organizations in which they participate professionally. Most committees, faculties, research institutes, and professional associations stum-

---

[9] This situation can be visualized in another way by means of the first proposition of Cyert and March. In their predictive model of organizational objectives with respect to a particular goal they propose that "In the steady state, aspiration level exceeds achievement by a small amount." Apparently a point-of-stress develops when this small difference is unstable or when its fluctuations include negative values. Richard M. Cyert and James G. March, "Organizational Factors in the Theory of Oligopoly," *Quarterly Journal of Economics,* Vol. LXX (1956), 44–64.

[10] Gresham M. Sykes, *The Society of Captives: A Study of a Maximum Security Prison* (Princeton, N.J.: Princeton University Press, 1958).

[11] Raymond W. Firth, *Malay Fishermen* (London: Trench, Trubner, 1946).

ble into the pitfall of factionalism. Their problems of stability, voluntarism, and achievement are secondary.[12]

Voluntarism has been shown as a point-of-stress in organizations as divergent as factory units,[13] labor unions,[14] civic associations,[15] and certain military units.[16]

Achievement is the point-of-stress for most small enterprises, for some scientific teams, for all symphony orchestras,[17] opera companies and law firms,[18] and for that small important category of organizations devoted to negotiation and keeping the peace.

Points-of-stress are not selected capriciously. The people involved are seldom free to designate the criterion on which they will concentrate their efforts. The selection is made for them by the institutional pattern and the environment. The consequences to be feared if the stressed criterion is not met are definite and real. Thus Sykes explains why most of the efforts of the official in the maximum security prison that he studied—and presumably in most other institutions of similar character—are concentrated on stability at the expense of alternative goals: [19]

> The prison exists as a dramatic symbol of society's desires to segregate the criminal, whatever reasons may lie behind that desire; and the prison wall, that line between the pure and the impure,

[12] See, for example, Robert S. Weiss, *Processes of Organization* (Ann Arbor, Mich.: Institute for Social Research, University of Michigan, 1956); Harry Eckstein, *Pressure Group Politics: The Case of the British Medical Association* (Stanford, Calif.: Stanford University Press, 1960); Oliver Garceau, *The Political Life of the American Medical Association* (Cambridge, Mass.: Harvard University Press, 1941); A. W. Gouldner, "Cosmopolitans and Locals," *Administrative Science Quarterly* (December, 1957–March, 1958); Harold Guetzkow and John Gyr, "An Analysis of Conflict in Decision-making Groups," *Human Relations,* Vol. VII, No. 3 (1954), 367–81.

[13] Elliott Jaques, *The Changing Culture of a Factory* (New York: Dryden, 1952), and Abraham Zaleznik, *Worker Satisfaction and Development* (Cambridge, Mass.: Harvard University Division of Research, 1957).

[14] Seymour M. Lipset, Martin Trow, and James S. Coleman, *Union Democracy* (Glencoe, Ill.: Free Press, 1956).

[15] David L. Sills, *The Volunteers* (Glencoe, Ill.: Free Press, 1957).

[16] Thomas T. Paterson, *Morale in War and Work* (London: Parrish, 1955).

[17] David Westby, *The Social Organization of a Symphony Orchestra* (unpublished thesis, University of Minnesota, 1957).

[18] Erwin O. Smigel, "Professional Bureaucracy and the Large Wall Street Law Firms" (paper presented at the St. Louis meetings of the American Sociological Association, 1961).

[19] Sykes, *op. cit.* The quotations are from pages 18 and 58.

has all the emotional overtones of a woman's maidenhead. One escape from the maximum security prison is sufficient to arouse public opinion to a fever pitch and an organization which stands or falls on a single case moves with understandable caution. The officials, in short, know on which side their bread is buttered. Their continued employment is tied up with the successful performance of custody and if society is not sure of the priority to be attached to the tasks assigned with prison, the overriding importance of custody is perfectly clear to the officials.

The situation of the prison with respect to the other three requirements is interesting. The criterion of integration is met very easily. It requires only passive acquiescence for an extensive network of social relationships to develop among the prisoners and for collusion to flourish between prisoners and guards.

> It is apparent, then, that the power of the custodians is defective, not simply in the sense that the ruled are rebellious, but also in the sense that the rulers are reluctant. We must attach a new meaning to Lord Acton's aphorism that power tends to corrupt and absolute power corrupts absolutely. The custodians of the New Jersey State Prison, far from being converted into brutal tyrants, are under strong pressure to compromise with their captives, for it is a paradox that they can insure their dominance only by allowing it to be corrupted. Only by tolerating violations of "minor" rules and regulations can the guard secure compliance in the "major" areas of the custodial regime. Ill-equipped to maintain the social distance which in theory separates the world of the officials and the world of the inmates, their suspicions eroded by long familiarity, the custodians are led into a modus vivendi with their captives which bears little resemblance to the stereotypical picture of guards and their prisoners.

The prison administrator—unlike the administrators of many other enterprises—need lose no sleep over the problem of inadequate communication, although he might be somewhat concerned about distorted communications.

The criterion of voluntarism is also easy for the prison to satisfy, but for a different reason. Although the program elicits little enthusiasm from either prisoners or guards, the amount of voluntarism required to keep it going is low. This is partly because of the norms of prison life, which assume resistance or apathy on the part of most prisoners, and partly because of the chronic oversupply of labor for the prison's work program. Even with minimum effort by the inmates, there is not enough work in the prison studied by Sykes to employ all the inmates or to keep those who are employed busy. The degree of voluntarism which satisfies the requirements of this particular prison is not much more than refraining from overt rebellion.

For different reasons, achievement does not represent a point-of-stress in the New Jersey State Prison. There are several kinds of required achievement, but all of them are easy. The principal organizational tasks are self-maintenance, punishment, and reform. For the first of these, as already indicated, manpower is always in long supply. The task of punishment is accomplished easily by incarceration, the task of reform is too ambiguously defined for achievement to be measured, and no penalties are specified for failure.

Voluntarism is likely to be the point-of-stress in organizations of two very different types. In voluntary associations, the continued existence of the organization depends upon the willing participation of members and the decision whether to continue participation is dependent on the satisfactions obtained. The association's resources are insufficient either to seduce or to coerce a member who loses interest. A major problem of voluntary associations is "apathy." Successful voluntary associations often escape from this threat by enlisting a cadre of militants or bureaucrats, for whom participation is a career. Voluntarism is also the point-of-stress in stable, highly integrated industrial enterprises where the efficiency of production is dependent on the workers' morale. Although there is a tendency to overestimate the correlation between activity and voluntarism (production and morale), any manufacturing program must guard against output limitation, nonconformity to rules, and sabotage.

Voluntarism is most likely to be a point-of-stress in enterprises with a status schism in which the identification of the lower stratum with the goals of the organization is inhibited by their sense of deprivation, and their lack of influence on the selection of goals.

An interesting study of workers' participation in the management of a Polish factory [20] showed that ". . . collective ownership as such, without proper provisions for communicative participation and

---

[20] Jiri Kolaja, "Workers' Participation in the Management of a Polish Textile Factory," *Human Organization,* Vol. XIX, No. 1 (Spring, 1960). The quotation is from page 16.

self-expression seems unable to overcome a social-relation dichotomy which is an outgrowth of the division of labor in an industrial organization." The workers in this Polish factory were faced with four distinct higher groups—the factory management, local party units, a labor union, and a workers' council—but tended to identify all of them as arms of the same authority and to resist commitment to any of them. The author suggests that an ideology that denies the existence of differing interests and opinions increases stress and threatens either rebellion or chronic apathy.

Finally, we come to organizations for which achievement is the point-of-stress. Most of them are small or middle-sized. Giant organizations are usually able to organize their environments so that minimum achievement is guaranteed, at least in the short run. Small business enterprises often fail to make a profit and disintegrate, the majority of failures occurring within a year after establishment. Great corporations persist indefinitely. When they deteriorate, they do so slowly and the decline is usually checked by merger or reorganization. Armies and navies and official bureaucracies are at least as durable as the states to which they belong, and conspicuously more durable than governments, but the fate of a small military unit or a small political party is often settled in a decisive hour.

The criterion of achievement is crucial only when (a) the probability of unsatisfactory performance is fairly high and (b) the consequences of unsatisfactory performance are predictably disastrous.

The symphony orchestra studied by Westby [21] provides a good illustration. During all its long history, it has survived precariously from year to year, dependent upon the donations of a large and shifting list of contributors. Their willingness to meet the annual deficit wavers at the first sign of any decline in the orchestra's musical quality or its national reputation. Artistic achievement is a pressing problem for the orchestra's management from season to season and even from concert to concert. It comes close to being the only problem.

Internal stability is attained very simply by giving despotic authority to the conductor. His status and salary are completely beyond the range of his musicians. His freedom to hire, fire, and assign personnel is unrestrained. The final decision on programs and schedules is reserved to him, and his voice is decisive on most other matters of administrative policy. The overwhelming concentration of power

[21] Westby, *op. cit.*

in the hands of the conductor nearly equalizes all subordinate statuses in the orchestra and guarantees adequate integration. Although factions may develop for purposes of sociability, they have no effect on the functioning of the orchestra. Musical policy is out of their reach, and power is not subject to manipulation. At the same time, voluntarism is easily maintained. Symphony musicians are adequately motivated by their private commitments to the norms of musical performance and their self-identification as professional performers. A conductor can be detested without much adverse effect on the orchestra's performance. So long as standards of achievement are maintained, the management need not give much thought to stability, integration, or voluntarism. However, if the quality of performance deteriorates, or approval by audiences and critics is withdrawn, the orchestra's ability to disregard problems of authority, communication, and morale disappears overnight.

There is no inherent reason why an organization must have a single point-of-stress. By empirical observation we discover that many do, but many others do not. In contrast to the small European political party with its stress on vote-getting achievement, the large-scale American party—Republican or Democratic—has chronic difficulty in satisfying all four of the criteria. Its ability to get votes for public offices is constantly checked by the other party. Its integration is weakened by permanent schisms on such matters as civil rights and by disagreements about particular political issues. The limited voluntarism of the party's precinct workers and registered voters is a constant problem. Stability is undermined by the competing claims of "office holders" and "politicians" to party leadership as well as by their uncertain control over the rank and file.

At another extreme, we can find organizations like the metropolitan bank described by Argyris,[22] which seem to have no points-of-stress at all. Organizations like this pursue their quiet ways for years on end with few disturbances and no problems more pressing than the selection of appropriate successors. They live in protected environments and are sheltered from the winds of change. Almost by definition, they are somewhat conservative and somewhat inefficient. In the "Friendly First Bank" stability is assured by having many

[22] Chris Argyris, *Organization of a Bank* (New Haven, Conn.: Labor and Management Center, Yale University, 1954).

officers, arranged in an intricate hierarchy, highly visible to each other, insulated from other employees, using impersonal means of control in place of direct orders. Integration is protected by procedures that require a minimum of personal communications. Voluntarism is assured by selecting employees with tractable and compliant personalities, and by a variety of devices to minimize turnover.[23]

The performance of the bank under these conditions is necessarily inefficient, but the profitability of a metropolitan bank is much more dependent on such outside factors as the business alliances of its directors and the growth of the principal local industries than upon the efficiency of its performance in the handling of money and accounts.

The identification of an organization's point-of-stress is made— more or less overtly—by the members themselves. The mere fact that a *new* point-of-stress has been identified has certain important consequences. Briefly summed up, these are as follows:

1. The status of those positions responsible for meeting the stress criterion tends to rise. Thus, for example, we may anticipate that as a university shifts its emphasis from integration to achievement, the relative influence of research scientists will tend to rise at the expense of teachers and humanists.[24]
2. The recognition of a point-of-stress tends to shift the existing balances in the organization between authority and consent, centralization and decentralization, tradition and innovation and other fundamental organizational dilemmas. Thus in the

[23] Confirmatory data is supplied in another study by Robert N. McMurry. See "Recruitment, Dependency, and Morale in the Banking Industry," *Administrative Science Quarterly,* Vol. III (June, 1958).

[24] Dubin provides a more exotic example:
"Missile janitors" have high power at launching sites because extreme precautions need to be taken to keep pipe lines at near-absolute cleanliness to prevent misfired rockets (an estimated three fourths of misfires at Cape Canaveral were due to "dirty" pipes in the rocket systems). These missile janitors are persons of relatively high power on the launching pads because of the criticalness, i.e. importance, of the functions they perform in the system.
Robert Dubin, "Business Behavior *Behaviorally* Viewed," in George B. Strother (ed.), *Social Science Approaches to Business Behavior* (Homewood, Ill.: Dorsey-Irwin, 1962). The quotation is from page 35.

internment camp described by Leighton,[25] the emergence of stability as a point-of-stress immediately split the camp administration into two new factions, one of which could be identified as conservative, authoritarian and centralist and the other as innovative, democratic, and decentralist.

HOW VALUES ARE GENERATED

Although the specific values held by organized groups are nearly as diverse as human life itself, it is nevertheless possible to identify universal elements. Taken at a certain level of abstraction, all organizations, regardless of their size, purpose, cultural setting or era, seem to show certain values related to the basic variables of stability, integration, voluntarism, and achievement. When internalized by the individual member for himself and accepted as imperative for other members, these become part of the organization's morality.

One set of values based on stability has loyalty as its central theme. All organizations make some sort of connection between acceptance of prescribed status differences within the organization and commitment to the collective goal. Omission of deference, or disobedience to superiors, is universally taken to imply at least a partial repudiation of membership. In this sense, loyalty is a universal value, although the forms by which it is expressed vary greatly.

The most important value generated by the criterion of integration is that members ought to prefer each other to nonmembers as interaction partners. This is not an unlimited requirement, but in organizationally relevant contexts it applies nearly without restriction and creates the classic distinction between in-groups and out-groups, us and the others, Greeks and barbarians. Its justification occupies a central place in the ideology of all organizations. The fury directed against traitors, heretics, and deserters is often out of all proportion to the practical significance of their offenses.

Most organizations support their own efforts to satisfy the criterion of voluntarism by defining themselves as attractive. This is the basis of the principle of self-aggrandizement discussed in the next chapter and the major element in such complex sentiments as patriotism, family pride, and school spirit.

Finally, an important set of values is derived from objective tasks.

[25] Alexander H. Leighton, *The Governing of Men* (Princeton, N.J.: Princeton University Press, 1945).

Whether the organization is a chess team or a shoe factory, it will honor prowess, style, and inventiveness in its central activities, and cults will develop around personages who embody these values to an unusual degree.

INTERDEPENDENCE OF VARIABLES

The relationships proposed among this second set of SIVA variables—stability, integration, voluntarism, and achievement—are similar to those proposed among the variables of the pair relationships—status, interaction, valence, and activity—subject to important qualifications.

First, we do not describe a condition with S equal to 0 in this second set, because when stratification reaches zero, the organization has disappeared and can no longer be treated as an equilibrium system. An organized peer group may show little stratification compared to a hierarchy, but it always has a discernible status order. Second, although an increase or decrease in I is again followed by an indeterminate change in V, this latter phenomenon is not exactly analogous to the ambivalence induced by changes in interaction in an unequal pair. Increasing the integration of a work crew may either raise or lower the level of voluntarism; in either case, there will be a net tendency rather than a tension of mixed motives.

On the other hand, since this second set of variables is an expansion of the simpler model, it shares many of the same characteristics. Again, its purpose is to predict the effect that a small increment of change in one variable, induced by outside forces, produces in the other three variables. It is again assumed that a small outside disturbance will be absorbed by the system, since a small change in a variable puts in motion a train of events whereby the variable tends to be restored to its original value. In the case of very large changes induced from outside, some of the same sequences will be observed, but the ultimate effect of the disturbance is to destroy or transform the equilibrium.

Although the model has much the same purpose as a system of differential equations, it is stipulated that the variables are incommensurate in the present state of knowledge. While the direction and the order of magnitude of variations are determinable, they cannot be precisely measured. Joint changes in two or more variables are treated in a similar way. We assume that if two variables are free to respond to a change in a third, the amount of variation in either of them will be less than if only one responded, but we do not know how much less. In describing secondary and tertiary effects, as when an increase in S is followed by a decrease in I, then in turn by a decrease in A, and thereafter by a decrease in S tending to restore equilibrium, we are again limited to specifying the direction of change and its order of magnitude, without being able to calculate the quantities involved.

The discerning reader will observe that this leaves no quantitative basis for the assertion that the train of disturbance culminates with the restoration of the precise, original values, and this objection is well founded. Whether improvement in methods of analysis will ever overcome this difficulty is a moot question. Conceivably, the relationships between organizational variables may be lawful and functional without the possibility of precise quantitative prediction.

Another feature of the model that needs to be emphasized is the expectation that at any given time a given variable may or may not be free to vary in one direction or both and that an observed change may or may not bring it close to the limit of variation permitted in that direction. For example, in a group whose output or achievement is fixed in the short run, a change in stability will have to be absorbed by changes in integration and voluntarism, since achievement may not vary. If, however, integration is already very low so that both horizontal and vertical communication are limited to the essential minimum, then the response to an increase in stability will be a decline in voluntarism, leading to a further increase of stability and, ultimately, a reduction of achievement will be forced in one way or another.

Although the model is not directly concerned with the ways in which changes are imposed on the variables from outside the system, such changes are not at all difficult to identify in the empirical case. In a factory crew, for example, stability may be increased by such diverse events as the appointment of an assistant foreman, a change in pay differentials, a grievance decision upholding the foreman, or the hiring of more apprentices. It might be decreased by a lay-off, by a public reprimand directed at the foreman, by a change in the incentive system, or by making the foreman report to an assistant superintendent instead of directly to the superintendent. Integration might be increased by the installation of quieter machinery permitting more conversation, by turning the foreman's desk around so that more of the shop floor falls under his observation, by scheduling department meetings every week instead of monthly, or by the establishment of a car pool that brings several of the senior men into closer contact. It might be diminished by a bitterly contested union election. Voluntarism might be increased by the engagement of the foreman's sister to one of the men, by the success of the department's bowling team in a plant contest, by the retirement of one party to a long-standing feud, or by designation of the crew as subjects for a sociological experiment. It might be diminished by the promotion of a popular foreman to a higher position, the reclassification of workers from piece rates to hourly rates, the introduction of new machinery considered to be dangerous, or the discharge of a long-seniority worker.

Achievement in factory work groups often varies for reasons outside any member's control. It increases with improvements in materials or machinery and with the efficiency of supplying departments. It decreases with a run of defective materials, a change from familiar to unfamiliar production methods, or the loss of a specialist. In many circumstances, achievement—as organizationally evaluated—can increase or decrease without any measurable change in output because of shifting standards. Thus the achievement of a factory work group increases, in effect, if its output remains unchanged while the output of comparable departments in the same plant declines.

The foregoing discussion emphasizes short-run changes, and the model itself refers only to changes in an existing equilibrium. It says nothing about the absolute values of the variables and makes no general statement about their intercorrelations. We cannot find in it the hypothesis of a general correlation between voluntarism and achievement or an inverse relationship between stability and integration, although there may be some temptation to do so.

Since the model contains no information at all about the absolute values of the variables and we have no way as yet of measuring stratification or integration on a single scale without regard to the type of organization involved, such statements cannot be derived. Common sense would seem to support the notion that an army is more stratified than a political party—but how much more? And is it more integrated at the same time?

These theoretical difficulties are largely removed when we deal with a set of similar organizations in which stability, integration, voluntarism, and achievement are measured by the same yardsticks and are known to show rather similar values and patterns of distribution. When these conditions are satisfied, it is permissible, or at least feasible, to examine the relationships between the variables in terms of small *differences* rather than small *changes*. Instead of observing that an increase of integration in organization X is followed at a short interval by an increase in achievement, we note that organization X, showing slightly more integration than organization Y, also shows slightly more achievement. This shift of viewpoint is obviously advantageous for such purposes as evaluating alternative styles of supervision. It has the great drawback of overlooking sequences of change in favor of static measurements. Nevertheless, it is the only way in which a substantial body of empirical evidence can be conveniently checked against the model.

WHY ORGANIZATIONS ARE PROBLEM-RIDDEN

Several investigators engaged in organizational case studies have amused themselves by asking a standard interview question such as, "What's this I hear about the recent crisis in your department?" and observing that practically all respondents find the question meaningful, even though the interviewer has no prior knowledge of any crisis. One of the most obvious features of the organization in action is its propensity to get into trouble. None of the organizations that have been closely studied seems to run smoothly for more than short intervals. A problem-free organization is as much a curiosity as a totally normal personality.

Organizational disturbances usually begin with some change in the external environment, and it is easy to see why environments never remain completely stable. It is not so clear why it is so difficult to make adaptations to change. Maladaptation is so common that it almost escapes notice. In comparing an organization to a machine, we are likely to forget how seldom it runs mechanically, and in comparing it to an organism, we are likely to overlook the continuously precarious state of its health.

The table showing the interrelationship of variables in the SIVA model gives us a number of clues to explain the susceptibility of organizations to crisis. The underlying problems seem to be:

1. Stability and voluntarism are positively correlated with achievement but are negative functions of each other. Thus, an increase in coercion ordinarily decreases the willingness to be coerced, or, on the other hand, an increase in voluntary cooperation tends to diminish the authority that sustains the whole system of cooperation.
2. Stability and integration are positive functions of achievement but negative functions of each other, so that the increase of communication ordinarily required to maintain an increased level of achievement weakens the status order, on which achievement also depends.
3. Integration and voluntarism are related in a very complex way, so that the increase in an organization's integration elicited by an emergency may also intensify dissension.

The central element in these problems, and indeed in the model itself, is that the coordination of human effort, the object of organization, is accomplished in every case partly by coercion and partly by contribution, partly in ignorance and partly with knowledge of the ends to be obtained, partly by fear and partly by love. The collective purposes that can be achieved without any compulsion do not require an organization, nor do those projects that can be carried out without the consent of the participants. An organization is a device to reconcile the two kinds of coordination and to adjust the discrepancies of interest that inevitably appear between the individual and the group in a persistent situation.

EMPIRICAL EVIDENCE (THE MICHIGAN STUDIES)

In 1947, the Institute for Social Research at the University of Michigan began a large-scale program of research "to discover the organizational structure and the principles and methods of leadership and management which result in the best performance. The general design of most of the studies has been to measure and examine the kinds of leadership and related variables employed by the best units in an organization in contrast to those used by the poorest." [26] Most

---

[26] Rensis Likert, *New Patterns of Management* (New York: McGraw-Hill, 1961), p. 5. The data presented are from many different studies, including those by Sudhansu K. Bose, Angus Campbell, Dorwin Cartwright, Lester Coch, H. C. Ganguli, D. M. Goodacre, Robert Kahn, Daniel Katz, Nathan

of the Michigan studies are focused on productivity as the dependent variable, and their results are obtained by comparing high-producing and low-producing sections in the same enterprise. The studies have been conducted in a wide variety of industries and in other large-scale organizations such as hospitals and government agencies.

The first group of findings described by Likert have to do with leadership and organizational performance. Among those relevant to our model are achievement as a positive function of voluntarism, achievement as a positive function of interaction, and achievement as a function of stability.

ACHIEVEMENT AS A POSITIVE FUNCTION OF VOLUNTARISM

When departments or work crews are arranged according to the amount of pressure the men feel for better performance, the departments that feel the most pressure (those having the lowest voluntarism) show much lower productivity, on the average.[27]

The sections of foremen who operate under general supervision show higher productivity, on the average, than those of foremen under close supervision.[28] This correlation may be partly due to the greater need for supervision shown by incompetent foremen, but not entirely so. There is evidence from various sources that close supervision is unfavorable to productivity. When factory departments in another study are grouped according to the extent to which the men feel free to set their own pace, the departments in which the men feel most free show higher productivity, on the average, than departments in which they feel less free.[29] Another study of supervisors [30] shows that those given more freedom than others to plan ahead are more likely than others to be high-producing. Nearly identical results were obtained in a national sample of research psychologists.[31]

Maccoby, Gerald Gurin, L. G. Floor, Nancy Morse, Rensis Likert, J. M. Willits, Floyd C. Mann, H. J. Baumgartel, James Dent, Everett Reimer, Donald C. Pelz, Stanley Seashore, Arnold S. Tannenbaum, and Marjorie Donald.

[27] *Ibid.,* p. 8.
[28] *Ibid.,* p. 9.
[29] *Ibid.,* p. 20.
[30] *Ibid.,* p. 21.
[31] *Ibid.,* p. 22.

A study of the relationship of insurance agency performance to management practices shows that "superior" and "mediocre" agencies differ widely as to whether the manager is unselfish, cooperative, and sympathetic in dealing with his agents, interested in their success, democratic in communicating with them, and enthusiastic about the importance of the work. The manager's helpfulness, knowledge, technical skill, and "personality" are less significant.[32]

A study of foremen's reaction to poor work in railroad maintenance-of-way crews shows that a significantly higher proportion of high-producing foremen than low-producing are nonpunitive and helpful when their men do a poor job.[33] Another study showed that those foremen considered promotable by management, presumably the most productive, are most likely to be characterized by their men as "pulling for the company." None of the promotable foremen are characterized as "pulling for the men." [34]

Pride in the work group was found to be positively correlated with productivity among clerical and railroad employees. But a number of studies show no correlation between section productivity and satisfaction with the company, the job, or its fringe benefits.[35]

One of the most interesting findings on the relationship between voluntarism and achievement is that the foremen of high-production work groups are much more likely to report that their crews perform well when they themselves are absent [36] than the foremen of low-production groups.

Likert discusses the findings of an ingenious investigation by Seashore in a heavy industrial company. In that setting, work groups with high peer-group loyalty and common goals were apparently effective in achieving their goals, regardless of whether they generally conformed to, or dissented from, managerial objectives. The higher the peer-group loyalty, the lower the variance of productivity within the group, and, in this particular company, the higher the average productivity. However, when the sample of work groups is divided into two clusters, based on the extent to which they accept or reject company goals, it is found that among work groups accepting company goals, high peer-group loyalty is associated with

[32] *Ibid.*, p. 10.
[33] *Ibid.*, p. 11.
[34] *Ibid.*, p. 29.
[35] *Ibid.*, pp. 14, 15.
[36] *Ibid.*, p. 28.

high productivity and among those rejecting company goals, high peer-group loyalty is associated with lower productivity.[37] This seems to suggest that the correlation between voluntarism and achievement in the industrial work group holds whether the group's achievement consists of supporting the company's larger program or of sabotaging it.

Various relationships are reported between voluntarism and indirect indices of achievement. Absenteeism, for example, is lower in work groups with high solidarity than in groups that lack solidarity.[38]

ACHIEVEMENT AS A POSITIVE FUNCTION OF INTERACTION

The classic experiment of Coch and French, in a textile factory where changes in production methods were to be installed, varied the degree of participation by workers in the planning and design of changes to be made in their own jobs. Increased participation was found to be favorable to productivity. Similar results have been obtained by half a dozen other investigators cited by Likert.[39]

ACHIEVEMENT AS A FUNCTION OF STABILITY

One relevant study was conducted in a company that operates nationally in a service operation. The data are from 31 geographically scattered departments having 15 to 50 employees each, all carrying out very similar operations. Continuous and comparable productivity and cost records are available for each department. The investigators asked both the men and managers to estimate their relative influence in their departments, the influence of plant management and of higher company management. They were asked to qualify this report by contrasting the influence desired with that actually exercised.

The results are consistent with the notion of stability as a system variable and of achievement as a function of stability. Both managers and men in the high-production sections attribute more influence to *every* level of supervision than is attributed in low-production sections. Even the distribution of *desired* supervisory in-

[37] *Ibid.,* pp. 31–32.
[38] *Ibid.,* p. 35.
[39] *Ibid.,* pp. 40–41.

fluence follows the same pattern, being consistently higher for every level in the high-production departments.

A complicated experiment carried out in a large corporation by Morse and Reimer shows the relationship of stability and achievement in detail. The study covered a large number of clerical employees in four parallel divisions engaged in a routine work process. Productivity could be rather accurately measured by the computation of unit salary costs. During the year that the experiment lasted, in two of the four divisions an attempt was made to change the mode of supervision so that decision levels were pushed downward, and group participation on all levels was increased. In our terminology, stratification was lowered and integration raised. In the other two divisions the experimental program called for increasingly close supervision, extensions of scientific management, and an upward movement of decision levels. In these cases, integration was lowered and stratification raised. The first program was called participative and the second hierarchic.

As so often happens in productivity experiments, both programs produced significant increases in productivity, the increase being slightly greater in the hierarchic program. The decrease in integration in the hierarchic program was "real" as shown by greater social distance between superiors and subordinates at the end of the experiment than at the beginning and by reduced in-group communication.[40]

A notable study of local chapters of the League of Women Voters by Tannenbaum, Donald, and James Likert shows regular and striking correlations between League effectiveness and the influence of unit leaders on members. However, members react negatively to pressure from presidents or board members.[41] There appears to be a negative correlation between the authority exerted or attempted by a chapter's higher officers and its achievement. The explanation seems to be that in a voluntary association, in which a member may withdraw participation without penalty, achievement cannot be raised by increasing stratification unless concomitantly some way is found for raising voluntarism.

The underlying reasons why stability and voluntarism are inversely related are suggested by a pair of very interesting studies

[40] *Ibid.,* p. 145.
[41] *Ibid.,* p. 144.

of military units by McGee.[42] The pilot study deals with sergeants in a National Guard artillery battalion. The respondent population in the principal study consists of all the commissioned officers of an Air Force division.[43]

McGee's technique was astonishingly simple. It consisted merely of ascertaining the number of superiors, equals, and inferiors with whom each subject habitually interacted in doing his job and of relating these numbers to measures of the subject's leadership, efficiency, and satisfaction. The central assumptions in this model are that:

. . . 1: There is a high, positive correlation between the number of superiors and the level of demands and pressures for expectation-fulfillment made by superiors on inferiors.

. . . 2: Any individual has a finite set of resources for making, fulfilling, or resisting demands and pressures for expectation-satisfaction; these include his personal characteristics, the support of his superiors, the assistance of his peers, and the labor of his inferiors to the degree that he is able to mobilize it to his end.[44]

The pilot study findings, based on a small sample of sergeants, provide striking confirmation for the existence of such effects. Inverse correlations appear between the official efficiency rating obtained by sergeants and the numbers of their inferiors. Self-ratings of satisfaction, on the other hand, are closely correlated with both the number of inferiors and the number of equals but unrelated to the number of superiors.

The much larger sample of Air Force officers in the principal study reveals a complex pattern of dependence between achievement and the environmental arithmetic. Dozens of highly significant associations are found between the number of superiors, equals, and inferiors and the subjects' efficiency, leadership, and satisfaction, measured in

---

[42] Reece J. McGee, "A Study in Ambience: The Numerical Analysis of Interaction Groupings in a Large Scale Organization" (unpublished dissertation, University of Minnesota, 1956), and "The Ambience Concept in Organizational Analysis," *Alpha Kappa Deltan,* Spring, 1958.

[43] Based on information gathered in connection with a previous project conducted under Air Force Contract No. 18 (600)–339 for the Human Resources Research Institute, Air Research and Development Command, U.S. Air Force, 1952–53, by Theodore Caplow, George A. Donohue, and Leo G. Reeder.

[44] McGee, "A Study in Ambience," pp. 64–65.

several ways and from various vantage points. The mere number of superiors, equals, and inferiors with whom an officer interacts significantly influences his ability to perform the duties and enact the roles of his position. Both the absolute number of persons he encounters in these three fundamental status categories and the ratios among them seem to be significant. In particular, the ratio of inferiors to superiors seems to measure the subject's ability to meet the whole range of demands placed on him by the organization.

This phenomenon may help to explain the commonplace finding that voluntarism in an organization increases with increasing rank—although the rewards reserved for higher status levels must also play a part. In general, the higher the status of a position, the lower the ratio of superiors to inferiors will be in the incumbent's ambience.

The promising leads provided by McGee's study have not yet been followed up. They suggest that certain kinds of structural analysis might be used for the direct comparison of equilibrium states in organizations of dissimilar types.

CONFLICTING EVALUATIONS OF SUCCESS

This discussion assumes that the success of an organization at any given moment can be measured with fair validity and reliability by means of devices provided for that purpose in the institutional pattern.

This assumption may strike the reader as excessively rational, and indeed it must be qualified in several ways. First, the relationship between an organization's program and its goals may not be simple. Many activities are based on demonstrably false estimates of causation and probability. An organization's goals may be illusory, inconsistent, or impossible, or its arrangement of activities may be inappropriate. Second, most important organizations have long lives, in the course of which they acquire a large assortment of goals, not all compatible and not all fully accepted. Third, the rationality of organizational action is diluted by the persistence of sentiments long after the situations that evoked them have disappeared or changed beyond recognition.

We must also examine the assumption that the blueprint (or institutional pattern) for a given type of organization includes devices for measuring achievement objectively. This phenomenon is easy to demonstrate and to understand. Purposive activity, by its nature, requires evaluation of results so that errors can be corrected and the level of achievement maintained or improved. The numerical evaluation of achievement is not unique to economic enterprises or to our number-minded age: Inca organizations kept quantitative records of output on knotted strings, churches count their communicants and measure their spiritual quality, military units recognize efficiency ratings in time of peace and casualty ratios in war, and almost all voluntary associations use attendance at meetings to measure achievement.

The yardsticks of organizational achievement are often multiple. Whenever the quantity of output is measured, there is also some possibility of measuring quality. Even in such sports as baseball or football, in which the numerical scores are specifically designed to provide a summary and final appraisal of each game, the participants and the more knowledgeable spectators habitually add measures of quality like the count of hits and errors in baseball or the yardage gained and lost in football. Some bureaucratic organizations have unbelievably complex systems of evaluating achievement. Thus, the performance record of interviewers in the small public-employment office studied by Blau [45] included eight separate indices—the number of interviews held, the number of applicants referred to a job, the number of successful job placements, the proportion of interviews resulting in referrals, the proportion of referrals resulting in placement, the proportion of interviews resulting in placements, the number of insurance notifications sent, and the number of application forms filled out.

Rating systems for larger organizations can be much more complex than this. It is a mistake to regard them merely as bureaucratic excesses. One of the major points of Blau's study is that the introduction of new performance indices changed the behavior of his subjects in the direction desired by the supervisors who installed the system.

In the next chapter, we shall see how the objectivity of achievement criteria is maintained in sets of organizations that resemble each other, interact with each other, and accept the same standards. We

[45] Peter M. Blau, *The Dynamics of Bureaucracy* (Chicago: University of Chicago Press, 1955), pp. 35–36.

shall see why any gross distortions in evaluating the achievement of one organization in such a set would threaten the other organizations. Institutionally provided yardsticks almost always measure achievement, but not stability, integration, or voluntarism. Organizations make these latter criteria the subject of independent study and occasionally of continuous measurement, but the normal mode of evaluation takes achievement as a measured, dependent variable and stability, integration, and voluntarism as independent, unmeasured variables. A crisis is ordinarily signaled by a decline in achievement, and remedial measures ordinarily consist of looking for a related decline in stability, integration, or voluntarism and attempting to reverse it.

There are several ways in which conflicting evaluations of organizational success develop. The least avoidable discrepancies in evaluation occur between (a) insiders and outsiders, (b) higher and lower status levels, and (c) the organization and its components.

The empirical evidence will be examined at length in Chapter Six. The evidence suggests general tendencies:

1. Members of an organization usually evaluate its achievement more highly than nonmembers.
2. Higher status members of an organization usually evaluate its achievement more favorably than lower status members.
3. Members of an organized component usually evaluate its contribution to the total program more favorably than nonmembers.

Needless to say, these discrepancies persist in the presence of objective yardsticks for measuring achievement. Discrepancies are not so likely to arise over the *measurement* of achievement as over its *evaluation* when measured. In the usual case, there is no room for disagreement about what the final score of the game was but considerable room for argument as to whether that score constituted a good or bad performance.

The evidence for discrepancies of evaluation between outsiders and insiders is presented at some length in the discussion of organizational sets in the next chapter, and we will restrict the discussion here to discrepancies between high- and low-status participants and between an organization and its components.

COMPLACENCY OF THE ELITE

In comparing its own performance with related groups higher or lower in the same hierarchy, each elite will want to overestimate its relative success. However, pretensions directed upward are likely to be corrected by superiors in defense of their own prerogatives. Pretensions directed downward are not ordinarily subject to as much control. Hence, officers observing the enlisted men under their command, teachers facing their students, and employers observing their employees are very likely to overestimate their own effectiveness. This leads them to ascribe their authority to leadership qualities and other personal factors, rather than to the specific devices provided by the organization for enforcing control.

The American Soldier [46] is a great compendium of information on the tendency for evaluation of one's own organization to be correlated with status. Officers were consistently and significantly more favorable than enlisted men in their evaluation of the army and various aspects of the military system.

On the other hand, particular situations of this kind must be interpreted with caution. The tendency for higher status members of an organization to evaluate its achievement favorably may be more than counterbalanced by the discrepancy between the evaluations of insiders and outsiders, in situations in which the higher status member is an agent of the larger organization responsible for enforcing its demands on a peer group of subordinates. A fascinating chart presented by Likert [47] shows what may happen under these circumstances. It gives the distributions of actual production and of estimates of reasonable productivity for several thousand workers in a large manufacturing company in which time standards had been set for most jobs. The foremen's estimates of reasonable productivity are consistently higher than the actual production of their sections. Their estimates of what management regards as reasonable productivity are higher still. Their estimates of what their men regard as reasonable figures are lower than their own standards but higher than the production achieved. Most of them in effect consider their own sections

---

[46] Samuel A. Stouffer et al., *The American Soldier,* Vol. I, *Adjustment During Army Life* (Princeton, N.J.: Princeton University Press, 1949). See especially pp. 89, 374, 417–23.

[47] Likert, *op. cit.,* pp. 48–51.

as substandard in productivity, regardless of the evaluator's vantage point.

The workers' estimates of reasonable productivity are mostly lower than their actual production. Moreover, these estimates are correlated with the actual production of the section to which they belong, so that, except in the very poorest sections, all workers are able to identify their own crews as highly productive. At the same time, they are aware that foremen have different standards of reasonable productivity and that their own foreman would not concur with their favorable self-ratings.

In another Michigan study, by Hamann,[48] 34 percent of the men say their foreman understands their problems well, while 95 percent of the foremen say they understand their men's problems well. Only 51 percent of the same foremen say that the general foremen understand their own problems well, but 90 percent of the general foremen claim they do so. Only 60 percent of the general foremen say that their own superiors understand their problems well.

As we have repeatedly stressed, all large organizations and many medium and small ones can be viewed as clusters of ramifying and overlapping component organizations. Although each component taken by itself may have adequate devices for evaluating its own achievement, there is no way in which consistency of evaluation among all components can be assured. On the contrary, some discrepancy is inevitable since one of the goals of a component organization is to protect its members against the requirements of the total organization, and one of the goals of the total organization is to protect its components against each other. The achievements of any component both contribute to and detract from the achievement of the total organization to which it belongs. Much the same can be said of a factional organization; even though its program is not part of the program of the total organization, it is likely to affect it both favorably and unfavorably. The balance between contribution and opposition depends on a multitude of factors, but it is usually possible to distinguish between the success of a branch, unit, or department in meeting its separate goals and its effectiveness as a cog in the total organization.

Even with respect to highly visible criteria of achievement, there may be room for complete disagreement between different levels of

[48] *Ibid.,* pp. 48–51.

the same organization. Roy, studying output limitation in a piecework machine shop, found the machine operators engaged in an elaborate game of subverting the formal rules and procedures.[49] Life in the shop was envisaged by the participants as a contest between technical management and the operators, a contest in which the goal of each faction was to frustrate the plans of the other. Yet, on closer analysis, the investigator is unable to say that the elaborate maneuvers of the operators reduce productivity. Instead, he finds a complex interplay in which both levels of the organization sometimes advance and sometimes impede the production of goods. He insists that any distinction between an economically rational management and nonrational work group is unjustified and that the labels could as well be reversed. The work group resists managerial directives in part because they are technically unworkable. Their circumvention of rules and regulations often contributes to maintaining the flow of production. The investigator suggests that management's "logics of efficiency" may be no more than "sentiments of efficiency" and sometimes no more than magical incantations.

A similar conclusion was reached by Shils [50] in a paper based on *The American Soldier,* and it is the dominant theme of several independent studies of the United States Navy that appeared after World War II.[51] The intricate relationship between the navy and its almost innumerable components can be understood only in terms of variations in the criteria of achievement. As Davis points out,

> The effective performance of the manifest functions of a military
> bureaucracy requires a certain type of occupational discipline and
> formal organization; these in turn tend to create inherent pressures

[49] Donald Roy, "Efficiency and 'the Fix': Informal Intergroup Relations in a Piecework Machine Shop," *American Journal of Sociology,* Vol. LX, No. 3 (November, 1954). See also his "Quota Restriction and Goldbricking in a Machine Shop," *American Journal of Sociology,* Vol. LVII, No. 5 (March, 1952), and "Work Satisfaction and Social Reward in Quota Achievement: An Analysis of Piecework Incentive," *American Sociological Review,* Vol. XVIII, No. 5 (October, 1953).

[50] Edward A. Shils, "Primary Groups in the American Army," in Robert K. Merton and Paul Lazarsfeld (eds.), *Continuities in Research: Studies in the Scope and Method of the American Soldier* (Glencoe, Ill.: Free Press, 1950).

[51] Arthur K. Davis, "Bureaucratic Patterns in the Navy Officer Corps," *Social Forces,* Vol. XXVII (December, 1948); Charles Hunt Page, "Bureaucracy's Other Face," *Social Forces,* Vol. XXV (October, 1946); Ralph H. Turner, "The Navy Disbursing Officer as a Bureaucrat," *American Sociological Review,* Vol. XII, No. 3 (June, 1947).

toward recession of goals, occupational ritualism, and professional insulation; which in turn may alter the actor's definition of the situation so as to impair systematically his effectiveness in carrying out the manifest functions of the bureaucracy.[52]

The study concludes with the suggestion that the effectiveness of military leaders tends to vary inversely with their exposure to a conventionally routinized military career.

Page's paper carries this emphasis somewhat further by emphasizing the informal elements in the naval bureaucracy.

Like the formal, it consists of rules, groupings and sanctioned systems of procedure. They are informal because they are never recorded in the codes or official blueprints and because they are generated and maintained with a degree of spontaneity always lacking in the activities which make up the formal structure. These rules, grouping, and procedures do, nevertheless, form a structure, for, though not *officially* recognized, they are clearly and semipermanently established. They are just as "real" and just as compelling on the membership as the elements of the official structure, and they maintain their existence and social significance throughout many changes of personnel.[53]

He goes on to point out the ways in which efficient solutions to bureaucratic problems are developed outside of the framework of the formal structure and to review the effect of informal procedures in various types of units. The study concludes with a suggestion that the bureaucratic and occupationally centered attitudes developed in the naval system may have negative consequences for society at large.

Turner's study is more specific. Concerned with the bureaucratic role of the navy disbursing officer, he too describes a system of informal relationships and distinguishes among friendship patterns, simulated friendship patterns, and the exchange system. He analyzes certain characteristic reactions of the disbursing officers to the strains and stresses created by the inconsistent demands of the official regulations and the informal rules.

Taken together, all three studies emphasize the extent to which compulsions and expectations not included in the official table of organization of the navy influence and modify the behavior of its officers. They may have been intended as studies of organizational

[52] Davis, *op. cit.*, pp. 143–53.
[53] Page, *op. cit.*, p. 89.

maladjustment or breakdown, but current theory puts the matter in a somewhat different light.

As Davis remarks, "Sociologically, a navy is a bureaucratic organization designed to operate under battle conditions which rarely occur." [54] The relevant test of achievement cannot be routinely made. Since the emergencies which are the organization's *raison d'être* occur rarely and may never occur at all, great importance is attached to actions that symbolize achievement. The informal norms of the officer corps reflect the attempt to develop substitute yardsticks to compensate for the inaccessibility of the criterion itself. This may be described as ceremonialism. In the absence of valid achievement measures, the performance of rituals is stressed instead. Ceremonialism declines sharply when units are engaged in combat for any length of time; achievement can then be measured directly.

Much of the contrast pointed up by Davis, Page, and Turner between the rigid formality of the larger organization and the spontaneity of officer peer groups arises from the fact that the latter *do* have effective ways of measuring achievement, even if the goals are as trivial as obtaining more canteen supplies.

Stability, integration, and voluntarism are meaningful criteria of success for both the navy and its components, but with different implications. A large body of regulations creates and supports the vast authority of the commanding officer. Many of the phenomena described in these studies—the avoidance of responsibility, the psychology of affirm-and-confirm, the deliberate insulation of naval personnel from the civilian world, of naval officers from their subordinates, and of commanding officers from their commands, and the impressive machinery of ceremonialism and differential privilege—have the purpose of maintaining the status of the commanding officer regardless of fluctuations in his interactions, valences, or activities.

Voluntarism is not a point-of-stress for the navy as a whole, despite certain precautions embodied in regulation and custom. The drastic control devices employed to maintain status reduce the need for voluntary maintenance of membership. However, the maintenance of valences is a vital function for many of its component organizations. The dangers created by nonparticipation, psychological withdrawal, and personal hostility scarcely touch the organization as a

---

[54] Davis, *op. cit.*, p. 145.

whole, but they are keenly perceived within each small component unit. Especially in wartime, when individuals are "processed" en masse, the components and factions must satisfy individual needs that would otherwise be overlooked. "The wartime services expanded so rapidly that they could attend only to categories and not to individuals. The imputed needs of the organization at the moment determined the disposition of resources. Most of the individual's vital interests—his work, friends, rewards, punishments—were largely outside his control." [55] It was to bring these matters back within the individual's control that many of the informal norms developed.

The principal threat to the maintenance of interpersonal valences was the mobility of personnel, since transfers were frequent and unscheduled. This threat was met by the diffusion throughout the navy of fixed patterns for unofficial organizations. Such patterns made the interchange among peer groups and other factional organizations as easy as the formal procedures for transferring the individuals among the official units. Membership in organized peer groups was not entirely involuntary, but it was strongly encouraged by the hostility between officers and enlisted men, between higher and lower ranks, between ship and shore services, and between different types of ship. As these forms of emulation were encouraged by the larger organization, the establishment of unofficial organizations was tacitly approved. Nevertheless, as the studies show, the privileges of peer-group membership were not granted casually. They tended to be proportioned both to length of service and to voluntarism. Page shows differences in peer-group acceptance of professional and nonprofessional officers and of regular and temporary enlisted men. In general, the unofficial organizations favored members having greater identification with the navy as a whole.

Because stability is a point-of-stress for the navy, it neglects somewhat the criteria of integration and voluntarism. Informal norms remedy the resulting deficiencies. Although the investigators agree that the navy does not conform to the ideal type of bureaucracy, this departure cannot be described as a breakdown. The functions that the large-scale organization is not capable of performing directly devolve upon its components and factions.

[55] *Ibid.*, p. 148.

CHANGES IN THE CRITERIA

So far, we have been concerned with organizations in equilibrium, those having more or less stable structures and pursuing their goals under fairly constant conditions. Whether this situation corresponds to equilibrium in the mathematical sense is an open question. The disturbances set in motion when an outside force impinges on one of the organization's variables are certainly self-damping, but they also leave some sort of mark on the system. A description of any organization in terms of the current values of its basic variables, omitting previous states of the system, is usually less explanatory than a similar instantaneous description of a physical or chemical system.

Although many different kinds of organizational change have actually been observed, sociological interest tends to focus on one very common situation, wherein an organization has two competing and partly inconsistent goals. The organization gives one goal higher priority than the other, and the people engaged in activities relevant to goal A enjoy a status advantage over those associated with goal B. It is usually also the case that the two groups constitute distinct or distinguishable factions.

Into this situation comes some outside influence tending to increase the importance of goal A and lessen that of goal B. The influence may consist of a new incumbent in a high-status position, a shift in the climate of outside opinion, or the outcome of a power struggle between parties identified with the two goals.

Analytic reasons alone do not explain the fascination that this simple plot holds for the social scientist. There is also an ideological element. In most of the case studies, the investigator has not been neutral with respect to goals A and B (this did not necessarily compromise the objectivity of his observations). As in most contests that arouse the emotions of the spectators, there is a hero and a villain. Again and again, the faction in the organization that attracts the investigator's sympathy is identified with "permissive," "democratic," "people-centered" or "consensual" goals and opposes a faction committed to "authority" or "efficiency."

The sociologist usually sides with those of his subjects who want more integration and less stability. In prisons and hospitals, he is likely to lean toward the goal of treatment rather than custody.[56] In industrial enterprises, he looks with a kinder eye on the establishment of norms by peer groups than by hierarchies, and in studying a hierarchy, he is more sympathetic to the staff than to the line.

Many of the best case studies are devoted to exploring the ways in which government depends upon the consent of the governed,[57] for example Jaques' study of organizational changes in the Glacier Metal Company,[58] Leighton's analytic account of resistance to authority in a Japanese internment camp,[59] McCleery's careful study of the change from custodial to treatment goals in Oahu Prison,[60] and Gouldner's description of the events following a change of administration in a gypsum plant.[61] All four of these important studies are concerned with situations of the classic type, and all four authors view their organizations as models of the larger society and derive generalizations about political processes from their data. McCleery traces the change from an authoritarian to a permissive regime in the prison. Gouldner describes a change in the other direction, from permissive to rigid enforcement of rules. Leighton tells the story of a divided camp administration in which both viewpoints were represented. Jaques belonged to a team of "action researchers" engaged by management to implement the transition from autocratic to consultative decision-making. The periods covered in these studies range from one to seven years. In every case, dramatic and unex-

[56] The correction movement in the United States, with special reference to California, is described in this way by Joseph W. Eaton, *Stone Walls Not a Prison Make* (Springfield, Ill.: Charles C Thomas, 1962).

[57] The classic Iowa studies had schoolchildren as subjects. They are extensively summarized and reinterpreted in Ralph K. White and Ronald O. Lippitt, *Autocracy and Democracy: An Experimental Inquiry* (New York: Harper, 1960).

[58] Jaques, *op. cit.*

[59] Leighton, *op. cit.*

[60] Richard H. McCleery, "The Governmental Process and Informal Social Control," in Donald R. Cressey (ed.), *The Prison: Studies in Institutional Organization and Change* (New York: Holt, Rinehart & Winston, 1961); also *The Strange Journey* (Chapel Hill, N.C.: University of North Carolina Extension Bulletin, 1953), and *Policy Changes in Prison Management* (East Lansing, Mich.: Governmental Research Bureau, Michigan State University, 1957).

[61] Alvin W. Gouldner, *Patterns of Industrial Bureaucracy* (Glencoe, Ill.: Free Press, 1954), and "The Problem of Succession in Bureaucracy," in Alvin W. Gouldner (ed.), *Studies in Leadership: Leadership and Democratic Action* (New York: Harper, 1950).

pected changes in equilibrium are known to have occurred *after* the period of observation closed.

The full findings of these studies are too extensive to be summarized here, but certain crucial and recurrent patterns should be noted.

THE PARADOX OF AUTHORITY VS. DEMOCRACY

We do not have to look very hard at the polar terms *authority* and *democracy* against the background of modern theories of administration to notice a curious feature: democratic decision-making, permissiveness with respect to rules, the displacement of authority by consultation, and group participation in setting and enforcing norms are all conceived as devices for extending the organization's control over the individual member. When they function successfully, they decrease his ability to hold private purposes opposed to those of the organization. The autonomy conferred on the individual in small matters reduces his opportunities to deviate from the main outline of the organizational program. Jaques, an eloquent advocate of this policy, puts the matter plainly:

> The nature of the interaction between authority and democratic sanctioning displays itself in the paradoxical relation between the scope of function of the consultative bodies and the strength of the executive. With democratic mechanisms through which all members are enfranchised, in the sense of having a say in policy, the authority of those in managerial roles is both questioned and yet upheld by those whom they control. The more far-reaching the control exercised by the consultative system, the more complete the authority invested in the executive system.[62]

This viewpoint was established by the Western Electric study [63] and reinforced by the work of Lewin and his students.[64] Under

---

[62] Jaques, *op. cit.,* p. 263.

[63] Elton Mayo, *Human Problems of an Industrial Civilization* (New York: Macmillan, 1933), Fritz J. Roethlisberger, *Management and Morale* (Cambridge, Mass.: Harvard University Press, 1941), Fritz J. Roethlisberger and William J. Dickson, *Management and the Worker* (Cambridge, Mass.: Harvard University Press, 1939), and Thomas N. Whitehead, *The Industrial Worker* (Cambridge, Mass.: Harvard University Press, 1938).

[64] Kurt Lewin, *Resolving Social Conflicts* (New York: Harper, 1948), and "The Practicality of Democracy," in Gardner Murphy (ed.), *Human Nature and Enduring Peace* (Boston: Houghton Mifflin, 1945); Henry S. Kariel,

various names, it enjoys a great vogue in American and European corporations. One management consultant calls it "freedom within law," another prefers "management by objectives." Packard, who has charted its incidence in industry, describes it thus:

> Under this concept of responsibility-without-strings, the superior's role is something like that of a lawyer with a client. Instead of being the daily order-giver and super-decision-maker, he plays a supportive role in helping the subordinate do his job by offering counsel, helping define problems, and making resources available. This is quite different from the usual idea that the subordinate is the superior's helper. In operating terms, this concept may mean that the superior will stroll to the subordinate's office rather than hold court in his own. They usually work together on the basis of mutual confidence rather than on the more traditional basis of authority.
>
> The superior's main function here is not to control people but rather to control the climate-or-environment in such a way that his people are able to grow. In this ideal climate, his group will function on an informal, relaxed basis. They will respect each other but not be disturbed by the appearance of disagreements. And group decisions most commonly will be made on the basis of a general, informal consensus.[65]

There are many contrary voices to question the benefits of these utopian procedures. Harrington [66] gives us a vivid, impressionistic account of life in a corporation governed by manipulated consent. He is puzzled by his own unhappiness in "a kindly, frustrating organization that asks of him but one concession—that he rein in his impulses to run free." He finds some fundamentally dissatisfying quality in the corporate routine, every detail of which is carefully contrived to prevent dissatisfaction. And like other observers, he is aghast at communication without meaningful content and the avoidance of hard decisions.

A more systematic critique by Thompson [67] identifies the ideology of substituting integration for stability as "managerial social psychology"; he criticizes it on several grounds. According to Thomp-

"Democracy Unlimited: Kurt Lewin's Field Theory," *American Journal of Sociology,* Vol. LII, No. 3 (November, 1956).

[65] Vance Packard, *The Pyramid Climbers* (New York: McGraw-Hill, 1962), p. 306.

[66] Alan Harrington, *Life in the Crystal Palace* (New York: Knopf, 1959), p. 25.

[67] Victor A. Thompson, *Modern Organization* (New York: Knopf, 1961), pp. 122–28.

son, theories of this kind divert attention away from the need for institutional change by emphasizing the possibility of adapting the individual to the existing structure. They are used by management to legitimize the status quo and to deny the existence of conflict by redefining it as individual maladjustment. This, he says, is accomplished in several different ways. First, the organization attempts to facilitate the formation of primary groups in order to provide a form of social control acceptable to potential deviants. Second, it encourages training in leadership skills on the theory that conflict may be prevented by skillful manipulation. Third, it employs every possible device to increase communication, enhance the individual's insight into himself and others, and encourage the development of a unified and officially sponsored image of the immediate environment. These efforts are discussed by Thompson as based upon the assumption that people are almost infinitely manipulable, aided by a venal social science that accepts the norms of management and seeks to hoodwink employees into conformity with them.

There are a number of paradoxes afoot in this area. Even an enlightened management could hardly be expected to believe that its functionaries are deluded in supposing themselves to be happy or that close working relationships based on good communication and mutual understanding are perverse. On the other hand, even the most sympathetic outside observer must gag occasionally at the bland tyrannies of the corporate world and marvel how human relations can induce such a state of fearful conformity that even minor, accidental features of the organization are held too sacred for criticism. There is a vast literature of protest on these points. They need not be labored here, but it may be useful to examine the paradox of democracy and autocracy in terms of our analytical variables.

Not only in the American corporation but throughout the Western world, this century has witnessed a fairly consistent decline of status differences. The reasons are multiple. *Abundance* lessens the dependence of every individual on his social superiors. The discharged employee no longer faces the danger of starvation; he may not even be threatened by discomfort. The same is true of the abandoned wife or child, the merchant whose customers forsake him, the outcast from church or village. *Mobility* has similar effects. The bad reference, the private blacklist, the anger of creditors, the lost reputation, or the criminal record can be escaped by moving away. *Mechanization* reduces the advantage of the strong over the weak in every

trade and of men over women. *Technical progress* reduces the value
of experience and tricks of skill. *Universal education* places a long
ladder of comparative advantage across the brutal gaps that formerly
stood between the lettered and the ignorant. The *increased scale* of
population diminishes all claims to personal or family superiority
except those supported by the mass media. The constant *growth of
the state* limits the personalized power of private and local magnates.
Secularization weakens every form of domination based on spiritual
or supernatural claims. Above all, the increasing *size* of organizations, partly due to population increase and partly to new inventions,
removes the rank and file in a factory, an army, or a school further
and further from those who exercise independent command.

All these factors are mutually reinforcing, tending to narrow the
status differences between pairs of positions in any established organization without reducing the desire of organizations to control the
behavior of their members. Indeed, they enhance it.

If stability declines steadily, achievement can be maintained only
by a continuous increase in integration and voluntarism. The fundamental devices for increasing integration and voluntarism—each correctly regarded as a function of the other—seem to be these:

1. Raising the level of interaction between unequals above the
   level technically required by the program of activity. Among
   the devices used are conferences, formal and informal consultation, group decision-making, periodic appraisals, and suggestion systems.
2. Reinforcement of primary groups by encouraging conversation
   at work, free choice of associates, homogeneity of individual
   characteristics, opportunities for group recreation, collective
   expressions of preference, and barriers against other peer
   groups.
3. Development of communication channels between top management and the rank and file, by such means as house organs,
   grievance systems, internal public relations, meetings, training
   films, personalized correspondence, and open-door policies.
4. Enforcement of loyalty to the organization's symbols and ideology by close surveillance.
5. Development of favorable environmental conditions and fringe
   benefits that offer comfort and security as rewards for continued
   participation.

A CASE IN POINT

McCleery's [68] study of the change in Oahu Prison from an authoritarian regime interested in maintaining discipline and preventing escapes to a liberal regime interested in treatment and rehabilitation has been diagrammed in a study by Allen H. Barton and Bo Anderson (see Table 4–2). For each of five stages described by McCleery the table gives qualitative estimates of the major variables involved. Although this classification of variables is different from ours, there is hardly any problem of translation. Table 4–2 shows how the shift

Table 4–2

OBSERVED CHANGES IN ATTITUDES OVER TIME
TOWARD TREATMENT GOAL

	AUTHOR-ITARIAN EQUI-LIB-RIUM	INITIA-TION OF RE-FORMS	EXTEN-SION OF RE-FORMS	SABO-TAGE AND REBEL-LION	LIB-ERAL EQUI-LIB-RIUM
1. ATTITUDES: *Concern with treatment goal among:*					
Administration	low	med	high	high	high
Custodial staff	low	low	low	low	med
Treatment heads	low	high	high	high	high
Treatment staff	low	med	high	high	high
Inmate elite	low	low	low	low	—
Inmate mass	low	low	med	med	high
2. COMMUNICATIONS: a. *Amount between:*					
Administration– Treatment	low	high	high	high	high
Administration– Custody	high	med	low	low	med

[68] McCleery, "The Governmental Process and Informal Social Control," *op. cit.*, and *The Strange Journey, op. cit.*

	AUTHOR-ITARIAN EQUI-LIB-RIUM	INITIA-TION OF RE-FORMS	EXTEN-SION OF RE-FORMS	SABO-TAGE AND REBEL-LION	LIB-ERAL EQUI-LIB-RIUM
Administration–					
Inmates	low	med	high	med	high
Custody–Treatment	high	high	low	low	med
Custody–Inmate elite	high	high	high	high	—
Custody–Inmate mass	low	low	low	low	—
Treatment–Inmates	low	med	high	med	high
Inmate elite–Inmate mass	high	high	med	low	—

b. *Degree of intermediate control by:*

	AUTHOR-ITARIAN EQUI-LIB-RIUM	INITIA-TION OF RE-FORMS	EXTEN-SION OF RE-FORMS	SABO-TAGE AND REBEL-LION	LIB-ERAL EQUI-LIB-RIUM
Custodial staff over administration-treatment staff communication	high	med	low	low	low
Custodial staff over inmate-administration and inmate-treatment communication	high	med	low	med	low
Inmate elite over inmate mass-administration and inmate mass-treatment staff communication	high	high	med	med	low

3. SANCTIONS AND RESPONSE:

Administration:

	AUTHOR-ITARIAN EQUI-LIB-RIUM	INITIA-TION OF RE-FORMS	EXTEN-SION OF RE-FORMS	SABO-TAGE AND REBEL-LION	LIB-ERAL EQUI-LIB-RIUM
Arbitrariness in discipline, assignments, etc.	high	med	low	low	low

	AUTHOR-ITARIAN EQUI-LIB-RIUM	INITIA-TION OF RE-FORMS	EXTEN-SION OF RE-FORMS	SABO-TAGE AND REBEL-LION	LIB-ERAL EQUI-LIB-RIUM
Treatment staff: Rehabilitative activities offered to inmates	low	med	high	high	high
Custodial staff: Maintenance of rituals of domination	high	high	med	med	low
Toleration of inmate elite privileges, power, rackets	high	high	med	med	low
Inmate mass: Participation in treatment program	low	med	high	low	high
Amount of disorderly behavior, violence	low	med	low	high	low

FROM a paper by Richard H. McCleery that was given limited circulation by the Bureau of Applied Social Research, Columbia University. See also Allen H. Barton and Bo Anderson, "Changes in an Organizational System: Formalization of a Qualitative Study," in Amitai Etzioni (ed.), *Complex Organizations* (New York: Holt, Rinehart & Winston, 1961).

from indifference to primary concern with the treatment goal was initiated by the administration and treatment staff and was resisted by the custodial staff and inmate elite. It shows also how the integration of the prison was sharply increased by shaking off the intermediate control of the custodial staff and the inmate elite over the interactions between administration and treatment staff, administration and inmates, administration and inmate mass, and treatment staff and inmate mass. We note the decline of the arbitrary discipline, rituals of domination, and inmate elite privileges, by which the former stratification was maintained, and, at the same time, the increase of "rehabilitative activities offered inmates," signifying an increase of integration. The last two items in the table show the irregular trend of voluntarism as integration increased and stability declined. Mc-Cleery attributes the period of rebellion to so sharp a reduction of stability that neither the inmate elite nor the custodial staff was able to control newly formed gangs of young reform-school graduates. A tantalizing footnote in one of the reports tells us that the prison erupted in a destructive riot at a still later stage, but McCleery was denied the opportunity to make a follow-up analysis, so that we do not know what sequence of events ultimately led to disequilibrium.

THE ALTERNATION OF GOALS

The foregoing discussion seems to exclude the possibility that the total achievement of an organization can be raised merely by taking thought. It seems also to exclude the possibility that an organization can pursue all of its goals at the same time with equal success. The reasoning behind these assertions needs to be made explicit.

A permanent increase in achievement requires corresponding increases in the total magnitudes of stability, integration, and/or voluntarism. Improvement of this kind can occur rather easily if membership is significantly expanded. To raise total achievement without an increase in size involves either an increase in the average activity of individual members or the development of new methods of coordination that are significantly more efficient than the old ways with respect to some goals without being less efficient with respect to other goals. This may be feasible in the long run, as technology advances and institutional patterns change. It is usually out of the question in the short run. Most organizations are not aware of alternative means of achieving their goals that are both superior to those they now employ and accessible.

The tendency toward expansionism, empire-building, and growth at any price that is so often remarked in business enterprises, government departments, and the headquarters of voluntary associations rests on an accurate perception of these principles and is seldom adverse to the organization's interests as defined by its own leaders, even when there are unfortunate consequences for the larger social system to which the expanding unit belongs.

It was noted above that organizations develop inconsistent goals. Some of these inconsistencies are attributable to uncertainties in the external environment. A combat organization must choose between defensive and aggressive strategies in preparing for a particular encounter. But the correct choice depends on unknown factors, such as the secret intentions of the enemy, and even on unknowable factors, such as the enemy's counterstrategy in response to the preparations.

March and Simon, in their brilliant analysis of organizational rationality,[69] call attention to certain limitations of the human mind that help to account for the alternation of goals. Following John R. Commons, who spoke of "limiting factors," and Chester Barnard, who identified "strategic factors," they show how rational behavior deals with a few components at a time. As they understand the process, the human minds that must cope with organizational problems are incapable of grasping them in their full complexity. Like sociologists, the managers of an organization can consider its problems rationally only by devising a simplified model that isolates the significant features of a problem without attempting to understand it fully. According to March and Simon, simplifications of this kind have several characteristics:

> (1) Optimizing is replaced by satisficing—the requirement that satisfactory levels of the criterion variables be attained. (2) Alternatives of action and consequences of action are discovered sequentially through search processes. (3) Repertories of action programs are developed by organizations and individuals, and these serve as the alternatives of choice in recurrent situations. (4) Each specific action program deals with a restricted range of consequences. (5) Each action program is capable of being executed in semi-independence of the others—they are only loosely coupled together.

The concept of a "repertory of action programs" is very useful in visualizing how the goals of an organization are modified from day to day, in response to the external environment or the internal calendar, without any loss of identity. It also helps to explain how goals that appear flatly contradictory—such as revenge and rehabilitation in a prison—can be pursued by a single organization.

March and Simon divide organization structure into three parts:

[69] March and Simon, *op. cit.*, Chapter 6, "Cognitive Limits on Rationality," especially pp. 169–71.

procedures for developing programs, procedures for deciding which program to apply at a given time, and the repertory of programs. This latter category they regard as the least stable. In evaluating an organization's effectiveness, they are inclined to attach more importance to its procedures for developing and switching programs than to the programs themselves.

STRATEGIC REPLACEMENT

In studying his gypsum plant, Gouldner was impressed by the wholesale turnover of supervisory personnel after the arrival of a new plant manager whose values differed from those of his predecessor. Gouldner calls this process strategic replacement. He shows how the new manager was at first impeded in his effort to improve production quotas by the old supervisors, who held values developed under the more voluntaristic regime of his predecessor. Their replacement by new men, attached to the new manager by personal obligations, not only furthered his program for raising production but also diffused a new set of attitudes through the interaction network.

All organizations, even the smallest, identify different members with alternative goals. A shift of stress from one goal to another subordinates one faction to another. If the shift is permanent, there is likely to be an exodus of those identified with the old goal and an influx of recruits sworn in advance to uphold the new. In McCleery's prison, the shift from custody to treatment started with the appointment of a new warden and led eventually to the resignation of most of the principal custodial officials and the appointment of new men dedicated to treatment and counseling. In Jaques' study of the development of labor–management consultation in a metallurgical plant, the system could not be made to work until union men moved into the representative positions originally held by management's loyal opposition. In Leighton's concentration camp each new turn of events in the inmates' campaign of resistance was accompanied by shifts of authority among both inmate and supervisor factions. In each of these cases, there were active alliances between factions in management and factions in the rank and file so that realignments anywhere in the status order were invariably reflected aloft and below.

There are several reasons why factions develop around each alternative goal and why the status of individuals rises or falls with the attention claimed by the goal of their faction. When emphasis shifts from one goal to another the primary responsibility for goal implementation shifts from one subdivision of the organization to another. This must occur because the optimum division of labor for the first goal cannot be appropriate for the second unless they are almost identical. With the new responsibility comes a rise in status, since the persons or units responsible for a stressed goal have a priority claim on the available resources. As they come to command more resources and to exert more influence in decision-making, their statuses rise along with those of their subordinates and allies. This is more than mere nepotism. As the new program is worked out, new positions are created and filled, and these are likely to require specialized training or experience that the displaced faction does not have. The rise in the status of the new faction is equivalent to a fall in the status of the old. The new channels of communication disrupt the old channels and reduce the integration of the old faction, who must choose between revolt and submission while a choice is still open. If they delay too long they may be unable to resist at all.

Consider again the four case studies. In the gypsum plant, the old supervisors resisted the new regime and were removed one by one. In the prison, the custodial force rebelled against the warden and sought outside support in the legislature but were defeated and ruined there. In the metal works and the internment camp, the displaced leaders seem to have withdrawn into sullen isolation.

The defending factions seem to be lured very frequently into a fatal miscalculation of their strength. Blocked from the new communication channels, they are often misinformed about the changes that have already taken place. Another handicap is their ideological commitment to the old methods and goals. They are lulled into overconfidence by their belief that the new methods are unworkable— the prisoners cannot be ruled by kindness, the miners cannot be made to obey safety rules, management never takes consultation seriously. Other defending factions gladly stake their futures on the certainty that the gasoline engine is a toy, that warships will never be obsolete, or that the social sciences are a passing fad. Whom the gods would destroy, they first make mad. A common form of organizational madness is the belief in one's own indispensability.

THE ORGANIZATION VS. ITS COMPONENTS

The previous discussion suggests that there may not be a close correlation between the success of an organization and of its components. In the long run, it is evident that an organization cannot survive unless many (not all) of its components are effective. In the short run and for small increments, however, there is only a slight relationship between the effectiveness of the total organization and any one of its components. The linkage between the two equilibriums is always complex and must be studied at close range to be understood at all. Thus, in Oahu Prison, the shift from custody to treatment was accompanied by a decrease in stability and an increase of integration and voluntarism for the prison as a whole. The consequences for component units were quite different. The warden's office seems to have experienced a decrease in stratification and an increase in integration, voluntarism, and achievement. All four variables declined for the custodial force while increasing for the treatment staff and declining to the point of disintegration for the old inmate community. The latter went out of existence and was replaced by new units centered on recreational activities and including staff members.

The opposition between the interests of organizations and those of their components appears in another light in "cumulative" tables of organization. In military forces, for example, a set of platoons makes a company, a set of companies makes a battalion, a set of battalions makes a regiment, and so on up through brigades, divisions, corps, armies, and army groups. There are similar patterns in many other institutions. Thus the Catholic, Orthodox, and Anglican churches follow the series: parish, diocese, archdiocese, metropolis. Higher education has the series: course, department, college, university. Official bureaucracies are usually built on a series such as: section, unit, office, division, branch, department, ministry. In cumulative arrangements of this kind, there is an unmistakable tendency for adjacent levels to alternate with respect to integration. Thus, brigades show low integration in armies with highly integrated regiments, departments are apt to be weakly integrated in well-integrated colleges, and so forth. Similar alternations between adjacent levels are often observed, although less regularly, with regard to stability and voluntarism. Since the achievement of each unit in an organization of cumulative form is conceived as approximately equal to the sum of the achievements of its components, the tendency of the variables to diverge in this way creates numerous stresses and strains.

The interests of an organization and of its own components are most consistently opposed with respect to reorganization. The changing needs of the parent organization continuously suggest, and sometimes require, the reorganization of components, which usually resist with all the means at their disposal. Thus, a really effective component organization will be able to maintain the integrity of its own structure, even if this should limit the effectiveness of its parent. Conversely, a really effective large-scale organization ought to have no components capable of defending themselves against reorganization. In a sense, the weakness of the components is a necessary condition for the strength of the whole. This factor alone is quite sufficient to insure a steady state of turmoil within any vigorous organization as it ambles along in rational pursuit of its goals.

CHAPTER FIVE

Making the Organization Man

SOCIALIZATION

The organizationally directed process that prepares and qualifies individuals to occupy organizational positions is called *socialization*.[1] It may be visualized as continuous, since the behaviors appropriate to an organizational position are not acquired once and for all when the position is assumed but are learned and relearned throughout the length of a career.[2]

Although the following pages will emphasize the positive features of the process—especially the behaviors *acquired*—it should be borne in mind that socialization implies losses as well as gains. The individual's entry into a new position usually coincides with his abandonment of an old one [3] and with some modification of his roles in other interaction networks.[4] Acceptance of any organiza-

---

[1] This chapter is considerably indebted to an unpublished manuscript, "Situational Forces in Adult Socialization," by Irving Rosow, which the author kindly sent me several years ago.

[2] For a good description of such long-term learning (in the French prefectoral career) see Brian Chapman, *The Prefects and Provincial France* (London: Allen & Unwin, 1955).

[3] A distinction is sometimes made between child and adult socialization on the grounds that child socialization involves basic character formation, a realm of fantasy, primacy in time, less free choice, fewer influential persons, higher levels of emotion, and an inexperienced subject. All of this may be so without establishing a difference of kind. There seems to be no reason why we cannot regard socialization into the family as a special case of socialization into an organization.

[4] This aspect of the process is vividly described in Rose Laub Coser's "The Socialization of Patients," Part 2 of *Life in the Ward* (East Lansing, Mich.: Michigan State University Press, 1962).

tional position creates a commitment to a consistent line of future activity that rules out many other alternatives, both known and unknown.[5] We shall consider, a little later on, some of the stresses that arise between the organization and the individual because of competing commitments.

WHAT SOCIALIZATION DOES

In every situation in which a member or an aspirant is to be transformed into a successful incumbent, there are at least four requirements that must be met. The candidate must acquire: (a) a new self-image, (b) new involvements, (c) new values, and (d) new accomplishments.

These requirements correspond in a general way to the familiar terms of organizational equilibrium. They amount to saying that the new man must be fitted into the status order, the interaction network, and the activities of the organization, while simultaneously acquiring the appropriate sentiments for each type of participation. Let us look at these requirements a little more closely.

The new self-image. The individual's recognition of himself in a new organizational position develops gradually. Only when the position has been held for some time and the incumbent has fallen into fixed habits can he take for granted who he now is and what others expect of him. Once developed, the self-image is not easily changed, although it may gradually be modified by the accumulation of incidents and the passage of time. The self-image of a fully socialized member mirrors the entire organization, although always imperfectly. It reflects a particular view of the organization's status order, interaction network, values, and activities. The sum of these perspectives gives every important organization a unique atmosphere and coloration that makes it different from anything else in the world, just as each individual, however fully explained, is a separate and unclassifiable experience to his intimates.

New involvements. Joining an organization involves an encounter with "new people," as does promotion or demotion or transfer.

[5] For an explanation of how this feature of socialization makes human behavior consistent, see Howard S. Becker, "Notes on the Concept of Commitment," *American Journal of Sociology,* Vol. LXVI, No. 1 (July, 1960).

Even former acquaintances seem to change. The incumbent of a new position sees them from a new angle, since they play different roles in relation to his present position than they did to his former position. The term *ambience* is used to denote the aggregate of individuals with whom a subject interacts in a given network.[6] In the course of socialization to a new position, the incumbent must begin to interact regularly with ambience associates who are prescribed in advance. Through these people, the organization's values are transmitted and the recruit's behavior is tailored to fit the required pattern. Their concensus eventually determines whether a particular instance of socialization is considered a success or failure; if it is successful, it is they who decide when the new identity has been fully assumed.

Socialization always involves something more than the development of new relationships; it also requires the abandonment of old ones. For the recruit, the convert, the newly elected, adopted, or graduated, there is always the awareness that becoming what one is now means forgetting what one was before. The bride is no longer a maiden; the new chief is expelled from the peer group. The extent and importance of the old relationships that are to be abandoned usually determine what kind of socialization process is necessary. In those cases in which socialization takes a drastic form, the severity of the experience is explained not so much by the difficulty of learning the new part as by the difficulty of forgetting the old.

New values. The values appropriate to a new position must be first communicated, then accepted, then internalized. It is often difficult to understand the mechanisms by which values are internalized or to measure the amount of internalization that occurs in a particular instance, but the fundamental concept is clear enough. In order for an individual to function as part of an organization, he must accept some of its purposes as his own. If nothing more, he must identify himself as a member and demonstrate minimum valences for other members. There is usually a great deal more. Even a small organization has an intricate complex of ideals and ideologies, of norms and standards, of beliefs and prejudices, of expectations

---

[6] A fuller definition of this concept is found in Theodore Caplow, "The Definition and Measurement of Ambiences," *Social Forces,* Vol. XXXIV, No. 1 (October, 1955), and in Theodore Caplow, Sheldon Stryker, and Samuel E. Wallace, *The Urban Ambience* (Totowa, N.J.: Bedminster Press, 1964).

and myths, so many in fact that they cannot be fully absorbed by any individual, however eager he is to conform. There are a few basic values on which all members agree as a condition of continued membership, a larger number that are fairly well accepted, and innumerable nuances that pertain to particular segments or factions but not to the organization as a whole.

New accomplishments. To occupy a new organizational position, it is not ordinarily sufficient to acquire the appropriate self-image, involvements, and values. Occupancy of the position also requires the accomplishment of specified tasks. The new incumbent in an organizational position does not stand still in it; he learns to act and move and manipulate the environment. His necessary accomplishments include the learning of skills with tools and techniques and of a special vocabulary for the matters to be communicated. One of the most important features of an organizational position is the length of time normally taken to acquire the necessary accomplishments. It may vary, among adjacent positions, from minutes to decades.

THE MODES OF SOCIALIZATION

There are fundamentally only a few modes of socialization, which appear again and again in ancient and modern societies and in organizations of every type. There is much less variation in the forms of the process than in its content. The apprenticeship of judges of high courts is similar in some ways to that of professional thieves. Initiation in a monastery resembles initiation in a military academy. The principal modes of socialization include schooling, training, apprenticeship, mortification, trial and error, assimilation, co-option, anticipatory socialization, screening, and nepotism.

Schooling is the systematic teaching of organizational behavior and values by a specialized agency. This has been carried further in our own society than in any other. The scope of general formal education is much broader than the needs of any particular organization. The educational institution prepares its students not for a particular socialization experience but for a vast number of such experiences with similar requirements.

Training ordinarily occurs within the organization in which the subject will eventually perform his tasks. The line between education and training is often hard to draw.[7] Training, like education, is never limited to its nominal objective. Organizations that conduct training programs conceive of them as imparting skills, but analysis of any particular training program always shows it to be concerned with the communication of values, the development of an ambience, the rejection of prior affiliations, and the development of an appropriate self-image. Hence the extraordinary extent to which success in training is often allowed to determine the subsequent career of the individual within the organization. Smigel [8] shows how the entire career of the lawyer in a large law firm is likely to be determined by his performance in the training period, just as his chance of being hired in the first place depended on his law-school record.

Apprenticeship is similar in purpose to training but utilizes a different agent of instruction. In apprenticeship, the responsibility for socialization is delegated by the organization to one of its members who serves as a model to a small number of successors. Apprenticeship is a preferred mode of socialization in systems in which the values to be communicated are as important as the accomplishments. In craft guilds skills are learned first, but the acquisition of a master's status waits upon a high degree of conformity to the expectations of the guild. Apprenticeship is often seen in the upper reaches of bureaucratic systems in which the holding of high office is so delicate a matter that only the successful official is considered competent to form his successor. In graduate schools and artists' studios, in executive suites and probably in harems, apprenticeship works either very well or very badly. There is no middle ground. Failures in apprenticeship are expensive to the organization and cannot be as readily salvaged as failures in training. Training is cheaper, more efficient, and infinitely more predictable than apprenticeship. It tends to displace apprenticeship, except for positions that are of the great-

[7] Shall we say, for example, that a Catholic theological seminary is a place for training, while an interdenominational Protestant seminary exemplifies education? From one standpoint, this is absurd; from another, it is quite plausible. The dossier of the candidate in the former case is continuous, and his performance in school is a much more important element in his subsequent career.

[8] Erwin O. Smigel, "Recruitment and the Large Law Firm," *American Sociological Review,* Vol. XXV, No. 1 (February, 1960). For additional evidence see Jack Ladinsky, "Careers of Lawyers, Law Practice and Legal Institutions," *American Sociological Review,* Vol. XXVIII, No. 1 (February, 1963).

est importance, or archaic, just as mass production replaces handicraft.

Mortification, as described by Goffman,[9] is the sequence of steps by which the recruit to a total institution is dispossessed of his previous roles and deprived of the self-image he brings with him from the outside world. It consists, Goffman says, of "a series of abasements, degradations, humiliations, and profanations of self." Among the standard features of this mode of socialization are admission procedures that simplify the recruit's appearance and remove some of his identifying characteristics, will-breaking contests, in which authority is exerted unreasonably and any defiance instantly punished, personal defacement or disfigurement, verbal and gestural profanations, physical and moral contamination, and minute subjection to routine. The common purpose of all these devices is to deprive the individual of control over his own activities and to make it impossible for him to resist the influence of the organization as it begins to shape his behavior in accordance with its own peculiar patterns.

Trial and error should not be overlooked as a mode of socialization. It is often the best means available, and for many positions in many organizations it serves as well or better than a deliberate course of preparation. The founders of organizations and the first incumbents of new positions must necessarily be socialized by trial and error. The vagaries of their experience are often carefully embalmed for future generations. The need for socialization is so overwhelming that even without accepted procedures it may take place with remarkable speed and smoothness. In a laboratory experiment by Blake and Mouton,[10] ten or twelve hours of autonomous in-group activity, followed by an election and a brief discussion, were sufficient to socialize representatives who showed unflinching loyalty to their own groups in subsequent intergroup competition.

Assimilation is another common mode of socialization. It is the

[9] Erving Goffman, "On the Characteristics of Total Institutions: The Inmate World" and "On the Characteristics of Total Institutions: Staff–Inmate Relations," in Donald R. Cressey (ed.), *The Prison: Studies in Institutional Organization and Change* (New York: Holt, Rinehart & Winston, 1961). The quotation is from page 23.

[10] Robert R. Blake and Jane S. Mouton, "Loyalty of Representatives to Ingroup Positions During Intergroup Competition," *Sociometry,* Vol. XXIV, No. 2 (June, 1961).

gradual, unscheduled acquisition of positional requirements by interaction and imitation and is the preferred mode where membership is not greatly prized, as in most civic associations. Assimilation is also typical of situations in which a great deal of time is available for socialization, as in some private clubs where privileges are determined by seniority and seniority measured in decades. There are some elements of assimilation in any sequence of education, training, or apprenticeship, since much of what the recruit must learn is not formally imparted but derived from casual and unscheduled contacts with others.

Co-option resembles assimilation but is essentially quite different. In this mode of socialization the new recruit is admitted from the outset to the privileges of membership in the group; he is excluded, however, from a dominant inner circle. The phenomenon is very common indeed. Zaleznik [11] describes a fully developed inner circle in a machine shop. The socialization process includes two overlapping sequences of events: one by which the new member acquires the values and behaviors of the whole organization, the other by which he is measured for membership in the inner circle. Rejection from the inner circle does not mean the end of membership in the larger organization, but it does signify a permanent limitation on the privileges of membership. Co-option is not always a one-sided procedure. There are always subtle ways of applying for membership in an inner circle and improving one's own chances of acceptance.[12]

Conversion is still another important mode of socialization. The term is used here to denote a sudden, drastic modification of values followed by an equally precipitate change in behavior. This may come about in a number of ways. Conversion in a revival meeting is more overtly emotional than in the Bahai temple. Conversion may be a social rather than an emotional experience, as in the case of the middle-class youth who joins a gang of lower-class delinquents and modifies his visible personality to render himself acceptable to his new peers. Something very like conversion occurs upon promotion

---

[11] Abraham Zaleznik, *Worker Satisfaction and Development* (Cambridge, Mass.: Harvard University Division of Research, 1957).

[12] Blau shows how "impression management" enables an individual who has some but not all of the characteristics desired by the inner circle to get himself co-opted. See Peter M. Blau, "A Theory of Social Integration," *American Journal of Sociology,* Vol. LXV, No. 6 (May, 1960).

to high office, particularly an office that places the appointee in a position of authority over his former equals and separates him from them in interaction. The explicit recognition of conversion as a "change of soul" is found in such ceremonies as coronation and consecration, and at times in initiation and graduation. Conversion need not be an isolated, individual experience. It may occur to an organized group or en masse. The Kamikaze Corps, recruiting Japanese flyers for suicide missions in 1944, was swamped with volunteers who adopted its unusual values without much hesitation.

> Some flyers sortied on their mission on the day after joining the Corps; none ever knew more than a day in advance when his time would come. Yet they studied, asked questions and showed intense eagerness to learn. Their attitude belied any aspect of gloom. They were cheerful and pleasant in company, but matter-of-fact, sincere, and industrious about their work. They were men with a job to be done.[13]

Anticipatory socialization rests on the identification of an individual with a group to which he does not yet belong but which he proposes to join. Drawing examples from *The American Soldier,* Merton and Kitt [14] discuss the case of the marginal enlisted man who adopts the official military mores as his own and rejects the surreptitiously rebellious values of the enlisted group. The marginal man rejects the values of his own group and perceives things from the viewpoint of those whom he aspires to join. He is not so much fixed between two groups as moving across a social no man's land from one group to the other. In the same essay, Merton and Kitt point out how this process is affected by the extent to which legitimacy is conceded to the existing status arrangements. Anticipatory socialization within a large organization is more complex than anticipatory socialization that involves movement between disconnected groups.

Screening is a method of reviewing candidates for a position and accepting only those with certain desired characteristics. Characteristics may be chosen either because they are useful to the organiza-

---

[13] Robert Pineau, "Spirit of the Divine Wind," *United States Naval Institute Proceedings,* Vol. LXXXIV, No. 11 (November, 1958). The quotation is from page 26.

[14] Robert K. Merton and Alice S. Kitt, "Contributions to the Theory of Reference Group Behavior," in Robert K. Merton and Paul F. Lazarsfeld (eds.), *Continuities in Social Research* (Glencoe, Ill.: Free Press, 1950). See especially pages 85–89.

tion or because experience has shown that people having them are the most assimilable. The screening process will ordinarily operate most smoothly when the selectors have themselves been screened for the same desired characteristics. There is always a tendency for organizations to drift toward a standard personality type even in the absence of a theory that this is beneficial. However, the theory is usually quick to appear.

Whether the screening process actually finds persons who resemble the desired image and who will behave in the manner anticipated depends mostly upon two considerations: whether the supply of applicants is large and whether selection is centralized. The larger the pool of applicants in proportion to the number of positions, the higher the probability that persons with the desired characteristics can be located. If the supply is relatively small, the practice of admitting exceptions and drifting into the use of other criteria than those originally proposed will become uniform. Decentralization limits a screening process because of the difficulty of communicating the model of a personality type. While this can be attempted with "psychometric instruments," it can be done better under the keen eye of an experienced recruiting agent who sets the candidate in interaction with himself to determine compatibility.

In its search for persons of conforming characteristics, the organization may by-pass individuals of greater ability than those it accepts. This almost undocumentable fact is very nicely documented in a study by Kelsall, who investigated the system of selecting higher civil servants used in Britain between 1870 and 1950.[15] He described the long struggle for appointment by merit, which followed the introduction of the civil service in England in the middle of the nineteenth century. Bit by bit, outside pressures forced down the barriers that formerly excluded applicants who did not have the same class and school origins as their examiners. Yet, after nearly a century, the process was far from complete. The effect of screening was to exclude many of the most able candidates and to impede the careers of those who were reluctantly admitted. Few organizations are exempt from that spontaneous chauvinism that makes the candidate with conforming traits look more talented than the outsider.

Nepotism, like screening, is more readily conceived as a procedure

[15] R. K. Kelsall, *Higher Civil Servants in Britain* (London: Routledge and Kegan Paul, 1955).

for designating candidates than as a method of socializing them. In two respects, however, it may be so considered: first, in that the inculcation of values and accomplishments is performed outside the organization—for example in the candidate's family—and, second, in that the nepotist assumes some responsibility for the performance of his protégé.

The most colorful instances of nepotism belong to former times, to the Renaissance Papacy, which gave us the word itself by showering ecclesiastical appointments on papal "nephews," or to the English navy of the eighteenth century, in which nepotistic appointment was the normal procedure.[16] Officers' commissions were awarded as a matter of course to children still in the nursery. One case is recorded of an infant commissioned on the day of his birth. The famous Admiral Wallace was entered on the navy's roster so early and retired so late that he drew pay for more than ninety years. Admiral Rodney managed to have his son promoted to a captaincy before the boy was sixteen. Nepotism in modern public services has grown more discreet, but it is by no means extinct; in many business and professional firms, it is a salient feature of the organizational tradition.

SOME EXAMPLES OF SOCIALIZATION

The United States Senate. The United States Senate has been called the most exclusive club in the world.[17] There is probably no other component of the Federal government that has changed so little since the Constitution was put into effect in 1789. Its conservatism is based on such factors as overlapping terms of office (one-third of the Senators are elected every two years), the tendency for men to advance to the Senate from positions in the House of Representatives or from governorships, the extraordinary devotion of the Senate to its own rules, and the tendency—rooted in the regional facts of American politics—for the more conservative Senators in both parties to enjoy longer tenure of office. As White shows,[18] the prevailing mode of socialization is co-option. What he calls the Inner Club is a very well-defined entity. A Senator must acquire some seni-

---

[16] Admirably described in E. S. Turner, *Gallant Gentlemen* (London: Michael Joseph, 1956).

[17] Originally said of the British House of Commons.

[18] William S. White, *Citadel* (New York: Harper, 1956).

ority before he can exercise much influence, either in the official committees or in the informal caucuses in which important decisions are made. But he may be repeatedly re-elected without ever gaining entry to the Inner Club or enjoying real influence among his colleagues. The co-option procedure is the more interesting because of the special circumstances. There are two Senators from each state, regardless of its population, so that a Senator from New York represents a constituency some fifty-nine times as large as that of a Senator from Nevada. The office stands high in the political status order, and incumbents often have effective control of the party machinery in their home states. The term of office is longer than those of other legislative and executive positions. Hence, a Senator, when elected, already enjoys a position of great prestige and some power outside of the organization. Within the Senate, the small size of the house and the principle of senatorial courtesy assure him substantial privileges from the outset, but with respect to the organization's principal business of legislation he is virtually helpless. He begins on the lowest rungs of the committee system and works his way upward by manifesting zeal, loyalty to the traditions of the Senate, the ability to associate with the members of the Inner Club on their own terms, and skill in debate, political maneuvering, and investigation. However, success in these matters is measured by the somewhat enigmatic criteria of the Senate itself and not by the standards of outside observers.

The Senate, White points out, is a "Southern-style institution." This is an historical accident. In the days before the Civil War, the men who fixed their stamp on the organization were predominantly Southerners, identified with the great plantation interests of the seaboard states. The historical accident is kept alive by certain features of the electoral system and by the rules of the Senate. Since the South had a one-party system and a limited electorate, while the rest of the country had a two-party system and nearly universal suffrage, and since it is usual in both parties for an incumbent to be nominated for re-election, southern Senators have had much higher probabilities of re-election than their northern colleagues. This means that the important posts on the major committees are mostly held by Southerners when the Democrats organize the Senate, and the weight of southern seniority is felt even when Republicans hold the committee chairmanships. Southern Democrats and northern Republicans are allied on many issues, so that although the power of seniority is less for Southerners during those sessions when the Republicans have a majority, their advantage over northern Democrats is not much reduced. The Inner Club, although it does not consist exclusively of Southerners, is characterized by a southern viewpoint. Southerners are likely to become members of the Inner Club soon after their first election, but Northerners must undergo a much longer period of probation.

White is hard put to explain the criteria of acceptance in the Inner Club for Northerners. Some liberals are fully accepted by the largely conservative insiders. Some men with no visible gift for gregariousness are preferred to others with great public charm. The aristocrats of the Inner Club have been known to exclude millionaires of good family, while accepting the sons of relief clients. What the members of the Inner Club have in common is a thorough commitment to the symbols of the organization and intolerance of any effort to change its customs.

This pattern is typical of co-option as a mode of socialization. First, selection is dependent on historical accident and the run of events. It is always partly accidental whether the new member who is unfamiliar with the standards of the inner circle (and may even be unaware of its existence) can meet the subtle preliminary tests. Second, the invariable qualification for admittance to an inner circle is adherence to the organizational status quo, especially to those arrangements that sustain the privileges of the inner circle. Third, there is a double set of criteria—note the easy acceptance of Southerners and reluctant acceptance of Northerners in the case of the Senate.[19] An inner circle, wherever it exists, is linked to some *illegitimate* mechanism for maintaining power, such as the southern one-party system. The automatic acceptance of inside candidates reflects this linkage, which also requires the co-option of outsiders. An arbitrary and unpredictable selection of outsiders protects the inner circle of the Inner Club. Outsiders cannot claim entry as a right but only as a privilege. In the Senate, all nonsouthern newcomers are reduced to the same state of dependent candidacy regardless of their qualifications. By maintaining enough flexibility to co-opt the leaders of any emergent opposing faction, the Inner Club has been able to maintain its com-

[19] Hollingshead found much the same thing in the high school cliques of Elmtown. August B. Hollingshead, *Elmtown's Youth* (New York: Wiley, 1949).

manding position in this delicately balanced situation for almost two centuries. It is interesting to note how quickly the system reconstituted itself after the interruption of the Civil War. Only a few years elapsed before the Senate again fell under the benevolent sway of of the Southerners.

The pilot's profession.   Samuel Clemens' *Life on the Mississippi* is a narrative account of river piloting by a participant observer with a genius for observation. (The extraordinary chapter "The Pilot's Monopoly" is one of the best available case histories of a conflict organization.) The earlier chapters contain a classic account of the author's apprenticeship as a pilot and his eventual acceptance into that closely guarded occupation.

In the little town of Hannibal, Missouri, where Clemens grew up, it was every boy's ambition to be a steamboat man. The steamboat pilot, with his princely wages and unchecked authority, stood at the peak of a pyramid in which even the lowest positions were glamorous. The influence of class stratification on recruitment for these positions is described with unerring eye. "Boy after boy managed to get on the river. The minister's son became an engineer. The doctor's and the postmaster's sons became mud clerks; the wholesale liquor dealer's son became a barkeeper on a boat; four sons of the chief merchant, and two sons of the county judge, became pilots." Eventually the author left home and sought training as a pilot. It took some months and many approaches before he found a pilot willing to accept him as apprentice and to teach him the Mississippi River from New Orleans to St. Louis for five hundred dollars, payable out of his first wages after graduating.

The neophyte pilot first discovers the need to know every turn and twist and bend in the river. When he has half mastered this knowledge, he is told that he must also be able to recognize them at night. Later, he is given the additional assignment of memorizing changes in banks and shoals. Step by step, further requirements are introduced, such as the identification of small signs on the surface of the water and the minute characteristics of the rough water above a reef. The finer points of instruction are described in a wonderful dialogue in Chapter 10:

> When I had learned the name and position of every visible feature of the river, when I had so mastered its shape that I could shut my

eyes and trace it from St. Louis to New Orleans; when I had learned to read the fact of the water as one would cull the news from the morning paper, and finally, when I had trained my dull memory to treasure up an endless array of soundings and crossing-marks, and keep fast hold of them, I judged that my education was complete; so I got to tilting my cap to the side of my head, and wearing a toothpick in my mouth at the wheel. Mr. Bixby had his eye on these airs. One day he said:

"What is the height of that bank yonder, at Burgess's?"

"How can I tell, sir? It is three-quarters of a mile away."

"Very poor eye—very poor. Take the glass." I took the glass and presently said:

"I can't tell. I suppose that that bank is about a foot and a half high."

"Foot and a half! That's a six-foot bank. How high was the bank along here last trip?"

"I don't know; I never noticed."

"You didn't? Well, you must always do it hereafter."

"Why?"

"Because you'll have to know a good many things that it tells you. For one thing, it tells you the stage of the river—tells you whether there's more water or less in the river along here than there was last trip."

"The leads tell me that." I rather thought I had the advantage of him there.

"Yes. But suppose the leads lie? The bank would tell you so, and then you would stir those leadsmen up a bit. There was a ten-foot bank here last trip, and there is only a six-foot bank here now. What does that signify?"

"That the river is four feet higher than it was last trip."

"Very good. Is the river rising or falling?"

"Rising."

"No, it ain't."

"I guess I am right, sir. Yonder is some driftwood floating down the stream."

"A rise *starts* the driftwood, but then it keeps on floating awhile after the river is done rising. Now the bank will tell you about this. Wait till you come to a place where it shelves a little. Now here: do you see this narrow belt of fine sediment? That was deposited while the water was higher. You see the driftwood begins to strand, too. The bank helps in other ways. Do you see that stump on the false point?"

"Ay, ay, sir."

"Well, the water is just up to the roots of it. You must make a note of that."

"Why?"

"Because that means that there's seven feet in the chute of 103."

"But 103 is a long way up the river yet."

"That's where the benefit of the bank comes in. There is water enough in 103 *now*, yet there may not be by the time we get there, but the bank will keep us posted all along. You don't run close chutes on a falling river, upstream, and there are precious few of them that you are allowed to run at all downstream. There's a law of the United States against it. The river may be rising by the time we get to 103, and in that case we'll run it. We are drawing—how much?"

"Six feet aft—six and half forward."

"Well, you do seem to know something."

"But what I particularly want to know is, if I have got to keep up an everlasting measuring of the banks of this river, twelve hundred miles, month in and month out?"

"Of course!"

The respect of the apprentice for his master is unconditional, and his dependence is nearly absolute. Even after a lapse of some thirty years, the description of Mr. Bixby which Clemens sets down in *Life on the Mississippi* is a paean of affectionate respect. All other pilots are depreciated. In one vivid scene, a gallery of visiting pilots assembles in the pilothouse while Mr. Bixby undertakes an especially difficult maneuver. We get a clear view of the apprentice's subordination and self-abasement before his master's peer group and of his negative judgment of his master's peers. The progressive imposition of responsibility on the cub-pilot is part of the instruction he receives. On a number of occasions, Mr. Bixby hides near the pilothouse to see how the apprentice handles a problem. At a later stage, he arranges a hoax and invites the captain and some passengers to watch the cub-pilot taking soundings and looking for shoals in the deepest part of the river. Yet these episodes create confidence. The apprentice is supported by the certainty that he will be rescued from any difficulty he falls into as long as he shows loyalty and zeal. In various episodes, the master protects his apprentice from other pilots, other crew members, outsiders, the hazards of the river, and the routine problems of the occupation itself. But he cannot protect him from the competition of his peers, and in two places Clemens reports rivalry between the apprentices attached to the two pilots who took alternate shifts on the same boat. An apprentice peer group is seldom well integrated. The antagonism toward superiors on which peer groups are founded is weak or lacking. The relationship with the master is far more important for the comfort and advancement of the apprentice than the support of his fellows. Since the former relationship is highly personal and includes a continuous evaluation of the apprentice, any attempt at output limitation is quickly observed.

At first sight, this account of piloting appears to contradict what we have said about the interaction of unequals. In apprenticeship, a high, sustained rate of interaction is not followed by a reduction of status difference. Nevertheless, the basic tendencies are still at work. It is precisely the purpose of the apprenticeship to bring the pupil to the level of the master and to make him a peer of the master. The ease with which status is maintained is explained by the apprentice's interest in reducing the status difference by the approved procedure that is opened to him.

Some ambivalence is reported at the very beginning of the Clemens narrative when the cub-pilot, alarmed by the requirements, doubts his master's competence and fervently hopes to see him run aground. In the later stages of the relationship, when the apprentice's transition to equality is virtually assured, ambivalence declines.

The fundamental feature of apprenticeship is that the organization's stake in the socialization of a recruit is entrusted to a single individual who enjoys considerable freedom of action. Those who take apprentices are necessarily of high status, and by doing so their status is further raised and their autonomy somewhat increased.

A military academy. Another variety of socialization is described in Dornbusch's account of the Coast Guard Academy.[20] There there are not only different modes of socialization but varying intensities also. Generally speaking, the process is intense when the behaviors to be learned are difficult to teach, when previous affiliations have to be discarded, and when close conformity is expected. All of these conditions are met in military academies.

The predominant modes of socialization in military academies are mortification, training, and anticipatory socialization. Experience

[20] Sanford N. Dornbusch, "The Military Academy as an Assimilating Institution," *Social Forces,* Vol. XXXIII, No. 4 (May, 1955).

in the Coast Guard Academy starts with the suppression of former affiliations. The new cadets, called swabs, are not allowed to leave the base or to have any interactions with outsiders. All swabs wear the same uniform. They are not permitted to receive money from home, and discussions of family background are taboo. This initiation produces a low-status peer group, without any outside sources of prestige.

The cadet is subject to two sets of rules: the "regulations" and the "traditions." A latent function of the regulations is to punish violators of the traditions. This is done by labeling any offense against the traditions as a breach of the regulations. The distinction between *formal* regulations and *informal* traditions is a little misleading. The traditions are norms enforced by peers, or by student superiors, rather than by instructors, and are informal only in this special sense. Although described as "unwritten rules," they are presented to new cadets *in writing* in the orientation manual. When there is a conflict between the regulations and traditions, the regulations are forced out of use. For example, when a swab violates regulations by carrying out the hazing orders given by an upperclassman, and receives demerits, the upperclassmen contrive to excuse him from other official infractions until his demerit account has been balanced.

The four classes in residence at any one time constitute a hierarchy, with the first class having almost complete control over the rest of the students and the classes in the middle having the responsibility (for so it is defined) of hazing the swabs. The first class insists that hazing take place and has the power to enforce this demand upon the other classes by giving demerits. In the face of the unpleasant and protracted experience of hazing, swabs develop very strong peer-group sentiments, some of which interfere with the program of classroom instruction. For example, if a cadet is unable to answer a question addressed to him, no other member of the class will answer. Together with the system of hazing and its *prescribed* infractions of the regulations goes a system of fraternization, which amounts to a *prescribed* violation of the traditions. This fraternization, whereby the hazers apologize for the aggressiveness they are compelled to display toward the swabs, is one element in the development of officer solidarity. Other elements are orientation to a common career and stereotyped antagonisms toward enlisted men, reservists, and civilians.

The homogenization of individuals begins upon admission and goes somewhat further in the Coast Guard Academy than in other military academies, perhaps because the prestige of Coast Guard officers is less secure than that of officers in the larger services. Throughout the cadet's career, he is taught to regard what happens to him as a function of his cadet status, not of his personality. Those who haze, says the observer, do not pretend to be personally superior to those who are hazed. Individual idiosyncracies may affect the type of hazing done, but not the amount. The homogenization of behavior and sentiments makes communication among cadets very easy and facilitates adjustment to the loss of status they undergo after graduation—the decline from the lofty student rank of first classman to the humble service rank of ensign.[21]

The status to which the candidates are being socialized is relatively high, and the origins of the students are such that many of them will have risen above the social class level of their families as soon as they are commissioned. The academy might not be able to attract suitable recruits if the status rewards offered by the organization were not substantial. On the other hand, while this socialization process enhances the apparent status of the positions the organization has to offer, it increases the apparent differences among those positions. An admiral is more exalted in the perspective of an ensign than from the viewpoint of a civilian. This principle seems to apply even in prisons and other punitive establishments, where the prestige of all participants is low by outside standards.

The general hospital.   The workings of assimilation as a mode of socialization are shown by a study of changes in the status attitudes of medical interns during their year of internship, reported by Seeman and Evans.[22] The interns were asked to fill out a status-commit-

[21] For a sophisticated description of socialization in the later stages of a military career, see Morris Janowitz, *The Professional Soldier* (Glencoe, Ill.: Free Press, 1960), especially Section 3, "Career Patterns."

[22] Melvin Seeman and John W. Evans, "Apprenticeship and Attitude Change," *American Journal of Sociology,* Vol. LXVII, No. 4 (January, 1962). The quotation is from page 376. Other findings of the same study are reported in their "Stratification and Hospital Care I: The Performance of the Medical Intern"; and "II: The Objective Criteria of Performance," *American Sociological Review,* Vol. XXVI, Nos. 1 and 2 (February and April, 1962), and in L. E. Rogers, *The Measurement of Status Relations in a Hospital* (Columbus, Ohio: Ohio State Engineering Experiment Station Bulletin No.

ment scale on the day of their arrival in the hospital and again a year later at the close of the internship. The scale has twenty-six attitude items measuring the respondent's "attitude toward stratification." The authors conceive of stratification as a composite of three status elements or subscores: power difference, social distance, and prestige distinction.

The results at first glance are not exciting. The correlation between scores obtained at the start of the internship and those obtained at the close is fairly high, and the mean score does not change significantly. In other words, over-all acceptance of the hospital status order does not shift very much during the year of internship, when considered either individually or collectively.

On closer analysis, this impression of stability gives way to a far more interesting pattern. First, the *undecided* responses to items in the status-commitment scale decrease significantly. The interns become more decisive in their status attitudes, whatever they are. Moreover, when the scale is rearranged to distinguish between items concerning the interns' relationships with their medical superiors, and those regarding their relation to subordinates, especially nurses, the apparent stability dissolves into two counter-balancing trends. With respect to their superiors, the residents and attending physicians, the interns have shifted toward "equalitarianism." With respect to their subordinates, the nurses, they express greater enthusiasm for status distinctions.

Whereas at the beginning of the year most of the interns could be classified as either equalitarian or segregationist,

> the predominant view at the end of the year is that the system should resemble neither an equalitarian team nor a three way system with the interns as an intermediate status group: it is now a two way stratification design composed of a homogenous group of physicians contrasted with the low status nursing staff.

This might be described as an instance of anticipatory socialization were it not for the fact that, as the authors show, the sentiments of the interns at the end of the year do not resemble those of the next higher stratum, the residents. They are actually less similar to those

175, May, 1959). For related findings, see various papers in Robert K. Merton et al., *The Student Physician* (Cambridge, Mass.: Harvard University Press, 1957), and Howard S. Becker, *Boys in White: Student Culture in Medical School* (Chicago: University of Chicago Press, 1961).

of the residents at the end of the year than at the beginning. The effect of assimilation for the interns is to accentuate their identification with physicians in general. Their attitudes shift so as to minimize their social distance from other categories of physicians while increasing their insulation from nurses and outsiders. When they become residents, and their self-images as physicians become more secure, some of these attitudes will be reversed. They will develop an interest in enlarging rather than diminishing the status difference between residents and interns.

The case suggests that susceptibility to aggrandizement effects is a function of socialization. The more thoroughly a member is socialized, the greater the perceptual distortion as he views his own organization against the background of the sets to which it belongs.

A metropolitan bank.   Screening as a mode of socialization is nicely illustrated by Argyris' study of the Friendly First Bank.[23] The procedure in this case is so simple that it hardly deserves a name, yet it is remarkably effective in fixing the character of the organization. In the Friendly First Bank, the hiring of new employees is in the hands of a personnel director and an assistant who mirrors his attitudes. These officials make their choices among job applicants on the basis of an image which they call the "right type." They are unable to describe the "right type" precisely, but they have no difficulty in determining whether a particular applicant matches the image. In one statement quoted at length, the personnel director reports his rejection of a high school student who smoked without permission during the course of the interview, of another candidate who arrived for the interview in the company of her strong-minded mother, and of other applicants who were talkative. He likes timid youngsters who do not do much talking, are somewhat nervous and quiet, and have a certain amount of poise. His assistant explains that dress is an important element in selection. He does not like candidates who are overdressed, flashy, sloppy or slick, or have dirty fingernails. He listens to the modulation of their voices and checks on

[23] Chris Argyris, *Organization of a Bank* (New Haven, Conn.: Labor and Management Center, Yale University, 1954). Another instance of "right type" selection—on a much larger scale—is described in Robert Heussler, *Yesterday's Rulers: The Making of the British Colonial Service* (Syracuse, N.Y.: Syracuse University Press, 1963).

the correctness of their grammar. He looks to see if they have filled out the application meticulously and submissively. From these and other interviews, the ideal type emerges: he is meek, quiet, obedient, tactful, cautious, careful, and nonaggressive.

The comments of officers and employees about their colleagues help to round out the picture. The people who work in the bank are not promoters, not go-getters, not gamblers, not competitive, not throat-cutters, uncomplaining, complacent, conservative, and submissive. The subjects describe themselves in the same way. Their favorite recreations are gardening, reading, and watching television.

Further exploration adds more characteristics of the "right type," such as a preference for working alone without supervision and a marked dislike of aggressiveness in others. Not unexpectedly, there are points of correspondence between this personality pattern and the organizational structure of the Friendly First Bank. Promotion is slow and heavily influenced by seniority. Wages are meager but secure; the bank is reluctant to fire an employee under any provocation. The officers are segregated from the employees and somewhat isolated from each other. They shrink from the exercise of personal authority as much as the employees dislike being supervised. The style of interaction emphasizes politeness, submissiveness to customers and superiors, the precise and accurate performance of routine duties, a low degree of initiative, resistance to change, and a taboo on institutional criticism.

There are refinements to the pattern. The personnel director's responsibility does not cease when a new employee is hired. He sees the employee in occasional compulsory interviews, usually on the employee's birthday. This "heart-to-heart talk" is painful and embarrassing to the employee. It is apparently intended to discover deviations from the behavior of the right type. Throughout the organization there is a curious tendency to suppress or ignore complaints and to understate or defer grievances. Fringe benefits, with respect to health, loans, and outside training, are liberal. There is little direct job training. Absorption by experience, the investigator remarks, is the usual way of learning the work. An emphasis on conformity pervades the entire organization.

Only where turnover is low, where the demands for achievement are easily satisfied, and where the organizational culture is somehow protected from change can this mode of socialization function successfully over a long period. The possibilities of innovation in the Friendly First Bank are limited. Any major changes would require the introduction of new persons who were incompatible with those of the "right type."

PROBLEMS OF SOCIALIZATION

Socialization has been discussed so far as if it always exemplified the easy fulfillment of social necessity and as if organizational requirements and individual aspirations were generally congruent. In real life these conditions are met imperfectly or not at all. The mutual adaptation of individuals and organizations creates enormous stresses for both. The following discussion touches lightly on some of the ways dysfunctions appear.

Obsolete socialization.   The changes that occur in an organizational program over a period of time sometimes have retroactive effects on processes of socialization long since completed. After members have been induced to accept certain values, it may happen that the organization itself abandons them. What was once adaptively useful now becomes an obstacle to adaptation. This may occur in many ways. Successful socialization sometimes lures the recruit into a situation that he finds progressively less satisfying with the passage of time. In Westby's [24] study of a symphony orchestra, the young and newly recruited musicians were found to be gregarious, occupationally satisfied, and generally well integrated into the organization, but their older colleagues were isolated, anomic, and frustrated. The symphony musician has an unusual career curve. He reaches his peak earnings and his terminal status very early in life, not much past the age of twenty. At that point, he may not be aware that his long-term prospects are unfavorable, especially if he hopes to become a soloist. Young musicians are persuaded to accept the occupation by the swift increase of salary and prestige at the outset of their careers; their subsequent advancement is likely to be disappointing.

Socialization may also become obsolete when promotion demands from the individual new values and accomplishments for which his former position may not have prepared him, or may even have dis-

[24] David O. Westby, "The Social Organization of a Symphony Orchestra" (unpublished thesis, University of Minnesota, 1957).

qualified him. The foreman whose major accomplishment was the tactful leadership of a peer group may find himself handicapped as superintendent by his tact and sensitivity. The meticulous craftsman promoted to a supervisory position, the careful bureaucrat who becomes chief executive and must acquire a flair for public relations, the obedient subordinate who rises to a position of independent responsibility and is called upon for bold tactical decisions—all of them are likely to be hampered by their prior successful adaptation to different demands in the same organization. This is one reason why civil-service systems often stop somewhat short of the top, and why, even in private companies, top management is often recruited on totally different principles than the lower echelons.

The disorienting shift need not be vertical; it is often horizontal. The decentralization of certain industrial firms has brought a host of problems to the decentralized people, whose urban capabilities are often misplaced in a rural setting. Even the local peculiarities of an organization may have this effect. In studying academic departments,[25] for example, we observed that men who acquire their academic habits in departments favoring team research are regarded as meddlesome and lacking in initiative when they move to departments that practice lone-wolf scholarship. Men brought up as lone-wolf scholars are apt to do badly in the departments with collaborative customs.

Role strain. Socialization within an organization never takes place without some reference to the subject's other memberships, the values of which must be rejected or accommodated to those being acquired. It is presumed by some students, although not by all, that in preliterate societies this problem is somewhat simplified by the tendency for all organizational patterns to be woven into what Redfield[26] calls a web or what Linton[27] characterizes as a system with few alternatives. Redfield describes a folk society in these terms:

> To the villager, however, sickness suggests that he has offended against the gods or the souls of the dead by some omission of ritual

[25] Theodore Caplow and Reece J. McGee, *The Academic Marketplace* (New York: Basic Books, 1958).

[26] Robert Redfield, *The Folk Culture of Yucatan* (Chicago: University of Chicago Press, 1941). The quotation is from page 211.

[27] Ralph Linton, *The Study of Man* (New York: Appleton-Century, 1936).

or pious duty; the diagnosis of the shaman-priest is likely to remind him of this conventional connection between sickness and religion; the religious connotations in turn depend upon the agricultural or beekeeping practices of the native. Thus, approaching the complex of ideas from the other end, when he cares for his bees or plants his corn, he will perform the customary rituals with a thought to the preservation of his health and that of his family.

Whether role strain between competing organizations is really low in folk societies, there can be no question that it is very high in our own. A good, although relatively trivial, example is provided by a study of the strain between the roles of clergyman and military officer among military chaplains.[28] The investigator was able to identify inconsistent prescriptions stemming from the two roles with respect to almost every feature of the chaplain's position. His prescribed position as an officer and his relationship to other officers and to enlisted men, his function as an intermediary between these groups and his function of moderating enforcement of military regulations, his religious principles, and his own personal needs all conflict. In addition to inconsistent prescriptions of overt behavior, the chaplain's situation requires acceptance of contradictory values about such matters as the relations between church and state and the morality of war. Burchard found that most of the chaplains in his sample suffered severely from role strains, which they attempted to resolve either by rationalization or by compartmentalizing their behavior. The net effect of these adjustments tended to reinforce the chaplain's role as an officer and to undermine his self-image as a minister.

A comprehensive theory of role strain is presented by Goode.[29] In summary, his basic theorem is that "the individual's total role obligations are overdemanding." In other words, the individual cannot possibly satisfy all of the obligations imposed by the several organizations in which he holds positions, the several roles that accompany each position, and the several activities belonging to each role. His problem is "how to allocate his energy and skills so as to reduce role strain to some bearable proportions." The organization's problem is how to integrate these individual allocations

28 Waldo W. Burchard, "Role Conflicts of Military Chaplains," *American Sociological Review,* Vol. XIX, No. 5 (October, 1954).

29 William J. Goode, "A Theory of Role Strain," *American Sociological Review,* Vol. XXV, No. 4 (August, 1960).

so that organizational goals are achieved. Goode identifies two sets of techniques that the individual can use to reduce role strain. The first set involves limits on the acceptance of roles, for example by delegating functions to others or by erecting barriers against intrusion. The second set involves a "role bargain" whereby the individual manipulates his own level of activity in each role relationship with the more or less deliberate intention of maximizing gratification and minimizing strain.

An interesting feature of Goode's theory is his view of the family as a "role budget center" for both adults and children; most individuals must account to their families for allocations of effort outside the family, and the family provides a vantage point from which all role prescriptions can be viewed in perspective.

There are probably other role budget centers as well. At least one study describes an adolescent peer group that served this purpose for its participants through schooling, military service, professional training, marriage, and career experience.[30] There are indications that industrial peer groups and even corporate hierarchies sometimes assume the allocation function for an individual's outside roles. (See Chapter Eight.)

This theory of role strain also helps to explain why promotion or demotion in an organization is often followed by more changes in the subject's interaction network than appear to be objectively required.

The dilemmas of succession. The dilemmas of succession are both quantitative and qualitative and are not theoretically solvable. Given the uncertainties of human health and tenure, there is no way of insuring that whenever a vacancy occurs there will be a suitable candidate to fill it, unless a great surplus of candidates is trained. If this is done, most candidacies will be frustrated, competition for promotion will be bitter, and the disappointed candidates will either leave the organization or remain as treacherous subordinates to their successful rivals. If it is not done, some people will be rewarded for unsatisfactory achievement by promotion to positions for which they are plainly unfit, and the legitimacy of the status order will be undermined. All organizations, large and small, are confronted from time

[30] Murray B. Seidler and Mel Jerome Ravitz, "A Jewish Peer Group." *American Journal of Sociology,* Vol. LXI, No. 1 (July, 1955).

to time with variants of this dilemma. Being immortal but staffed with mortal men, they develop vacancies periodically. For some openings there will be too many candidates, for others too few. The career system of any large organization is *necessarily* unfair, since individual advancement will be affected by accidents of timing.[31] Some men rise easily with the help of successive coincidences. Others, equally deserving, can hope for promotion only after long delay.

Even if the number of positions should match the number of candidates (a condition sometimes approached in rapidly expanding organizations), there remains the difficulty that a change of status usually involves a change of activity and that the correlation between performance in one activity and performance in another is imperfect. Indeed, performance tends to be most unpredictable at just those critical points at which promotion involves a great increase in responsibility. The incompetent director, manager, commander, or president can demoralize or even destroy a thriving organization. Unfortunately, there is no sure method by which his incompetence can be foreseen.

This brings us to the qualitative dilemma that arises because a successor is always evaluated in comparison with his predecessor. A change of style seems to be called for if the predecessor was highly successful (because another performance in the same style will be invidiously compared), and also if he was unsuccessful (the style stands discredited and the mechanisms that defeated the predecessor are still intact). This is vividly shown in the two available case studies of succession in industrial management, those of Gouldner and Guest.[32] The two successors in these studies were faced with nearly identical situations: production had been declining in their respective plants and they were assigned to improve it. Gouldner's successor tried to increase stratification, with doubtful results. Guest's successor fostered integration, with conspicuous suc-

---

[31] The effect of various age gaps on succession and replacement has been explored, only half humorously, by C. Northcote Parkinson, *Parkinson's Law and Other Studies in Administration* (Boston: Houghton Mifflin, 1957), and again in his *Inlaws and Outlaws* (Boston: Houghton Mifflin, 1962).

[32] Alvin W. Gouldner, *Patterns of Industrial Bureaucracy* (Glencoe, Ill.: Free Press, 1954), and Robert H. Guest, *Organizational Change: The Effect of Successful Leadership* (Homewood, Ill.: Irwin-Dorsey, 1962). The point at issue here is discussed by Guest in "Managerial Succession in Complex Organizations" and by Gouldner in a "Comment" on Guest's paper, *American Journal of Sociology*, Vol. LXVIII, No. 1 (July, 1962).

cess. Both authors explain how the behavior of the successor was conditioned by that of his predecessor. Gouldner's predecessor was well known and highly respected in the close-knit community surrounding the plant. The legitimacy of succession was questioned from the outset. Guest's predecessor was a nervous authoritarian, very similar to Gouldner's successor; he left no cadre of loyal retainers behind him. In this case, the successor began with the tentative support of all his subordinates, who hoped for some improvement over the predecessor's unsatisfactory ways. Gouldner's successor faced the active opposition of workers and supervisors alike; both groups were firmly committed to the predecessor's managerial style and feared change. The personalities of the new men must certainly have played a part in the respective outcomes, but it is at least conceivable that the results would have been reversed had each been given the other's predecessor. Gouldner makes the interesting comment that

> The administrative constraints on, or opportunities available to, a successor will differ radically with the structural arrangements prevailing under his predecessor. For example, the successor who follows a situation in which punishment-centered bureaucracy was established has an opportunity to recharge subordinates' motivations by withholding or reducing the constraints previously in effect. The very possibility of the *success* of a representative bureaucracy may depend on the subordinates' experience with the prior, less gratifying organizational structure. If, however, a successor enters a situation in which representative bureaucracy had prevailed, it may be more difficult for him to improve upon the prior level of gratifications supplied subordinates. The latter may come to take the gratifications which they had previously experienced for granted, and there may be a tendency for their motivation (to conform and to produce) to run down even in a representative bureaucracy, perhaps thereby readying the organization for a swing back to more punishment-centered forms.[33]

The dilemmas of succession are so threatening to the organizational program that—for small organizations at least—a low rate of succession seems to favor a high level of achievement. In very large organizations, on the other hand, there appears to be an inverse correlation between size and the rate of succession in top

[33] Gouldner, "Comment," *op. cit.,* p. 55.

positions. Grusky,[34] whose studies have focused on this point, suggests that the largest business corporations are capable of routinizing succession and thus of decreasing its disruptive aspects. It has also been suggested that very large organizations require rapid succession at the top in order to maintain a suitable rate of adjustment to their very complex environments.

The local and the cosmopolitan.[35] The interesting distinction between the local and the cosmopolitan has been applied principally to academic men, especially to research scientists, but seems to be relevant in some degree for other professionals, businessmen, artists, journalists, and even craftsmen. The *local* is committed to a particular organization, such as a research institute, the cosmopolitan to a field or to a set of organizations. The ambitious local wants to be made department head or director; the cosmopolitan dreams of gold medals or an office in a national society. The local, when he is successful, enjoys a personal reputation that cannot be transferred to another milieu, since it rests on his past contributions to the organization and his special knowledge of it. The cosmopolitan is known everywhere his art is practiced and has relatively few roots in his particular job, even after he has held it for half a lifetime.

The dichotomy is not absolute, of course, but rather a continuum

[34] Oscar Grusky, "Managerial Succession and Organizational Effectiveness" (paper presented at the 1962 meetings, American Sociological Association), "Administrative Succession in Formal Organizations," *Social Forces,* Vol. XXXIX, No. 3 (December, 1960), and "Corporate Size, Bureaucratization, and Managerial Succession," *American Journal of Sociology,* Vol. LXVII, No. 3 (November, 1961). See also Louis Kriesberg, "Careers, Organization Size, and Succession," *American Journal of Sociology,* Vol. LXVIII, No. 3 (November, 1962), and Bernard Levenson, "Bureaucratic Succession," in Amitai Etzioni (ed.), *Complex Organizations: A Sociological Reader* (New York: Holt, Rinehart & Winston, 1961).

[35] The terms were devised by Robert K. Merton, *Social Theory and Social Structure* (rev. ed.; Glencoe, Ill.: Free Press, 1957). For various applications see Herbert Shepard, "Nine Dilemmas in Industrial Research," *Administrative Science Quarterly,* December, 1956; Hollis W. Peter, "Human Factors in Research Administration," in Rensis Likert and Samuel P. Hayes, Jr. (eds.), *Some Applications of Behavioral Research* (UNESCO, 1957); Alvin W. Gouldner, "Cosmopolitans and Locals: Toward an Analysis of Latent Social Roles," *Administrative Science Quarterly,* March, 1958; David Riesman, *Constraint and Variety in American Education* (Lincoln, Nebr.: University of Nebraska, 1956); Barney C. Glaser, "Some Functions of Recognition in a Medical Research Organization" (unpublished dissertation, Columbia University, 1961), and "The Local–Cosmopolitan Scientist," *American Journal of Sociology,* Vol. LXIV, No. 3 (November, 1963).

from one polar type to the other. It reflects both the structure of organizational sets and of individual careers. There is a tendency for low-ranking organizations in a set to be staffed by locals, partly because they are less qualified for cosmopolitan competition and partly because achievement in a low-prestige organization has little exchange value. As we move up the prestige order of the set, the proportion of cosmopolitans increases; but it may decline again at the top, where the highest-ranking organizations offer sufficient rewards to discourage outward mobility.

Almost by necessity, the modes of socialization for locals and cosmopolitans differ. Over and above the training that is technically required, cosmopolitans are developed by apprenticeship and their careers depend on the continued support of sponsors in the same discipline. Locals discover their roles by assimilation, and their security is based on extensive interaction within a single organization. Whenever both types are represented in the same situation, those in the minority are likely to get hard treatment. This is the case in graduate schools of high prestige, for example, where the student preparing for a local career is forced to satisfy cosmopolitan requirements in a clumsy and time-consuming fashion.

RESISTANCE TO SOCIALIZATION

Adaptation and nonadaptation. The prevailing typology of resistance to socialization is set forth by Merton in his classic essay on social structure and anomie.[36] Five modes of adaptation are listed as follows:

Table 5–1

A TYPOLOGY OF MODES OF INDIVIDUAL ADAPTATIONS

MODES OF ADAPTATION	CULTURE GOALS	INSTITUTIONALIZED MEANS
I. Conformity	plus	plus
II. Innovation	plus	minus
III. Ritualism	minus	plus
IV. Retreatism	minus	minus
V. Rebellion	plus/minus	plus/minus

[36] Merton, "Social Structure and Anomie," in *American Sociological Review,* Vol. III, No. 5 (October, 1938).

Although this typology refers to individual adaptations in social systems (a higher level of abstraction), it applies without any revision to the possible outcomes of socialization. The conformer, the innovator, the ritualist, the retreatist, and the rebel can be readily identified in case studies of organizational careers.

Modes of nonadaptation are not distributed randomly. The mode of nonadaptation appears to be determined by the mode of socialization. In the Coast Guard Academy case previously described, the cadet's time is controlled too rigidly to permit much innovation or ritualism, and the legal code makes rebellion very dangerous. Retreatism is the only mode of nonadaptation permitted, and it is prevalent—two out of three students drop out before completing the course.

Among the river pilots in Clemens' account, retreatism was unusual; the occupation was too rewarding in pay, prestige, and enjoyment. Rebellion was nearly impossible, since the apprentice could not change masters or become a pilot without a master's approval. Ritualism was inhibited by the continuous presence of an audience—pilots, officers, passengers, crew—before whom the goal of safe passage could not be questioned. Innovation was possible and frequent. Both apprentices and pilots dressed oddly and affected eccentricities. They innovated continually in their work, each apprentice being expected to develop a style of his own.

In the Senate, the Inner Club is organized in a way that does not give new Senators much scope for innovation or for ritualism. They cannot hope to change the existing structure in the short run, and there are no rituals available for outsiders to follow. The alternatives—as in most situations involving an inner circle—are retreatism, if the candidate contents himself with his membership in the outer circle, or rebellion, if he challenges the legitimacy of the whole arrangement.[37]

The Friendly First Bank obtains an unusually high degree of conformity. Rebellion is unthinkable in its genteel corridors. Retreatism is rare; few employees ever resign, presumably those who might do so having been excluded in the initial selection. Innovation,

---

[37] Senator Joseph S. Clark of Pennsylvania attacked the Senate's inner circle in March, 1963, describing it in a speech from the floor as "a self-perpetuating oligarchy with overtones of plutocracy." *Newsweek*, March 11, 1963.

repressed by a variety of devices, elicits immediate disapproval. Ritualism then is the sole available mode of nonadaptation and is of such common occurrence in the daily operations of the Friendly First Bank that it can hardly be distinguished from conformity.

Likewise, among the interns, rebellion, retreatism, and innovation seem to be effectively blocked as modes of adaptation, leaving ritualism as the prevalent expression of nonadaptation.

From the standpoint of the organization the intermediate types of nonadapters, the innovators and the ritualists, are not complete liabilities. They are not actively antagonistic toward the program and they bring it some support. However, in contrast to fully socialized members, they cannot be counted upon in episodes of crisis: they lack the predictability of the fully socialized. In the case of the innovators, a change of goals will not necessarily be followed by changes in the individual's behavior that are appropriate from the organization's point of view. In the case of the ritualists, the change in activity required by some modification of the organizational program will not necessarily be followed by an appropriate readjustment of values.

The loss of idealism. One of the most curious aspects of the socialization process in large organizations is that it is often observed to involve the progressive abandonment of the organization's major values. The phenomenon has been reported in detail for army recruits, physicians in training, and college students.[38] In the light of our previous discussion, it must appear very strange that successful socialization may lead to the rejection of organizational values already internalized.

The key to the understanding of this paradoxical question seems to be found in analyzing unresolved contradictions between formal and informal goals, inconsistencies between the organization's creed and its program.[39] The displacement of "idealism" by "cynicism"

---

[38] The taboo on expressions of patriotism among combat soldiers is described in Samuel A. Stouffer et al., *The American Soldier* (Princeton, N.J.: Princeton University Press, 1949) and other studies; the development of cynicism about medicine in Merton et al., *The Student Physician, op. cit.;* the college student's alienation from educational values in Philip Jacobs, *Changing Values in College* (New York: Harper, 1957).

[39] For a full discussion of conflicts between organizational creeds and programs, see Thurman W. Arnold, *The Folklore of Capitalism* (New Haven,

in the course of socialization can usually be traced to increasing familiarity with illegitimate elements whose existence and purposes are unfamiliar to outsiders. In the course of socialization, the recruit learns that he must participate in the illegitimate activities and follow sequences of activity that cannot be justified by the goals the organization displays to the outside world. The discovery may be disturbing to him. In rejecting the ideal of optimum patient care, the medical student experiences some anxiety. Unpatriotic soldiers or students to whom education has become a game of tactics played for grades are similarly affected. When the inconsistency between creed and program is not acute, they can be reconciled by a rationalization or a ceremony. When they are blatantly inconsistent, the exposed individual is often moved to reject the values of the organization altogether, and, in extreme cases, to construct a negative ideology in which the terms of the original creed are displaced by their opposites to make a sort of organizational Black Mass. The cynicism of the veteran reporter, disillusioned politician, thirty-year soldier, or weary and overexperienced professional in any field may be counterbalanced by a secret adherence to some purified form of the creed the vulgar version of which he derides. The number of such negative adherents who can be accommodated in a given organization depends upon the nature of its program and the stability of its goals.

Conn.: Yale University Press, 1937), pp. 356 et seq., and Robin M. Williams, Jr., *American Society* (New York: Knopf, 1952), p. 356.

CHAPTER SIX

Organizational Sets

WHAT IS AN ORGANIZATIONAL SET?

An organizational set consists of two or more organizations of the same type, each of which is continuously visible to every other. The sociology departments of major universities constitute a set. So do the Protestant churches in a small city, the baseball teams in the American League, the teen-agers' clubs at a settlement house, or the leading manufacturers of electrical equipment. The members of a set are organizations, not people. The set itself may be organized, as in the case of the American League, but this does not influence its structure as a set as much as might be expected.

For reasons that will presently appear, it is almost impossible to discover an organization that does not belong to any set; but some sets are much more important than others, just as some of an individual's reference groups are more important than others. Some organizations are much more influenced by their sets than others, just as some individuals are more influenced by their reference groups. An organization is usually identified with more than one set at a time, some of them overlapping. For example, Columbia College in New York City belongs to a set of colleges called the Ivy League, to another set identified as eastern men's colleges, to the set of liberal arts colleges located in the city, and to the set of colleges that are part of Columbia University.

Not every group of organizations constitutes a set. The organizations may be very similar in structure but blocked off from continuous communication. Or they may be in continuous communication but differ in some crucial way that prevents comparison between them. Comparison is the essential function of an organizational set, and every set generates a prestige order that is recognized by participants and usually by an outside audience as well.

Prestige, as we understand the term, can be analogous to status but is not at all the same thing. Status is a measure of the influence explicitly assigned to a given position in a given organization. Prestige is a composite of opinion about the relative value of an individual or a group or a symbol in a given context. Whereas status is fixed and verifiable, prestige is inherently subjective and can never be determined unequivocally. The status of an individual in an organization is the same regardless of the observer, but his prestige varies with different observers and even with the moods of an observer.

On the other hand, prestige is no less real for being vague. Prestige orders are as essential as status orders in a social system. Their functions are different but equally crucial. Moreover, since there is always some important relationship between status and prestige in a particular situation, we cannot fully understand one without taking account of the other.

The functions of a prestige order for an organizational set are roughly analogous to the functions of a status order for an organization. According to Barnard,[1] the functions of status in cooperative systems are (a) facilitating communication, (b) providing incentive, and (c) imposing responsibility. The dysfunctions are (a) distorted evaluation of individuals, (b) restriction of mobility, (c) injustice, (d) the exaggeration of authority, (e) oversymbolization, and (f) limited adaptability.

Following this outline, the primary functions of prestige in organizational sets are: (a) facilitating communication among the organizations in the set and with outside audiences, (b) providing competitive incentives, and (c) regulating cooperation and conflict among the member organizations.

The dysfunctions of prestige for an organizational set are similar to the dysfunctions of status for a single organization. The prestige

[1] Chester I. Barnard, "The Functions of Status Systems," in Robert K. Merton, Ailsa P. Gray, Barbara Hockey, and Hanan C. Selvin (eds.), *Reader in Bureaucracy* (Glencoe, Ill.: Free Press, 1952), pp. 242–55.

order (a) leads to unrealistic definitions of situations, (b) hampers mobility between organizations, (c) rewards equal performance unequally in different places, (d) exaggerates the importance of strong organizations at the expense of the weak, (e) induces the sort of organizational paranoia discussed at length in the next section, and (f) limits the plasticity of organizational structure in relation to a changing environment. Some of the least excusable patterns of human irrationality arise from prestige orders in organizational sets, including the worst follies of nationalism.

The reasons that make organizations responsive to the prestige order and that motivate the struggle for prestige in a set are parallel to those that explain the striving for status within the individual organization. Prestige is a scarce good. The scarcity of high prestige is self-evident from the rank order itself. The higher an organization's prestige, the more it can influence the formation of standards of achievement in its set and therefore the greater its ability to meet those standards. Prestige is also valued because, as we shall presently see, it determines the exchange value commanded in the general society by the statuses of a given organization.

The available empirical evidence suggests that all organizational sets develop a prestige order. This means that a large proportion of the members of each organization are able to compare their own and other organizations on general prestige. The highest-ranking organization in a set is visualized as "better" or "higher" or "stronger" than the others, as well as being evaluated on specific characteristics. In addition to the organizations involved, there are often outside audiences interested in the prestige order of a set.

The reliability of prestige ranking varies from one set to another and is subject to certain peculiar distortions that will be discussed a little later. Different audiences sometimes develop quite different prestige orders for the same set of organizations, but this is an unusual and unstable condition. Most prestige orders command fair but not overwhelming agreement from the different audiences concerned and show moderate reliability of rating. There is usually better agreement about the highest and lowest rankings than about intermediate places. Perfect consensus as to which organization occupies the first place in the set is not unusual.

The fact that organizational sets have a number of major and important functions explains their ubiquity. They include: (a) the transmission and refinement of the institutional model, (b) the allocation of scarce resources, (c) procedural experimentation, (d) comparative appraisal of achievement, (e) diffusion of inventions and discoveries, and (f) exchange of personnel.[2]

Organizations, as we know, are designed according to an institutional pattern that is part of a relevant culture. The institutional pattern may be visualized as a kind of blueprint that tells the naive founder of an organization how to go about his work and enables him to discover later at what points he deviated from the perfect plan. But since one would search the cellars of the culture in vain for an actual repository of such blueprints, the matter is not a simple one. Even when organizations have written constitutions and bylaws and formal specifications of procedure, these turn out not to be very informative. New organizations, it appears, are usually designed to imitate existing organizations. They are staffed by people experienced in these other organizations and who carry the patterns in their heads. Thus a new precinct club or juvenile gang or international bank is least likely to be innovative when it first appears.

Useem, Useem, and Gibson, in an admirable study of neighboring, show how the upwardly mobile middle-class family moves through successive sets of neighbors in the course of its self-advancement, learning from each set in turn the life style that is appropriate for a nuclear family of that particular time, place, and socioeconomic level.[3]

> . . . the residential neighborhood has become, for upwardly mobile men stripped of kin and whose values stem primarily from the work role, the locus for working out the supporting framework for the functioning of their nuclear family and the basis for entrance into other supporting institutions of church, school, clubs, etc. The high preoccupation of the men with the social and status characteristics of their neighbors and neighborhood is understandable, for it stems from their need to have consistency and mutually reinforcing life segments.

[2] The religious *denomination* is a type of organizational set that displays these latter functions with unusual clarity. See, for example, David O. Moberg, *The Church as a Social Institution: The Sociology of American Religion* (Englewood Cliffs, N.J.: Prentice-Hall, 1962).

[3] Ruth Hill Useem, John Useem, and Duane L. Gibson, "The Function of Neighboring for the Middle-class Male," *Human Organization*, Vol. XIX, No. 2 (Summer, 1960). The quotation is from page 69.

Incredibly subtle resemblances appear in a set of suburban families, or of passenger liners on the Atlantic run, or of companies in a new industry, or of the separated barracks in an internment camp. The organizational set is rapid and sensitive in its transmission of instructions for building and remodeling tables of organization. These instructions are usually only advisory, but in the presence of an exigent outside audience they may be compelling.

Thus Coleman,[4] in his study of secondary schools, discovered that the status system in private schools and for girls in public schools (in his sample) was free to "wander" according to local conditions, with more weight given to academic achievement in some schools and more to sociability in others. The status system for boys in public schools was comparatively uniform and based on interscholastic athletics. The presence of an outside audience imposes requirements on the set that shape the status system of each school.

> . . . A school and the community surrounding it cannot hold its head up if it continues to lose games. It *must* devote roughly the same attention to athletics as do the schools surrounding it, for athletic games are the only games in which it engages other schools and, by representation, other communities.

The influence of an outside audience on the internal structure of organizations in a set has also been described in detail by Perrow,[5] in his study of a general hospital. This is one of the few studies so far that have focused directly on the way in which a prestige order influences the goals of the organizations in a set.

> If an organization and its product are well regarded, it may more easily attract personnel influence, relevant legislation, wield informal power in the community, and insure adequate numbers of clients, customers, donors, or investors. Organizations may be placed along a continuum from unfavorable to favorable public images. A predominantly favorable image we shall call "prestige," and it may range from low to high.

[4] James S. Coleman, "The Adolescent Subculture and Academic Achievement," *American Journal of Sociology,* Vol. LXV, No. 4 (January, 1960). The quotation is from pages 346–47.

[5] Charles Perrow, "Organizational Prestige: Some Functions and Dysfunctions," *American Journal of Sociology,* Vol. LXVI, No. 4 (January, 1961). The quotation is from page 335.

In the hospital he studied, Perrow discerns the deflection of effort from intrinsic to extrinsic standards for measuring achievement— for example, a preference for research and clinical activities that can be publicized. Throughout his analysis, he shows how these deflections are related to the competitive process. The client, consumer, or donor has a choice of organizations to support and makes that choice in accordance with his own perception of the prestige order in the set.

Because prestige orders govern the allocation of resources in most sets, they are self-reinforcing, and, in the absence of countertendencies, the prestige differences in a set may be expected to grow wider with time. In fact this often does occur, particularly in organizations that are conservative in outlook and have limited possibilities of structural change, such as museums and the standing committees of legislatures. In many sets of this kind the reinforcement of differences proceeds so far that the prestige order becomes nearly as explicit as a status order.

Another tendency that is constantly at work to freeze existing prestige differences is for the institutional model to be transmitted from the top downward. There are no literal blueprints for building organizations of a particular type or for reconstructing them as the institutional pattern slowly shifts. What happens instead is that each organization in a set functions as a partial model to those below it while continuously imitating those above. The leading organization in any set (the Boston Symphony, General Motors, the New York Yankees) comes to be regarded as the embodiment of the pattern. Since other organizations in the set lose prestige by deviating from the procedures of the leading organization, the latter may exercise an influence over its followers and competitors that at times approaches outright control. A famous study by Harbison and Dubin [6] shows how collective bargaining between one automobile manufacturer and one union local, each first in its own set, determined the outcome of negotiations throughout the automobile industry and, to some extent, throughout the national economy. Competition for available resources is also regulated in more subtle ways. The prestige order

[6] Frederick H. Harbison and Robert Dubin, *Patterns of Union-Management Relations* (Chicago: Science Research Associates, 1947).

in an organizational set, by its very nature, defines and limits subsets.[7] For example, the set of manufacturers in an industrial market almost always includes a recognized subset of two to five market leaders, another subset of small but solidly established competitors, and another subset of marginal low-quality producers who are viewed with some hostility by the others. Indeed, a meaningful division, something like this, is made in nearly any set with a sufficient number of members, while much more intricate subdivisions occur in large sets.

The effect of the prestige order is to limit competition, decrease its costs, and impose order on the allocation process. Both the strong and the weak compete for the most part with others like themselves and measure their gains and losses of prestige in relation to their near neighbors in the prestige order.

Fortunately for the cause of social change, there are also tendencies at work in organizational sets that reduce prestige differences and permit organizations to change places. Often these are external: the environments of some may become less favorable while others are finding new resources. For example, the fortunes of a community hospital are affected by changes in the community population over which the hospital staff has no control.

Another source of instability is the tendency for decisive innovations to enter the institutional pattern through organizations of intermediate prestige. This tendency admits of many exceptions and is difficult to describe because it has not yet been studied in detail. Innovations introduced in an organization of intermediate prestige are often then adopted by imitators at adjacent prestige levels, taken up after considerable lag by some of the leaders in the set and, finally (by being incorporated in the institutional pattern), diffused downward to the remaining members of the set. This path has been followed again and again in the introduction of new academic subjects into the college and university curriculum. New subjects are usually introduced on the restless campuses of middling colleges and universities. Some of them die there; others are imitated on adjacent levels of academic prestige; while a few are ultimately adopted by one or another of the great universities and then diffuse downward

---

[7] Shown with special clarity in Erwin O. Smigel, *The Wall Street Lawyer: Professional Organization Man?* (New York: Free Press, 1964).

again to become standard subjects in every curriculum. The leading universities, which are not usually associated with this missionary effort, may be the last finally to adopt the new subject. This has been the sequence followed by sociology, among many other subjects. Introduced first at Brown and Nebraska in the 1880's, it spread rapidly through the state universities of the Midwest and upper South, was endowed with respectability by Yale, Columbia, and Chicago, and then slowly diffused down the long, long ladder of academic prestige. It still has not reached the last of the small, denominational colleges. As is typical, some of the leaders excluded themselves from the adoption process or endorsed alternative approaches. Sociology, in its current form, was not established at California and Princeton until after World War II.

Similar sequences of adoption can be traced in their respective sets for such varied innovations as automation in steel-making, the double-wing back formation in football, and cost accounting in hospitals.

Needless to say, not all innovations are successful. The great majority of inventions, both technical and social, that are introduced in any institutional context never take root. Such experiments are observed by other organizations. The costs of experimentation in a well-integrated set are greatly reduced by the fact that each organization provides a laboratory for all of the others and enables them to assess the merits of proposed innovations or to compare alternative innovations before installing them.

The organizations in such sets are also training and proving grounds for each other's personnel. The individual's career is jointly determined by the prestige order of the set and the status orders of the organizations in which he participates. The career of the symphony musician provides an admirable example.[8]

There are several hundred units in the set of American symphony orchestras. All of them perform orchestral pieces drawn from the same repertory.[9] The repertory itself is a unified body of cultural material, the composers and works of which are his-

[8] See, for example, John H. Mueller, *The American Symphony Orchestra: A Social History of Musical Taste* (Bloomington, Ind.: Indiana University Press, 1951), John J. Sherman, *Music and Maestros* (Minneapolis, Minn.: University of Minnesota Press, 1952).

[9] Mueller, cited above, describes this configuration of composers and works and accounts for its development.

torically and culturally interdependent. The nature of the repertory imposes a common structure on every symphony orchestra. They are all, for example, divided into the same sections—first violins, second violins, cellos, flutes, trumpets, percussion, and so forth— and although the membership of an orchestra varies between forty and about one hundred and twenty, the relative size of sections remains fairly constant. All symphony orchestras concentrate overwhelming authority in the conductor and limit the section heads to minor technical and administrative matters. Most of them have the same small roster of nonplaying positions, such as business manager and librarian.[10]

There are several other reasons why the organizations in this large set follow a uniform institutional pattern. The pattern is old, as modern institutions go. The composition of the orchestra has not changed significantly since the early 1800's, after being in constant flux during the three previous centuries. The age of the pattern in itself contributes to stability. Communication in the set is extraordinarily good, largely because of the traveling soloists who crisscross the country and the world, some of them playing with more than a hundred orchestras in the course of a year. The major sources of recruitment are a handful of music schools—Curtis, Juilliard, Eastman, and the European national conservatories—so that orchestral musicians throughout the country are linked together by friendships formed in training. The rate of movement of musicians among orchestras is high, partly because the overwhelming authority of the conductor precludes job security, partly because the opportunity for mobility is defined as an occupational advantage. Many musicians participate regularly in several orchestras. Finally, the curious fact that orchestras normally operate at a deficit, since box-office receipts are seldom sufficient to cover production costs, makes the orchestra particularly sensitive to the exigencies of its audience, and this audience is conservative in its musical preferences and generally opposed to institutional innovations.

[10] For the historical development of existing institutional patterns see, among others, L. A. Coerne, *The Evolution of Modern Orchestration* (New York: Macmillan, 1908), Paul Bekker, *The Story of the Orchestra* (New York: Norton, 1936), Arthur Loesser, *Men, Women and Pianos* (New York: Simon and Schuster, 1954), Theodore Caplow, "The Influence of Radio on Music as a Profession" (Paris: *Cahiers d'Etudes de Radio–Television*, Nos. 3–4, 1955), and Jacques Barzun, *Music in American Life* (New York: Doubleday, 1956).

Within the total set of American symphony orchestras, three subsets are distinguishable. At the top of the prestige order are a dozen major orchestras. The typical major orchestra was founded in the nineteenth century and has been led by a series of internationally famous conductors. Its audience is wealthy and solidly established. It has its own hall and a fringe of auxiliary associations. The procedure for meeting the annual deficit has been so well routinized that organizational survival is seldom in doubt. Its recordings are much in demand and are made with the best of the world's soloists. The musician in the major orchestra is seldom paid enough to live without outside employment, but he has a wide range of possibilities for extra work, and if he takes pupils, commands high fees.

The next subset includes about a hundred fully professional orchestras. Most of them are located in small cities that have an enthusiastic but somewhat undependable audience. They play in rented halls or public auditoriums, make few recordings, and economize in their choice of soloists. Their seasons are short. Most members are paid the minimum union scale and supplement their earnings by outside employment, often in a nonmusical occupation, as well as by music teaching and arranging or jobs playing jazz and popular music.

The largest and lowest subset consists of civic orchestras, staffed mainly by amateurs playing for pleasure, with a few paid professionals in key positions. These orchestras play only a few concerts a year, although they may rehearse regularly. Box-office receipts are very low, the survival of the orchestra from year to year is always in doubt, and deficits are met either by the amateur members of the orchestra or by local subsidies. Participation in the civic orchestra is only another occasional job for the professional musician, although he may derive some prestige from it as a conductor or soloist.

When we examine the marketplace for orchestral musicians, we discover that it is governed by a number of definite principles that may be summarized in the concept of the *exchange value of statuses*.

In every organizational set that allows individuals to move from one member organization to another or that expects individuals from two or more organizations in the set to meet and interact, people in these categories will be able to evaluate the status conferred by the organization to which they belong in relation to the statuses conferred by other organizations in the same set. In the example we have been using, a musician will not voluntarily move from one orchestra to another unless the status of his new position is at least as valuable as that of the position he now holds. He must be able to make this kind of evaluation in order to make a rational decision. The orchestra seeking to hire him does not want to offer a status less valuable than he now holds, which he may be expected to refuse, nor to offer much more than the minimum necessary inducement, since overrewarding newcomers will make established members restless and turn their eyes to greener pastures. Both orchestras and musicians need a method of evaluation, and not any method will do. The results must accord with the perceptions of the people involved.

In a milieu in which personal mobility in all directions is high and informal interaction between relative strangers is frequent, it is very important for individuals meeting outside the boundaries of their own organizations to be able to assess each other's professional standing, identify themselves as equal or unequal and, if unequal, to estimate the difference.

The solution to these problems is one of the key functions of the organizational set, and in this case, perhaps its *raison d'être*. The solution consists of taking organizational prestige as a kind of coefficient to be applied to organizational status. The product is the exchange value of an individual's status. It measures what status is worth outside the organization, but still in the same set, when compared with the claims of others who have had comparable achievements.

A numerical example will illustrate how the exchange value of a status is calculated. The example given below is made up out of whole cloth, since the research necessary for accurate estimation has not been carried out. As a further caution, it should be recalled that prestige is a composite of opinion that fluctuates from one observer to another and from one time period to the next, so that all numerical estimates of prestige are somewhat unreliable. On the other hand, the rank orders of status and prestige in the example do command high consensus, and the fact that the numbers given are arbitrary estimates should not affect the demonstration of how such mechanisms work.[11]

[11] The somewhat similar mechanisms that govern the exchange of scholarly personnel among universities are analyzed at length in Theodore Caplow and Reece J. McGee, *The Academic Marketplace* (New York: Basic Books, 1962), especially Chapter 4, "How Performance Is Evaluated."

The arbitrary estimates are as follows:

ORCHESTRAS	RELATIVE PRESTIGE (*estimated*)
Boston Symphony	100
Cleveland Orchestra	50
Indianapolis Symphony Orchestra	30
Duluth Civic Orchestra	5

POSITIONS	RELATIVE STATUS (*estimated*)
Conductor	10
Assistant conductor	3
First desk	2
Section man	1

First let us see what these assumptions mean with regard to the exchange of personnel. Informal interaction and the appraisal of experience will follow the same lines and need not be separately considered. An interesting complication omitted in the interest of simplicity is that the sections of an orchestra themselves constitute an organizational set with their own prestige order in which, for example, cellists stand higher than bass players. Consider first the extreme points of the illustration. The Boston conductor with an exchange value of 1000 cannot receive a serious offer from anywhere else in the system; the Cleveland conductor (500) would be strongly lured by the Boston conductorship but by no other position. The assistant conductor at Boston (300) would probably leap at the Cleveland conductorship and be torn by indecision if offered the same post at Indianapolis (300). At the other end of the scale the conductor at Duluth (50) would not accept an offer as a simple section man at Indianapolis (30), but he would probably consider a first desk there (60) and ought to find a first desk offer from Cleveland (100) irresistible. In need of a conductor, Duluth (50) might hope to attract a section man from Indianapolis (30) or even from Cleveland (50), but except for the conductorship, it would not hope to recruit anyone at all from the other three orchestras since its next best position, assistant conductor, has only half the exchange value (15) of the lowest-ranking position at Indianapolis (30). Conversely, Boston, Cleveland, and Indianapolis can easily make an irresistible offer to anyone else at Duluth.

Boston can ordinarily take whom it pleases from Indianapolis (except for the Indianapolis conductor) since a Boston section man (100) has a higher exchange value than the assistant conductor at Indianapolis (90).

Systems such as these have very long ramifications. Besides the exchange value of a position in the organizational set, positions also have a kind of exchange value in the general society, in which information about any organization and the set to which it belongs is much more vague and evaluations rely heavily on specific titles. For this reason, there are many sets in which men refuse to move to a position with a lower title in a parallel organization, even though the new position has a higher exchange value. This is the case in the academic system, for example, where it is rare for a full professor to accept a new position as an associate professor. The exchange values of the set continue to govern offers and acceptances, but certain exchanges are permanently blocked off.

THE AGGRANDIZEMENT EFFECT

The aggrandizement effect is the upward distortion of an organization's prestige by its own members. The distortions are often spectacular. Studying sets of squadrons at two Air Force bases, Mack found more than half of the squadrons were ranked first in prestige by their own members.[12] In a study of 122 university departments, 51 percent of the departments sampled were rated by their own chairmen as among the first five in the country and only 5 percent as having lower than average prestige in the set to which they belonged.[13] In a study by the author of a sample of sets representing 33 different types of organization,[14] raters overestimated the prestige

[12] Raymond W. Mack, "The Prestige System of an Air Base: Squadron Rankings and Morale," *American Sociological Review,* Vol. XIX, No. 3 (June, 1954).

[13] Caplow and McGee, *op. cit.* Table 5–5 shows the upward deviation of actual from expected ratings when chairmen evaluated their own departments.

[14] Unpublished manuscript, 1959. Fifty-five sets of six organizations each composed the sample. The types of organization represented were: fraternities, sororities, adolescent clubs, Protestant churches, Catholic churches, public high schools, denominational colleges, dance studios, nursing schools, hospital wards, restaurants, savings and loan associations, pest-control crews, community centers, country clubs, fashion shops, advertising agencies, Camp-

of their own organization (as seen by outsiders) eight times as often as they underestimated it. Similar results were obtained in a study of college sororities [15] and in numerous studies of occupations and professions.[16]

The aggrandizement effect typically has the following interesting characteristics:

1. An organization will be given a higher place in the prestige order of its set by its own members than by outsiders, including members of other organizations in the same set.
2. Members of an organization, while disagreeing with outsiders about the prestige of their own organization, will agree with them more or less about the prestige of all other organizations in the same set.
3. The amount of upward distortion when members evaluate the prestige of their own organizations will be roughly constant throughout the prestige order of a given set.[17]

The arithmetical consequences are curious. If the upward distortion is constant throughout the set, an array of ratings of organizations by their own members will show exactly the same prestige order as an array of ratings of the same organizations by outsiders. The bias, being uniform, cancels itself out and self-ratings may then be used to confirm the prestige estimates obtained from outside ratings.

fire Girl groups, YMCA branches, photographic crews, church clubs, banks, supermarkets, printeries, employment agencies, architectural offices, foreign-student clubs, Skid Row missions, trucking crews, department stores, religious foundations, and university departments.

[15] Ben Willerman and Leonard Swanson, "Group Prestige in Voluntary Organizations: A Study of College Sororities," *Human Relations,* Vol. VI, No. 1 (1953).

[16] Especially Peter M. Blau, "Occupational Bias and Mobility," *American Sociological Review,* Vol. XXII, No. 4 (August, 1957); Salomon Rettig, Frank N. Jacobson, and Benjamin Pasamanick, "Status Overestimation, Objective Status, and Job Satisfaction Among Professions," *American Sociological Review,* Vol. XXIII, No. 1 (February, 1958); and Alvin Zander, A. R. Cohen, and E. Stotland, "Power and Relations Among Professions," in Dorwin Cartwright (ed.), *Studies in Social Power* (Ann Arbor, Mich.: Institute for Social Research, University of Michigan, 1959).

[17] Except perhaps at the extremes. Mack, *op. cit.,* reports less than normal aggrandizement at the bottom of a prestige order, and the occupational studies just cited may be interpreted as showing less aggrandizement at the top.

At the same time, whenever the prestige of an organization, as perceived by its own members, is compared with the prestige conceded to it by another organization in the same set, there is certain to be some discrepancy. Since this latter kind of comparison will inevitably occur whenever the two organizations come into contact, the aggrandizement effect builds a solid basis for misunderstanding into the structure of any set.

The inflated appraisals of organizations by their own members may be viewed either as organizational fictions or as a kind of ignorance. According to Dubin [18] the functions of organizational fictions are to facilitate organizational change, to organize the future, to support organization offices and other elements of the structure, and either to facilitate or paralyze organizational action. Moore and Tumin,[19] in a classic paper, enumerate the functions of ignorance as the preservation of privileged positions, the reinforcement of traditional values, the preservation of fair competition, the preservation of stereotypes, and the provision of appropriate incentives for effort.

The consequences of the aggrandizement effect fit readily into both of these theoretical frameworks since the overestimate of an organization's prestige is equivalent to an inaccurate, favorably biased evaluation of its achievement. It makes leadership seem more effective than it has been, favors established procedures over innovations, exaggerates the value of membership, and reduces the attractiveness of outside affiliations. It may even bridge periods of crisis by concealing organizational failure. Above all, the aggrandizement effect enables an organization to satisfy its members more economically than would be possible if achievement were accurately evaluated. The self-aggrandizing organization places a perpetual premium on everything it has to offer and persuades its members to accept its dross as gold.

So much for the functions of the aggrandizement effect. It also has dysfunctions. By falsifying the measurement of performance, it diminishes the possibility of improvement. By raising the barriers to

---

[18] Robert Dubin (ed.), *Human Relations in Administration* (2d ed.; Englewood Cliffs, N.J.: Prentice-Hall, 1961), pp. 435–36.

[19] Wilbert E. Moore and Melvin M. Tumin, "Some Social Functions of Ignorance," *American Sociological Review,* Vol. XIV, No. 6 (December, 1949). See also Louis Schneider, "The Role of the Category of Ignorance in Sociological Theory: An Exploratory Statement," *American Sociological Review,* Vol. XXVII, No. 4 (August, 1962).

mobility, it tends to maintain less efficient organizations at the expense of the more efficient and to misallocate personnel and resources. Above all, by precluding a common frame of reference in the mutual dealings of parallel organizations, the aggrandizement effect introduces an undercurrent of dissension that is often fatal to peaceful cooperation.

XENOCENTRISM

The phenomenon of being oriented to a group other than one's own works in the direction opposite the aggrandizement effect and is much weaker. It was named by Kent and Burnight,[20] who paraphrased the definition of *ethnocentrism* in William Graham Sumner's *Folkways,* the "view of things in which one's own group is the center of everything, and all others are scaled with reference to it."

There is no doubt that organizational raters sometimes respond in this way. Mack, in the study cited above, shows how low-ranking food service and air police squadrons chose to identify with high-prestige bombing squadrons.[21] Merton and Kitt, in a famous discussion of positive orientation to nonmembership reference groups,[22] show how an individual may adopt the values of a group to which he aspires but does not belong. This anticipatory socialization serves the double purpose of aiding his rise into that group and of easing his adjustment after he has joined it. Xenocentric ratings of this kind seem to occur constantly in organizational sets such as country clubs or Protestant churches, in which mobility from lower- to higher-ranking organizations is encouraged.

In sets in which interorganization mobility is discouraged or prohibited, the admission of inferiority to an outside organization high in the prestige order often appears as a device for denying inferiority with reference to adjacent organizations or for rejecting any comparison at lower levels of prestige.

Another function of xenocentric rating is the disruption of com-

---

[20] Donald P. Kent and Robert G. Burnight, "Group Centrism in Complex Societies," *American Journal of Sociology,* Vol. LXVII, No. 3 (November, 1951). The quotation is from page 256.

[21] Mack, *op. cit.*

[22] Robert K. Merton and Alice S. Kitt, "Contributions to the Theory of Reference Group Behavior," in Robert K. Merton and Paul F. Lazarsfeld (eds.), *Continuities in Social Research* (Glencoe, Ill.: Free Press, 1950).

placency in an organization for the sake of internal reform. A conspicuous example has been the ascription of superiority to the Soviet educational system by American educators pressing for reforms in the curricula of their own schools.

THE DETERMINANTS OF PRESTIGE

The problem of explaining how organizational prestige is determined is similar to the problem of accounting for the prestige of a given organization in a given set or of explaining the class position of a particular individual in a particular community. The dimension measured has the same character in all three cases, since it is a composite of opinion based on a number of interrelated characteristics, each of which is interwoven with all the others but not completely predictable from them. In all three cases, the prestige variable itself has a margin of indeterminacy, varies somewhat according to the observer and the situation, and is better ascertained from real than hypothetical behavior.

Among the factors often correlated with organizational prestige are those that measure importance (age, size, wealth), those that measure internal equilibrium (stratification, integration, voluntarism, achievement), and those that evaluate the organization's present condition in the light of its own history (growing, declining, stable). The prestige of any organization is also affected by its alliances and affiliations with other organizations and by the prestige its members import from other contexts.

So much for the general process. In detail, there is room for considerable variation, and any one of these determining factors may be suppressed or reversed or specially weighted. Size may be inversely correlated with prestige in a set of private clubs or honorary societies. The effectiveness of a unit had no influence on prestige at the RAF base described by Paterson,[23] where prestige was a function of involvement in combat flying. There are not usually any affiliated organizations from which teen-age gangs can derive support, and we have mentioned how carefully all marks of outside status are suppressed among the students of a military academy. The method of determining prestige in any given set can be understood only after

---

[23] Thomas T. Paterson, *Morale in War and Work* (London: Parrish, 1955). Mack, *op. cit.*, reports partly comparable findings for an American air base.

close examination. Yet most of the factors listed above are correlated with organizational prestige in most sets.

There is, of course, a two-way connection between the status of individuals and the prestige of organizations. In the case of the business organization, for example, some writers view with alarm the individual's dependence on the organization for status and self-esteem, identifying it as a pathology due to overspecialization, mechanization, and alienation from work.[24] The status transaction between the individual and the corporation is seen as illicit and unwholesome: "The demand for status often expresses itself in sustained efforts to borrow prestige from whatever source possible. Organizations of many kinds now 'sell' prestige to their members, and employees borrow status from the company in which they work."[25]

Meanwhile, in a work published almost simultaneously, Packard documents and deplores the tendency to limit eligibility for executive positions in American companies to WASP's (White Anglo-Saxon Protestants), thus excluding a large proportion of the available talent and energy.[26]

Others, more neutral minded, regard the interlocking of nominally independent status and prestige orders as the key to understanding modern communities, an approach that is admirably summarized in Lamb's "Suggestions for a Study of Your Hometown."[27] This so-called reputational technique has been vigorously both criticized and defended, but the arguments have challenged the relationship of reputation to community power, not the fact of status consistency.[28] The tendency for status and prestige orders to converge in modern

[24] C. Wright Mills expands this theme eloquently in *White Collar: The American Middle Classes* (New York: Oxford University Press, 1951), quoting Karl Mannheim and others.

[25] Robert Presthus, *The Organizational Society: An Analysis and a Theory* (New York: Knopf, 1962), pp. 152–53.

[26] Vance Packard, *The Pyramid Climbers* (New York: McGraw-Hill, 1962), Chapter 3.

[27] Robert K. Lamb, "Suggestions for a Study of Your Hometown," Chapter 31 in Richard N. Adams and Jack J. Preiss, *Human Organization Research: Field Relations and Techniques* (Homewood, Ill.: Dorsey, 1960).

[28] For positions pro and con, see William V. D'Antonio and Eugene C. Erickson, "The Reputational Technique as a Measure of Community Power: An Evaluation Based on Comparative and Logitudinal Studies," *American Sociological Review,* Vol. XXVII, No. 3 (June, 1962), and Robert Dahl, "Equality and Power in American Society," in William V. D'Antonio and H. J. Ehrlich (eds.), *Power and Democracy in America* (Notre Dame, Ind.: University of Notre Dame Press, 1961).

communities has been studied very extensively.[29] It may be summarized by the following propositions:

1. The statuses of all the positions occupied by an individual tend to be (or become) consistent, that is, to have the same exchange values. Perfect status consistency [30] in a community would mean that the status difference of any two individuals, A and B, would be identical in every organization to which both of them belonged. Since status orders are often not comparable and any prestige measurement has a margin of uncertainty, perfect status consistency is never achieved in civil society, although it is closely approached in some special communities, such as the Foreign Service. Under most conditions, the practical limit of status consistency is a condition whereby an individual A who is superior to another individual B in the status order of one organization, is never inferior to B in the status order of another organization.

There is good evidence that inconsistent relationships are experienced as uncomfortable by the parties concerned.[31] This discomfort involves a problem for both organizations—specifically because each participant tries to withdraw from his less favorable situation and generally because status inconsistency induces restlessness and dissatisfaction.[32]

[29] A complete bibliography would occupy many pages. It would begin with two pivotal works, Pitirim Sorokin, *Social Mobility* (New York: Harper, 1927), Robert S. Lynd and Helen M. Lynd, *Middletown* (New York: Harcourt, Brace & World, 1929), and continue without interruption to the latest community survey. The most complete documentation of these cross-connections is in the series of Yankee City studies published by Lloyd Warner and his associates under various titles in the 1930's. The theory of status consistency is given in Elton F. Jackson, "Status Consistency and Symptoms of Stress," *American Sociological Review*, Vol. XXVII, No. 4 (August, 1962).

[30] A number of other terms have been used for the same concept, including *status crystallization* (Gerhard E. Lenski), *class crystallization* (Werner S. Landecker), *status congruency* (Stuart N. Adams), and *equilibration* (G. H. Fenchel, J. H. Monderer, and E. L. Hartley). *Consistency* seems to be gaining general acceptance.

[31] One recent investigator even finds evidence that status inconsistency produces "psychophysiological symptoms," Jackson, *op. cit.*

[32] As shown for example in Irwin W. Goffman, "Status Consistency and Preference for Change in Power Distribution," *American Sociological Review*, Vol. XXII, No. 3 (June, 1957), and B. B. Ringer and David L. Sills, "Political Extremists in Iran," *Public Opinion Quarterly*, Vol. XVI, No. 2 (Winter, 1952–53). The correlation between status inconsistency and dissatisfaction,

2. It follows from the above that persons who occupy positions of high status in high-prestige organizations will also tend to occupy positions of high status in other high-prestige organizations; that persons who occupy positions of low status in low-prestige organizations will tend to occupy similar positions in other low-prestige organizations and tend to be excluded altogether from high-prestige organizations; that persons who occupy positions of low status in organizations of high prestige will be able to claim positions of high status in organizations of low prestige; and that persons who occupy positions of high status in organizations of low prestige can only enjoy low status in organizations of high prestige.

By similar reasoning we might expect that persons having high status in high-prestige organizations would be excluded altogether from organizations of low prestige, while persons having low status in low-prestige organizations would be ineligible for organizations of high prestige. This, in fact, seems to be the case, subject to these qualifications:

1. There is a tendency, as the Yankee City studies show, for communities to display two distinct types of organizations: those limited to particular class levels, so that membership is equivalent to acceptance in a social class, and those that intentionally include representatives of several social classes and allow for a considerable range of social distance among members.

2. The absolute amount of participation is correlated with prestige, so that persons of high prestige will participate in more organizations, on the average, than persons of low prestige, and there will be proportionately more organizations with restricted upper-class membership than with restricted lower-class membership.[33]

---

enlarged to a grand scale, has been put forth as the primum mobile of economic history by Everett E. Hagen in his *Social Change* (Homewood, Ill.: Dorsey, 1962).

[33] Indeed, some studies have found practically no voluntary associations among the lowest socioeconomic groups. However, Minnis argues that many lower-class women's organizations are overlooked by investigators because of their limited means of publicity. Mhyra S. Minnis, "Cleavage in Women's Organizations: A Reflection of the Social Structure of a City," *American Sociological Review*, Vol. XVIII, No. 1 (February, 1953). Likewise, the findings of several studies comparing Negro and white participation in vol-

On the basis of the foregoing assumptions, we would expect to find a heavy concentration of high-status positions in a small circle of high-prestige people with multiple memberships but a tendency for the leadership of large-scale organizations to devolve upon persons of intermediate class position, who are able to participate in a maximum proportion of the total number of organizations. Mills' description of the participation of white-collar employees in the civic associations of middle-sized cities shows precisely this pattern:

> White-collar employees have no leaders active as their representatives in civic efforts; they are not represented as a stratum in the councils; they have no autonomous organizations through which to strive for political and civic ends; they are seldom, if ever, in the publicity spotlight. No articulate leaders appeal directly to them, or draw strength from their support. In the organized power of the middle-sized city, there is no autonomous white-collar unit.
>
> The few organizations in which white-collar employees are sometimes predominant—the Business and Professional Women's Clubs, the Junior Chamber of Commerce, and the YWCA—are so tied in with business groups that they have little or no autonomy. Socially, the lower white-collar people are usually on "the Elk level," the higher in the No. 2 or 3 social club; in both they are part of a "middle-class mingling" pattern. They are "led," if at all, by higher-income salesmen and other "contact people," who are themselves identified with "business," and whose activities thus lend prestige to businessmen rather than to white-collar people.[34]

We take the local community as our unit of discussion only because the implications of status consistency are more readily traceable within the highly visible boundaries of a town or small city than in a large unit. The principles involved are universal. The need for status consistency is felt whenever there is a possibility that individuals A and B, who interact in one organization, will also encounter each other in another organization. It even holds—although with much less force—when pairs of individuals who interact in an organization encounter each other in another organizational set. Thus, some pressure for status consistency can be discovered in the big city, the nation, the world—indeed, in any territorial or social

untary associations are mutually contradictory. See Nicholas Babchuk and Ralph V. Thompson, "The Voluntary Associations of Negroes," *American Sociological Review,* Vol. XXVII, No. 5 (October, 1962).

[34] Mills, *op. cit.,* p. 251.

community characterized by overlapping organizational memberships. On the other hand, the less the amount of overlapping, the
fewer the requirements for consistency. Metropolitan communities
harbor discrepancies of status that could not possibly occur in a
smaller and more autonomous place.[35]

A curious aspect of status consistency is discussed by Homans,
interpreting a study by Zander, Cohen, and Stotland,[36] on status and
valence differences among psychiatrists, psychologists, and social
workers. It appears that interprofessional contact was desired by
high-status psychiatrists and by low-status psychologists and social
workers but was avoided by the low-status members of the high-
prestige professions and the high-status members of the low-prestige
professions. Homans points out that

> . . . the members of the upper class who stood lowest within their
> class were most anxious to avoid contacts with members of the
> lower class, presumably because they might have had a hard time
> maintaining, over against these others, a superiority they were far
> from feeling within their own group. But the members of the upper
> class who were firmly established as high in status and the members
> of the lower class who were firmly established as low had nothing
> to lose by the contacts and welcomed them at least as a possibility.
> These people were more congruent in status than the others, who
> were either low men in a high group or high men in a low group.[37]

The concept of congruence is here given a further extension with
the suggestion that both "low men in high groups" and "high men
in low groups" are subject to something like status inconsistency when
they interact with people from other organizations in the same set
and isolate themselves from such contacts as far as circumstances
permit. The idea of exchange value may be usefully brought in
again. The men in each of these groups have statuses the exchange
value of which is much more typical of other organizations in the set
than of the one to which they belong. They are often in the curious
situation of dealing with "discordant equals," who have similar ex-

[35] Robert W. Hodge, "The Status Consistency of Occupational Groups,"
American Sociological Review, Vol. XXVII, No. 3 (June, 1962).

[36] George C. Homans, *Social Behavior: Its Elementary Forms* (New York:
Harcourt, Brace & World, 1961). The data were drawn from Zander, Cohen,
and Stotland, *op. cit.*

[37] *Ibid.,* p. 333.

change values based on quite different combinations of individual status and organizational prestige. This interesting concept suggests several lines of empirical research.

HOW TO RECOGNIZE ORGANIZATIONAL SETS

At the beginning of this chapter a set was defined as two or more organizations of the same type, each of which is continuously visible to every other. The key words in this definition are *of the same type*. One of the rare references to organizational sets in the sociological literature identifies a set as any cluster of related organizations, for example a business, its suppliers, its customers, its unions, and the government agencies with which it negotiates.[38] A moment's reflection will show that clusters of this kind are not like the organizational sets we have been discussing—they are not discrete entities, their boundaries are nebulous, and they do not have well-developed prestige orders.

The question remains: What is meant by organizations *of the same type?* The problem is trivial in a set of symphony orchestras; all of them have approximately the same table of organization, all perform the same activities, all are evaluated by the same standards and, at least in theory, their parts are interchangeable. The case is less clear if we consider the squadrons at an air base. Their tables of organization are similar but not identical. They have some activities in common but others (bombing, maintenance, supply, administration, security) that are quite dissimilar. Some of their personnel, such as squadron clerks, are interchangeable. Others, such as bombardiers, are not.

The problem lies not with our categories but with the nature of

[38] Blau and Scott use the term in this sense:

> By extension, one can speak of organization-sets or webs of organization, thus referring to the various other organizations to which any one organization is related, like the persons who form an individual's role-set, these organizations often make conflicting demands on a particular organization. For example, a business concern may find that it is linked with a large number of organizations and groups—competing firms, suppliers, customers, the board of directors representing the stockholders, government agencies, unions, professional associations, and possibly consumer organizations.

Peter M. Blau and W. Richard Scott, *Formal Organizations: A Comparative Approach* (San Francisco: Chandler, 1962), p. 195.

reality. We discover, on closer view, that no two organizations, even symphony orchestras, are likely to retain identical structures for very long. Diversity is as fundamental a feature of the organizational set as is the prestige order. What enables us to identify a set is the presence of a prestige order that is recognized by most participants, the interchangeability of *some* personnel, and the engagement of each organization in *some* important activities common to all members of the set. There is no hard and fast line between a set and a mere aggregate of organizations, but the more imperfectly the condition of similarity is met, the more indefinite becomes the prestige order and the less significant the function of the set in transmitting and modifying a common organizational culture.

The strain toward structural differentiation in ostensibly identical organizations deserves a little more attention. Barnard once wrote, referring to the company over which he himself presided:

> Suppose the Germans should drop a highly selective lethal gas on New Jersey that destroyed only the entire management organization of the New Jersey Bell Telephone Company (except the president, who has to be retained as a nucleus of a new organization). Now the scheme of organization of Bell Telephone companies is nearly standard, the New Jersey company is about one twentieth or one twenty-fifth of the whole system, so that, with some straining, it would in principle be feasible immediately to replace lost personnel by borrowing men from other companies. The replacing persons would know the formal organization, they would know the relations of their respective positions to all others relevant to their work, and each would possess adequate and tested technical competence for his position. How long would such an organization be able to function effectively? I would guess not more than twelve hours.[39]

Thompson [40] studied the operation of two Air Force wings, intended to be identical, with the same regulations, directives, and charts, reporting to the same headquarters, and comparable in equipment, personnel, length of time in existence, and mission. They even operated under similar weather conditions. He found major differences in the allocation and use of authority, the relative importance

[39] Chester I. Barnard, "Education for Executives," *Journal of Business*, Vol. XVIII (October, 1945).

[40] James D. Thompson, "Authority and Power in 'Identical' Organizations," *American Journal of Sociology*, Vol. LVII, No. 3 (November, 1956).

of positions in the command hierarchy, the functions attached to each position, the amount of administrative communication, and the pattern and direction of interaction between positions.[41]

The reasons for these differences were not completely discovered, although the personal characteristics of officers in the key positions seemed to have some effect. The commander of Wing A preferred to let his subordinates make decisions. He held them responsible for the conduct of operations and limited his authority to a veto power over their decisions. His opposite number in Wing B took more initiative and exercised more authority. Observation over a longer period might have shown other factors at work. Conceivably, what the observer perceived as personality traits were modes of behavior shaped by the necessities of their situations. With one exception, no senior officer in Wing A reported to the same superior position as his opposite number in Wing B.

An equally interesting case, on a much smaller scale, is described by Blau [42] in his study of employment interviewers in a state employment service. In this agency, the principal criterion of achievement was the number of placements made. The goal was unequivocal for the agency since legislative appropriations took the number of placements into account. It was emphasized for individuals by giving it heavy weight in their civil-service ratings. Blau discovered that two parallel units engaged in the referral of job applicants had devised quite different modes of maximizing the number of placements. The rank order of competitiveness was almost the same as the rank order of productivity in section A, but there was no relation between competitiveness and individual productivity in section B. The competitive interviewer in section B had no particular advantage. Competitive practices worked in section A but not in section B. Closer observation showed the investigator that section A functioned competitively, while section B had developed a cooperative system under which interviewers divided job openings, shared information about applicants, and kept track of each other's placements in order to show uniform output.

The differing values of the two sections affected many aspects of

[41] There were also some changes in the official table of organization which appeared spontaneously in *both* wings.

[42] Peter M. Blau, *The Dynamics of Bureaucracy* (Chicago: University of Chicago Press, 1955). The relevant data appear in a table on page 53.

their work. Productivity and popularity were related in section A but not in section B. Indeed, the members of section B disapproved of high output. One female interviewer discussed a male colleague, whom she considered the best interviewer in the section, with the observer. She remarked that he did not make many placements and that this was to his credit because the person who does the better job necessarily has fewer placements. Thus, the official values were reversed.

Curiously enough, the competitive section was much less effective than the cooperative section. Blau supposes that the hoarding of job openings interfered with operating efficiency. In any case a higher proportion of the job openings received in section B were successfully filled.

The difference between the two sections had some influence on all aspects of their members' working lives. The members of section B usually spent their rest periods together; the members of section A did not. Those in section A even avoided the company of employees from elsewhere in the division. The observer recorded 2625 interactions occurring during the busy hours of a single week and classified these as either official or private contacts. In section A, the competitive section, he found a virtually perfect correlation (+.98) between an interviewer's official contacts and his productivity. In section B, the correlation was negligible (+.08). It appears that in the competitive section, extensive communication to retrieve job openings hoarded by others enabled the interviewer to make a good record. In section B, obtaining cooperation in official duties demanded no special effort by the interviewer.

There was more to this pattern, however. In section A, the frequency of nonofficial contacts was also related to productivity. There was no such correlation in section B. Blau suggests that the more productive members of the competitive section needed to compensate for their aggressive behavior toward their colleagues by the expression of friendliness.[43]

[43] A much more elaborate case of diverse development from a nearly identical structure is provided by Vallier in a comparison of the missionary systems of Mormons and Reorganites. Ivan Vallier, "Church, Society and Labor Resources: An Intra-denominational Comparison," *American Journal of Sociology*, Vol. LXVIII, No. 1 (July, 1962). Two Indian textile mills provide still another example. See K. Chowdhry and A. K. Pal, "Production Planning and Organizational Morale," *Human Organization*, Vol. XV, No. 4 (Winter, 1957).

Even when elaborate efforts are made to obtain identical organizations for experimental purposes, small variations of development lead to major differences in structure. In a summer-camp experiment in group relations undertaken by Sherif in 1953,[44] the subjects were boys, all about the same age, from middle-class Protestant families. These characteristics were chosen to minimize variance. Psychological tests were administered to exclude deviants. The boys were of similar educational level and somewhat above average in intelligence, and for two days they engaged in activities involving the entire camp.

> This was done so that the group formation to follow could not be attributed to friendship clusters which might form spontaneously on the basis of personal affinities and common interests and without manipulation of experimental conditions. Following this brief period, the boys were divided into two experimental groupings made up so as to *split budding friendship clusters* and to *be as similar* as possible in athletic ability, personality characteristics, and prior acquaintanceship.

Despite these elaborate precautions, almost the first observations of the investigators showed differences in status and solidarity between groups, and the organizational structures they eventually developed were strikingly different.

One common feature of the foregoing cases deserves special attention. Their tables of organization remained identical while dramatic differences developed in their equilibrium variables. The table of organization is visible to outsiders; the configuration of variables is not. The members of other organizations in the same set have even less opportunity than strangers to observe the organization in motion, since their mere presence on the scene involves the organization's prestige and transforms whatever situation is under way. Additionally, because competition is continuous in most sets, rules of secrecy develop so that commonplace information about the inner workings of an organization cannot be passed to an outsider from the same set without bringing the loyalty of the informant into question.

The main effect of these concealments is that the members of one organization in a set are likely to visualize any other organization in the same set in terms of their own and to perceive it as more

[44] Muzafer Sherif, B. J. White, and O. J. Harvey, "Status in Experimentally Produced Groups," *American Journal of Sociology*, Vol. LX, No. 4 (January, 1955). The quotation is from page 374.

similar to their own than it really is. This leads to all sorts of complications when the two organizations interact. It frequently happens, for example, that the wrong agents are approached for liaison, that the persons responsible for an action are incorrectly identified, or that communication on some subject becomes unintelligible because the language of one organization is at variance with the language of the other and their representatives have no way of discovering the difference.

CHAPTER SEVEN

Organizational Improvement

THE CASE OF THE CORPORATION

The large industrial corporation is often regarded as the dominant type of organization in our society. It probably attracts more interest and systematic study than all other organizations combined. As the vehicle of a rapidly changing technology it has a commitment to continuous innovation in social as well as technical arrangements. Some of these innovations are local; they consist of reorganizations or reorientations in a single enterprise. Some of them are industry-wide and follow from the introduction of new manufacturing methods or materials. Other changes sweep across the entire industrial system and are felt in all the far corners of the economy.

From the foundation in 1791 of the first U.S. manufacturing cor-poration, the Society for Useful Manufactures of New Jersey, the importance of corporations in this country has increased without interruption.[1] By 1813, manufacturing corporations were numbered

[1] The best short summary of the historical development of corporations in the United States is Abram Chayes' Introduction to the 1961 edition of John P. Davis, *Corporations: A Study of the Origin and Development of Great Business Combinations and Their Relation to the Authority of the State* (New York: Capricorn Books, 1961, originally published by Putnam, 1905). The standard descriptive work on the corporation is A. A. Berle, Jr., and Gardner C. Means, *The Modern Corporation and Private Property* (New York: Commerce Clearing House, 1932) supplemented by Berle's *The Twentieth Century Capitalist Revolution* (Harcourt, Brace & World, 1954) and *The American Economic Republic* (Harcourt, Brace & World, 1963).

229

in hundreds. The substitution of general incorporation or incorporation by legislative charter began with a New York act in 1811 and spread fairly rapidly to all of the states.

By 1885, according to Ely, corporations held one-fourth of the total value of all properties in the United States and were rapidly increasing their proportionate share.[2] Before the turn of the century, the characteristic modern apprehension about the suppression of individualism by corporations was in the air.

> As one of the evil effects of corporate organization we shall have, in place of the independent business men of today, each gaining his livelihood by his success in a wide range of thought and action, a body of clerklike functionaries, each of whom will do a certain limited kind of work at the command of his superiors.[3]
>
> In 1800 we were a few millions of people and we loved liberty. In 1900 we are nearly a hundred millions of people and we love money. Most of this money is invested in what are called corporations. From a handful of individuals we have become a nation of institutions. The individual counts for less and less, organizations for more and more.[4]

In the 1960's, the five hundred largest business corporations in the United States account for about two-thirds of the national product, excluding agriculture, and about 130 of the manufacturing corporations produce half of the total manufacturing output.[5] There are more than five hundred corporations with five thousand employees; the largest has nearly a million.[6]

The corporation looms large in its own right, but its dominance as a type is shown by the tendency of other institutions to take on quasi-industrial forms. The staff divisions in the headquarters of a religious denomination are likely to be closely patterned on an industrial prototype, down to such details as the accounting system and the furnishing of executive offices. Military leaders, philanthropists, and the operators of criminal syndicates adopt styles of executive behavior that originate in the great corporations. University administration has

[2] Richard T. Ely, "The Growth of Corporations," *Harper's Magazine*, June, 1885.

[3] Charles Francis Adams, quoted by Davis, *op. cit.*, p. 5.

[4] Henry Watterson, quoted by Davis, *op. cit.*, p. 4.

[5] As shown by the annual listings of the five hundred largest corporations prepared by *Fortune* magazine.

[6] Bureau of the Census, *Company Statistics,* Bulletin CS–1, 1958.

taken on the same appearance, and the college weakly attempts to imitate the factory in the measurement of teaching productivity and the classification of personnel. Even the family shows such tendencies; the earliest writings of the scientific-management movement included books on the scientific management of the home and these have since expanded into an enormous literature.

Not only the methods of corporate management but its myths and values are transferrable to other spheres. Drucker sees the enterprise as displacing the community.[7] He believes that other major institutions are weakening so rapidly that corporate enterprise will eventually have to take over the functions they perform. Riesman [8] suggests that values derived from the enterprise are given precedence over values derived from other types of organizations.

> Our definitions of work mean that the housewife, though producing a social work-product, does not find her work explicitly defined and totaled, either as an hour product or a dollar product, in the national census or in people's minds. And since her work is not defined as work, she is exhausted at the end of the day without feeling any right to be, insult thus being added to injury. In contrast, the workers in the Detroit plant who finish their day's production goal in three hours and take the rest of the day off in factory loafing, are defined as eight-hour-per-day workers by themselves, by their wives, by the census.

Whyte,[9] studying the Park Forest and other suburbs populated by rising young executives, shows how their neighborhood patterns, their churches, and even their barbecue parties are shaped by the requirements of the corporation. He has also studied corporate efforts to control the family lives of employees.[10] In the novels of J. P.

[7] Peter F. Drucker, "The Employee Society," *American Journal of Sociology,* Vol. LXIII, No. 4 (January, 1953). See also his *The New Society* (New York: Harper, 1949).

[8] David Riesman, with Nathan Glazer and Reuel Denney, *The Lonely Crowd* (New Haven, Conn.: Yale University Press, 1950). The quotation is from pages 300–01.

[9] William H. Whyte, Jr., *The Organization Man* (New York: Simon and Schuster, 1956).

[10] As in "The Wives of Management," *Fortune,* October, 1951. The startling willingness of corporate executives to accept such control is shown in an attitude study by Edgar H. Schein and J. Steven Ott, "The Legitimacy of Organizational Influence," *American Journal of Sociology,* Vol. LXV, No. 6 (May, 1962).

Marquand, the forms taken by this control are described in a number of different settings.[11] Tumin deplores the assimilation of corporate values by the family,[12] and Hutchins,[13] among others, deplores the subordination of the intrinsic values of higher education to those of the corporate enterprise, continuing a theme that can be traced back two generations in the writings of Thorstein Veblen, Upton Sinclair, and E. A. Ross. Recent studies of corporate influence on community affairs show how corporate delegates, participating under orders, distort the duties of citizenship. Hughes [14] writes of the "intertwining of government and business" and of the relation between public enterprises and private bureaucracies.

Meanwhile, the great corporations continue to grow in size, to increase their share of the national wealth, and to give ever more attention to their own structures and functions. When we examine the enterprise in the United States, we find it in a fever of self-improvement, or what its managers conceive as self-improvement.[15] Besides the need to adapt to technical and scientific discoveries, a number of other factors are at work.

Among the long-term influences are what I have elsewhere described as differentiation, aggregation, and rationalization.[16] *Differentiation* refers to the steady increase of the division of labor, as shown by a title such as Vice President in charge of Cookie Mix Production or by a factory devoted entirely to the manufacture of hubcaps. *Aggregation* is the tendency for enterprises and their components to grow indefinitely in size. *Rationalization* is the substitution

---

[11] John Phillips Marquand, *The Late George Apley* (Boston: Little, Brown, 1937); *Point of No Return* (Boston: Little, Brown, 1949); *Sincerely, Willis Wayde* (Boston: Little, Brown, 1955).

[12] Melvin Tumin, "Some Disfunctions of Institutional Inbalance," *Behavioral Science*, Vol. I (1956).

[13] Robert Maynard Hutchins, "The Democratic Dilemma," in *Freedom, Education, and the Fund* (New York: Meridian Books, 1956).

[14] Everett C. Hughes, "Disorganization and Reorganization," *Human Organization*, Vol. XXI, No. 2 (Summer, 1962).

[15] European experience is not so different, as described for example in Georges Friedmann's *The Anatomy of Work: Labor, Leisure, and the Implications of Automation* (New York: Free Press, 1961).

[16] Theodore Caplow, *The Sociology of Work* (Minneapolis, Minn.: University of Minnesota Press, 1954; New York: McGraw-Hill, 1963), Chapter 2. For a more specific view of trends in corporate enterprise in the United States, see Wilbert E. Moore, *The Conduct of the Corporation* (New York: Random Rouse, 1962), especially Chapters 14 and 15.

of prescribed behavior for spontaneous human activity. It includes the standardization of the working environment and the substitution of impersonal for personal judgments.

There is still another factor that should be taken into account. Some of the innovation observed in the industrial world is a kind of play. It arises in part from the monotony of executive work, which can be as real as the monotony of work on the assembly line, in part from the temptation to spend corporate surpluses extravagantly. It may have something to do with the marginal utility of innovation. In operations already at high efficiency the cost of obtaining additional increments of efficiency by conventional methods may be prohibitive, and the inducement to try new methods becomes very great.

The industrial corporation is often discussed as if it had no other goal than efficient production. Nothing could be further from the truth. Experiments in self-improvement have been equally concerned with integration, voluntarism, and stratification. Indeed, many of the slogans of modern management theory are variations on the theme that human relations are more important than technical processes. The germ of truth in these slogans is that the modern enterprise is usually able to satisfy the criterion of achievement more easily than the other criteria of organizational effectiveness. However, this observation refers to the long run and the large picture. In the short run, the efforts to improve voluntarism and integration are usually based on the assumption that they are closely correlated with achievement—or can be made to correlate if the right formula is found. As this hope has lessened in sophisticated managerial circles, there has been no lessening of interest in the perfectibility of the organization. Steadily increasing output is nearly taken for granted in the giant manufacturing enterprise as something that can be routinely achieved by appropriate staff work. The planning emphasis falls instead on such matters as executive development, the choice between centralization and decentralization, and the "human aspects of automation."

The vast movement toward corporate self-improvement has more facets than can be conveniently summarized. It evokes a steady barrage of criticism from within and without, and is thought by some observers to be more pernicious than the earlier industrial practices which have gradually been replaced. Although a catalog of all the theories and methods involved in this movement would be encyclopedic, the major lines of effort can be conveniently categorized. Some attempts to raise achievement in the industrial enterprise are focused on activities, as in time-and-motion studies and work-flow analysis. Others are aimed at interactions (group dynamics), statuses (decentralization), or valences (incentive plans). The improvement of integration has sometimes aimed directly at interactions, as in communication programs, but often indirectly at valences (compatible work teams), activities (suggestion systems), and statuses (conference methods). Voluntarism is fostered directly by fringe benefits and other morale-building measures; indirectly through modification of activities (job enlargement), interactions (selective recruitment), and statuses (personnel development programs). The stability of an enterprise can be maintained by manipulating rewards and punishments, or by working indirectly on interactions (internal public relations), valences (training in supervisory technics), or activities (job classification). The more coherent of these approaches will be considered separately in the following pages.

Raising the Level of Achievement

SCIENTIFIC MANAGEMENT

Taylor's theories of functional foremanship and the span of control have been generally discarded, but his three major discoveries have each given rise to separate schools of experts. What Taylor discovered was that

1. Human capabilities in work must be determined experimentally. They are not intuitively obvious either to the worker or to an observer.
2. The worker's maximum output at a given job cannot be achieved without systematic training. Such training rests upon a method of decomposing the job into its component parts and analyzing each of them separately and in sequence.
3. Individual differences in output are accentuated, not removed, by training.[17]

[17] Frederick W. Taylor, *The Principles of Scientific Management* (New York: Harper, 1911) and *Shop Management* (New York: Harper, 1911).

Presumably, all this was known for centuries to men who had the knack of command in workshops. However, it is one thing for isolated individuals to have a bit of practical knowledge and another for general principles to be discovered. The first of these principles developed into the large and flourishing specialty of human engineering.[18] The next principle, on the need for training, led in one direction to the development of industrial psychology and, in another, to the ill-famed but indispensable art of time-and-motion study. In other directions, it stimulated a proliferation of training methods.

The last of Taylor's principles led to personnel studies, personality and aptitude testing, promotional selection devices, and all the rest of the elaborate machinery for evaluating, sorting, and distributing persons in the modern enterprise. The use of these methods was subject to corruption from the beginning, and current practices involve many violations of decency. Packard in *The Pyramid Climbers* [19] and Whyte in *The Organization Man* [20] give hair-raising examples, and the author knows of a California corporation whose executives are compelled to undergo a session with a psychoanalyst every month to keep their personnel records up-to-date. Some of these aberrations result from attempts to push the available measuring and predictive devices far beyond their statistical limits and to use them as means of discipline. But even when employed with restraint, "scientific" personnel methods have the fundamental defect that the low probabilities generated by the modest correlations between predictive tests and subsequent performance are interpreted as if they were certainties. Men may be rewarded for their skill in meeting personnel requirements rather than for their usefulness to the organization.

THE HUMAN-RELATIONS APPROACH

Whyte [21] has summarized the contribution to industrial management made by Mayo in *Human Problems of an Industrial Civilization,*[22]

---

[18] See Ernest J. McCormick, *Human Engineering* (New York: McGraw-Hill, 1957), or Edwin S. Rescoe, *Organization for Production* (Homewood, Ill.: Irwin, 1963).

[19] Vance Packard, *The Pyramid Climbers* (New York: McGraw-Hill, 1962).

[20] William H. Whyte, Jr., *op. cit.*

[21] William F. Whyte, "Human Relations Theory—a Progress Report," *Harvard Business Review,* Vol. XXXIV, No. 5 (September–October, 1956).

[22] Elton Mayo, *Human Problems of an Industrial Civilization* (New York: Macmillan, 1933).

published in 1933. Mayo, he says, established the propositions that
(a) the economic incentive is not the only motivating force to which
the worker responds; (b) the worker does not respond as an isolated
individual, but as a member of a work group; (c) extreme functional
specialization does not necessarily lead to maximum efficiency.

This summary can be restated in more positive terms. Although
the Mayo school did not enunciate many formal propositions, their
subsequent studies accustomed all later investigators to the implicit
propositions that:

1. There is a social system consisting of established informal relationships between particular persons in any live organization,
   and this system invariably has important consequences for
   achievement. Improvement of the organization's achievement
   will be either impossible or extremely difficult if informal relationships are not taken into account.
2. Peer groups form in work situations whenever the opportunity
   exists. They control production by limiting output and by modifying prescribed work procedures.
3. The output of the individual worker is influenced by his emotional state, which in turn is influenced by the emotions of his
   peers. Technological changes cannot be smoothly introduced
   unless the emotional consequences of an innovation are taken
   into account.

The crucial discovery was of the ubiquity of output limitations—
that is, of the establishment of standard ranges of work performance
by peer groups, in opposition to managerial directives. Output
limitation can only be said to occur when the achieved output is
well below the output that could be obtained in the absence of group
controls. In most situations of this type, the limitation of output also
involves standardization. The agreed output is set at some point
within the capacity of the least competent members of the group
and enforced on them as a minimum standard, while it functions for
the others as a maximum. Absolute standardization, with every
worker on a crew turning in the same number of pieces for each
period, is not uncommon, but usually there is some slight variation.
The rationale of output limitation in the factory is the fear that a
higher level of performance will lead to lower pay per unit of work.
This apprehension is often well grounded.

Output limitation is maintained by a number of devices. Men who have finished the day's quota may simply avoid doing any more work. Work above quota may be transferred to the credit of the slower members of the group or saved for another day. Breakdowns of machinery or delays in the transfer of work may be arranged as necessary. The methods differ from plant to plant and from shop to shop, but the purposes are usually the same.[23]

Output limitation has been most thoroughly investigated in the factory,[24] for obvious reasons. It seems to occur in every other kind of large organization as well, in schools and colleges, in political parties, and in military units. The military occupation itself is identified with output limitation in the term *soldiering*. Even churches and voluntary associations appear to have their share (although the evidence is widely scattered and not readily amenable to citation). Nevertheless, the ubiquity of limitation can be exaggerated. It can probably be found in every large organization but not in all of the components of any large organization. A number of work groups composed of women have been closely studied without revealing any restrictive norms.[25] In many corporations in which competition for succession to executive posts is intense, there is little output limitation in the upper echelons. A few companies encourage limitation by rules about "leaving the job in the office."

There is some tendency in the managerial literature to treat the limitation of output as a waywardness in the souls of workers, capable of being cured by the shrewd application of human-relations therapy. A more balanced view of the problem must start with the functions of output limitation and the reasons for its appearance.

[23] The rate-buster is a worker who disregards the limitations imposed by his social peers under a piece-work system and produces as many units as he can. As might be expected, he turns out to have distinct asocial and unsociable characteristics. Melville Dalton, "The Industrial 'Rate-buster': A Characterization," *Applied Anthropology*, Vol. VII, No. 5 (Winter, 1948).

[24] The pioneer work on the subject was published before the findings of the Western Electric study. S. B. Mathewson, *Restrictions of Output Among Unorganized Workers* (New York: Viking, 1931). Of the dozens of more recent publications dealing with the topic, see especially Donald Roy, "Quota Restrictions and Goldbricking in a Machine Shop," *American Journal of Sociology*, Vol. LVII, No. 2 (March, 1952) and C. Arnold Anderson, "Sociological Elements in Economic Restrictionism," *American Sociological Review*, Vol. IX, No. 3 (August, 1944).

[25] The relay assembly test room at Western Electric, Homans' cash posters, and the first Amicon tube crew.

Output limitation is a way in which the peer group asserts its autonomy in the face of excessive control from above. It may also serve the larger organization by standardizing output at a predictable guaranteed level. Output limitation is not so much a matter of waywardness as a transaction between the organization, which claims an unlimited right to dispose of the energies of its members, and the members, who deny that right and regard the organization as an instrument for their own purposes. Between these irreconcilable objectives, the balance is struck at some point determined by the relative strength of the parties. What kind of balance it is depends on the history and goals of the peer group. Sayles distinguishes four types: [26]

1. The *apathetic* group, whose members may be dissatisfied but are so divided against themselves that they are unable to take concerted action.
2. The *erratic* group, which swings from passivity to outbursts of aggressive action—often on issues that seem trivial.
3. The *strategic* group, which seeks to improve its position through carefully calculated, united action.
4. The *conservative* group, whose members are capable of concerted action but who are generally satisfied enough so that they do not take the trouble to make themselves heard.

The leading concepts of human relations have diffused through the industrial world along many different paths, starting with the counseling program at Western Electric and ending with the almost universal recognition by managers trained in the modern manner that peer groups hold a veto power over all technical directives and that the emotions of the worker are factors to be included in the calculation of output.

FIELD THEORY AND GROUP DYNAMICS

After Taylor and Mayo, the most influential figure in the background of corporate self-improvement is Kurt Lewin.[27] His followers,

[26] Leonard R. Sayles, *Behavior of Industrial Work Groups* (New York: Wiley, 1958).

[27] His relevant writings include: *Dynamic Theory of Personality* (New York: McGraw-Hill, 1935), *Principles of Topological Psychology* (New York: McGraw-Hill, 1936), "Field Theory and Experiment in Social Psychology:

perhaps because of their special interest in cohesiveness, have remained more united than most other schools of social science, and much of their work has been done in centers established to develop and propagate Lewinian theory.[28] The major applications to industrial problems may be briefly summarized as follows:

1. The individual's willingness to cooperate in a program of activities depends on his perception of the environment and his own place in it, his "life-space." [29]

2. The individual's perception of his own situation (his life-space) is largely determined by his primary-group membership and his interaction with others in primary groups, the "social field of force."

3. Low morale and substandard achievement in an industrial work group result from the frustration experienced by individual workers when conflicting valences develop in their situation—simultaneous positive and negative valences, for example, toward interaction with unequals.

4. The introduction of technical or procedural changes in a working situation will be met by resistance because the new goals and the paths leading to them will be inconsistent with those already established.

5. The individual's perception of a situation can be most effectively modified by the influence of the primary groups to which he belongs. The most economical way of overcoming resistance to production goals in industry is to reinforce primary

Concepts and Methods," *American Journal of Sociology,* Vol. XLIV, No. 5 (November, 1939), "Time Perspective and Morale," in Goodwin B. Watson (ed.), *Civilian Morale* (New York: Reynal, 1942), "Patterns of Aggressive Behavior in Experimentally Created Social Climates" (with Ronald Lippitt and R. K. White), *Journal of Social Psychology,* Vol. X (1939), *Resolving Social Conflicts* (ed. G. W. Lewin and Gordon W. Allport) (New York: Harper, 1948), "Frontiers in Group Dynamics" and "Constructs in Field Theory" in Dorwin Cartwright (ed.), *Field Theory in Social Science* (New York: Harper, 1951).

[28] The Research Center for Group Dynamics, located first at M.I.T. and later at the University of Michigan, the Tavistock Institute of Human Relations, the National Training Laboratory at Bethel and the Human Relations Research Group at U.C.L.A.

[29] The life-space is visualized by Lewin as an area that has regions representing activities or statuses, valences standing for motives of all kinds, the possibility of locomotion from one region to another, barriers blocking locomotion, and additional dimensions representing reality and time.

groups and encourage their participation in production planning.

6. Groups with a democratic and permissive atmosphere, whose members participate in determining their own goals, will have higher morale and more commitment to the organization than those directed by authoritarian leaders. Under some conditions, the amount of participation will determine the group's level of achievement.

These ideas have stimulated many laboratory studies of social processes in small, problem-solving groups, mostly composed of students. Another series of studies, beginning in the 1940's, has involved experiments with, and observations of, primary groups in real industrial situations.[30] Some findings of these investigations were discussed in the previous chapter. In general, they support the view that the effective cooperation of a work group rests upon group consent, and that consent to new work methods is most easily obtained when the group participates in planning them. Efforts to increase productivity *without* new work methods are even more likely to arouse resistance. Hence, they require group consent and autonomous decision-making to an unusual degree.[31] The most interesting applications of these findings have been made by industrial supervisors for practical, not scholarly, purposes.[32] By slow and untraceable diffusion, such technics have become the common property of sophisticated managers throughout American and European industry. They have even been treated as trade secrets.

A number of other offshoots of Lewin's work have attracted wide interest among managers bent on self-improvement. One of these is action research, in which the roles of management consultant and social scientist are combined, usually in a program of raising output by democratizing work relations.[33] Another is the conference

[30] This work, except for the most recent developments, is summarized in Harold H. Kelley and John W. Thibaut, *The Social Psychology of Groups* (New York: Wiley, 1959).

[31] Admirably summarized in Rensis Likert, *New Patterns of Management* (New York: McGraw-Hill, 1961). See the discussion in Chapter Four above.

[32] For example, the methods developed by Howard Kahn to encourage the spontaneous reorganization of work groups in his laundry and dry-cleaning plants.

[33] Elliott Jaques, *The Changing Culture of a Factory* (New York: Dryden, 1952), is still the best published example.

method, a system of teaching individuals to organize permissive and leaderless conferences. The spirit of these "group-centered approaches" is cultic as well as scientific, full of solemn references to "true democracy," "personal growth," [34] and assertions of the superiority of the group over the individual in learning, problem-solving, and "creative self-realization."

THEORY Y

From the amount of corporate interest in the theory and methods of democratic work relations, we begin to get some notion of the massive pressures on the modern industrial enterprise to decrease or conceal status differences and to give more autonomy to subordinates in order to reduce the discrepancy between individual motives and organizational goals. McGregor, whose work is written for executives rather than social scientists, calls the viewpoint underlying this program "Theory Y" and summarizes it as follows:

1. The expenditure of physical and mental effort in work is as natural as play or rest. The average human being does not inherently dislike work. Depending upon controllable conditions, work may be a source of satisfaction (and will be voluntarily performed) or a source of punishment (and will be avoided if possible).

2. External control and the threat of punishment are not the only means for bringing about effort toward organizational objectives. Man will exercise self-direction and self-control in the service of objectives to which he is committed.

3. Commitment to objectives is a function of the rewards associated with their achievement. The most significant of such rewards, e.g., the satisfaction of ego and self-actualization needs, can be direct products of effort directed toward organizational objectives.

4. The average human being learns, under proper conditions, not only to accept but to seek responsibility. Avoidance of responsibility, lack of ambition, and emphasis on security are generally consequences of experience, not inherent human characteristics.

5. The capacity to exercise a relatively high degree of imagination, ingenuity, and creativity in the solution of organizational problems is widely, not narrowly, distributed in the population.

[34] For example, Helen Irene Drive, *Multiple Counseling—A Small-Group Discussion Method for Personal Growth* (Madison, Wisc.: Monono Publications, 1958), and Chris Argyris, *Understanding Organizational Behavior* (Homewood, Ill.: Dorsey, 1960).

6. Under the conditions of modern industrial life, the intellectual potentialities of the average human being are only partially utilized.[35]

An organization accepting Theory Y, according to McGregor, will not assume without question that the requirements set up by its program take precedence over the needs and desires of its members. Promotions and transfers, for example, will not be made by unilateral management decision. The preferences of the individual will be given equal weight with those of the company. Work objectives and means of reaching them will be determined in consultation with all the people involved. Managerial and staff activities are redefined as services rather than controls and the manager is enjoined to restrict his own authority to essentials. Throughout this development, the goals of the larger organization remain unchanged and unchallengeable. The manager following Theory Y is measured by how well he maintains the valences of his subordinates in place of, and in preference to, maintaining his own status.

In practice, few industrial managements are tempted to adopt Theory Y wholesale, but many companies apply it self-consciously at certain points, particularly at the executive level just below top management. In that region, good human relations and a cooperative atmosphere are likely to be especially valued by presidents and vice-presidents looking down from a vantage point slightly above. Their own statuses, heavily anchored outside the immediate organization, are not seriously reduced in an egalitarian atmosphere.

OTHER LEADERSHIP STUDIES

A somewhat calmer view of the choice between stratification and voluntarism is taken by many writers who regard leadership as specific to a situation and assume that the balance of status interaction and valence that will maximize activity in a given relationship is not a constant formula but varies from one situation to another.

The best exposition of supervisory alternatives appears in a management manual by Pieper.[36] He distinguishes between directive lead, which is authoritative and instructional, and creative lead, which

[35] Douglas McGregor, *The Human Side of Enterprise* (New York: McGraw-Hill, 1960), pp. 470–78.
[36] Frank Pieper, *Modular Management and Human Leadership* (Minneapolis, Minn.: Methods Press, 1958).

enlists cooperation and support and provokes autonomous action based on group discussion. Either the supervisor or the supervisee may have learned to prefer either directive lead or creative lead and to dislike the opposite. The supervisor, in adapting himself to the situation, must take account of his own disposition, the preferences of the people supervised, and the objective requirements of the situation. Leadership always necessitates an intricate adaptation. The leadership appropriate to a particular work situation cannot be completely specified in advance except for such extreme cases as volunteer aid, in which a creative lead may be the only way of eliciting any cooperative effort at all, or a display of discipline, such as a military parade, in which a directive lead is absolutely required. Ordinarily, the special characteristics of the leader and the followers must both be taken into account to achieve what is called effective leadership or, in plainer terms, the maximum output of which that group is capable under those circumstances.

Improving Horizontal and Vertical Integration

HOLDING THE LARGE-SCALE ORGANIZATION TOGETHER

The perception that achievement can be raised by improving integration often leads to the adoption of integration as an end in itself rather than a means. The search for cohesion is perhaps the most salient feature of current managerial ideologies.[37] Bendix refers to the development of "managerial collectivism in large-scale economic enterprises." [38] Whyte scorchingly satirizes the corporate creed of

---

[37] The emphasis on cohesion in the corporate enterprise is readily imitated by other institutions, sometimes with techniques adopted directly from the business world. Thus, we find team research and interdisciplinary instruction displacing the individual scientist and teacher in educational institutions. Group therapy is advocated as a substitute for psychoanalysis, group work for individual counseling. Army officers are taught to do strategic planning by the conference method. Even families are exhorted to develop programs for increasing togetherness.

[38] Reinhard Bendix, *Work and Authority in Industry* (New York: Wiley, 1956), p. 337.

"belongingness" and "togetherness." [39] "Belongingness," "togetherness," and "scienticism" mark for him the decline of the Protestant ethic and the beginnings of a society in which moral goals are to be replaced by conformity for conformity's sake. Packard writes that "Individualists frequently talk wistfully about the need for men who are tigers. What they really want are cooperative tigers, tigers who come quickly to heel and can get along nicely with other tigers. They want tigers who fit in." [40]

Bendix lays the responsibility for this trend on the doorstep of Mayo. Whyte is inclined to blame it on the suburban philosophy that he calls the social ethic. Riesman [41] ties it to rates of population growth and the other-directed personality pattern. All of these are relevant, but a number of more limited factors have played a part. Perhaps the most important of these is the expansion of management itself. The increase in numbers of managerial personnel has been enormous, both absolutely and relatively, and promises to continue. It is paralleled in the general society by the increase in the proportion of white-collar workers, and among white-collar workers by the increasing ratio of technical to clerical jobs. General Electric, the company used by Bendix to exemplify managerial collectivism, had at the time of his writing more than twenty thousand executives. In a large European enterprise (as formerly in American companies) the proportion would be very much smaller, [42] and the managerial stratum would be held together by class or family ties, their awareness of common interests reinforced by a common way of life.

The professionalization of management threatens corporate integration in many ways. Specialization increases the possibility of moving from one company to another. Rationalization affects many firms and many industries in a similar way. The traditional manager owed much of his competence to knowledge of a local milieu; the modern professionalized manager is likely to be an expert in marketing or personnel administration, and his skills may be usable in hundreds of different places. This development has had a double-barreled effect. On the one hand, each enterprise attempts by in-

---

[39] William H. Whyte, Jr., *op. cit.*
[40] Packard, *op. cit.,* p. 115.
[41] Riesman et al., *op. cit.*
[42] See Roy Lewis and Rosemary Stewart, *The Managers* (New York: New American Library, 1961).

doctrination to develop a cohesive spirit that will help to hold its personnel. On the other, the high rate of inter-enterprise mobility makes it extremely important for the mobile individual to fit easily into new companies or to leave them without feelings of bereavement.

The best-substantiated sociological proposition about the integration of the large-scale corporate enterprise is that the enterprise is a cluster of organized groups. The individual acts more often than not as a group representative. The practical consequences of this statement can be understood only against the background of the older individualistic ideology which persistently—in the face of common sense and everyday knowledge—regarded the individual employee as moved only by his personal interests.[43]

Disclosure of the extent to which the individuals in a large-scale organization respond to events as members of peer groups, cliques, factions, departments, and other component units is perennially surprising. There appears to be literally no end to the development of internal loyalties. Furthermore, the study of reference groups makes it necessary to take account of a kind of representation that does not depend on membership.[44] The individual may respond to events in the organization by expressing the attitudes of groups to which he does not belong but to which he has developed an attachment.

SELECTION OF A UNIT OF EMOTIONAL AFFILIATION

Inconsistency between the goals of the large organization and its components often develops in the selection of a unit of emotional affiliation by members. The principle involved here has not been very closely studied, and it rests for the present upon a scattering of indirect evidence.[45]

Most large organizations seek an emotional and moral commitment from their members. Indeed, considering what organizations

---

[43] See Bendix, *op. cit.*, for a full discussion.

[44] See the classic discussion in Robert K. Merton and Paul F. Lazarsfeld (eds.), *Continuities in Social Research* (Glencoe, Ill.: Free Press, 1950).

[45] The largest of these fragments of evidence comes from *The American Soldier.* One of its most striking findings was that the American soldier in World War II fought an almost totally nonideological war, and that it was not the nation, the armed services, the fleet or the force but the company or squadron or platoon that became the focus of his loyalties.

do and their impact upon the lives of their members, it is easier to understate than to exaggerate the strength of the emotional bonds that develop in their interaction networks. These bonds, however, are subject to certain structural necessities.

Each membership affiliation divides a member's universe into an in-group and an out-group. Some degree of antagonism to members of the out-group is the necessary reverse of the coin of loyalty and confidence in the in-group. The development of emotional attachments in one direction prevents, or at least discourages, the development of attachments in directions that might have a conflicting pull. The presence of a status order in the large organization means, among many other things, that the emotional affiliations of individuals are worked out within limited zones of freedom. To be loyal at the inappropriate level, or to prefer the larger group to the smaller, will often by perceived as insubordination by a superior or as treason by a peer group. The upshot of all these considerations is that the member of a large organization is ordinarily drawn or coerced into the selection of one subdivision of the organization as his primary unit of emotional affiliation. The soldier can never be expected to divide his loyalties among the army, the corps, the division, the regiment, the platoon, and the squad. In some circumstances (Napoleon's Grand Army) he identifies primarily with the army; in other circumstances (Rogers' Rangers or Stonewall Jackson's Corps) the unit of identification will be a division or a corps; in another situation (the British Army in India) the emotionally significant unit will be the regiment; among the American infantrymen studied by Stouffer and the Research Branch, it was the company or the squad. All of the pyramided components may have flags of their own, but there is seldom more than one flag for which men are willing to die.

The primary unit of emotional affiliation is not necessarily well integrated. It may be torn with dissension and conflict, as are many staff sections and work crews in industry. It may even be hated by many of its members. Nevertheless, in the division of the world into "we" and "they," which is a prerequisite for any kind of organizational action, we can usually discern a "we" which is fundamental and through which the demands of larger units claiming loyalty must be channeled. The corporation's insistence on emotional solidarity and on being one big happy family often amounts to a plaintive protest against its employees' devotion to their own units.

MARGINAL MEN IN INDUSTRY

Marginality of identification may be illustrated by the case of the foreman. Like the noncommissioned officer, prison guard, office supervisor, precinct committee man, or anyone else in an analogous situation, he is caught between the demands of his superiors that he identify with management and embody authority to his men and the demand of the men that he assist them to evade the rules and maintain peer-group solidarity. The dilemma appears to be inseparable from the function of foremanship. If it cannot be detected in the position labeled *foreman,* it will ordinarily be found one step above or below. Whoever it is who finally transmits the program of the enterprise to the persons who actually carry out the physical operations, he is certain to be pulled in two directions.[46] This is undoubtedly the reason why a very large proportion of the total effort to induce cohesion in the enterprise has been focused on foremen or first-level supervisors. They have been the principal targets of supervisory training, conference systems, performance appraisals, and so on, just as in an earlier era functional foremanship and the span-of-control theory were intended to resolve the marginality of the foreman. In time, such devices diffuse further up the administrative line—almost, if not quite, to the top—and the same history repeats itself at each level. Marginality, it turns out, is not limited to the foreman. It occurs in more subtle forms at other levels of the hierarchy—between top and middle management, between staff and line, between sales and production, between research and operations, even between the advisor and the decision-maker.[47] The effort in some companies to create a kind of managerial caste is often frustrated by the tendency for marginality to spread upward to junior executives and middle management. With what religious zeal the pursuit of a common identification is undertaken may be inferred from the credo read to executives of a great American corporation at the moonlight ceremony welcoming them to a training session:

[46] The best exposition of how this process works is to be found in a study that has nothing to do with corporate enterprise but that contrasts American prisons and Soviet labor camps—Donald R. Cressey and Witold Krassowski, "Inmate Organization and Anomie in American Prisons and Soviet Labor Camps," *Social Problems,* Vol. V, No. 3 (Winter, 1957–58).

[47] Lyman Bryson, "Notes on a Theory of Advice," in Robert Merton et al. (eds.), *Reader in Bureaucracy* (Glencoe, Ill.: Free Press, 1952).

Screened with care for character, drafted for dependability, mustered together for your minds and hands—you are the framework upon which the future must be made to take shape and substance.

Those who guide and guard this company; those who light and lead the way will give unto you full measure of their strength and courage; full measure of abundance of resource . . . for ideas, vision, and breadth of mind. Measure for measure, they will give, for loyalty and devotion. Such compromise builds upon Faith in God, in our country and in our Company. . . .

ORGANIZATIONAL CONFLICT

A small volume by Selznick [48] provides an ideology to support sentiments like those expressed in this credo. His thesis is that every successful organization develops a unique organizational character. He distinguishes between the mere administrator who heads an organization and the statesman who protects the uniqueness of an institution. Character, according to Selznick, is a historical product, integrated, functional, and dynamic. His essay is admirably documented with examples drawn from government agencies and the armed forces. There are relatively few illustrations from industry, perhaps because industrial enterprises tend, in fact, to be far less distinctive than government departments. Nevertheless, the basis for a new corporate faith is laid down in eloquent terms.

> The integrity of an enterprise goes beyond efficiency, beyond organization forms and procedures, even beyond group cohesion. Integrity combines organization and policy. It is the unity that emerges when a particular orientation becomes so firmly a part of group life that it colors and directs a wide variety of attitudes, decisions, and forms of organization, and does so at many levels of experience. The building of integrity is part of what we have called the "institutional embodiment of purpose" and its protection is a major function of leadership.

Logic and frame of reference in groups. It is now a sociological truism that a difference of interests between groups will be accompanied by differences in ideology and perspective that interfere very seriously with mutual understanding. Because each group per-

---

[48] Philip Selznick, *Leadership in Administration* (Evanston, Ill.: Row, Peterson, 1957). The quotation is from pages 138–39.

ceives a different scene and a different setting, the actions of the other are likely to appear irrational or malicious.[49] The introduction of conferences and committees is intended in many cases as an antidote to this effect. By "bringing people together" to "exchange viewpoints," the conference is intended to reconcile divergent frames of reference and to develop a common logic that will be shared by opposing groups, at least to the extent of their common responsibilities in the corporate program. This is the legitimate use of conferences. There is also an illegitimate mode, in which executives enforce conformity upon their subordinates by conferences that are ostensibly intended for an exchange of viewpoints between different status levels but in fact serve as occasions for the promulgation of official doctrine and for the detection and suppression of heresy.[50] The line between legitimate and illegitimate is often hard to draw. The observer, too, has his own logic and frame of reference.

The rule-making function and group interests. Although only a few studies have been focused directly on rule-making,[51] the insights obtained from various investigations have had a notable effect upon the kind of rules that are promulgated in enterprises. As a result of the findings, conceptions of industrial rules borrowed from the common law have given way to the view that rules are instrumental, relative, and subject to systematic evasion. The arbitrary commandments of an earlier era are being replaced by less punitive and more detailed directions. Authority tends more and more to invite consent, and negative rules are restated in positive terms whenever possible.

The following propositions appear to be fairly well established:

1. Rules are ordinarily promulgated by one group to control the behavior of another group in the presence of a conflict of interests.

[49] See Jaques, *op. cit.*

[50] Warren Breed, "Social Control in the Newsroom," *Social Forces,* Vol. XXXIII, No. 4 (May, 1955).

[51] Alvin W. Gouldner, *Patterns of Industrial Bureaucracy* (Glencoe, Ill.: Free Press, 1954). See also Robert Dubin, *The World of Work* (Englewood Cliffs, N.J.: Prentice-Hall, 1958) and Victor A. Thompson, *Modern Organization* (New York: Knopf, 1961) for more general discussions of rule-making and enforcement.

2. Rules cannot be enforced unless they have been accepted by the subjects.
3. Acceptance of new rules depends to a large extent on how they have been formulated and introduced, and particularly on whether or not the subjects participated in the formulation.
4. Any set of rules that requires enforcement by outsiders provokes systematic evasion.
5. The routine enforcement of rules consists of maintaining an existing level of partial compliance.
6. When rule evasion has been systematized, there will ordinarily be collaboration between those charged with enforcement of the rule and those responsible for its evasion, in an effort to maintain the status quo.

Inconsistencies between the organization's goals and those of its components or factions result in norms of rule evasion. For example, many working establishments have No Smoking rules. These are seldom consistently obeyed except where they are based on the danger of explosion, as in powder plants and on airport aprons. The reasons for No Smoking rules are diverse and not always self-evident. Manifest motives range from the danger of fire to the desire for decorum. Latent motives range from a mere wish to assert authority to the desire to increase productivity by keeping the worker's hands free. Whatever the motives may be in a particular situation, it is predictable that they will not win full support from those concerned. There will probably be smoking in the establishment the halls of which are placarded with No Smoking signs. The important point is that the amount of smoking, the places for it, the designation of those who may smoke and those who may not, the devices used to conceal smoking from supervisors or visitors, and the type of resistance opposed to enforcement will be governed by the norms of organized groups as well as by the impulses of individuals.

We do not fully understand why some rules are enforceable and others are not, or why the pattern of evasion for some rules differs from that for others. The plant studied by Gouldner had a No Smoking regulation that was ignored. Managers and workers agreed in regarding the No Smoking rule as something imposed by the insurance company. This view was reinforced by the circulation of a warning and the temporary enforcement of the rule during the periodic visits of the insurance inspectors. Gouldner comments that because the rule was neither enforced by plant management nor obeyed by plant workers, it provoked little conflict between the two factions and may even have enhanced their solidarity. "Both the customary violation of the rule, as well as the occasional enforcement of it, were buttressed by the informal sentiments and behavior of the participants." [52]

Evasion of the No Smoking rule had a further basis in this case. Under the fire-insurance policy, smoking in the plant office was allowed by a special permit, so that, had the rule been enforced, existing status differences would have been sharpened by allowing privileges to office workers which were denied to the manual workers in the plant. The egalitarian attitudes that prevailed in the company were unfavorable to this sort of discrimination.

Other patterns of compliance in Gouldner's study are more complex. The plant is divided into a surface factory and an underground mine. There is a rather high level of conformity to all rules in the surface factory and consistent disregard of rules in the mine. Although the level of compliance differs between surface and mine, the same categories of rule enforcement can be observed in both places. Gouldner describes these somewhat awkwardly as three "patterns of bureaucracy." The first is the *mock pattern,* already described in connection with the No Smoking regulation. The second is the *representative pattern,* illustrated by safety rules developed under pressure of both union and management and supported in operation by both factions. Rule enforcement in this category, however, is by no means perfect. The values of management and workers about safety diverge enough to generate some tension, if little conflict. The third pattern is *punishment-centered;* two examples are given—the rule against absenteeism, initiated by management, and the rule awarding job choices by seniority, initiated by the union. These are straightforward examples of goal inconsistency. In each case, one faction considers the rule legitimate; the other concedes it only on the grounds of expediency and conforms reluctantly, so that enforcement is a continuous source of conflict.

[52] Gouldner, *op. cit.,* p. 186.

THE IMPORTANCE OF COMMUNICATION

If there is a single word that epitomizes the wide effort to improve industrial efficiency by taking account of human factors outside the usual sphere of engineering, it is *communication*. Half a dozen specialities have contributed to the magic aura that surrounds the word: sociology, psychology, cybernetics, semantics, psychiatry, operations research. Innumerable social inventions have been tried, from simple planning conferences in the middle reaches of management to elaborate systems of mutual criticism.[53]

What is wishfully called the theory of communication[54] remains so far in a fragmentary state. Its principal propositions appear to be these:

1. Communication in any large-scale organization is imperfect because the meaning of a message transmitted up or down the chain of command necessarily changes. Only by the application of many safeguards and correctives can this distortion be held to a reasonable minimum. The fundamental reason why distortion occurs is that as orders proceed down the line they must be vastly expanded and translated into specific directives. As reports flow up the line, they must be condensed in order not to overwhelm the ultimate recipients at the top of the organizational pyramid. Like all translations, these involve some shifts of meaning.

2. The willingness of persons in organizations to communicate or to receive communications cannot be taken for granted. Most communications have emotional significance. Transmission and reception are seriously curtailed when the consequences are perceived, however faintly, as unpleasant.

3. Component and factional organizations routinely erect barriers to prevent the passage of information wanted by the larger organization, whose transmission is regarded as injurious to the suborganization.

4. The technical requirements for an effective system of com-

[53] William F. Whyte et. al., *Money and Motivation* (New York: Harper, 1955), especially Chapter 14.

[54] For another version of communication theory, with emphasis on encoding and decoding, see William V. Haney, *Communication: Patterns and Incidents* (Homewood, Ill.: Irwin, 1960).

munication are severe. All organizational networks have mechanical defects so that messages go astray, lag excessively, are misunderstood or distorted without any intention. In the admirable jargon of cybernetics, any message includes a component of noise.

5. What is communicated has both a manifest and a latent content. Even if the manifest content is perceived identically by persons occupying different positions in the organization, it is impossible—by virtue of the fact that they occupy different positions—for them to perceive the same latent content.

Whether the problem of distortion is critical in a given situation depends upon an empirical finding that what is communicated does, or does not, allow the organization to function above a minimum level of effectiveness. Even in a smooth-running organization distortion will appear whenever messages are exchanged between people of different statuses or between equals who are not in continuous interaction. Indeed, these distortions provide a key to the outside observer as he collects expressions of attitudes or reports of behavior at various points in the network of communication. An investigator who receives identical reports about any situation from people viewing the situation from different positions may be certain that something is amiss. Variation in frames of reference is inherent in all status orders.

It is also important to observe that the communication system of any organization includes *information screens*. These are intended to prevent the flow of messages in certain directions, just as channels of communication facilitate the movement of information in other directions. In a study of the academic labor market, for example, it was discovered that reliable market information is not generally available to academic men.[55] Standard information screens prevent the dissemination of certain information entirely or distort it so that it becomes unreliable. Those that came to light in the course of the study included:

1. An information screen concealing reasons for departure from colleagues when a faculty member resigns to take a position in another academic department.

[55] Chapter 3, "How Vacancies Occur," in Theodore Caplow and Reece J. McGee, *The Academic Marketplace* (New York: Basic Books, 1958).

2. An information screen concealing the terms and conditions of a new position accepted elsewhere from the former colleagues of the migrant.
3. An information screen obscuring the subsequent career of a migrant from his former colleagues.
4. An information screen surrounding all of the official personnel actions of superiors in the academic hierarchy.
5. An information screen concealing from faculty members the criteria by which they are officially evaluated in the administrative processes of the university.

Information screens protect an organization from unwanted outside evaluations and protect peer groups and status levels from each other. Thus, the information screen that obscures the later career of a professor from his former colleagues enables them to maintain the myth that resignations are prompted by the lure of better positions elsewhere, not by dissatisfaction within their own department. By blocking subsequent communication with the departed man or his new friends, the information screen also reduces the consequences of having departmental secrets carried outside the department or communicated to persons whom the department does not control.

The information screen that surrounds the personnel actions of administrative officers in the academic hierarchy is one of the main sources of their authority. Since the relationship between evidence and decision is not known, the people affected cannot challenge a decision on rational grounds, and their ability to manipulate decisions in their own favor is severely limited. In an organization in which authority is ambiguously defined, secrecy is one of the mainstays. The information screen by which departments conceal their operations from administrative superiors allows them to present the appearance of unanimity.

One of the best studies of communication problems in an organizational context is Ronken and Lawrence's case history of a factory work group assigned to the production of a new kind of electronic tube.[56] The authors are able to show in detail how and why communications between unequals are distorted. For example,

[56] Harriet O. Ronken and Paul R. Lawrence, *Administering Change: A Case Study of Human Relations in a Factory* (Boston: Harvard Graduate School of Business Administration, 1952). The quotations are from pages 294–97.

in the relationship between a foreman and a group of girls who had recently been transferred to his department:

> When Lou said, "Yes, I know about that problem," his ambiguous remark could have meant many things. In view of what we know about Lou's frame of reference, we might hear him say, "Yes, I know that that is a problem. Because I do not yet have any idea how to handle it, I do not dare discuss it with you, for fear of appearing ignorant." In view of the girls' own frames of references, however, they heard him say something quite different. What they heard was more like this, "I know a great deal more about it than you do. I do not need you to point this out. I will take care of it myself." When, then the problem was not immediately "taken care of," but remained to annoy them, the girls blamed Lou.

Dozens of similar examples lead to these empirical generalizations:

> 1. Everyone we saw on the Amicon tube project brought to the situation a picture of himself in relation to the world, a way of interpreting his experiences, a set of feelings, assumptions, and expectations—in short, a frame of reference from which he looked at the world. These factors were prime determinants of what was communicated in any given interaction: what was "said," what was "heard," and what was "done."
>
> 2. Communication was impaired when the demands of the job brought together people with frames of reference which were incompatible (i.e., which led them into behavior that seemed to deny the validity of one another's feelings, assumptions, and expectations). Under those circumstances people tended to have no more contact with one another than was strictly necessary, to dislike, discount, resist ideas from, and even resent one another, and to make comparatively little progress on the task at hand.
>
> 3. Communication was facilitated when the demands of the job to be done brought together people with complementary frames of reference. Under those circumstances people tended to see more of one another than the necessary minimum, to like and respect one another, and to get more work done.
>
> 4. Communication was facilitated when there was in the situation someone who was able to recognize and accept a frame of reference different from his own; who was sufficiently free from preoccupation with the intent of his behavior to be able to see its effect on someone else; and who was able to state his point of view in terms that made sense from the listener's frame of reference.
>
> 5. Communication was facilitated when there was in the situa-

tion someone who had some insight into his own frame of reference, who recognized that his own feelings affected his perceptions, who was aware that he had to be perceived as a source of help before he could be helpful.

The authors remark in conclusion that the distinction between objectivity and subjectivity in behavior is one of our cultural myths; that we have been trained to distinguish between fact and emotion, or between reality and opinion, without realizing that the external reality we perceive in an interactive situation is a function of the frame of reference we bring to it.

INTERACTION NETWORKS

Present knowledge about interaction networks in large corporations rests on several distinct groups of studies: empirical charting of the flow of information through vertical and horizontal channels,[57] experimental studies of the relative efficiency of task groups having different types of communication nets,[58] descriptive studies of supervisory behavior,[59] and interaction process studies, using rather

[57] See the papers by A. M. J. Chorus, Keith Davis, Peter M. Blau, Albert H. Rubenstein, and Theodore Caplow in Section 4, "Communication," in Albert H. Rubenstein and Chadwick J. Haberstroh (eds.), *Some Theories of Organization* (Homewood, Ill.: Irwin, 1960).

[58] The classic papers are Alex Bavelas, "Communication Patterns in Task Oriented Groups," in Dorwin Cartwright and Alvin Zander (eds.), *Group Dynamics* (Evanston, Ill.: Row, Peterson, 1953); Harold H. Leavitt, "Some Effects of Certain Communication Patterns on Group Performance," *Journal of Abnormal and Social Psychology*, Vol. XLVI, No. 1 (1951); George A. Heise and George A. Miller, "Problem Solving by Small Groups Using Various Communication Nets," *Journal of Abnormal and Social Psychology*, Vol. XLVI, No. 4 (1951); Harold Guetzkow and Herbert A. Simon, "The Impact of Certain Communication Nets upon Organization and Performance in Task-oriented Groups," *Management Science*, Vol. I, No. 3 (April, 1955) and Vol. I, No. 4 (July, 1955); Harold Guetzkow and William R. Dill, "Factors in the Organizational Development of Task-oriented Groups," *Sociometry*, Vol. XX, No. 2 (June, 1957); Robert Dubin, "Stability of Human Organizations," in Mason Haire (ed.), *Modern Organization Theory* (New York: Wiley, 1959); Mark Mulder, "Communication Structure, Decision Structure and Group Performance," *Sociometry*, Vol. XXIII, No. 1 (March, 1960).

[59] A full bibliography of the empirical studies reporting the interactions of executives and supervisors is given in Robert Dubin, "Business Behavior Behaviorally Viewed," in George B. Strother (ed.), *Social Science Approaches to Business Behavior* (Homewood, Ill.: Dorsey-Irwin, 1962).

elaborate systems of coding and quantification.[60] This substantial body of empirical work supports a number of tentative conclusions.

1. The largest share of the time of managers at every level is spent in face-to-face interaction, that is, talking to superiors, inferiors, and peers. The proportion of time spent in talk increases with status, so that the highest-ranking executives in many corporations have virtually no time at all for reading, writing, or solitary reflection.

2. The proportion of time spent with superiors seems to increase as one moves upward through the organizational pyramid. (This is merely a tendency, and some exceptions are noted.) In effect, those having high status spend more of their time looking downward in the organization than those of low status; those of low status look mostly upward.

3. The proportion of total interaction involving peers seems to decrease with status, but it is substantial at all levels. Indeed, the interaction network in most enterprises cannot be understood from the table of organization alone. Such tables emphasize interaction between superiors and subordinates. They understate or omit interaction between peers and unscheduled interaction across department lines, but the necessary coordination of effort in an enterprise could not be carried on at all without a large volume of "horizontal communications." [61]

4. In addition to horizontal communication about work, all large-scale organizations seem to develop grapevines to diffuse information of general interest, that is, to carry news, gossip, and rumors. In stable organizations, the grapevine is rapid, highly

[60] See the numerous publications of Eliot D. Chapple and his associates, especially his "Quantitative Analysis of Complex Organizational Systems," *Human Organization,* Vol. XXI, No. 2 (Summer, 1961) and Eliot D. Chapple and Leonard R. Sayles, *The Measure of Management* (New York: Macmillan, 1961). A quite different system of coding has been used by Robert F. Bales and his students; it is fully explained in his *Interaction Process Analysis: A Method for the Study of Small Groups* (Cambridge, Mass.: Addison-Wesley, 1949) and "The Equilibrium Problem in Small Groups," in Talcott Parsons, Robert F. Bales, and Edward A. Shils, *Working Papers in the Theory of Action* (Glencoe, Ill.: Free Press, 1953).

[61] Henry W. Riecken, "The Effect of Talkativeness on Ability to Influence Group Solutions of Problems," *Sociometry,* Vol. XXI, No. 4 (December, 1958), as well as a number of experiments reported by Robert F. Bales.

selective of messages and recipients, and surprisingly accurate. Individual and group differences in participation are conspicuous. The process whereby a few "liaison individuals" come to play a disproportionate part in every grapevine is not entirely understood, but the phenomenon has been repeatedly observed, together with an unequal distribution of information that keeps certain segments of the organization better informed than they apparently need to be, while isolating or bypassing others.

5. In horizontal communication, increases of interaction appear to be unequivocally favorable for the status of individuals and the prestige of groups. The experimental studies of small groups show that participants who are talkative exert more influence than those who are quiet. The observational studies of peer groups show that higher status is usually accompanied by more interaction and especially by greater "receipt of contacts" from peers than is true of low status.

6. Both individuals and groups appear to develop habits of interaction, for example competitiveness or impatience, that persist over time and may not be relevant to the immediate situation. The irregular appearance of many interaction networks is due to the fact that the ability of any pair of positions to communicate depends on the accidents of matching.

SERIAL, CIRCULAR, AND RADIAL NETWORKS

In Leavitt's original experiment, five subjects were seated around a table, separated by partitions, and restricted to written communication. By opening and closing slots in the partitions, the interaction networks could be experimentally manipulated. Four patterns were tested: the *circle,* which allowed each subject to pass notes to one other subject on either side; the *chain,* a version of the same pattern with two closed ends; the *wheel,* having one subject at the center who could exchange messages with all of the others, who were unable to communicate directly among themselves; and the "Y," consisting of a four-member chain, plus a fifth subject who could exchange notes only with one of the inner members.[62]

[62] Leavitt, *op. cit.*

In another early study, Heise and Miller [63] used five triads having all the possible combinations of one- and two-way channels among three positions. Guetzkow and his collaborators [64] used the wheel and circle and, as a third type, an *all-channel* network, in which each of five positions could communicate directly with any other. Other small group experimenters have introduced minor variations.

Davis,[65] in his descriptive study of an industrial grapevine, distinguishes four types of network: the *single strand,* identical with Leavitt's chain; the *gossip chain,* identical with the wheel as described above; the *probability chain,* in which subjects communicate randomly to some but not all of the adjacent persons; and the *cluster chain,* based on liaison persons, each of whom communicates to at least one nonliaison person and to no more than one other liaison person.

Dubin [66] discusses organizational stability in terms of three fundamental types of linkage: *serial* linkage, which is the same as the chain; *radial* linkage, which is the same as the wheel; and *circular* linkage, which is the same as Guetzkow's all-channel network. It does not correspond to the circle network in the earlier small group experiments. He also presents combinations of these basic types.

The Bavelas-Leavitt experiments show that the wheel-shaped groups performed their simple tasks best in all respects, working faster and making fewer errors than any of the other sets. The circle was least efficient, while the Y and the chain fell in between. Heise and Miller obtained results consistent with these. Their Figure 3, which corresponds to the wheel, was superior in most respects to the other nets; they make an interesting comment that

> The man in position A of net 3 is forced by his central position to become a coordinator. He usually warns the other two members at the beginning of a trial, and takes charge of any procedural matters that arise during the trial. When asked at the conclusion of the experiment which position in the network they preferred, all subjects chose this central position.[67]

[63] Heise and Miller, *op. cit.*
[64] Guetzkow and Simon, *op. cit.*, and Guetzkow and Dill, *op. cit.*
[65] Davis, "Management Communication and the Grapevine," in Rubenstein and Haberstroh, *op. cit.*
[66] Dubin, "The Stability of Human Organizations," *op. cit.*
[67] Heise and Miller, *op. cit.*, p. 331.

Figure 7–1

TYPES OF INTERACTION NETWORKS

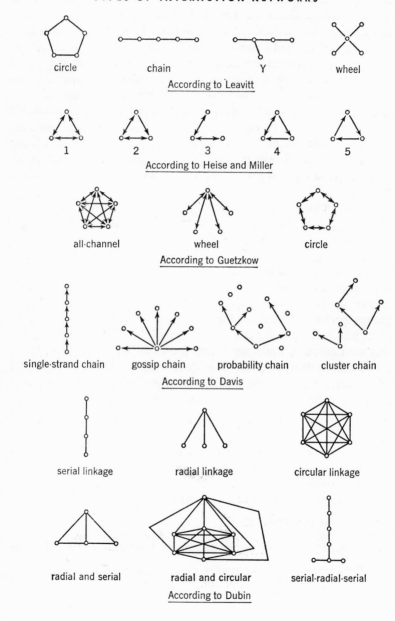

circle   chain   Y   wheel

According to Leavitt

1   2   3   4   5

According to Heise and Miller

all-channel   wheel   circle

According to Guetzkow

single-strand chain   gossip chain   probability chain   cluster chain

According to Davis

serial linkage   radial linkage   circular linkage

radial and serial   radial and circular   serial-radial-serial

According to Dubin

The Guetzkow-Simon experiments confirm these results but move to a new kind of explanation. Once again the wheel permits the fastest problem-solving with the fewest messages, the circle is least efficient, and the all-channel structure is close to the wheel. These investigators, however, attribute the differences to the initial difficulty experienced by the circle groups in working out a stable organizational arrangement. Imposing the wheel net on the subjects enabled them to settle very quickly on a "stable two-level hierarchy"; in other words, to agree on a pattern of exchanging information through a leader. The circle and all channel groups were initially handicapped. These networks are much more difficult to convert into an efficient arrangement for the exchange of information than the wheel is. When the subjects did succeed in working out a hierarchy and a stable method of exchanging information, the circle and channel turned out to be no less efficient than the wheel groups. In the Guetzkow and Dill experiments the subjects were given more scope to restructure their own networks between trials than in the other studies, and most of the groups moved rapidly toward the simplest possible wheel.

Leaning heavily on this evidence, and on the theoretical assumption that the stability of an organization demands the minimum number of links among its components, Dubin concludes that radial linkage is inherently more effective than serial, circular, or compound linkages because it minimizes the number of bonds required to hold the organization together and, by implication, the cost of organizing. The hypothesis is interesting but essentially unsupported. True, radial linkage appears to be advantageous in small task groups, but all-channel linkage, which ought to be the least effective under Dubin's assumptions, is nearly as efficient as the wheel and plainly superior to the chain or circle. In addition, the leap from small ad hoc experimental groups to giant organizations is too long to take without additional evidence.

Other network experiments underline the importance of what might be called the *organizability* of the experimental group. Shaw [68] found indications that while his wheel groups were faster than circle groups in solving simple problems, they were slower in solving com-

[68] M. E. Shaw, "Some Effects of Problem Complexity upon Problem Solution Efficiency in Different Communication Nets," *Journal of Experimental Psychology,* Vol. XLVIII (1954).

plex problems. He proposes the explanation that the central subject in the wheel becomes saturated with information. This view has been challenged by more recent studies,[69] which seem to show that the weakness of the wheel network in coping with complex problems is temporary and can be explained by the need to develop authority (a "centralized decision structure") first, which takes time.

We are left with a reasonable certainty that the shape of the inter-action network influences both the productivity of a group and its ability to reorganize itself. It also seems to be well established from these experiments that a maximum volume of communication is anti-thetical to high output. A status order, even if rudimentary, appears to facilitate any task performance. The reduction of interaction for a given level of activity follows immediately as soon as a coordinating position can be designated and a division of labor begun. Dubin's minimum-linkage hypothesis would open up all sorts of new possi-bilities of organizational engineering, if it could be substantiated. For the moment, however, it does not rest on much firmer ground than the intuitive propositions of other writers about the optimum span of control. Although there have been many managerial ex-periments in flattening the organizational pyramid and increasing the number of subordinates reporting to one supervisor—to as many as fifty, or even more—[70] we still lack the knowledge that would make it possible to plan an interaction network for maximum achieve-ment.

Improving Voluntarism

INDIVIDUAL ADJUSTMENT IN THE ENTERPRISE

A situation is defined as a problem when someone wishes to change it or believes that it ought to be changed. Thus, in the relationship between an individual and an organization, some features of the relationship may be perceived as a problem by the individual but not by the organization, and vice versa. Even when a given situation is

---

[69] See Mulder, *op. cit.*

[70] See James C. Worthy, "Organizational Structure and Employee Morale," *American Sociological Review,* Vol. XV, No. 2 (April, 1950).

viewed by both parties as a problem, their reasons are likely to be quite different.

The opposition between the corporate enterprise and the individuals who compose it, or who must deal with it, is one of the most discussed topics of our time. Even under the best conditions, large-scale organizations do not serve the ends of all their members equally well. At the other extreme, an enterprise may be heartily detested by most of its members and its program may be carried on by people who abhor its goals.

With some risk of oversimplification, the problems of the individual in an organization and the related but incongruent problems of the organization vis-à-vis the individual may be captured by a model that assumes a single pair relationship between the individual and the organization as a whole. Like simpler pair relationships, this one may be described by the analytic variables of status, interaction, valence, and activity. However, for convenience, we will give them slightly different names. The variable S in the generalized pair relationship between the individual and the organization is a measure of the individual's *subjection* to organizational control; the variable I is a measure of his *involvement;* the variable V measures the *volition* of the individual; and the variable A is a measure of his *adaptation* to the organizational program.

A problem is defined, according to this model, whenever the value of any variable is perceived by either party (or an interested observer) as too high, too low, or too unstable. This perception is admittedly and explicitly subjective, dependent on the desires of the definer, and not capable of complete validation. However, partial validation may occur in various ways—for example, when both the individual and the organization agree that a given variable is too high, too low, or too unstable, or when impartial observers agree that a particular relationship is greatly out of line with others in the same organization or the same set. Even in these instances, the problem remains essentially subjective. A variable may be characterized as too high by the individual and at the same time as too low by the organization, and either party may perceive a problem where the other recognizes none at all. Even when the individual and the organization happen to agree that one of the variables of their relationship is too high, too low, or too unstable, the problems they perceive as arising from this condition are not necessarily the same. For example, when men are worked too hard in a factory (A is too high) they complain of exploitation, while management sees problems of turnover and absenteeism. Incongruence in an individual's organizational status (S is unstable) leads him to perceive injustice in situations wherein the organization notices only a lack of predictability.

Table 7–1, "Stresses in the Relationship Between an Individual

Table 7–1

STRESSES IN THE RELATIONSHIP BETWEEN AN INDIVIDUAL AND AN ORGANIZATION

CONDITION	EXAMPLE OF INDIVIDUAL'S PROBLEM	EXAMPLE OF ORGANIZATION'S PROBLEM
1. S too high	coercion	threat of rebellion
2. S too low	ambiguity	lack of flexibility
3. S unstable	injustice	low predictability
4. I too high	loss of autonomy	deflection of goals
5. I too low	anomie	low participation—"apathy"
6. I unstable	disorientation	tendency to factionalism
7. V too high	sacrifice of values in other systems	resistance to innovation
8. V too low	alienation	noncooperation—sabotage
9. V unstable	susceptibility to crisis	unreliable support
10. A too high	exploitation	turnover and absenteeism
11. A too low	boredom	low productivity
12. A unstable	insecurity	underutilization of resources

and an Organization," shows some of the problems that occur for individuals when each of the four variables are perceived as too high, too low, or too unstable and, in another column, it shows the quite different problems recognized by organizations under the same conditions. None of the problems shown in the table are rare. Indeed, the case literature of industrial sociology includes empirical examples of every one of them.[71] Yet the distribution of urgency is not quite

[71] For example, following the numbers of the table: (1) Chowdhry and Pal's Mill A, (2) Argyris' Friendly First Bank, (3) Homans' Ledger Clerks, (4) Roethlisberger's Bank Wiring Room, (5) Jaques' Glacier Works Council, (6) Ronken and Lawrence's Amicon Project Crew, (7) Harrington's Crystal

so symmetrical. If we examine the organizational pyramid with reference to this model, we note that moving from bottom to the top the relationships between individuals and the organization as "a generalized other" show changes of form. A relationship at the top of the pyramid, compared to a relationship at the bottom, is likely to rate lower on Subjection and higher on Involvement, Volition, and Adaptation. The vulnerability to specific problems differs accordingly. Executives are far more likely than laborers to suffer from role ambiguity and to sacrifice their family life to corporate values. But laborers are much more likely to experience resentment and boredom.

In the case of the business enterprise, the organization and the individual are not fully committed to each other. To some extent, each views the other as an instrument to help him achieve goals he imports from other systems. Hence, the organization looks for means of increasing the individual's dependence on itself, while the individual seeks to free himself as far as possible from the attachment. The enterprise is tempted to regard any existing level of Involvement, Volition, and Adaptation as too low and it grapples the individual with steel hoops. The individual is likely to regard the same levels as too high; he would prefer to be free. Managers and managerial experts concentrate on the discovery of new incentives to raise low productivity and to enlist emotional support for the goals of the enterprise, while spokesmen for the individual, such as William F. Whyte and David Riesman, are concerned with the loss of individual autonomy and the subtle, modern forms of exploitation.

Since our immediate concern is with the self-improvement of the industrial enterprise, the following discussion will consider several major lines of effort, accompanied by appropriate theorizing, whereby managers have sought to raise the level of voluntarism.

THE DESIGN OF INCENTIVES

Enormous ingenuity and contrivance have gone into the development of incentives for those industrial workers whose wages are determined on the basis of their output.[72] A piecework plan consists of

Palace, (8) Chinoy's Automobile Workers, (9) Zaleznik's Machine Shop, (10) Walker and Guest's Assembly Line, (11) Barnes' Research Laboratory, and (12) Archibald's Wartime Shipyard.

[72] For an interesting discussion of incentive systems as exchange transactions between the individual and the organization, see Nathan D. Grundstein, "Pro-

an output standard based on time-and-motion study, with individual or group bonuses for output above the standard and penalties for failing to make the standard.[73] Profit sharing is a variant of the same principle, and in a few instances, as in the famous Scanlon Plan, the production group to which the incentive applies is the entire work force.[74]

Although piecework wages have been paid since before the beginning of the Industrial Revolution, and bonuses were known in the nineteenth century, incentive schemes of this kind developed in the wake of Frederick W. Taylor's discoveries. Subsequently, it became apparent that money is by no means the only incentive to which workers are sensitive. Surveys sometimes found wage rates ranking seventh or eighth among desired conditions of work. There were even tendencies in management circles to dismiss monetary incentives as unimportant, but these tendencies were quickly corrected by experience.

The design of incentives is haunted by three distinct types of uncertainty. First, although the theory of wage incentives assumes that normal achievement can be objectively determined, this is seldom the case.[75] There is no method of determining normal or maximum output a priori for most industrial jobs, even when they are decomposed into separate operations. Hence, standard rates must be set on the basis of the measured performance of workers on the job or in some comparable work. Such measurements establish a minimum-output rate only. The maximum cannot be located unless the workers who are studied are too skillful for any improvement. This condition is seldom met in the real industrial world, hence the output standard for most jobs is firmly anchored in thin air.[76]

Another sort of relativism arises from the impossibility of determining—except in a rough and ready way—the most attractive distribution of incentive payments. The puzzle is almost unsolvable.

legomena to Ethics for Administrators," in Harlan Cleveland and Harold D. Lasswell (eds.), *Ethics and Bigness* (New York: Harper, 1962).

[73] Explained in Adam Abruzzi, *Work Measurement* (New York: Columbia University Press, 1952).

[74] Frederick G. Lesieur (ed.), *The Scanlon Plan* (New York: Wiley, 1958).

[75] A thorough discussion of this point will be found in Edward Gross, *Work and Society* (New York: Crowell, 1958), pp. 530–47.

[76] This fact is often dramatically illustrated when production processes are transplanted from one country to another. The work standards established in the new country are sometimes much higher for certain operations than those in the home plant.

Steeply graded incentive payments are the most effective in the short run, but they disturb the congruence of status and wages. The most important source of uncertainty is that incentives are usually appraised by the people concerned in terms of relative advantage and deprivation.[77]

The guiding principles may be summed up as follows:

1. Wages are evaluated by wage earners in relation to a reference group of peers, competitors, or acquaintances. Privileges and status symbols are also evaluated relatively rather than absolutely.

2. The reference groups used for the evaluation of wages are not whimsically selected by the individual, and they cannot be ascertained casually. It often takes a good deal of investigation to discover what standards are actually in use for measuring relative advantage and deprivation.

3. Improvement in the payments or privileges of some members of a reference group will be perceived as a deprivation by their fellows when their own treatment remains unchanged and even when it is improved but to a lesser degree.[78] The resistance to relative deprivation is stronger than the attraction of an equivalent relative advantage.

4. It follows from the foregoing that an incentive system in which earnings fluctuate about an average will be less effective than one in which earnings are stable at the same level.

5. Since the earnings of a worker under an incentive plan cannot fall in relation to those of his reference group without imposing a relative deprivation on him, or rise without imposing a relative deprivation on others, the incentive plan itself includes powerful dis-incentives and encourages the control of output by peer groups.[79]

[77] The concept of relative deprivation was developed in *The American Soldier*. The complementary concept of relative advantage was added by Merton and Kitt in their restatement and clarification of the original analysis, Robert K. Merton and Alice S. Kitt, "Contributions to the Theory of Reference Group Behavior," in Merton and Lazarsfeld, *op. cit.*

[78] For the history of such a case, see Leonard R. Sayles and George Strauss, "Conflicts Within the Local Union," *Harvard Business Review*, Vol. XXX, No. 6 (November–December, 1952).

[79] Whyte remarks that

. . . men are concerned about their pay in relative as well as in absolute terms; the point is obvious to anyone with industrial experience, yet all

LONG-RANGE INCENTIVES

Lewin [80] was the first to point out that the morale of individuals in an organization is not explicable by their situation at a given time but is heavily affected by their "psychological future" and to a lesser extent by their past. He cites the findings of Farber's study of suffering in prison: the prisoner's daily routine had no appreciable correlation with the amount of his suffering, but there was a definite relationship between the amount of suffering the prisoner reported and his attitudes about the justice of his sentence and his chances of parole.

The implications of time perspective for the industrial enterprise are diverse. It should be noted that:

1. Long-run satisfaction with an organizational career depends on whether the subject's initial level of aspiration is achieved or exceeded. The expectations acquired in the course of socialization are crucial in establishing the demand, so to speak, which the individual makes on the organization in the course of his subsequent participation.
2. Aspirations are developed in various ways and are partly independent of an individual's actual prospects.

What happens when aspirations are frustrated has been extensively investigated. Although it is an unresolved question whether the mobility chances of industrial workers have suffered a long-term decline,[81] the chance of promotion from the shop floor in the mass

---

too often we fail to draw the conclusions which logically follow. This means that, in planning the introduction of an incentive system, management cannot afford to concentrate its attention on the problem of motivating one particular group of workers alone. It must, at the same time, recognize the place these workers occupy in the status and pay system of the plant.
William F. Whyte, "Human Relations Theory—A Progress Report," *Harvard Business Review*, Vol. XXXIV, No. 5 (September–October, 1956), p. 128.

[80] Kurt Lewin, *Resolving Social Conflicts* (New York: Harper, 1948), especially Chapter 7, "Time Perspective and Morale."

[81] For varying viewpoints see W. Lloyd Warner, "The Corporation Man," in Edward S. Mason (ed.), *The Corporation in Modern Society* (Cambridge, Mass.: Harvard University Press, 1960), Robert C. Stone, "Factory Organization and Vertical Mobility," *American Sociological Review*, Vol. XVIII, No. 1 (February, 1953), and J. O. Hertzler, "Some Tendencies Toward a Closed Class System in the United States," *Social Forces*, Vol. XXX (March, 1952).

industries is certainly slight. Chinoy [82] studied the aspirations of automobile workers and concluded that they "face a patent disparity between the promises of the tradition of opportunity and the realities of their own experience." Within the organization, they meet this disparity by reducing their aspirations and redefining success as the achievement of modest, small goals. More important, perhaps, is the process of displacement by which aspirations are transferred outside of the factory to the acquisition of possessions, vocational ambitions for children, and the goal of leaving the factory for a small business venture.

Guest [83] reaches parallel conclusions in another study of automobile workers. He attributes even more dissatisfaction than Chinoy does to the discrepancy between limited opportunity and the tradition of unlimited opportunity.

A finding on which Chinoy and Guest agree is restated by Riesman and Bloomberg in their study of leisure and work in the industrial population.[84] They note a trend away from exclusive work emphasis, a diminishing amount of time actually spent at work, the increasing importance of nonwork life, a growing variety of leisure activities, the delaying of entrance into the working force, and the increasing preference for early retirement, and they conclude that the industrial enterprise is becoming emotionally neutral for blue-collar workers, and perhaps for lower-echelon managers. It provides income and an occupational identification for the individual, but his real life-interests lie elsewhere, sometimes in another occupation.[85]

The incentives that the modern corporation offers to its executives are very different from those that it offers to its workers. Executives are hired, in theory, for an indefinite continuous tenure, and their long-term incentives are offered in the form of status gains. Salaries and fringe benefits are contrived to match statuses; they are not

[82] Ely Chinoy, "The Tradition of Opportunity and the Aspirations of Automobile Workers," *American Journal of Sociology,* Vol. LVII, No. 5 (March, 1952) and *Automobile Workers and the American Dream* (New York: Doubleday, 1955). The quotation is from page 453.

[83] Robert H. Guest, "Work Careers and Aspirations of Automobile Workers," *American Sociological Review,* Vol. XIX, No. 2 (April, 1954).

[84] David Riesman and Warner Bloomberg, Jr., "Work and Leisure: Fusion or Polarity?" in Conrad M. Arensberg et al. (eds.), *Research in Industrial Human Relations: A Critical Appraisal* (New York: Harper, 1957).

[85] It is estimated that nearly one-third of the workers in American automobile factories hold a second paid job. The practice is known as "moon-

visualized as independent inducements. The executive's whole time belongs to the company, and any outside activity that does not contribute to corporate purposes may be viewed with suspicion. Considerable attention is given to long-range incentives, such as retirement annuities and stock options, that discourage mobility by making it costly.

The situation of the industrial worker is totally different. Although he may work an uninterrupted lifetime for the same company, there is no expectation that he will do so and no obligation on the part of the company to keep him continuously employed. In the normal course of events, lay-offs of varying duration for the company's convenience will be part of his work history. With the growth of social security and unemployment insurance, his incentives for remaining in one employment decline, and most corporations do not try to reinforce them. The company's claim on him is limited to his paid working time. There are very few added incentives outside of the immediate work situation.

THE PLANNING OF EMOTIONS

Here again, the pioneer work of Mayo and Lewin set the tone for much of what was to follow in research and industrial practice. Both of them advanced the view that a high level of voluntarism in the enterprise depended on binding the individual worker into a primary group of work associates and converting the solidarity of that group into support for the corporate program. Riesman and Bloomberg comment:

> Whereas Marx saw the factory as disorganizing, Mayo, examining the anxious reveries of middle-aged Polish women in the Hawthorne Plant, saw it as the source of leadership and the countervailing power to *anomie,* with the sociability of the factory workgroup as a kind of enclave of leisure within work—releasing the latter's tensions and allowing for a smoother, less insistently sabotaged output.[86]

This is the key to many tangled situations that would formerly have seemed enigmatic or irrational. The hope that employee discontents

---

lighting." Others operate small businesses or develop hobbies to the point where they become vocations.

[86] *Ibid.,* p. 4.

can be resolved by judicious staging of face-to-face interaction pervades much of the literature of industrial sociology and psychology.

Thus, when Wilensky and Wilensky [87] analyzed the counseling program that figures so largely in the famous studies at the Hawthorne Plant of Western Electric [88] they discovered that:

> The redirection of employee attention away from his original definition of his grievance through the "multi-valued way of talking" is held up as an ideal to the counselor. Especially in crisis periods—like a mass layoff—is the counselor able to adapt his techniques to serve company ends. . . . Counseling has helped to protect management's freedom to promote, downgrade, transfer, train, discipline, lay off, apply a variety of rewards and sanction (with a minimum of interference from a relatively cooperative union)—in short, it has helped the company retain its control over the worker.

This line of criticism has been carried furthest by the nonacademic sociologist Whyte in *The Organization Man,*[89] a somewhat humorous and sometimes bitter description of the way in which the large corporate enterprise has extended its influence and its passion for conformity over an ever widening area of its employees' lives. Whyte is troubled to find that this extension of control is welcomed by most of those concerned. To justify his concern about the loss of an autonomy which the losers do not seem to regret, he proposes a bill of particulars against the "social ethic." It is redundant, he says, for society to stress extrovert values that are easily developed and to protect itself against individual initiative and imagination, which are always in short supply. The social ethic prematurely separates technique from conduct and the skills of adjustment from the purposes of adjustment. Morale and team spirit are adopted as ends in themselves.

The social ethic is delusory, says Whyte, because the interests of the individual and society are never entirely compatible and when the individual surrenders his right to judge into the hands of an

[87] Jeanne L. Wilensky and Harold L. Wilensky, "Personnel Counseling: The Hawthorne Case," *American Journal of Sociology,* Vol. LVII, No. 3 (November, 1951).

[88] For a philosophical discussion of the issues raised by the Western Electric studies, see Georges Friedmann, *Industrial Society* (ed. Harold L. Sheppard), (Glencoe, Ill.: Free Press, 1955) and his *Le Travail en Miettes* (Paris: Gallimard, 1956).

[89] William H. Whyte, Jr., *op. cit.* Whyte's "social ethic" is almost synonymous with Riesman's "other directedness." Riesman et al., *op. cit.*

organization, it will do crooked justice, looking after its own interests. The social ethic is static because organizations in themselves have no ultimate aims. It is self-destructive because the quest for normalcy leads to neuroses and the social ethic makes them worse. The norms of conformity, by inviting individuals to seem more like each other and the common standard, make it ever more difficult for them to live with their different selves.

> The skills of human relations easily tempt the new administrator into the practice of a tyranny more subtle and more pervasive than that which he means to supplant. No one wants to see the old authoritarian return, but at least it could be said of him that what he wanted primarily from you was your sweat. The new man wants your soul.[90]

Perhaps the most extreme form of the social ethic—which has manifold forms—is "sensitivity training for executives and supervisors" as developed by followers of Lewin at the Institute of Industrial Relations of the University of California, Los Angeles.[91] The assumptions of the movement are that face-to-face interaction, especially in groups, is the fundamental activity of supervisors, that effectiveness in face-to-face interaction depends upon "interpersonal skill" (also called social sensitivity and empathy) and that interpersonal skill is developed by training and leads to "behavioral flexibility." Many incidental advantages are claimed for sensitivity training—the development of self-understanding, insight into the motives of others, understanding of intergroup processes, awareness of the organizational culture and, above all, greater influence over people.

The fundamental procedure for this training is a series of meetings of a small group with a nondirective trainer.[92] The fundamental activity of the group is the discussion of itself and its own processes —an experience that ultimately generates a good deal of emotion among the participants. A kind of mystical efficacy is attributed to

[90] William H. Whyte, Jr., *op. cit.,* p. 397.

[91] Robert Tannenbaum, Irving R. Weschler, and Fred Massarik, *Leadership and Organization: A Behavioral Science Approach* (New York: McGraw-Hill, 1961).

[92] The procedure was originally developed at the National Training Laboratory in Group Development at Bethel. Its partisans acknowledge the influence of Freudian psychoanalysis and Rogerian nondirective therapy as well as group dynamics.

the groupness of the group. The account of one series of thirty meetings ends with the comment of the official observer that:

> They had been through much together. They were a "group"—whether they knew it or not, whether they liked it or not. In one way or another, they all had changed. . . . The group seemed to be saying—and for once with the kind of consensus unknown to it during its lifetime—that the end was only apparent; more than likely it was really a beginning.[93]

The typical crises in sensitivity training meetings are struggles between the group and a defiant member, made restless either by the frustration of the blank agenda or by personal criticism. The desired outcome is the individual's renunciation of his defiance and his penitent re-entry into the group.

Sensitivity training is probably the most extreme form of the social ethic. It has had fairly wide acceptance in industry. Milder forms of training—such as the "conference method"—are more widely diffused. They involve similar but less severe spiritual exercises.

The fundamental perceptions underlying the exaltation of the primary group in modern industrial management are supported by a great deal of evidence. Reduced to simplest terms, these perceptions may be summarized as follows:

1. The enterprise cannot expect the high level of achievement its program specifies without high levels of activity on the part of its members.
2. The activity of individual members is a function of status, interaction, and valence in pair relationships.
3. Many of the individual's pair relationships in a large organization occur within the framework of an organized primary group, composed of peers or of near superiors and inferiors.
4. The rewards and punishments administered by a primary group are more effective in controlling behavior than those administered by a large organization.
5. The most economical and effective way of incorporating the individual in the program of a large organization is through the mediation of a primary group.

[93] Tannenbaum et al., *op. cit.*, p. 166.

6. Primary groups can be trusted to support the organizational program if they are given enough internal autonomy and allowed organizational rewards in return for their contributions.

The entire mechanism turns on this last principle—the discovery that small components and segments develop organizational interests apart from the interests of their members, interests that higher management is often able to satisfy.

THE SELECTION OF COMPATIBLES

"Group-centered" supervision is intentionally designed to develop uniform ways of thinking, feeling, and acting among group members. Conversely, there is overwhelming evidence to show that:

1. The formation of an integrated primary group in any organizational setting is facilitated by homogeneity of characteristics among the potential members and hindered by heterogeneity. Given a cluster of work associates who are equal in status, all male, all white, all Protestant, of similar ethnic origin, and about the same age, the formation of a highly integrated primary group is almost inevitable. Given a cluster of associates who were heterogeneous on *all* of these traits, the maintenance of any interaction network at all would be difficult.
2. Groups with high integration, voluntarism, and achievement are most readily formed from "natural" sociometric pairs—that is, from persons who have high valences for each other. Sociometric choice is correlated with similarity of individual characteristics, and valences tend to be highest in homogeneous pairs.
3. The obvious way to obtain an organizational population in which primary groups form readily and develop high integration is to recruit individuals who resemble each other as much as possible.

Consciously or unconsciously, this set of assumptions has come to dominate the recruitment of executives by large corporations and, where circumstances and hiring practices allow, the recruitment of workers also.[94] The art or pseudoscience of personnel selection con-

[94] Unless solidarity in the work force is more feared than desired, in which case personnel may be carefully selected for *heterogeneity*.

sists very largely of devices for reducing the range of personal variability among the recruits to a group.

Whenever any hiring process is formalized, the first step is usually some restriction of variability. Most of the criteria used are not technically relevant, but they serve the purpose of recruiting compatibles. There is no technical reason why janitors should not be female or Catholic or college educated, yet it is typical for an employer to consider only those janitor applicants who are male, white, married, age 45 to 55, immigrants of north European origin, without college education or craft training, having an I.Q. between 90 and 110. Packard [95] shows that in many corporations the candidate for a junior executive position must be male, a college graduate, white, Protestant, married, native born, within a narrow age range, not too short or too tall, even having an appropriate face. He must also be in good health, inactive in politics, lacking a criminal record, not closely related to anyone with a deviant history, and without any jarring peculiarities such as vegetarianism or an interest in porcelain. His wife, too, must pass a screening along the same lines. Much more subtle devices, such as interest inventories and personality profiles, are used to protect the corporation against the possibility of hiring someone who resembles the standard executive externally but conceals some unexpected variation in his psyche.

The persons recruited by these procedures are indeed compatible and form primary groups very readily, but they sometimes lack imagination, talent, or willingness to disagree with their compatible associates. [96]

[95] Packard, *op. cit.*

[96] Hughes shows, in a survey of industrial development throughout the world, that the factory is almost everywhere an agent of racial and ethnic discrimination. Ethnic exclusiveness, he notes, tends to develop at all levels of colonial industrial hierarchies, the dominant functions remaining in the hands of the founding ethnic group. The necessity of keeping a full labor force operates against exclusiveness in those categories in which large numbers are required—that is to say at the lower levels of skill—but even there:

> The sponsoring power of lower ranks may be less, but is by no means completely lacking in many situations. Coal miners and railroad workers notoriously have great sponsoring power. And even in the colonial regions the members of an ethnic group or clan, or the inhabitants of a village, may have in effect, the power to recruit new workers. In a sense, when industry brings in some new ethnic group it has to do it in opposition to the present workers.

Everett C. Hughes, "Queries Concerning Industry and Society Growing Out

JOB ENLARGEMENT

Perhaps the most interesting effort to improve voluntarism in the industrial enterprise is the world-wide movement toward job enlargement. This movement is a reaction against excessive specialization and what is sometimes called the *micro-division of labor*.[97] Adam Smith's [98] classic case of pin-making in Glasgow two centuries ago is a full-fledged example of micro-division. His analysis suggests that the advantages of increasing specialization increase indefinitely; the fewer operations performed by the worker, the greater his dexterity and the less time wasted in changing operations. This principle was literally accepted from Eli Whitney to Charles Bedault, and as factories grew in size and machines in complexity, the micro-division of factory labor was frequently carried to the point at which the worker was a simple moving part. The process was limited only because the most simplified jobs could often be replaced by mechanical devices. But as fast as this occurred, new micro-divisions took place.

This is still the general situation in modern industry. The overwhelming majority of factory jobs require less than a day's training, and are simple, monotonous, and highly repetitive. Nevertheless, task simplification is no longer accepted as unlimitedly advantageous. Once again, discoveries about actual behavior have modified the basis of industrial rationality. The most important discoveries have been that:

1. The micro-division of labor induces fatigue, boredom, distraction, accidents, and anxieties. The indirect costs of these conditions are reflected in such things as spoilage and turnover. They are likely to outweigh the savings obtained in the last few stages of specialization.
2. Moderately complicated tasks resist interruption and generate psychological impulses toward their own completion (the

---

of Study of Ethnic Relations in Industry," *American Sociological Review,* Vol. XIV, No. 2 (April, 1949), 220.

[97] Admirably documented in Friedmann, *The Anatomy of Work, op. cit.* See also Robert K. Merton, "The Machine, the Worker and the Engineer," in *Social Theory and Social Structure* (Glencoe, Ill.: Free Press, 1957).

[98] Adam Smith, *The Wealth of Nations* (1776).

Zeigarnik effect [99]). This effect is slight or lacking altogether in highly simplified or repetitive tasks. Hence, excessive specialization diminishes the inherent incentive of work.

3. Men, unlike most machines, work more efficiently at a variable than at a constant rate. A constant rate of output cannot much exceed the minimum phase of a more natural, variable rate. Variable work rates are difficult to arrange in an oversimplified job, but they are normal in complex jobs.

4. When work is minutely subdivided, the voluntarism of workers with regard to the enterprise is constantly threatened by the status loss they experience through the degradation and reduction of their skills and the loss of the public identity of their jobs.[100]

5. The loss of identification with the product reduces the worker's ability to take any autonomous purposive action with regard to the productive process. Quality suffers because "nobody is watching," and errors in the production process remain uncorrected because "nobody cares."

6. Excessive specialization reduces cooperation and teamwork, so that under some conditions the worker is isolated from primary-group contacts, and under others the primary groups that form are hostile to the production program.

The net effect of these tendencies is that the micro-division of labor is sometimes—not always—more costly than a lesser division which leaves the individual worker with a more complex and interesting task. Friedmann describes experiments in job enlargement in the United States, Great Britain, France, Belgium, Germany, and Italy. The results are usually favorable to complexity, provided that the enlarged jobs are socially meaningful units and involve real increases in responsibility and pay. The experiment demonstrates that semi-

---

[99] B. Zeigarnik, "Ueber das Behalten von erledigten und unerledigten Handlugen," *Psychologische Forschungen,* Vol. IX (1927); and M. Rickers-Ovsiankina, "Die Wiederaufnahme unterbrochener Handlugen," *Psychologische Forschungen,* Vol. XI (1928). These studies are cited and summarized by Friedmann in *The Anatomy of Work, op. cit.* A more recent study is M. Rickers-Ovsiankina, "Studies in the Personality Structures of Schizophrenic Individuals: II, Reaction to Interrupted Tasks," *Journal of Genetic Psychology,* Vol. XVI (1937).

[100] Merton, *op. cit.*

skilled and unskilled machine operators are capable of performing many of the tasks associated with highly skilled occupations, that the rate of production can often be increased beyond accepted ceilings, that the reduction of constraint is highly favorable for such authoritarian functions as inspection and, once again, that technical innovations can be more effectively introduced with than without the participation and consent of the workers concerned.

RESISTANCE TO CHANGE

Any organization must find the means of maintaining its structure while adapting to changes in the external environment and to the unanticipated consequences of its own growth. The size of a corporate enterprise generally determines how well it is able to do this. The largest corporations, the prototypes of all the others, may be said to have solved the problem.[101] As we descend the scale of size, self-maintenance becomes an increasingly serious problem, down to the bottom of the ladder, where small business enterprises are mostly unstable and short-lived.

The stratification of the large enterprise is seldom threatened from within, but its maintenance in the face of unpredictable changes in the economic environment, like the swings of the business cycle and the transitions between war and peace, is an organizational *tour de force,* achieved by simple and ruthless means. Changes in market conditions require violent oscillations in the volume of production. To reduce the disturbance of its own structure, the corporation divides its employees into two groups. The first consists of managers, technicians, and certain clerical workers and skilled craftsmen, whose tenure is not affected by fluctuations in production. They are hired for continuous employment, and as far as possible their work is arranged to be independent of the volume of production or the profitability of the enterprise from month to month. The other, and much larger, group consists of machine operators, semiskilled artisans, and some clerical and supervisory workers, who are added to, or subtracted from, the payroll as they are needed. The insecure tenure of these people is the price paid for the stability of the entire structure.

---

[101] So far as the enterprise as a whole is concerned; component units are subject to much more uncertainty.

The other principal threat to the stratification of the enterprise is technological change. Improvement in manufacturing methods is nearly continuous under current conditions. The entire industrial system is oriented to a yearly increase in productivity that can be accomplished only in this way. Technological change displaces people, devaluates skills, creates new jobs, modifies the relative prestige of occupations, and revises the norms of component units of enterprise. Automation is a case in point; its effects have been outlined by a number of studies, the major findings of which seem to be these: [102]

1. Any major innovation in production methods will be followed by a period of disorganization during which achievement and voluntarism are sharply lowered and it is impossible to evaluate the success of the innovation. This sequence is described in loving detail in Walker's study of the automation of a mill making seamless iron pipe. His conclusions include a set of general recommendations for managerial policy in the interim period: [103]

   a. Train and educate the men in everything about the new process through repeated meetings in the earlier phases of the changeover
   b. Encourage nonfinancial incentives to develop
   c. Reinforce personal contacts between supervisors and each member of the crew
   d. Develop a special incentive plan for the interim period which takes account of the indirect labor cost of the changeover
   e. Take care of the men displaced in a manner satisfactory to those remaining.

2. It is almost certain that *any* proposed change in the structure of a large organization will be perceived by some of the per-

---

[102] See Georges Gurvitch (ed.), *Industrialisation et Technocratie* (Paris: Librairie Armand Colin, 1949), Charles R. Walker, *Toward the Automatic Factory* (New Haven, Conn.: Yale University Press, 1957), Floyd C. Mann and Laurence K. Williams, "Observations of the Dynamics of a Change to Electronic Data Processing Equipment," *Administrative Science Quarterly*, Vol. V (1960), and Alain Touraine, *L'Evolution du Travail Ouvrier Aux Usines Renault* (Paris: Centre National de la Recherche Scientifique, 1955).
[103] Restated from Walker, *op. cit.*, p. 159.

sons involved as a threat of status loss.[104] The pattern of resistance to an innovation cannot be understood without reference to the distribution of such perceptions. The status threat, of course, may be either real or illusory, but there are few innovations that do not have adverse effects for someone.

The resistance to status threat often makes it very difficult to accomplish such "legitimate" managerial objectives as the consolidation of redundant units. A reorganization may be flatly impossible when the statuses of the persons who would have to carry out the plan are threatened.[105] The popularity of industrial decentralization in recent years is partly explained by the fact that decentralization requires additional positions and raises the status of existing positions. Under decentralization, executive positions in each local unit acquire more autonomy and rise in status. At the same time, the status of executives in the home office is enhanced, even if their operating responsibilities are reduced, because they now have a greater number of subordinates. Frequent reorganizations along these lines lead to an exploding population of vice presidents in large corporations.

STATUS SCHISM

Some degree of antagonism between positions of different status is an inevitable feature of organizational life, but the horizontal division of an organization into two distinct and sharply separated strata, so that all members of the management stratum have higher status than any member of the labor stratum,[106] is a special phenomenon.

Status schism is not merely a differentiation between two broad categories of organizational membership. It is a peculiar type of rela-

[104] For an interesting analysis of organizational changes initiated by outsiders in the name of broad social values, see Ronald Lippitt, Jeanne Watson, and Bruce Westley, *Planned Change: A Comparative Study of Principles and Techniques* (New York: Harcourt, Brace & World, 1958).

[105] Nicely expressed in the comment of Dan Willard of the Baltimore and Ohio on the prospects of consolidating competing railroads: "No one likes to consolidate himself out of a job." *The Reporter,* August 7, 1958, p. 24.

[106] Other examples of status schism will be remembered: officers and enlisted men in military service, faculty and students in a college, masters and slaves in a plantation, guards and prisoners in a penitentiary, staff and inmates in a mental hospital.

tionship that resembles the relationship between rulers and ruled in societies established by conquest, or the endogamous castes developed as an aftermath of slavery.[107] The essential elements of status schism are a set of practices that appear to have two purposes: first, to limit the amount, the form, and the content of interaction between members of the two groups; second, to establish the unequivocal superiority of all members of the upper group in any interaction with members of the lower group. The reasons for these objectives are fairly clear. They appear in situations in which the upper stratum enjoys enormous advantages over the more numerous lower stratum, to which the latter cannot be expected to give full consent, so that a constant danger of rebellion or desertion is apprehended by the upper stratum. In a fully developed status schism, the following features invariably appear:

1. The members of each stratum are clearly identified by insignia, dress, manners, appearance, and location, so that the possibility of misidentification is minimized. There are rituals of recognition between members of the two groups, including some norms of obsequiousness from the lower to the upper. The personal possessions, tools, and furniture of the upper stratum are distinguished as far as possible from those of the lower, being more elaborate or costly. Insofar as possible, the work places of the two strata are separated. Members of the upper have freedom of movement in the territory of the lower stratum, but members of the lower are either restricted entirely from the territory of the upper stratum, or allowed there only with express permission.

2. Communication between the strata is hedged by many restrictions, and the peer groups both above and below the status barrier are concerned with maintaining them. There are particular rules against fraternization, limiting the sociable contacts of individuals across the gap. These rules apply most rigorously to intimate association outside of the work situation. Communication from upper to lower is familiar and stereotyped; from lower to upper it is deferential but equally stereotyped.

[107] John Dollard's *Class and Caste in a Southern Town* (New Haven, Conn.: Yale University Press, 1937) contains a full description of such a caste system.

3. One of the most interesting features of status schism is the standardized mythology that emerges from the confrontation of the two strata. The myth about the lower stratum held by the upper includes: lack of responsibility, lack of commitment to distant goals, childishness or childlikeness, physical strength and endurance, limited intelligence, and the desire to be dominated. The members of the upper stratum are seen by the lower as corrupt, lazy, vain, arbitrary, and ineffectual.

4. In a perfect status schism, there is no mobility whatever between the strata. This condition is actually realized in some American and many European companies, although not in all. Even in those corporations in which it is possible for a few individuals to ascend from the labor to the management stratum, movement in the other direction is completely banned;' executives never become workers.

It is striking how many of these elements appear in situations that are otherwise far apart. Historically, status schisms are associated with the recruitment of members of organizations from distinct classes of the population. Even in the modern enterprise, inherited and acquired differences in social class distinguish the two strata. Almost all executives and very few workers are college graduates, for example. However, the explanation cannot stop here, if only because some companies with this pattern of recruitment have only rudimentary status schisms while others, such as the great electrical manufacturers, have developed them to an extraordinary degree.

It has been suggested that status schisms are created to sharpen the inequality of reward, that is to say, to guarantee to the upper stratum a larger share of the available rewards than they could otherwise obtain. At the beginning of a long controversy on the necessity of stratification, Davis and Moore proposed that stratification was essential in any society [108] (and by inference in any organization)

[108] The controversy began with a paper published by Davis and Moore in 1945 and continues to this day. The basic positions are contained in Kingsley Davis and Wilbert E. Moore, "Some Principles of Stratification," *American Sociological Review,* Vol. X, No. 2 (April, 1945), and Melvin M. Tumin, "Some Principles of Stratification: A Critical Analysis," *American Sociological Review,* Vol. XVIII, No. 4 (August, 1953). The subsequent course of the debate is summarized in Moore's "But Some Are More Equal Than

to persuade persons having scarce talents to devote them to collective goals. They suggested that systems of differential rewards, including material luxuries, "humor and diversion," and ego advantages, are both functional and inevitable. Tumin took the contrary position, claiming to show that all or most forms of unequal reward are dysfunctional. He maintained that there is a marked loss of conscientiousness in any system of unequal positional rewards, that this loss would be considerably reduced if identification with collective goals were increased at all levels of talent, and that equal rewards for equal conscientiousness would probably maximize identification.

None of the sociologists taking the Davis–Moore position are able to specify *how much* inequality of reward is necessary or desirable in a given context. They cannot, therefore, answer the question that is raised here—whether the sharp inequality of a status schism is more or less favorable for organizational achievement than the milder inequality of a status order without a schism.

The problem is not well understood. We have no general theory for systems of unequal reward,[109] but we may find some explanatory clues by examining the actual operation of status schisms. We note that members of the lower stratum are compensated in money, not in status or status aspirations; that efforts are made to keep their aspirations low and that the enterprise holds out no offer of permanent employment in return for faithful effort. Members of the lower stratum are expected to develop some hostility to the company and to join organizations that will bargain with it on their behalf. The worker is responsible to the company only for his conduct on the job and for a certain number of working hours. The company is indifferent to his outside activities and interests. The rewards he receives are categorical rather than personal, and they are limited by the requirement that all members of the upper stratum, except trainees, receive more in money and perquisites than any worker. In the upper stratum, by contrast, rewards are defined primarily in terms of status, and income is conceived as a means of supporting one's status with

Others," Tumin's reply "On Inequality," and Moore's "Rejoinder," all in *American Sociological Review*, Vol. XXVIII, No. 1 (February, 1963).

[109] No one so far has been able to explain the distribution of occupational incomes in an industrial economy by any single principle or to propose a consistent ideal distribution. The problem is discussed in Theodore Caplow, *Sociology of Work* (Minneapolis, Minn.: University of Minnesota Press, 1954, and New York: McGraw-Hill, 1963), Chapter 7.

an appropriate style of life. The corporation encourages aspiration and rewards effort individually; it extends a wide control over the life of the executive and his family and insists on having his loyalty.

It is clear that the status schism insulates these incompatible systems of reward from each other and by doing so enables justice, in the sense of equal return for equal activity, to be rendered in each stratum separately, while making the comparison between strata as difficult as possible.

The fact remains, of course, that members of the upper stratum are much more lavishly rewarded for their efforts than members of the lower. We need not go so far as Tumin, who seems to regard all status differences as wicked, to observe that the enterprise has no machinery for limiting inequality of reward to an economic optimum.[110] The distribution is arranged much more pragmatically.

The corporation starts by paying the going wage rates to its workers. These are determined partly by collective bargaining, partly by legislation, partly by custom, and partly by supply and demand in the local market for manual labor. Disregarding some marginal cases—senior foremen, specialized artisans, executive trainees, and staff professionals—the scale of executive compensation starts at a point above the maximum earnings of a worker. Subsequent increments are governed by the requirements that every status difference should be recognized by a salary difference and that executives of equal status should receive approximately equal salaries and those of unequal status should receive clearly unequal salaries. Given the tendency of an enterprise to multiply status levels, the distribution is nearly self-adjusting, although the total salary range has a tendency to lengthen indefinitely in order to accommodate additional status differences. At the very top, the distribution disappears in the clouds. The only factor limiting the corporation's rewards to top executives is its unwillingness to make them financially independent of itself. In the case of family-controlled companies in which this factor does not operate, remuneration—largely in the form of stock rights—is limited only by the solvency of the business and the possible objections of minority owners.

For a number of reasons, the special forms of remuneration at the top of the executive stratum are not easily measured. They

---

[110] The consequences of this situation are elegantly analyzed in Wilbert E. Moore, *The Conduct of the Corporation* (New York: Random House, 1962), especially Chapter 1.

include investment plans, stock options, insurance and annuities, the use of corporate facilities, and the intangibles of power and privilege. As we examine these distributions of reward, we note that the implications of very high status in an enterprise do not seem to have been changed very much by the ideology of human relations or the emphasis on the reduction of status differences that operate further down the pyramid. Some writers even hint at a kind of conspiracy:

> . . . members of the middle and lower ranks actually have an organization "mentality" which those few at the top only appear to have. These few are predominantly princes. . . . The human relations enthusiasts placed the primacy of the group before the executive as an obstacle to hurdle. But unwittingly, they gave the prince a concrete and convenient unit whereby he could advance his own individual interests.[111]

ARE CORPORATIONS BUREAUCRATIC?

The concept of bureaucracy in its modern sense is derived from the work of Weber,[112] for whom the term preserved its original connotations of public administration. Many, if not most, American sociologists classify the corporate enterprise as a bureaucracy and stress the resemblances between corporations and government bureaus rather than their differences.[113]

Bureaucracy of the ideal type, according to Weber, is founded on legal authority, which implies acceptance of the following interdependent ideas: [114]

[111] Eugene E. Jennings, *An Anatomy of Leadership: Princes, Heroes, and Supermen* (New York: Harper, 1960), pp. 190–91.

[112] Max Weber's analysis of bureaucracy is found in his *Theory of Social and Economic Organization* (ed. Talcott Parsons) (New York: Oxford University Press, 1947), and Hans Gerth and C. Wright Mills (eds.), *From Max Weber: Essays in Sociology* (New York: Oxford University Press, 1946). A full account of the uses which American sociologists have found for Weber's ideas would require a sizeable volume.

[113] This viewpoint pervades some general works on organization, such as Victor A. Thompson, *Modern Organization: A General Theory* (New York: Knopf, 1961), and Robert Presthus, *The Organizational Society: An Analysis and a Theory* (New York: Knopf, 1962), as well as scores of research reports, such as Alvin W. Gouldner's *Patterns of Industrial Bureaucracy* (Glencoe, Ill.: Free Press, 1954).

[114] Abstracted almost verbatim from Weber, *The Theory of Social and Economic Organization, op. cit.,* pp. 329–40.

A legal norm, however established, has a claim to the obedience of the members of the organization that enacts the norm and to that of the other persons within the sphere of power of the organization. Every body of law is a consistent system of abstract rules, and the administration of law consists in the application of these rules to particular cases. An official in such a system has all of his actions, including exercises of authority, determined by his status and subject to the impersonal demands of the total system. The person who obeys authority does so as a member of the organization, and what he obeys is the norm, not the person enforcing it. The obligation of obedience is limited to the specifically prescribed authority created by the organization in a particular relationship.

The table of organization of a bureaucracy shows a continuous series of official functions bound by rules. Each position has a definite sphere of competence, with specified task obligations, a specified degree of authority, and the means of compulsion to enforce its authority. Positions are organized hierarchically, each lower position being under the control and supervision of a higher. Special training is necessary to qualify the incumbents of most positions, so that they are capable of following the technical or normative specifications for their behavior. Persons occupying positions in the organization do not have rights of ownership over the means of production or administration. Furthermore, there is a complete separation of personal from official property and of home from work place. The incumbent does not own his position, and he cannot sell, lease, or bequeath it. Administrative acts, decisions, and rules are formulated and recorded in writing, even in cases in which discussion is also required.

In the purest type of bureaucracy, officials are appointed, and they function according to the following criteria: They are personally free and subject to authority only with respect to their impersonal and official obligations. Their positions are arranged in a well-defined status hierarchy. Each position has a definite assignment of tasks and authority. Appointments to positions are based on free contractual relationships. Candidates are selected on the basis of merit, verified by objective evidence. They are appointed and not elected. Each position has a fixed monetary salary and there is a system of retirement pay. The position constitutes the primary or sole occupation of the incumbent. Officials ordinarily join the organization for life. The sequence of positions they occupy constitutes a career. There is a system of promotion by seniority, or merit, or both. Promotion is dependent upon the judgment of superiors, and he is subject to strict and systematic discipline in the performance of his duties.

Although the applicability of the bureaucratic frame of reference to corporations can hardly be questioned in the light of its long and successful use, there are a number of points at which the bureaucratic model does not fit the industrial enterprise perfectly. The major departures of the corporation from the ideal type are partly matters of substance and partly of emphasis. The following points appear the most significant:

1. Only the upper stratum of the corporation is bureaucratized. The rank and file of workers are neither officials nor clients, in the Weberian sense, and their participation in the organization is not a career commitment.
2. The emphasis on legality, and the application of a consistent body of law to particular cases, is much less marked in corporations than in government agencies. The few empirical studies on this point indicate more dependence on norms of reciprocity and less on the written rules.
3. The separation of personal from official property and of home from work place is much less marked in the case of the corporation than it is in the government agency. Instead, as we have seen, there is a tendency for corporate control to overflow into other areas of life.
4. Authority tends to be impersonal when applied to the non-bureaucratic employees of the corporation, but it becomes much more personalized in the higher levels of the business hierarchy than in the corresponding levels of the government agency.
5. The most important and most intangible difference is that corporations have much less operational inertia than government agencies. Their problems of overmaintenance and red tape are likely to be much less severe. The modern corporation attaches relatively little importance to precedents, and it values innovation to such a point that although each position may have a definite sphere of competence, no position is certain to retain the same sphere indefinitely.

SOME LONG-TERM TRENDS

We have examined in some detail a number of the devices by which the corporate enterprise attempts to improve or maintain its stratification, integration, voluntarism, and achievement. To the extent that these devices work, they establish certain long-term trends that are easy to describe and difficult to interpret.

Interchangeability of human parts. The crushing insistence on adaptability, on getting along with people, on belongingness and togetherness, is—from a functional viewpoint—only one phase of the method by which the enterprise assures itself a supply of interchangeable managers. What has been accomplished for manual workers by the breakdown of skilled into semiskilled occupations, the standardization of jobs, and compulsory education beyond the minimum of literacy is accomplished for the higher echelons by college education, executive training, human relations techniques, and the increasing standardization of executive tasks from one industry to another.

Standardization. The interchangeability of human parts is fostered by the standardization of positions, functions, equipment, methods, titles, and objectives. A personnel-classification director, for example, may be able to move from a steel company to a grocery chain to the Pentagon to a state university to a pharmaceutical house without much new training. Standardization across company and industry lines extends to quite minor details of equipment and procedure. It is facilitated by the quasi-professionalization of managerial specialties, by the widespread use of standardized office machines and procedures, and above all by the ideology of the Organization Man with its systematic inculcation of the virtues of adaptability.

Mobility. The large-scale enterprise in its typical form not only permits a high rate of mobility but arranges it. It is not unusual for young executives to be rotated to a new job in a new community every two or three years. Mobility for the manual worker is assured by job standardization, seasonal fluctuations in production, and the system of casual layoff. Frequent office reorganizations and the practice of recruiting executives by raiding competitors make promotions and transfers matters of daily occurrence in large companies.

Pluralism. Modern American society is seen as pluralistic by many of its keenest observers.[115] Its distribution of power resembles more a vast network than a neat pyramid. The same may be true of the enterprise in its emerging form. The separation of ownership and management, decentralization, even the human-relations approach itself (by allowing for the expression of divergent viewpoints) have contributed to an arrangement whereby every significant faction in the enterprise has some voice in determining policy. Corporate decisions are often reached by a measurement of opposing forces rather than by fiat. The model executive may become so receptive to the viewpoints of various factions that he is incapable of adopting any views of his own.

Rationality. Many of the problems of the large corporation arise out of its attempts at rational self-improvement, such as the introduction of new machinery to increase output. If its faults result from imperfect rationality, the remedy may be more rationality. As new problems appear, even such very subtle problems as finding a balance between individualism and conformity, there is a tendency for new solutions to be sought, for long-range planning to be extended, for scientific or quasi-scientific methods to be further adapted. There is apparently no limit to the current impulse toward rationality. Semantic theories are put to work in the training of telephone operators. Esoteric methods of economic analysis are applied to the accounting ledgers of lamp factories. Wherever commitments to the past survive, like grass growing through cracks in the pavement, they are likely to be uprooted by the next consultant. Looked at in this light, the guiding principle of the corporation is change, and its mode of progress is from one unstable equilibrium to another. It is the very antithesis of utopia.

With its apparently limitless capacity to increase man's control

---

[115] See, for example, C. Arnold Anderson and Harry L. Gracey, review of Mills' *The Power Elite, Kentucky Law Journal,* Vol. XLVI, No. 2 (Winter, 1958).

over the environment, its rapid abandonment of machines and customs that are still useful, its tendency to adopt and discard weird ideologies, its curious ability to satisfy and frustrate the aspirations of its participants at the same time, the modern corporation is a serviceable monster—alarming, indispensable, and sometimes comical as well.

CHAPTER EIGHT

The Utopian Formula

THE POSSIBILITY OF UTOPIA

The preceding chapter considered some of the problems of perfecting an organization. The chapter that follows will discuss organized conflict. The analysis of utopia falls naturally between these two topics. Utopian organizations are, by definition, perfect and therefore free of internal conflict. The utopian program is designed to serve a transcendent goal. It does not evolve out of the organization's history and it is not supposed to develop spontaneously. The distinction between formal and informal elements of structure disappears in a utopian organization. With only a slight margin for error, expected and observed behavior coincide—else it is no utopia.

The utopian organization has some resemblance to Redfield's "little community," [1] the identifying characteristics of which are distinctiveness, smallness, homogeneity, and self-sufficiency. These characteristics appear in hundreds of thousands of villages all over the world. According to one estimate, three-quarters of the human race live in rural villages, and the little community is still the principal theater of human life, as it has been throughout history.

The utopian organization differs from the little community in sev-

[1] Robert Redfield, *The Little Community* (Chicago: University of Chicago Press, 1955). For an admirable systematic analysis of the larger scheme from which Redfield draws the concept of the little community, see Horace Miner, "The Folk-Urban Continuum," *American Sociological Review,* Vol. XVII, No. 5 (October, 1952).

eral ways. It is the result of planning, not of spontaneous development, and it is founded at a given moment. In contrast to the ethos of the little community, the utopian organization is dominated by an explicit theory of the good life and of the final end of man which it is the purpose of the organization to realize in action. Instead of the diffuse conservatism of the little community, the utopian organization sets itself consciously against unscheduled change. It may be viewed as a device for controlling innovation or for maintaining a set of values by insulating them from random events.

Utopian organizations cannot be analyzed without some reference to Goffman's masterly discussion of *total institutions*.[2] He includes in this category all the organizations that constitute a complete world for their members, involving them with their fellows day and night and segregating them from the outside world—those organizations, in sum, that have *inmates*. Among them are homes for the helpless, hospitals and sanatoriums, prisons and concentration camps, barracks and boarding schools, convents and other cloisters. Any utopia, as we are using the term in this book, is necessarily a total institution, but only a small proportion of total institutions are utopian, despite some curious resemblances that connect them all. Goffman uses many examples from convents and monasteries, juxtaposing them with others from mental hospitals and concentration camps. He is primarily interested in the machinery used to assure the obedience of individual to the organizational norms—not in the goals and purposes on which the present analysis is centered.

The organizations we are going to discuss also bear a family resemblance to sects and social movements. Like the sect, the utopian organization embodies transcendental goals—ends in themselves—acceptance of which is required of all members and sets them apart from the rest of society. Only because of the transcendent goal can probationers be attracted to a way of life involving so many renunciations.[3]

[2] Erving Goffman, "On the Characteristics of Total Institutions," Chapters 1 and 2 in Donald R. Cressey (ed.), *The Prison: Studies in Institutional Organization and Change* (New York: Holt, Rinehart & Winston, 1961).

[3] Renunciations, that is, of goals accepted in the environing society. Benedict's Apollonian-Dionysian dichotomy seems relevant here. A society dominated by Apollonian values, like the Pueblo, provides a natural approximation to utopia. Indeed the Pueblos go even further than our utopians in some respects. For example, they ban the best runners from races because they might

Historically, there has been a close association between one type of Protestant sectarianism and utopian experimentation. However, most sects do not have a total design for living. Their structures are more fluid than fixed; they emphasize growth rather than stability, and their isolation from the surrounding society is incomplete.[4]

The utopian organization resembles a social movement in its insistence on a single formula for social improvement. The connection between utopianism and the major social movements of modern times has been very close. The Anabaptist movement stimulated the foundation of utopian colonies and also ushered in the Reformation. Socialism and Communism as modern political movements emerged partly in continuation of nineteenth-century utopian theory and partly in reaction against it. Marx and Engels welcomed the social criticism of their predecessors, the so-called utopian socialists, but rejected their peaceable methods for achieving socialism in favor of revolutionary violence. The rejection was so emphatic that the label "utopian" became an epithet in Marxist terminology and continues to be unfavorably contrasted with "scientific," "hard-headed," or "practical" socialism. One curious consequence of this attitude was that neither Marx nor his successors followed the utopian practice of describing the desired postrevolutionary conditions in detail. It became a mark of orthodoxy to eschew a detailed vision of the successful socialist society.[5] There does not seem to be any Marxist

spoil the contest for others. See Ruth Benedict, *Patterns of Culture* (Boston: Houghton Mifflin, 1934).

[4] For discussion of sects and the church–sect typology see H. Richard Niebuhr, *The Social Sources of Denominationalism* (New York: Holt, 1929); Liston Pope, *Millhands and Preachers* (New Haven: Yale University Press, 1942); Charles S. Braden, "The Sects," *Annals of the American Academy of Political and Social Science,* Vol. LVI (March, 1948); Elmer T. Clark, *The Small Sects in America* (rev. ed.; Nashville, Tenn.: Abingdon-Cokesbury Press, 1949); Harold W. Pfautz, "The Sociology of Secularization: Religious Groups," *American Journal of Sociology,* Vol. LXI, No. 2 (September, 1955); Benton Johnson, "A Critical Appraisal of the Church–Sect Typology," *American Sociological Review,* Vol. XXI, No. 1 (February, 1957); and Peter L. Berger, "Sectarianism and Religious Sociation," *American Journal of Sociology,* Vol. LXIV, No. 1 (July, 1958).

[5] The few early Marxian writers who sketched the profile of the future limited themselves to the revolution and its immediate aftermath, neglecting the working arrangements of the socialist state. For example, Emile Pataud and Emile Pouget, *Syndicalism and the Co-operative Commonwealth,* trans. Charlotte and Frederic Charles (Oxford: New International Publishing Co., 1913).

doctrine at all on such fundamental questions as the determination of differential wages or the urban–rural balance under mature socialism.

In the great currents of ideas that furnish the motive force for religious and political development, utopian, sectarian, and revolutionary thought are intertwined. Mannheim uses the term *utopia* to denote not a form of organization but a theory favoring social change. It is paired to ideology as a theory in defense of the status quo.[6] He identifies four historical stages in the "configurations of the modern utopian mentality." The first was the *orgiastic Chiliasm* (concentrated on an immediate and emotional religious experience) of the Anabaptists. The second was the liberal humanitarianism that guided the American and French revolutions. The third was the conservative counterutopia, developed as a means of defense by the dominant classes in the nineteenth century. The fourth is modern socialism. The utopian socialism of Owen, Fourier, and Saint-Simon is classified in the second stage, as an aspect of liberal humanitarianism.[7]

There is a large mixed category of organizations that contain both utopian and nonutopian elements. The Church of Jesus Christ of the Latter Day Saints cannot be considered as a utopian organization because many aspects of Mormon life are unplanned or left outside the jurisdiction of the Church, but it abounds in utopian elements. The same might be said of the Virginia Colony or Plymouth Colony in their early years, despite some expectations of growth

[6] Karl Mannheim, *Ideologie und Utopie* (Frankfurt: Schulte-Bulmke, 1952). (*Ideology and Utopia,* trans. Louis Wirth and Edward Shils [New York: Harcourt, Brace & World, 1936].) Also see Chapter Four above. For a modification of the ideology–utopia distinction see *Individualism Reconsidered,* pp. 70–71. Mannheim's formulation includes some elements of value judgment. Riesman's distinction between utopia and ideology is frankly evaluational. He defines utopia as a rational belief that is in the long-run interest of the holder and an ideology as an irrational belief, *not* in the interest of the holder, but "sold to him by a group which has an interest in swindling him."

[7] Mannheim's discussion is almost exclusively in terms of European experience. American social movements are summarized in Thomas H. Greer, *American Social Reform Movements* (New York: Prentice-Hall, 1949). For a brief schematic treatment which takes account of both European and American experience, see Rudolf Heberle, "Observations on the Sociology of Social Movements," *American Sociological Review,* Vol. XIV, No. 3 (June, 1949).

and change.[8] Other examples of partially utopian organizations are as various as Versailles under Louis XIV, the Heavens of Father Divine, the house parties of the Oxford movement, and Alcoholics Anonymous. Each of these has some characteristics of utopia but lacks others.

IMAGINARY UTOPIAS

The student of utopian organization finds a fascinating double tradition—on the one hand a long series of real-life experiments, and on the other a long series of philosophical–fictional accounts. The two traditions are of equal antiquity and have always been closely related. The oldest of the great imaginary utopias, Plato's *Republic*, appears to have been patterned on a real utopian experiment in Sparta, under the laws of Dycurus. (Plutarch gives an account of it in which fact and imagination appear to be mingled in approximately equal parts.) The best known of the Renaissance utopias, the book that gave its name to the entire species, was Thomas More's *Utopia,* published in Latin in 1516. Morgan[9] argues that More's imaginary island resembles the real Inca empire of Peru too closely for coincidence; he supposes that More's symbolic narrator, Raphael Hythloday, may have been a real informant who made an early unpublicized voyage to South America. James Harrington's *Oceana,* published in 1656, is known to have influenced William Penn's constitution for the quasi-utopian colony of Pennsylvania in 1682. The dozens of Fourierist communities that sprang up in the United States in the nineteenth century were based on a fictional model. The ideas of Bellamy in *Looking Backward*[10] were tried out in the cooperative settlements of the Farm Security Administration.[11]

---

[8] There are a few sociological analyses of these quasi-utopian societies. See Louis Taylor Merrill, "The Puritan Policeman," *American Sociological Review,* Vol. X, No. 6 (December, 1945), Clifford Dowdey, *The Great Plantation* (New York: Rinehart, 1957), and Sigmund Diamond, "From Organization to Society: Virginia in the Seventeenth Century," *American Journal of Sociology,* Vol. LXIII, No. 5 (March, 1958).

[9] Arthur Morgan, *Nowhere Was Somewhere* (Chapel Hill, N.C.: University of North Carolina Press, 1946).

[10] Edward Bellamy, *Looking Backward 2000–1887* (Boston: Houghton Mifflin, 1926). Published originally in 1888.

[11] Edward C. Banfield, *Government Project* (Glencoe, Ill.: Free Press, 1951).

The literature of imaginary utopias is enormous. One anthology [12] lists more than a hundred major works published between 1850 and 1950; the latter date marked the approximate beginning of a new wave of utopian publication presented as science fiction. The more serious of the imaginary utopias show remarkable similarities. It is curious how many parallels appear in such widely separated classics as Plato's *Republic,* More's *Utopia,* Bellamy's *Looking Backward,* and Huxley's *Brave New World.*[13] We hear in each case of an organized urban community with a stable population, the abolition of private property, the assignment and rotation of work by a central committee, a strict status order, public dining halls, few and drastically enforced laws, deliberate cultural isolation, and the severe repression of innovations. The subordination of the individual to the good of the community is explicit in each case. As Plato wrote, "At present, I take it, we are fashioning the happy State, not piecemeal, or with a view of making a few happy citizens, but as a whole. . . ."

The four books are equally uncompromising on the equality of the sexes. Women are trained as soldiers in the *Republic* and *Utopia* and as industrial workers in *Looking Backward* and *Brave New World.* The *Republic* has a system of publicly assigned matings. More's *Utopia* enforces absolute monogamy, as does Bellamy's Boston in a different fashion. The inhabitants of *Brave New World* enjoy compulsory promiscuity. In every case, the responsibility of supporting and training children rests with the community rather than the married pair.

The similarities that appear repeatedly in imaginary utopias suggest that these literary fantasies are in some way responsive to a principle of limited possibilities. The few exceptions to the prevailing uniformity of structure represent shifts from the sociological to the psychological or philosophical level. An example of the first type is Wright's remarkable *Islandia,*[14] an imaginary society devoted to the refinement of emotional relationships. The classic example of the second type is still Francis Bacon's *New Atlantis.*

[12] Glenn Negley and J. Max Patrick, *The Quest for Utopia* (New York: Henry Schuman, 1952).
[13] Aldous Huxley, *Brave New World* (New York: Harper & Row, 1953).
[14] Austin Tappan Wright, *Islandia* (New York: Holt, 1958).

The common strain in imaginary utopias can be seen in resemblances such as these:

> Citizens, we shall say to them in our tale, you are brothers, yet
> God has framed you differently. Some of you have the power of
> command, and in the composition of these he has mingled gold,
> wherefore also they have the greatest honour; others he has made
> of silver, to be auxiliaries; others again who are to be husbandmen
> and craftsmen he has composed of brass and iron; and the species
> will generally be preserved in the children. But as all are of the
> same original stock, a golden parent will sometimes have a silver
> son, or a silver parent a golden son [*The Republic*].[15]

> Husbandry is a science common to all men and women. In this
> they are instructed from their youth, brought up not only behold-
> ing the use of it but practicing it also. Besides husbandry, every
> one of them learns his own craft, commonly clothworking, masonry,
> the smith's craft, or the carpenter's science. For the most part, every
> man is brought up in his father's craft; but if a man's mind stand
> to any other, he is by adoption put into a family of that occupation
> [*Utopia*].

> The full workmen are divided into three grades, according to
> efficiency, and each grade into a first and second class, so that there
> are in all six classes, into which the men fall according to their
> ability [*Looking Backward*].

> Alpha children wear grey. They work much harder than we do,
> because they're so frightfully clever. I'm really awfully glad I'm a
> Beta, because I don't work so hard. And then we are much better
> than the Gammas and Deltas. Gammas are stupid. They all wear
> green, and Delta children wear khaki. No, no, I *don't* want to
> play with Delta children. And Epsilons are still worse [*Brave New
> World*].

The fictional utopia abolishes conflict or keeps it under the
strictest control. Conflicts over goods, status, or sexual objects are
prevented by such complementary devices as celibacy and promiscuity, by hereditary assignment of functions or by rotation of work,
by the community of property or its abolition. Conflict over belief
is repressed by the universal enforcement of a single creed, and by
closing the borders against new ideas. Conflict over power is checked

15 Benjamin Jowett, trans., *The Republic* (Cleveland: World Publishing Co.,
1946).

by the rigidity of a social structure in which mobility is impossible or limited to a select group.

In a brilliant essay on literary utopias, Ruyer [16] isolates a number of their typical characteristics, including:

1. *Symmetry.* Almost all the utopian worlds are arranged with a passion for regularity and geometric neatness. The cities have gridiron street-plans and identical houses. The status hierarchies are always regular progressions. They have, says Ruyer, a "nonorganic" character.

2. *Uniformity.* Together with the passion for regularity goes a predilection for uniformity, homogeneity, and interchangeability. Even those utopias that have social classes insist on uniformity within the classes. There are no dissidents, no oppositions, no parties, no minorities. Although More preached tolerance and religious freedom, he did not permit the public practice of dissident religions. There is always something totalitarian about the fictional utopia.

3. *Belief in education.* The passion for homogeneity involves an extraordinary belief in the efficacy of education. Most utopias have an elaborate educational system with extraordinarily specific objectives. The extreme, perhaps, is *Brave New World,* where pedagogy is carried beyond instruction to the conditioning of reflexes before birth and through childhood.

4. *Hostility to nature.* This is another general characteristic discerned by Ruyer. Inspecting his sample of fictional utopias in an existentialist spirit, he finds them partial to plastic and synthetic materials, hostile to wood and stone. They likewise constructed languages and formal gardens.

5. *Authoritarianism.* Subjection to governors nearly always prevails, except in a small number of "counterutopias" such as Rabelais' *Abbey of Thélème* and Wright's *Islandia.* This authoritarianism is often at odds with the democratic prejudices of the utopian author. It seems to arise from a lack of confidence in spontaneous growth or natural equilibrium. The architect of a world, Ruyer remarks, does not want his materials to amuse themselves. Literature and art are usually

[16] Raymond Ruyer, *L'Utopie et les Utopies* (Paris: Presses Universitaires de France, 1950).

subject to the same absolute control as politics and domestic life.

6. *Collectivism.* A consequence and accompaniment of these authoritarian tendencies is the collective character of utopian life. "An individual family is a refractory unit to absorb in the unity of the state." The general warehouse appears very frequently in the fictional utopias as a substitute for the family cupboard.

7. *Isolation.* Fictional utopias have this as a fixed feature. A desert island, a hidden valley reached through a cleft in the rocks, future time, another dimension, or another planet are favorite sites. Remoteness protects the artificial society against contamination by the real world.

8. *Asceticism.* Despite their interest in the standard of living, there is a certain miserliness in these ideal communities. Asceticism is normal. Profusion is frowned upon. Waste is disapproved. Utopian authors who happen to think of the cycle of fashion promptly put a stop to it. Luxury is too irrational and perhaps too individualistic for the utopians. The good life they depict is a life of quiet happiness, with nothing heroic or ecstatic about it.

It would be entertaining to linger for further analysis of these works. They are interesting in themselves, and the best of them are full of profound commentary on real societies. Indeed, their usual purpose is to expose the weak points of a contemporary society by comparison with an idealized model. However, the sociological study of imaginary utopias cannot lead to firm conclusions. A sufficient number of real utopias are available for analysis and some of them have been carefully studied.

REAL UTOPIAS

We shall consider four examples of real utopian communities: the Oneida Community, the convent of cloistered nuns, the Israeli kibbutz and the Hutterite Brotherhood. These cases are selected partly because of available documentation and partly to illustrate the range of possibilities.

Oneida was one of hundreds of utopian colonies founded in the

United States from the settlement of the Labadists at Bohemia Manor in 1769 to those still in the course of formation.[17] The vast majority of these experiments failed. As in the case of Brook Farm, their failures often had important consequences. Nine colonies achieved some degree of permanence. Three of them—the Ephratans, the Shakers, and the Inspirationists—lasted more than a century. Oneida flourished as a utopian colony for forty years. After its conversion into a joint stock company in 1880 the company prospered, and some elements of the original organization have lingered on to this day.[18]

The Catholic contemplative orders go back to the early centuries of the Christian era, to the Egyptian Pachomius in the early fourth century and to St. Basil a little later. The organizational structure in its present form was developed by St. Benedict of Aniane and refined by St. Benedict of Monte Cassino more than a thousand years ago.[19] There are many variations of monasticism within the Catholic church. Even among the purely contemplative orders the rules differ in severity, and the degree of conformity seems to vary considerably from one house to another.[20] Monica Baldwin, whose account of convent life is perhaps the most complete, describes an establishment in which conformity to the written rules was extremely high.[21]

[17] One account describes eighteen modern utopian colonies and refers to many others in California alone. Robert V. Hine, *California's Utopian Colonies* (San Marino, Calif.: Huntington Library, 1953).

[18] A detailed description of the postcommunal history of Oneida may be found in Walter D. Edmonds, *The First Hundred Years* (Oneida Ltd., 1948). The best source for the whole movement of which Oneida was a part is Mark Holloway, *Heavens on Earth* (London: Turnstile Press, 1951), which also contains an excellent bibliography of older writings. John Humphrey Noyes, the founder of Oneida, was the author of one of the most interesting of these, *The History of American Socialism*, published in Philadelphia in 1870. A firsthand survey of the same era is Charles Nordhoff's *Communistic Societies of the United States* (London: Redway, 1900). See also William Alfred Hinds, *American Communities and Co-operative Colonies* (2d rev.; Chicago: Charles H. Kerr, 1908) and Everett Webber, *Escape to Utopia: The Communal Movement in America* (New York: Hastings House, 1959).

[19] Valentine Theodore Schaaf, *The Cloister* (Cincinnati, Ohio: St. Anthony Messenger, 1921), *The Rule of Saint Benedict* (London: Chatto & Windus, 1925). This latter is extraordinarily enlightening. The specifications of positions and roles in the Benedictine cloister, developed a generation after the extinction of the Roman Empire of the West, are still in current use.

[20] Howard M. Vollmer, "Member Commitment and Organizational Competence in Religious Orders," *Berkeley Publications in Society and Institutions*, Vol. III, No. 1 (Spring, 1957).

[21] Monica Baldwin, *I Leap Over the Wall* (New York: Rinehart, 1950).

McCabe,[22] who reported on life in a Franciscan monastery in England about two generations ago, described a good deal of rule evasion, informal adaptation, resistance to authority, and substitution of goals. The observer of a cloistered order must necessarily have been a member, but his observations are usually written after he has ceased to be one. The narratives of monastic life are relatively few and tend to be strongly biased in one direction or the other. We do not have enough data to estimate the extent of nonconformity in monastic orders, which emphasize conformity more than any other human organization.[23] The enormous age of the monastic institution is matched by its extraordinary capacity to resist change. The convent described by Baldwin is closer to the medieval world in program, calendar, language, and visible appearances than any other living form of organization.

The kibbutz (sometimes written kvutza) is very modern by contrast. The first kibbutz was founded in 1908 at Kinnereth in Galilee. There are now more than two hundred of these colonies in existence. They differ somewhat in detail and in political orientation, but the fundamental structure is remarkably uniform and has shown stability through violent political and social changes. The survival of the kibbutz from the days of Turkish rule in Palestine through the British mandate, the Arab-British war, and into the era of Israeli independence is an interesting demonstration of the viability of a utopian design. We are fortunate in having a careful and highly detailed study of one community and a number of other technically oriented observations.[24]

[22] Joseph McCabe, *Life in a Modern Monastery* (London: Grant Richards, 1898).

[23] Besides those already cited, our principal sources have been L. Gregory Smith, *Christian Monasticism* (London: A. D. Innes, 1892), Thomas Merton, *The Seven Storey Mountain* (New York: Harcourt, Brace & World, 1948), Henry Marc-Bonnet, *Histoire des Ordres Religieux* (Paris: Presses Universitaires de France, 1949), and Kathryn Hulme, *The Nun's Story* (Boston: Little, Brown, 1956).

[24] Melford E. Spiro, *Kibbutz: Venture in Utopia* (Cambridge, Mass: Harvard University Press, 1956). Two other volumes of great interest are Henrik F. Infield, *Co-operative Living in Palestine* (New York: Dryden, 1944), and Gideon Baratz et al., *A New Way of Life* (London: Shindler and Golomb, 1949). A description of the background of events against which the kibbutz developed can be found in S. N. Eisenstadt, "Israel," in Arnold Rose (ed.), *The Institutions of Advanced Societies* (Minneapolis, Minn.: University of Minnesota Press, 1958). See also Yonina Talmon, "Aging in Israel: A Planned Society," *American Journal of Sociology*, Vol. LVII, No. 3 (November. 1961).

Our fourth specimen of utopian organization is the Hutterite Brotherhood of South Dakota and western Canada. The Hutterische Bruder were founded in 1528 in Moravia, at the peak of the Anabaptist movement. They migrated to Transylvania and Wallachia in the seventeenth century, to Russia in the eighteenth, to South Dakota in the nineteenth, and to Canada in the twentieth—always moving as a colony or cluster of colonies. The present membership is about nine thousand persons living in about a hundred communal hamlets. The Hutterites are the most stable representatives of that German pietism which produced so many utopian colonies. They are related historically and ideologically to the Doukhobors,[25] the Amish and Brethren of Lancaster County,[26] and somewhat more remotely to Ephrata, the Rappites, Zoar, Bethel, and Aurora.[27] The reasons why community experiments under the aegis of Moravian piety are so durable have not been systematically explored, although we do have two excellent studies of the Hutterites in modern times, one by Deets, based on observation in the 1920's,[28] and another by Eaton and Weil twenty years later.[29]

Like the Catholic orders, the Hutterites deliberately maintain the style of an earlier era. By steady resistance to innovation, they seem to have preserved the language, the folkways, the costume, and even the physiognomy of their founders. The Hutterites, however, engage in agriculture and are economically involved with the larger society; they are, therefore, much more vulnerable to cultural pressures than the monastic orders. Eaton has described their system of "controlled acculturation" [30]—how the Hutterites offer a flexible resistance to

[25] H. B. Hawthorn, "A Test of Simmel on the Secret Society: The Doukhobors of British Columbia," *American Journal of Sociology,* Vol. LXII, No. 1 (July, 1956).

[26] Charles S. Rice and Rollin C. Steinmetz, *The Amish Year* (New Brunswick, N.J.: Rutgers University Press, 1957).

[27] For a careful analysis of the relationship between ideology and social structure in Ephrata and Bethel, see Eugene E. Doll, "Social and Economic Organization in Two Pennsylvania Communities," *American Journal of Sociology,* Vol. LVII, No. 2 (September, 1951). A good historical account is Robert J. Hendricks, *Bethel and Aurora* (New York: Press of the Pioneers, 1933).

[28] Lee Emerson Deets, *The Hutterites: A Study in Social Cohesion* (Gettysburg, S.Dak.: Times and News Publishing Co., 1939).

[29] Joseph W. Eaton and Robert J. Weil, *Culture and Mental Disorders: A Comparative Study of the Hutterites and Other Populations* (Glencoe, Ill.: Free Press, 1955).

[30] Joseph W. Eaton, "Controlled Acculturation: A Survival Technique of the Hutterites," *American Sociological Review,* Vol. XVII, No. 3 (June, 1952).

innovation, for example by allowing buttons to replace hooks and eyes on their clothing only after buttons have been replaced by zippers—and then permitting only black buttons.

Studying these four utopian organizations, we shall try to see how each of them defines its goals and sets about maintaining stratification, integration, and voluntarism. In this way, it may be possible to show how the interrelationship of these basic variables is affected when the impingement of the external environment is sharply reduced.

RULING GOALS

Each of our specimen cases has unique goals to which all of its norms are related in some way. These goals are capable of succinct expression, and they stand for the community's protest against the world, at once the excuse for its isolation and the justification for its special way of life. The goals of Oneida were embodied in the doctrine of Perfectionism, which placed the Second Coming of Christ in the past, held that original sin had been abolished, and imposed on its believers the obligation to live sinlessly. The goal of the contemplative convent is to provide the kind of life that will enable the religious to make direct, mystical contact with God. The goal of the kibbutz is the promotion of Zionism by the building of a Jewish homeland and the defense of its political autonomy. The goal of the Hutterites is to live according to *Die Glauben,* instructions for peaceable and communal living that they believe have been specially imposed upon them and must be obeyed "even to martyrdom."

In all four cases socialization is a long and arduous process, and there is a long term of probation. At Oneida the period of probation was apparently varied to fit the applicant, but sometimes lasted for many years. The probation of convent nuns is severe; five full years are ordinarily spent in the noviceship. The period of candidacy in the kibbutz is ordinarily six months, but it may be much greater; Infield reports the case of a probationer who served seven years and was then refused. The probationary procedure of the Hutterites is elaborate. Even though the candidate has been born into the organization and brought up entirely within its special culture, the doctrine of adult baptism permits his rejection.

In all four cases there are procedures for the expulsion of full members, and expulsion is not infrequent. Deviant opinion is considered sinful or immoral. Everyday rules of conduct are written down in minute detail. The convent goes furthest of all in specifying behavior:

> From the moment of awakening, till the hour when at last you are permitted to fall asleep, the Rule holds you in its grip.
> Nothing, except the degree of obedience to what is commanded, is left to individual choice. Not only what you do, but when, and even how, you do it is meticulously prescribed. . . .
> Each moment of the day is provided for. One prays, reads, eats, walks in the garden, at the appointed hour; no religious is allowed to follow her own inclinations in the disposal of her time.[31]

The promiscuity of Oneida differs greatly from the celibacy of the cloister, and the formal authoritarianism of the Hutterites from the formal egalitarianism of the kibbutz. Nevertheless, the similarities are as striking as the differences. The nuclear family is effectively replaced in all four utopian organizations. The formation of cliques or organized peer groups is prevented. All four colonies hold property in common. In the convent, this is carried to such an extreme that one speaks of "our" comb or "our" knife and fork, never of "mine and thine." In all four cases, food is served in collective dining halls, not in family groups. The Hutterites come closest to a conventional domestic arrangement. Their families are very large, averaging ten children per completed family, and occupy separate apartments in communal houses. These do not have kitchens, and they are open to outsiders. In the kibbutz, children are placed in a children's house at birth; in Oneida, after weaning; among the Hutterites, the care of infants is shared and kindergarten begins soon after the age of two.

The four colonies are widely different in their regulation of sexual relationships, but the effect in every case is to increase the dependence of the individual on the organization as a whole and to minimize the possibility of conflict arising out of sexual jealousy or competition. The most intricate and spectacular sexual arrangements were those of the Oneida Community. By developing the practice of coitus interruptus into a doctrine, Noyes was able to separate love-making from procreation. Any member of the society might apply through an intermediary to sleep with another, and individual preferences were

[31] Baldwin, *op. cit.*, p. 64.

respected, except for the interesting provision that the community might interfere to separate a couple who showed a tendency to develop "exclusive affections." [32] Procreation, however, was a matter of assignment—under a system that Noyes called *stirpiculture* and which he likened to the selective breeding of livestock. One of the points of this system was to choose parents who differed in age and temperament. The general testimony of participants is that the system worked reasonably well, although it is not clear whether it yielded in the end to external criticism or internal dissatisfaction.

The following excerpt suggests the seriousness with which the Perfectionists took their own principles:

> Not only temperament, but tendencies that were in any way objectionable, were recognized as being undesirable qualities to intensify by uniting of two parents having the trait in common. Both Charles C and Miss B having been under criticism for a tendency to drift into exclusive relations in such manner as to jeopardize communistic love, it was found wrong to place them in conditions of stronger temptation; so the moral interests outweighed those of exclusive affection. This may have been a trial for Charles B, but *he never harboured a jealous thought of the man who was united to the same woman; on the contrary, their common love was a bond of union, and after the child was born he loved it as tenderly and cared for it as devotedly as if it were his own.* Miss B had been an object of admiration not only to Charles C but to many of us. She was a young lady of great beauty. Her easy grace, her kind disposition and fine accomplishments made her very much beloved in the family. Motherhood ripened her into a most charming woman, and my friendship gradually grew into courtship.
>
> Although Charles C was aware of my affection for Miss B, he was so far from evincing the least resentment that our relations continued to be those of the most heartfelt friendship.
>
> Not having been reared among the Perfectionists, I was not sufficiently imbued with their spirit to understand fully their utter unselfishness in love; I was, therefore, unprepared to credit Charles C with the full measure of his noble nature; consequently, when visiting Miss B, whose room was on the same corridor with Charles C, I was conscious of wishing to avoid observation while passing his

[32] The reasons why this device promoted community integration are explained at length by Philip E. Slater, "On Social Regression," *American Sociological Review*, Vol. XXVIII, No. 3 (June, 1963). Note the reference to Oneida, p. 349.

door, and if Charles C appeared when I was in company with B I invariably withdrew. In later years I learned that my consideration caused the pain I had sought to avoid, for Charles C felt grieved that his relations with Miss B should be so construed as to curtail our freedom on his account.

One evening, when I was in Miss B's room, her child was so fretful that our efforts failed to soothe it. The door opened and Charles C, taking the child from its crib so quietly that we were scarcely aware of his presence, carried it into his own room. Not a word was spoken; but his action, trifling in itself, was to me a revelation of such nobility of character as I had scarcely supposed possible. His solicitude lest our courtship be interrupted, his manly, yet delicate way of acting on so generous an impulse, made an impression on my heart that can never be effaced. I was covered with shame at having even harboured a doubt as to the unselfishness of his love. It is needless to add that we were even firmer friends from that time forward.[33]

The celibacy of a convent is absolute, of course, and some authors state that even those who leave by permission and obtain a papal dispensation from their vows of poverty, obedience, and enclosure are never dispensed from the vow of chastity.

Marriage in the kibbutz, according to Infield, is reduced to a rooming arrangement with a minimum amount of joint activity.

The selection of a mate is determined only by personal attraction. If this is great enough to lead to a common life, a room is requested from the "econom." With the moving of the beds, the marriage status is achieved. . . . Marriage does not alter the social status of the spouses. The wife continues to use her name; the husband acquires no new obligations. They simply are recognized as belonging to each other. The terms "husband" and "wife" are not used either in the Kvutza or in pioneer Palestine generally. "My girl" or "my boy" are preferred. . . . Married life does not change the private habits of the wedded. Each makes his own bed and arranges his things as before. Their meals are taken in the dining hall, they attend meetings as equal members, and whether they go to theatre or cinema is decided by the group.[34]

And Spiro remarks that:

[33] Allan Estlake, *The Oneida Community* (London: Redway, 1900), pp. 75–77.
[34] Infield, *op. cit.*, pp. 99–100.

It was, therefore, important for a person who had acquired a "companion" to emphasize the fact that he had not divorced himself from the group life, and he was not creating a private life or developing private interests that would sever his ties with the group.[35]

Here, too, procreation is subject to committee control. Conception is permitted or prohibited according to the colony's economic circumstances.

Among the Hutterites, stability appears to be achieved by the combination of very strict norms and the highest birth rate of any contemporary population. Marriage is nearly compulsory for normal individuals. The sex ratio is stable; there are few unmarried women and most of the married women are continuously involved in childbirth. The opportunities for sexual distraction are limited, and the rules offer no provision for divorce.

MAINTAINING ACHIEVEMENT

All four colonies approach the division of labor in the same spirit. Edmonds writes of Oneida that ". . . in assigning work they try to eliminate possible feelings of discrimination by rotating jobs from year to year as widely as individual abilities permitted, and at one time or another, practically everyone had to take his turn at the inevitable drudgery of the household." [36] Baldwin, in whose convent there was an annual change of office, explains the theory of *la grace d'état*. A nun appointed to any office will acquire the competence it requires by grace if she prays and does her best. On this principle, a young and inexperienced nun may be put in charge of the training program and another appointed as infirmarian without any nursing experience.

In the kibbutz, the rotation of work is carried to such an extreme degree as to threaten productivity.

> So far as is practicable, experts . . . are retained in their specialty. Nevertheless, they must (like all other members) take turns in chores such as kitchen duty, serving as waiters, and laundry work. The unskilled members form a sort of mobile reserve which the

[35] Spiro, *op. cit.*, p. 114.
[36] Edmonds, *op. cit.*, p. 18.

Committee of Work assignment directs to specific daily tasks. Every evening a list of these assignments is posted at the entrance of the dining hall. From this list, each member learns his next day's tasks and his station. Exemptions are rare. They comprise the sick, invalids, children and women in the last weeks of pregnancy. Even guests, should they remain more than three days, are expected to pick up the shovel.[37]

Similarly, among the Hutterites, work is systematically rotated, so that, for example, each woman may spend one week out of twelve in the kitchen, one week in the bakery, four weeks milking cows, and the remainder of her time at seasonal tasks. These arrangements limit efficiency by preventing the development of specialized skills or the rational allocation of available talent. In a colony engaged in simple agriculture and housekeeping the effect is by no means disastrous. The lowered achievement is presumably compensated by heightened voluntarism, which indeed is one of the purposes of the procedure. Stability cannot be modified by individual differences in productivity, and this is another reason for rotation.

In the kibbutz, which relies on machines more heavily than do the other groups, the rotation procedure involves great strain and is readily abandoned with respect to certain indispensable specialties such as bookkeeping and tractor repair. The consistent failure of utopian factories is explained by the virtual impossibility of rotating jobs in any production process with an advanced technology. Without rotation, the stability of a utopian organization is inevitably compromised by status modifications based on the division of labor.

MAINTAINING STABILITY

The convent is so hierarchical that no two nuns can ever be equal. The egalitarianism of the kibbutz rejects the concept of leadership altogether. Yet certain common elements may be discerned in both organizations. In the first place, seniority seems to count very heavily. Whether this is due to the inherent conservatism of these colonies, to the long process of socialization, or to the natural drift of any social system in which the recognition of individual merit is restrained, the fact is that elders receive unusual respect in utopian organizations.

[37] Infield, *op. cit.*, p. 41.

In Oneida, despite an elaborate scheme of committee management, power lay in the hands of an inner circle of elders who made all decisions concerning the propagation of children and were responsible for the system of mutual criticism. Seniority is always recognized in the convent. The precedence of each nun is determined by the date when she takes her vows. Her place in the choir and at the refectory table will always be between her immediate junior and her immediate senior, and the distribution of privileges is adjusted to seniority. A Hutterite community is managed by a group of elders, presided over by a minister who is himself an elder. In the kibbutz, the suppression of other forms of stratification seems to emphasize the dependence of status upon seniority. Spiro remarks that the social structure of the kibbutz is designed to implement the values of the oldest stratum—the founders—and that leadership stems primarily from their ranks.

In three of the four cases, authority is centered in a single person, although resting in principle on general consent. The kibbutz is an exception; its egalitarian values seem to rule out a single, strong leader. Noyes had virtually complete control over Oneida from its founding until his attempted retirement in 1876. It was transformed into a manufacturing company when the leadership of his son proved unacceptable. Although Noyes was not formally elected, only those entered the colony who wished to be his followers and his rule was never seriously questioned until close to the end of his life.

In the convent, the power of the superior is as absolute as the rules can make it. Baldwin describes the Prioress:

> Her position was less that of mistress than of mother to the community. The extreme respect shown to her was based upon the idea that in the monastery she held the place of Christ. The nuns, until they had been for a certain number of years in the community, always knelt when she spoke to them. When she passed, they had to rise and bow to her as she went by. For anything that was in any way an exception to the Rule, her leave had to be asked. Her will was supreme.[38]

The Prioress is elected every three years by the general vote of the choir nuns, however, and they also elect at that time a sort of council of sixteen or seventeen members who are consulted by the Prioress

[38] Baldwin, *op. cit.*, pp. 69–70.

and even asked to vote when decisions of importance are to be taken.

The spiritual leader of a Hutterite colony is the preacher. Preachers are selected, usually for life, by an interesting method which combines appointment, voting, and chance. When a minister is to be chosen, a list of nominees is prepared after long consultation with members of the colony and of related colonies. These candidates are voted on in a public meeting, and the names of candidates who receive five or more votes are thrown into a hat or box. The name of the winning candidate is then drawn by lot. According to Deets, the preacher ". . . tends to absorb in a patriarchal way the authority of the father." [39] Legislation for the whole brotherhood is adopted at intercolony meetings of preachers and then submitted to the governing assembly of male members in every colony for acceptance or rejection by majority vote. In the recorded history of the colonies studied by Eaton, no formal proposal of the preacher assembly has ever been voted down.

Leadership in utopian organizations is ordinarily charismatic. Indeed, the possibilities of charisma are pushed to extremes in colonies of this type, and the divinization of the leader has occurred frequently in the course of the American experiments. The Shakers, for example, regarded their Mother Anne as the female counterpart of Christ.

MAINTAINING INTEGRATION

Unlike many imaginary utopias, our real utopias are not found on remote islands or reached through clefts in mountain walls. They have a surprising amount of contact with outsiders. According to Estlake,[40] people came from all parts of the world to see the Oneida Community, and hundreds of visitors were sometimes entertained in a single day. On occasion, the rush was so great that work had to be suspended. Visitors were always welcomed and entertained.

In the convent, the seclusion of the nuns within their enclosure is usually complete and is prescribed by sweeping laws. As Schaaf describes it:

> In the cloisters of nuns there are no "neutral" places to which both
> nuns and outsiders have access. What are such in monasteries of

[39] Eaton, *op. cit.*, p. 334.
[40] Estlake, *op. cit.*

male regulars, e.g., the public church and its contiguous sacristy, are outside the enclosure of nuns and, as we shall see below, no nun is allowed to go to these places except in the cases specified by law or by papal dispensation. The nun's choir lies within the cloister and is closed to outsiders. It must be separated from the church by a screen. In this screen, there is a small window which the nuns approach for communion, investiture, profession and the like. This window is fitted with two doors; the key to the outer one is in the keeping of the confessor, that to the inner one is in the keeping of the abbess. The roof also lies outside the cloister . . . so, too, the parlor to which visitors have access.[41]

The nuns in the convent described by Baldwin, however, keep a school and are in daily contact with pupils from the outside.

The Hutterite colony receives a fair number of visits from the outside world: salesmen, agricultural agents, doctors, and neighbors. The kibbutz has a guest house and is not at all secluded from visitors. At least three of our specimen organizations employ hired laborers who are not full members. The number of hired hands at Oneida was sometimes greater than the number of colonists. Hired hands were always supervised by members. The convent described by Baldwin includes a group of lay sisters who are responsible for the heavier services of the house and are not admitted to all of its privileges, besides a certain number of ordinary employees. The studies are silent on whether the Hutterites employ outside labor. The kibbutz routinely does so.

Frequent, intimate, and exclusive interaction is the fundamental device for maintaining integration in these organizations. Most of the members of the Oneida colony lived in a single house, as do all the nuns of the convent. Although the kibbutz and the Hutterite colony have several buildings, they are closely clustered.

All four institutions show well-developed rituals of solidarity, in which music has an important part. At Oneida there were daily evening meetings attended by the whole colony. The nuns are almost constantly in convocation. The kibbutz has at least one general assembly a week and innumerable special meetings occupy the leisure time of the members. Most of the Hutterites attend church services every day.

[41] Schaaf, *op. cit.,* pp. 106–07.

MAINTAINING VOLUNTARISM

There are certain distinctive devices for maintaining voluntarism that seems to differentiate the successful utopian experiment from similar unsuccessful attempts. These include methods for working directly upon the ego of a potentially dissident member, simultaneously chastising him for his errors and reassuring him of group support. The system at Oneida, like so many of Noyes' social inventions, was simple and ingenious.

> At Oneida, Mutual Criticism was the medium of all discipline. Usually a member who was confronted with a moral problem or who was conscious of some form of guilt would request a criticism; but sometimes the treatment was administered as a corrective for unacknowledged delinquency; and it was even used, as psychoanalysis is now used, as a cure for physical ailments—apparently with a number of satisfactory results. The person to be criticized would sometimes appear before the entire society, but more often before a committee selected from those who knew him best. Each member would then state quite frankly the faults and merits of the persons concerned, while he sat in silence. Any tendency to spitefulness or prejudice on the part of a member of the committee would be corrected by other members, and by the knowledge that such conduct would in itself call for criticism. At the end of the session, the chairman of the committee would usually sum up and offer such advice, reproof, or encouragement as seemed necessary. No ill-feeling was provoked in the "victim," who almost always emerged from the ordeal with a clear knowledge of how to repair his faults or avoid the causes of his distress.[42]

The convent has an exercise called the "Examine of Conscience," which takes place daily and requires the systematic listing of one's own faults. This is supplemented by weekly confessions and public penances.

In the kibbutz,

> When the pressure of public opinion, exerted in informal and in semiformal ways, is not effective, the kibbutz has recourse to more formal procedures. These procedures are resorted to when a serious breach of kibbutz norms has occurred—such as refusal to abide by an official decision of the kibbutz, or a violation of some

[42] Holloway, *op. cit.*, pp. 186–87.

part of its moral code. The first procedure is to bring the person's dereliction to the official attention of the kibbutz at a town meeting. This is a powerful sanction, and the very threat to use it is usually efficacious in this community where people are so sensitive to public opinion.[43]

Among the Hutterites:

> According to rigorously observed Hutterite ethics, it is the duty of all members to be informers regarding the behavior of each other. If an offender does not reform after being admonished by the minister, he is required to appear before a week-day evening religious meeting and ask forgiveness of the members, after which he is given public admonition. If, now a recidivist, he still continues, he is required to appear before the Sunday morning religious meeting in daylight. If all the series of graduated pressures are of no avail, he is excommunicated. This means that he is socially isolated from the community. His whole world turns against him. He must eat alone. No one may talk to him. He is treated as if he were not a member of the community. After a week or ten days of such treatment most members reform. Those who do not reform, find life in the community unbearable and leave.[44]

THE PROS AND CONS OF UTOPIA

Much more evidence could be presented to demonstrate the practicability of utopian organization. Utopia is not some hypothetical, implausible condition of the general society. It is a definite formula for small communities—with recognizable advantages and disadvantages. The variations of detail are infinite, but the general pattern persists through all the variations. Many of the failures are explained by omission of essential elements in the utopian formula. Let us see if we can recapitulate what these elements are.

The utopian organization replaces the individual's private purposes with its dominant goals. The resulting program requires nearly absolute conformity. Members must look alike, act alike, express the same attitudes, and follow the same daily routine. Discipline and subjection to rule are invariably required. Rabelais' *Abbey of Thélème,* with its motto of "Do what thou wilt," is the perfect counterutopia.

[43] Spiro, *op. cit.,* p. 101.
[44] Deets, *op. cit.,* pp. 46–47.

Utopian conformity is not achieved by consent alone nor completely imposed by coercion. The frequent combination of autocratic headship and democratic election is significant. The individual voluntarily assigns to the organization a general right to police him and cooperates in group exercises to make him less resistant to policing. In the successful utopias, the rules are internalized to an extraordinary degree.

Human nature is evidently not too selfish or individualistic to stand this kind of discipline. Although there is certainly a selective factor in the recruitment of members for utopian organizations, we do not have enough data to assess its importance. Sex, race, and even cultural background are not essential criteria. The Catholic monastic system has been successfully established almost everywhere in the world. The kibbutzim drew recruits at first from all parts of the Western world and later from oriental countries without fundamental modifications.[45]

Monasteries, cooperative colonies, and tribal societies of utopian type appear in many civilizations. The problem of recruiting appropriate personality types is serious but not desperate. All four of our specimen utopias were successful in transforming the personalities of their members. Observers agree that there was very little interpersonal friction in Oneida. "A crowd in a convent consists," says Baldwin, "with very few exceptions, of people who are more concerned that others shall have the first places than themselves." [46] The Hutterites, says Deets,

> . . . exhibit a degree of peacefulness, social harmony, and cohesion which by contrast with our society is very striking. Within their order they have collective security. . . . Crime, either against our society or their own, is very rare. Divorce is unknown. Almost all members of Hutterite society have extraordinary mental health and freedom from mental conflicts and tensions. Family quarreling of any kind is extremely rare. Suicide has never occurred. Insanity is almost non-existent. . . . Lonesomeness and friendlessness are practically unknown.[47]

[45] For a lively description of the changes that did occur, see Horace M. Kallen, *Utopians at Bay* (New York: Herzl Foundation, 1958).

[46] Baldwin, *op. cit.*, p. 112.

[47] Deets, *op. cit.*, pp. 1–2. Eaton and Weil discovered an appreciable incidence of psychotic and neurotic disorders among the Hutterites but confirmed that antisocial, violent, or acutely aggressive behavior was unknown.

The kibbutz has some factionalism, but personal enmities are not tolerated, and do not seem to occur.

The most important achievement of utopian organizations is the suppression of internal conflict.[48] Conflict *can* be abolished, or nearly abolished, if the organization commands the total adherence of its members free from conflicting valences. This explains why every utopian organization must exclude or undermine the nuclear family. Some of the conditions of a utopia are satisfied within a happy family, and utopian organizations like to visualize themselves as large, artificial families. It is not merely coincidental that in all four of these cases members address each other as Brother or Sister.

Not only do the goals of the utopian organization take precedence over personal ambitions, but the structure itself is highly valued. Technical innovation is restrained as far as possible from having any social consequences. There is always a drift toward anachronism in a successful utopia, as there probably is in any long-established prosperous family. The institutional pattern as a whole is cherished by the members, and they are unwilling to separate its essential from its fortuitous elements, even if the separation were possible.

What are the disadvantages of utopia? Why, in the face of repeated demonstrations that segments of society are perfectible, is there so little interest in perfectionism? Why has the contrast between the cloister and the world persisted, even when the cloister, like Oneida, is cheerfully hedonistic? What is the relevance of utopian organization in an era of large-scale enterprise and government?

The first disadvantage is that of scale. A utopia cannot be very large, if its members are not to have competing affiliations. The utopian formula is applicable only to small settlements, although these may combine into larger federations. All four of our specimen cases belong to federations—the Benedictines have hundreds of houses, Hutterite villages are units of a brotherhood, Oneida had several branches, every kibbutz is federated. The extension of utopian organization on a very large scale, although somewhat unlikely, is not inconceivable.[49]

[48] External conflict is not incompatible with utopian organization. Military orders such as the Knights Templars loom large in the early history of Christian monasticism. Some of the kibbutzim are frontier defense units.

[49] Note the Chinese attempt in the late 1950's to reorganize agricultural villages into quasi-utopian collectives. This program appears to have had mixed success without acquiring a definite utopian character. See W. R. Geddes,

Another drawback is that the time and energy spent by the utopian organization on its own maintenance is disproportionate to its resources. The rituals, the convocations, the ceremonies, the long indoctrination, the punishment of minor deviations, the conservation of obsolete methods and ideas, are all very costly. Oneida, it is true, was eventually successful in its manufacturing ventures, but it had the benefit of a large initial investment and unusual technical talent. Even so, income appears to have risen sharply when the community was converted into a stock company and relieved of some of the burden of maintaining its utopian structure. Convents and monasteries are usually not self-supporting, and depend on contributions of outside capital. The kibbutzim have been continuously subsidized by contributions from abroad. Despite very arduous efforts, their standard of living is still rather low. The prosperity of the Hutterites rests on the acceptance of austere conditions as well as hard work and thrift.

Aside from the direct costs of internal maintenance, utopian organizations tend to be inefficient because achievement is not stressed. The problem of maintaining integration and voluntarism at very high levels takes precedence over problems related to achievement. Utopian experiments in urban factories have been short-lived and rather pathetic.[50]

A utopian organization needs an overwhelming incentive. It is misleading to discuss our utopias in terms of structure alone. Their members are animated by a powerful faith—in Perfectionism, in the mystical body of Christ, in Zionism, in the Moravian Creed. They subordinate themselves to the organization for the sake of a goal that takes precedence over any other. Each of these movements is universalistic in its intentions, if not in its program. The improvement of each utopian colony is identified with the betterment of the great world. Its time perspective extends far beyond the individual lifespan—backward into a glorified past, and forward into an idealized future.

Present Life in Communist China (Ithaca, N.Y.: Society for Applied Anthropology, 1963), for one of the few available accounts.

[50] Watson Thomson, *Pioneers in Community* (Toronto: Ryerson Press, 1949), especially the history of the Columbia Conserve Company.

CHAPTER NINE

Organized Conflict

THE PROBLEM OF CONFLICT

Conflict is the central problem of human society. It has always been so, but in our time it assumes a special urgency because the survival of mankind probably depends upon the development of better means for the resolution of conflict than are now available. These means may, conceivably, be discovered by sociological analysis. The work that has so far been done is altogether trivial compared to the universal emergency confronting us, but it is better than nothing at all.

The discussion of conflict in this chapter is limited to situations in which the antagonistic parties are organizations. Many phenomena that are commonly described as conflict do not fall within the scope of this definition, for example the tension of inconsistent motives within the individual, family discord, population pressure, race prejudice, and intellectual debates.[1]

Even with these exclusions, organizational conflict is a very complex phenomenon. Sociological textbooks, following Park and

[1] Current theories of conflict do not distinguish sharply between organizational conflict and other forms. See, for example, Kenneth Boulding, *Conflict and Defense: A General Theory* (New York: Harper, 1962), and Anatol Rapoport, *Fights, Games and Debates* (Ann Arbor, Mich.: University of Michigan Press, 1960). The former work contains separate chapters on the individual, the group, and the organization as parties to conflict. The latter is explicitly addressed "to any serious student of human conflict on the intrapersonal, interpersonal, organization, social or international level" (p. vii).

Burgess,[2] have distinguished conflict from competition and cooperation, but it is one of the commonplaces of social science that these processes form a continuum. Coser quotes four of the founding fathers of American sociology—Cooley, Small, Ross, and Sumner—to this effect.[3] A hundred years before, Clausewitz insisted that "war is only a part of political intercourse, therefore by no means an independent thing in itself." [4] Georg Simmel, who first outlined the theory of organizational conflict, laid great stress on the point that conflict sustains and facilitates cooperation, and he showed what this involves. Some cooperation between antagonists is required in order to stage a fight, and, conversely, a struggle for advantage always takes place when two groups cooperate. Virtually every conflict of organizations involves some external scarce goal over and above the mutual animosity of the parties. In virtually all competitive situations, some degree of hostility develops between the competitors as soon as they are aware of each other's existence.

Scarcely an author who has written on this subject has failed to propose a typology of conflict. Rose writes: "A survey of historical and contemporary group conflicts suggests the following working classifications: (1) political, or conflict over scarce values; (2) ideological, or conflict over ways of life; and (3) racist, or conflict over biological dominance." [5] This is a classification by the bone of contention. A classification by common sense categories would include wars, feuds, strikes, elections, field games, commercial rivalries, bureaucratic intrigues, schisms, gang fights, conspiracies, litigation, rebellions, revolutions, *coups d'état,* community controversies, and many miscellaneous forms. Conflicts may also be classified as violent or nonviolent, by the degree of external regulation, by whether the goals are aggressive or accumulative, and as limited or total.

There have been several attempts to adapt Kurt Lewin's model of psychological tension to group conflict. Levinger [6] describes relation-

[2] Robert E. Park and Ernest W. Burgess, *Introduction to the Science of Sociology* (Chicago: University of Chicago Press, 1921).

[3] Lewis A. Coser, *The Functions of Social Conflict* (Glencoe, Ill.: Free Press, 1956).

[4] Carl von Clausewitz, *On War* (new and rev. ed.; London: Kegan Paul, Trench, Trubner, 1911), III, 121.

[5] Arnold M. Rose, *Sociology: The Study of Human Relations* (New York: Knopf, 1956), p. 506.

[6] George Levinger, "Kurt Lewin's Approach to Conflict and Its Resolution: A Review with Some Extensions," *Conflict Resolution,* Vol. I, No. 4 (December, 1957).

ships involving compatible goals as "plus-plus conflicts" or trade relationships and those having incompatible goals as "minus-minus conflicts" or fight relationships. The third type of relationship suggested by the topological model is "plus-minus conflict," in which the individual is both attracted and repelled by the forces emanating from the same region.

Andrzejewski, in a chapter entitled "Omnipresence of Struggle," brings together the whole range of conflict behavior in the assertion that "the struggle for wealth, power and prestige . . . is the constant feature of the life of humanity. . . . [W]hether we like it or not the fact is that no society, no group however small has ever been heard of where such a struggle would be altogether absent." [7]

Rapoport [8] makes an interesting distinction among fights, games, and debates. In fights, the object is to harm, destroy, subdue, or drive away the opponent. In games the opponent is an essential part of the situation, rather than a nuisance, and he is seen as a mirror image who has similar but incompatible interests. In debates the object of each party is to persuade, rather than to harm or outwit, the other.

In recent years, game theory has been the preferred model for conflict analyses in the United States. Game theorists classify a conflict situation by the mathematical model used to analyze its strategy. Indeed, this sort of classification is the principal device for applying game theory to real conflicts.[9] The fundamental dichotomy is between zero-sum games—what one player wins the other loses—and non-zero-sum games, which involve some element of mutual dependence. The limiting case of the non-zero-sum game is the pure cooperation game, which has been extensively studied and found to have all sorts of unexpected properties, such as the possibility of reaching agreement without any communication at all. The most interesting recent discussions of conflict strategy focus on what Schelling calls bargaining or mixed-motive games, which contain elements of both conflict and mutual dependence. Virtually all or-

---

[7] Stanislaw Andrzejewski, *Military Organization and Society* (London: Routledge & Kegan Paul, 1954), p. 7. Anthropological evidence for this assertion may be found in L. T. Hobhouse, "Pattii, Peace and Order Among the Simplest Peoples," *British Journal of Sociology,* Vol. VII, No. 2 (June, 1956).

[8] Rapoport, *op. cit.,* Introduction.

[9] John McDonald, *Strategy in Poker, Business and War* (New York: Norton, 1950).

ganizational conflicts fall into this category when considered strategically.[10]

Another interesting taxonomy was derived by Ephron [11] from the works of sociological theorists. Although intended to apply only to organizational conflict between component units of a larger organization, it is probably capable of being extended. The three models of conflict are the *administrative model,* which involves mutual dependence on limited resources and interdependence of the timing of activities, the *political model,* which involves resistance to authority and the measures taken to overcome it, and the *coercion model,* which centers on the incompatibility of interests and values between the conflicting parties.

What is there in this diversity that enables us to talk intelligibly about organizational conflict in general? Georg Simmel, the first sociologist to answer this question in detail, did so with his usual mixture of razor-edged insight and discursiveness. Simmel's contributions to the theory of conflict have been codified in a remarkable essay by Coser, in which he discusses and rephrases propositions drawn from Simmel's work.[12] Not all of these propositions are relevant to our present inquiry. Both Coser and Simmel take conflict in a broader sense than we do here and devote a good deal of attention to the class struggle. The most important of the relevant propositions are these:

> Conflict with other groups contributes to the establishment and reaffirmation of the identity of the group and maintains its boundaries against the surrounding social world. . . . Aggressive or hostile "im-

10 The best single discussion is Thomas C. Schelling, "The Strategy of Conflict: Prospectus for a Reorientation of Game Theory," *Conflict Resolution,* Vol. II, No. 3 (September, 1958). Other relevant papers appear in almost every issue of the same journal.

11 Lawrence R. Ephron, "Group Conflict in Organizations: A Critical Appraisal of Recent Theories," *Berkeley Journal of Sociology,* Vol. VI, No. 1 (Spring, 1961). The administrative model is credited mainly to James G. March and Herbert A. Simon, the political model to Philip Selznick, and the coercion model to Rolf Dahrendorf. A parallel treatment of conflict within a bureaucratic structure is Eugene Litwak, "Models of Bureaucracy Which Permit Conflict," *American Journal of Sociology,* Vol. LXVII, No. 2 (September, 1961).

12 Georg Simmel, *Conflict,* trans. Kurt H. Wolff (Glencoe, Ill.: Free Press, 1955), and Coser, *op. cit.* The propositions that follow are taken from Coser, and each sentence is a direct quotation, although they are not continuous in the original.

pulses" do not suffice to account for social conflict. Hatred, just as love, needs some object. Conflict can occur only in the interaction between subject and object: it always presupposes a relationship. . . . Realistic conflict need not be accompanied by hostility and aggressiveness. "Tensions" in the psychological sense are not always associated with conflict behavior. . . . Greater participation in the group and greater personality involvement of the members provide greater opportunity to engage in intense conflicting behavior and hence more violent reactions against disloyalty. It is in this sense that intense conflict and group loyalty are two facets of the same relation. . . . A conflict is more passionate and more radical when it arises out of close relationships. The coexistence of union and opposition in such relations makes for the peculiar sharpness of the conflict. Enmity calls for deeper and more violent reactions, the greater the involvement of the parties among whom it originates. . . . Loosely structured groups and open societies, by allowing conflicts, institute safeguards against the type of conflict which would endanger basic consensus and thereby minimize the danger of divergences touching core values. The interdependence of antagonistic groups and the criss-crossing within such societies of conflicts . . . "sew the social system together" by cancelling each other out, thus prevent disintegration along one primary line of cleavage. . . . Groups . . . not involved in continuous struggle with the outside . . . are more likely to be large. Such groups are able to resist outside pressures successfully by exhibiting elasticity of structure and allowing an area of "tolerated conflict" within. . . . Groups engaged in continued struggle with the outside tend to be intolerant within. They are unlikely to tolerate more than limited departures from the group unity. . . . The only way they can solve the problem of dissent is through the dissenter's voluntary or forced withdrawal. . . . Rigidly organized struggle groups may actually search for enemies with the deliberate purpose or the unwitting result of maintaining unity and internal cohesion. . . . The evocation of an outer enemy or the invention of such an enemy strengthens social cohesion that is threatened from within. Similarly, search for or invention of a dissenter within may serve to maintain a structure which is maintained from outside. Such scapegoating mechanisms will occur particularly in those groups whose structure inhibits realistic conflict within. . . . Conflict with another group leads to the mobilization of the energies of group members and hence to increased cohesion of the group. Whether increase in centralization accompanies this increase in cohesion depends upon both the character of the conflict and the type of group. Centralization will be more likely to occur in the event of warlike conflict and in differentiated structures requiring marked division of labor. . . . Despotism seems to be related to lack of cohesion; it is required for carrying out hostilities where there is insufficient group solidarity to mobilize energies of group members. . . . Conflict consists of a test of power between antagonistic parties. Accommodation between them is possible only if each is aware of the relative strength of both parties. However, paradoxical as it may seem, such knowledge can most frequently be attained only through conflict since other mechanisms for testing the respective strength of antagonists seem to be unavailable. . . . If a relative balance of forces exists between the two parties, a unified party prefers a unified opponent.

The central theme that runs through this theory is that conflict can unify social groups as well as destroy them.[13] It is the indispensable process for the maintenance of boundaries. The threat of conflict reinforces the structure of the organizations involved by immediate preparatory increases in stratification, integration, voluntarism, and, often, the achievement of nonconflict goals. Simmel also sees conflict as a means of adjustment and distribution, the indispensable instrument for ascertaining the relative strength of two organizations and allocating scarce resources between them. The benefits of conflict account for the tendency of organizations to seek out new antagonists, to encourage the unification of enemy groups, and even to invent imaginary enemies when real ones are scarce. Most of the propositions we have omitted have to do with a set of consequences more or less beneficial to individuals. The expression of antagonism releases destructive impulses and permits the reestablishment of relationships threatened by an accumulation of hostile feelings.

[13] The classic American expression of this viewpoint was Sumner's:
> The relation of comradeship and peace in the we-group and that of hostility and war towards others-group are correlative to each other. The exigencies of war with outsiders are what make for peace inside, lest internal discord should weaken the we-group for war. . . . Loyalty to the group, sacrifice for it, hatred and contempt for outsiders, brotherhood within, warlikeness without—all grow together, common products of the same situation.

William Graham Sumner, *Folkways* (Boston: Ginn, 1906), pp. 12–13, 1940 edition. A greatly expanded statement of this position is contained in the section on "Antagonisms" in Chapter 14 of William Graham Sumner and A. E. Keller, *The Science of Society* (New Haven, Conn.: Yale University Press, 1927).

Simmel's ideas are extremely perspicacious, and they serve to correct the curious view of conflict as a psychological aberration that sometimes finds its way into sociological textbooks. They do not go very far, however, toward enabling us to evaluate the consequences of an organization's involvement in a particular conflict in a given set of circumstances. To do this requires a kind of empirical evidence that, until recently, was not available and is still very scarce.

CASE STUDIES

Until about 1950 case studies of conflict situations by sociologists were almost unknown.[14] Since that time, there has been a great upsurge of interest—related to, but not wholly explained by, the wholesale involvement of social scientists in nuclear strategy—and we now have a fair assortment of empirical case studies. Only a few of them, however, enable us to follow changes in the variables of conflict from point to point or to observe the immediate effects of tactical decisions.

There is a massive and rapidly growing literature on war as a social phenomenon,[15] and there are many studies of soldiers and their special occupational problems,[16] but there is still no sociological analysis of a battle to be had, although several historic battles have recently been reconstructed in unprecedented detail.[17]

[14] Jesse Bernard, "Where Is the Modern Sociology of Conflict?" *American Journal of Sociology*, Vol. LXVI, No. 1 (July, 1950). The only important exception at the time was the case study of a strike included in the Yankee City investigation, and that was centered on the historical background rather than the sequence of events. W. Lloyd Warner and J. O. Low, *The Social System of the Modern Factory* (New Haven, Conn.: Yale University Press, 1947).

[15] See especially Quincy Wright, *A Study of War* (Chicago: University of Chicago Press, 1942), and Lewis F. Richardson, *Statistics of Deadly Quarrels* (Chicago: Quadrangle Press, 1960).

[16] Besides the landmark study by Samuel A. Stouffer et al., *The American Soldier* (Princeton, N.J.: Princeton University Press, 1949), Janowitz, writing in 1959, was able to cite more than a score of sociological reports on the U.S. armed services and others on foreign forces ranging from Germany to Malaya. Morris Janowitz, *Sociology and the Military Establishment* (New York: Russell Sage Foundation, 1959).

[17] Two distinguished examples of sociologically oriented battle histories are Cecil Woodham-Smith, *The Reason Why* (New York: Dutton, 1960), on the Charge of the Light Brigade, and Garrett Mattingly, *The Armada* (Cambridge, Mass.: Riverside Press, 1959), on the naval battle of 1588. The major battles of the American Civil War have been described in closer detail

The material on political contests is a good deal fuller than that on war. There are a number of thorough, excellent studies of electoral campaigns and parliamentary episodes.[18] We have a number of empirical studies of bureaucratic conflict,[19] but almost nothing on commercial rivalry or athletic contests.[20] The effects of victory and defeat on the internal structure of a football team are still as unknown to social science as the demography of Mars. A number of community controversies have been reported and analyzed in full detail.[21] There are a few recent studies of the mechanisms of re-

than any other large-scale events in human history. See, among almost innumerable other works, Bruce Catton, *Glory Road* (Garden City, N.Y.: Doubleday, 1952), Clifford Dowdey, *Death of a Nation* (New York: Knopf, 1958) and *High Tide at Gettysburg* (Indianapolis, Ind.: Bobbs-Merrill, 1958), all of which contain extensive bibliographies on the battle of Gettysburg.

[18] Especially R. B. McCallum, *The British General Election of 1945* (New York: Oxford University Press, 1948), Bernard R. Berelson, Paul F. Lazarsfeld, and William N. McPhee, *Voting: A Study of Opinion Formation in a Presidential Campaign* (Chicago: University of Chicago Press, 1954), Angus Campbell et al., *The Voter Decides* (Evanston, Ill.: Row, Peterson, 1954), W. H. Morris-Jones, *Parliament in India* (New York: Longmans, Green, 1957), Duncan MacRae, Jr., *Dimensions of Congressional Voting* (Berkeley, Calif.: University of California Press, 1958), Constantin Melnik and Nathan Leites, *The House Without Windows: France Selects a President* (Evanston, Ill.: Row, Peterson, 1958), Eugene Burdick and Arthur Brodbeck (eds.), *American Voting Behavior* (Glencoe, Ill.: Free Press, 1959), Georges Dupeux, *Le Front Populaire et les Elections de 1936* (Paris: Armand Colin, 1959), Paul F. Lazarsfeld, Bernard Berelson, and Hazel Gaudet, *The People's Choice* (New York: Columbia University Press, 1960), W. J. Mackenzie and K. E. Robinson, *Five Elections in Africa* (Oxford, Eng.: Clarendon Press, 1960), Paul Tillett (ed.), *Cases on Party Organization* (New York: McGraw-Hill, 1963).

[19] Elliot Jaques, *Changing Culture of a Factory* (New York: Dryden, 1952), Philip A. Selznick, *TVA: The Grass Roots* (Berkeley, Calif.: University of California Press, 1949), Marshall E. Dimock, *Administrative Vitality* (New York: Harper, 1959), Harrison White, "Management Conflict and Sociometric Structure," *American Journal of Sociology*, Vol. LXVII, No. 2 (September, 1961), Melville Dalton, *Men Who Manage* (New York: Wiley, 1959).

[20] For the first modest approaches to the sociological analysis of team sports, see Oscar Grusky's forthcoming papers and Dale Ordes and Fred Suffet, "Tendencies Toward Deviance in Competitive Sports," Columbia University, *G. S. S. Journal*, Vol. II, No. 1 (December, 1962).

[21] For a summary of those published before 1957, see James S. Coleman, *Community Conflict* (Glencoe, Ill.: Free Press, 1957). The most informative single study of a community controversy is Martin Meyerson and Edward C. Banfield, *Politics, Planning and the Public Interest* (Glencoe, Ill.: Free Press, 1955).

bellion,[22] a small but growing literature on the modes of conflict in simple societies,[23] and a handful of experimental studies, notably by Sherif.[24]

The problems of studying conflict situations objectively at close range are formidable.[25] Timing is critical. In unscheduled conflicts, such as riots and political crises, the investigator does not know when or where to anticipate the occurrence of his subject matter. Even if he is able to get to the site in time, it is difficult for him to plan for the observation of a sequence of events the schedule of which is unknown. Revolutions, for example, do not wait upon the observer. Crucial events often happen very fast. Direct observation is difficult and more subtle methods of study may be out of the question.

Another obstacle to the empirical study of conflict is a feature of the phenomenon itself. As a situation of this kind moves toward its climax, neutrals are excluded. Their presence compromises secrecy and reduces internal integration. Objectivity, however inconspicuous, is a threat to the insulation of an embattled group. These objections obtrude even when the investigator or the research team is

22 Notably Alexander H. Leighton, *The Governing of Men* (Princeton, N.J.: Princeton University Press, 1945), and D. J. Goodspeed, *The Conspirators* (New York: Viking, 1961).

23 Summarized in the special issue of the *Journal of Conflict Resolution,* Vol. V, No. 1 (March, 1961) on *The Anthropology of Conflict.* The value of intercultural comparisons is shown by several of the included papers, especially Igor Kopytoff, "Extension of Conflict as a Method of Conflict Resolution Among the Suku of the Congo," and N. A. Scotch, "Magic, Sorcery and Football Among the Urban Zulu." See also Peter Matthiessen, *Under the Mountain Wall* (New York: Viking, 1962).

24 Muzafer Sherif, Jack B. White, and O. J. Harvey, "Status in Experimentally Produced Groups," *American Journal of Sociology,* Vol. LX, No. 4 (January, 1955); Muzafer Sherif, "Superordinate Goals in the Reduction of Intergroup Conflict," *American Journal of Sociology,* Vol. LXIII, No. 4 (January, 1958); Muzafer Sherif, *Intergroup Relations and Leadership: Approaches and Research in Industrial, Ethnic, Cultural, and Political Areas* (New York: Wiley, 1962); and Muzafer Sherif et al., *Intergroup Conflict and Cooperation: The Robbers' Cave Experiment* (Norman, Okla.: University of Oklahoma Institute of Group Relations, 1961).

25 But not insuperable. Similar problems beset disaster research, in which, nevertheless, there has been a notable series of empirical studies. See Allen H. Barton, *Social Organization Under Stress: A Sociological Review of Disaster Studies* (Washington, D.C.: National Academy of Sciences—National Research Council, 1963) and George W. Baker and Dwight W. Chapman (eds.), *Man and Society in Disaster* (New York: Basic Books, 1962).

willing to confine its efforts to a single side. They become nearly insuperable when it is proposed to observe both sides simultaneously. The mere establishment of a line of communication between the enemy camps is perceived as a danger by the combatants, and this perception is probably not unsound. Hence, those few studies which contain first-hand accounts of conflict situations have been produced by participants whose objectivity cannot be definitely established. Some, like Leighton and Meyerson, were administrators actively involved in the situations they report. Jaques was the head of an action research team working to solve the problems described. Only Sherif and his associates,[26] whose hostile groups of campers had been created experimentally, could combine objectivity with unlimited access to both camps. In the face of these barriers, it is perhaps remarkable that anything at all has been discovered about organized conflict, however meager our present knowledge may seem.

THE VARIABLES OF CONFLICT

A conflict relationship between two organizations resembles a cooperative relationship in that the parties have equal or unequal power to influence each other's activity, remain aware of each other and in contact for the duration of the relationship, and develop sentiments toward each other in accordance with the expectations of the larger system in which the relationship occurs. The two relationships differ in ways that can be conveniently expressed by a change of sign. Achievement in a cooperative relationship is measured by progress toward common goals. Conflict efforts are directed toward mutual hindrance. Similarly, cooperation is facilitated by effective communication between the parties, and conflict is facilitated by insulation of the parties from each other's influence. The sentiments that support cooperative activity are predominantly (although not entirely) friendly. The sentiments that sustain conflict are predominantly hostile.

In the next few pages, we shall try to sketch out a very tentative model of conflict based on four SIVA variables. Like our previous models of cooperative activity and similar in form, this model too is

---

[26] Sherif, White, and Harvey, *op. cit.*, and Sherif et al., *op. cit.*

conceived to be culture-free and applicable to organizational conflict regardless of time or place, to have "stability in the small" without "stability in the large" and to enable us to make useful but imperfect predictions about events in the real world.

As a mnemonic device, the four variables of the conflict model are denoted by terms having the same initial letters as those used to describe the dimensions of cooperation. We shall discuss conflict between organizations in terms of Subjugation, Insulation, Violence, and Attrition.

Subjugation denotes the quantitative difference, however measured, between the ability of organization A to interfere with the program of organization B and B's ability to interfere with A's program, when A and B are in contact and have incompatible goals. Like status, it represents a difference in the ability of the parties to influence each other and control each other's behavior.

Insulation, as a variable, measures the extent to which communications between organizations in conflict (and between their respective components or members) are blocked. This is achieved in various ways—by forbidding that messages be sent or received, by cutting available channels of communication, by mistranslating and distorting messages, or by punishing communicators. The immediate product of insulation is dissensus between the organizations in conflict about something or somebody in their perceptual field. The effects of insulation exactly reverse the effects of interaction.

Violence, as a variable, is a measure of the overt hostility that each organization develops toward the other. It may be conceived as a sum of negative valences.[27] Sentiments, of course, can be experienced only by individuals—although they can be attributed to collectivities. The level of violence in a conflict indicates the extent to which members of the conflicting organizations have come to hate each other as individuals.

---

[27] This meaning of *violence* differs somewhat from its common meaning but is by no means unprecedented. Compare the following: "Nonviolence never calls for destroying an invader. . . . It seeks to destroy his motivation (his patriotic justification) by dealing fairly with him. In this it may be contrasted with violence, which characteristically refuses to grant any merit to the opponent and by its very nature unleashes its own injustice on the innocent and guilty alike within the enemy country." D. Dellinger, quoted in *Current,* No. 34 (February, 1963).

Attrition is the cost of a conflict to the protagonists, measured by the price of the damage they inflict on each other. Depending upon the type of conflict, attrition may be measured in lives or goods or prestige or any other scarce and valued resource. Like activity in the cooperative model, attrition is a measure of output, *not* input. As our era knows so well, the invention of new weapons can increase attrition in a spectacular way without much increase in cost.

The conflict model, like the model of cooperation, is concerned with relationship and, in its present form, ignores differentials between the parties, without supposing that they are nonexistent or trivial. The level of violence in one party may be quite different from that in the other. One side may be better insulated than the other. The burden of attrition may weigh more heavily on one of the parties than on the other. These differences are recognized but left out of account for the time being.

In this respect, too, the conflict model resembles the model of cooperation. In the former, with status equal to zero, the two members of the interacting pair tend toward symmetrical patterns of interaction, valence, and activity. As S increases, their differentiation on each of these dimensions increases also. Similarly, when conflicting organizations are evenly matched and subjugation is equal to zero, the two parties will not ordinarily show much differentiation with respect to insulation, violence, or attrition. As S increases, the implications of the conflict become more and more dissimilar for the protagonists. Richardson's theory of war,[28] which is centrally concerned with differential values of what we have called subjugation, insulation, violence, and attrition, presents substantial evidence that such differences are important. Boulding,[29] considerably influenced by Richardson, proposes the matrix analysis of differentials among nations with respect to the three dimensions of strength–weakness, exclusiveness of territorial occupation, and hostility–friendliness, which seem to be precisely equivalent to S, I, and V.

Table 9–1 gives a rough typology of antagonistic relationships between organizations, based on a dichotomous classification of insula-

[28] Richardson, *op. cit.*
[29] Kenneth E. Boulding, "National Images and International Systems," *Journal of Conflict Resolution*, Vol. III, No. 2 (June, 1959). See also his *Conflict and Defense, op. cit.*

Table 9–1

A ROUGH TYPOLOGY OF ANTAGONISTIC RELATIONSHIPS
BETWEEN ORGANIZATIONS

	INSULATION	VIOLENCE	ATTRITION
Conflict	high	high	high
Accommodation	high	high	low
Competition	high	low	high
Disorder	low	high	high
Exploitation	low	low	high
Prejudice	low	high	low
Coexistence	high	low	low
Peace	low	low	low

tion, violence, attrition—in each case as high or low. Without finer measurements than high and low, the typology does not allow us to classify particular cases, but it does show the kinds of transformation that are likely to occur. For example, starting with a peaceful relationship, a rise in attrition leads to exploitation, a rise in both attrition and insulation to competition and a rise in all three variables to conflict. Similarly, a sufficient decrease in attrition transforms conflict to accommodation; a decline in both attrition and violence leads to coexistence and a further decline in insulation culminates in the blessed condition of peace.

Table 9–2 presents the fundamental relations of the SIVA model of conflict in their barest form. The necessary assumptions are that:

1. Insulation, violence, and attrition are each a function of the others when subjugation is zero, that is, when the opposing parties are evenly matched. An increase in subjugation tends to decrease insulation and attrition but has an indeterminate effect on the level of violence. The reason for this indeterminacy is that increased subjugation simultaneously multiplies the opportunities for violence and its hazards.

2. An increase in insulation, other things being equal, is followed by a reduction of subjugation or an increase of violence or an increase of attrition.

Table 9–2

A MODEL OF ORGANIZATIONAL CONFLICT

DIRECTION OF CHANGE	RESULTING TENDENCY *			
	SUBJUGA-TION	INSULA-TION	VIOLENCE	ATTRITION
Subjugation plus	—	minus	indeterm.	plus
Subjugation minus	—	plus	indeterm.	minus
Insulation plus	minus	—	plus	plus
Insulation minus	plus	—	minus	minus
Violence plus	indeterm.	plus	—	plus
Violence minus	indeterm.	minus	—	minus
Attrition plus	plus	plus	plus	—
Attrition minus	minus	minus	minus	—

* In one variable at a time, holding the others constant.

3. An increase of violence has an indeterminate effect on subjugation, but tends to increase insulation or attrition.
4. An increase of attrition, other things being equal, will be followed by a decrease of subjugation or an increase of insulation or an increase of violence.
5. The greater the subjugation in a conflicting pair, the less insulation will accompany a given amount of attrition and the less change in insulation will follow a given change in attrition. Conversely, if subjugation is increased, the amount of attrition associated with a given degree of insulation will also increase.
6. An increase of violence is also anticipated when either attrition or insulation is increased, but we cannot predict, without more information, the effect of an increase in subjugation on an existing level of violence.

PATTERNS OF CONFLICT

There have been a number of attempts to work out typical patterns of conflict and to improve the predictability of outcome for particular struggles. Perhaps the most useful classification of conflict for our present purposes is by the underlying pattern of the conflict situation itself. In another context, I have tried to present a classification of conflict situations as *episodic, continuous,* and *terminal,* noting that the most probable strategy followed by the members of a triad in seeking coalitions will differ sharply among these conditions.[30]

In *episodic* conflicts, the contest for power continues over an extended time, the means of conflict are determined in advance, and the object of struggle is to secure an advantage in distributions of reward that occur periodically and under predetermined conditions. Episodic conflicts occur on schedule and are subject to regulation either by superior authority or by agreement of the parties. Elections exemplify this type of conflict. So do athletic contests and some forms of collective bargaining.

In *continuous* conflicts, the object of struggle consists of rewards that are found within the situation, such as ordinary commercial rivalry. There are no scheduled episodes of conflict, and the means to be used are not specified in advance. Continuous conflict is unspecialized and limited in scope. It often occurs between organizations in a set. Examples are bureaucratic rivalry, competition among oligopolists, and international relations in peacetime.

In *terminal* conflicts, the object is a single redistribution of power. The outcome is conceived as permanent because it disables or dissolves one of the parties or leads to some accommodation that precludes continuation of the conflict. The best example and the most important case is war between sovereign national states. Other examples are community controversies, feuds, and revolutions.

The distinction among conflicts arose originally out of the analysis of coalition formation, when a triad consisting of three unequals, no one of which is greater than the other two combined, was used to illustrate the strategy of coalition (Figure 9–1). The probable coalitions were at first supposed to be AC or BC, on the reasoning that A would seek to join both B and C, and C would seek to join both A and B, but B would have no incentive to enter a coalition with A, and A would have a very strong incentive to enter a coalition with C. After considerable laboratory experimentation, it became

[30] Theodore Caplow, "Further Development of a Theory of Coalitions in the Triad," *American Journal of Sociology,* Vol. LXIV, No. 5 (March, 1959).

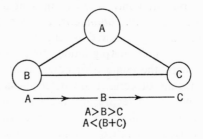

Figure 9–1

THE STRATEGY OF COALITION

evident that this strategy refers only to the continuous situation.[31] The episodic situation is resolved in a different fashion. All coalitions are equally advantageous. Since each episode of conflict is an independent event, no member of the triad can win without entering a coalition and any member is certain to win by entering a coalition with any other. Thus each member regards either coalition partner as equally advantageous and the three possible coalitions, AB, BC, and CA, are equally probable. In the terminal situation, when it is clearly recognized, it is unlikely that any coalition at all will be formed, since the object of a coalition would be to destroy the isolated member of the triad, and once this was accomplished, the weaker member of the triumphant coalition would be left at the mercy of the stronger. If the coalition of B and C is successful in partitioning A, it must be on the basis that C receives a share sufficiently larger to bring him up to dyadic equality with B, and so to avert the danger that once the coalition has completed the destruction of A, B will proceed to subjugate C. B, however, is unlikely to agree to a division of spoils that gives the lion's share to the initially weaker C, and it is therefore improbable that any coalition at all will be formed. This is one of the fundamental forms of the balance of power.

[31] The highlights of the discussion will be found in Theodore Caplow, "Theory of Coalitions in the Triad," *American Sociological Review,* Vol. XXI, No. 4 (August, 1956), and "Further Development of a Theory of Coalitions in the Triad," *op. cit.;* W. E. Vinacke and A. Arkoff, "An Experimental Study of Coalitions in the Triad," *American Sociological Review,* Vol. XXII, No. 4 (August, 1957); Sheldon Stryker and George Psathas, "Research on Coalitions in the Triad: Findings, Problems and Strategy," and Harold H. Kelley and

It is possible for the same pair of organizations to engage in episodic or continuous or terminal conflict, depending upon the circumstances. Under conditions we shall presently examine, one type of conflict may readily change into another. Even total war, the extreme case of the terminal situation, is no exception to this rule. Episodic war has occurred very often in history, as in the wars of the eighteenth century. Continuous conflict between armies, described as an uneasy truce or as guerrilla warfare, is a common occurrence in the modern world.

The factors that determine which type of conflict will take place between unions and management are analyzed in detail in Golden and Parker's collection of present case studies of thirty collective bargaining relationships characterized by episodic instead of continuous or terminal conflict.[32] Kerr remarks that:

> We do not find in this series of cases any of the following: Small, competitive employers and a dominant union which take advantage of an inelastic demand for the product or service to organize a collusive system to gouge the consumer [0]; or a group of miscellaneous or minor or occasional purchasers of a type of skilled labor who hire this labor according to a price list announced by the union [0]; or a union torn with internal factionalism or facing a life-or-death struggle with a competitive union [T]; or a casual labor market organized through a hiring hall [0]; or highly marginal firms [0]; or an industry of such importance to the public that its industrial relations are dominated by government boards [C]; or a national pattern-setting relationship [C].[33]

The items in the foregoing list marked "0" represent the absence of labor–management conflict; those marked "T" indicate situations of terminal conflict; those marked "C" show continuous conflict.

A. J. Arrowwood, "Coalitions in the Triad: Critique and Experiment," both in *Sociometry*, Vol. XXIII, No. 3 (September, 1960); William A. Gamson, "A Theory of Coalition Formation" and "An Experimental Test of a Theory of Coalition Formation," *American Sociological Review*, Vol. XXVI, No. 3 (June, 1961) and Vol. XXVI, No. 4 (August, 1961); Richard H. Willis, "Coalitions in the Tetrad," *Sociometry*, Vol. XXV, No. 4 (December, 1962); William H. Riker, *The Theory of Political Coalition* (New Haven, Conn.: Yale University Press, 1962).

[32] Clinton S. Golden and Virginia D. Parker (eds.), *Causes of Industrial Peace Under Collective Bargaining* (New York: Harper, 1955).

[33] Clark Kerr, "The Collective Bargaining Environment," in Golden and Parker, *op. cit.*, p. 21. I have added the markings in brackets.

The three types of conflict may also be distinguished in another way. If we visualize subjugation as ranging from zero, at which the opponents are evenly matched, to unity, at which one party is completely at the mercy of the other, then we observe that episodic conflict is characterized by fairly regular fluctuations of this variable, subjugation being close to zero at the beginning of each episode, rising close to unity at the end of each episode, and reverting to zero again for the beginning of the next episode. Continuous conflict, by contrast, occurs under circumstances in which the complete subjugation of either party is very unlikely—for example, in the rivalry of bureaucratic departments. Equality of strength is also unlikely in continuous conflict because of the structure of organizational sets. Hence, the history of a continuous conflict is usually characterized by irregular oscillations in intermediate values of subjugation. Terminal conflict is characterized by the expectation that subjugation will eventually lead to unity; that is, one party will be completely defeated and rendered incapable of further offensive action.

As might be expected from the model, the other variables follow parallel trends when we compare the three types of conflict within the same organizational set. Thus, insulation in episodic conflicts rises sharply at the beginning of each episode and falls at the end; in continuous conflict, insulation is lower but remains fairly constant; in terminal conflict, insulation seems to rise in the early stages while mobilization is still under way but falls sharply as the conflict nears its end. Violence is episodic in episodic conflict, moderate and fairly constant in continuous conflict, and likely to increase up to the end of a terminal conflict. Attrition in episodic conflict is virtually limited to the active episode; it is lower and more constant in continuous conflict; it usually rises throughout the course of a terminal conflict.

Although the direct evidence is much less than we really need, we turn now to analyze each type of conflict in greater detail, leaning on a small number of studies as well as some inferences drawn from general observation. If we lack reliable data on certain points, at least it is certain that everyone in our society has ample opportunity for participant observation of organizational conflict.

EPISODIC CONFLICT

Our central illustration of episodic conflict will be taken from Duverger's work on political parties.[34] He begins by noting that parties in the modern sense are a modern phenomenon the origins of which go back no further than the nineteenth century. The term covers a number of distinct organizational types, including the middle-class party, the activity of which is entirely directed toward elections and parliamentary alliances; the mass party (like European socialists), the disciplined dues-paying members of which are organized into large local branches with extensive programs of extrapolitical activity; and the totalitarian party, which is highly stratified, autocratically controlled, and based on small, well-integrated local cells. In addition to these major types there are a number of variants, such as labor parties that depend directly on union membership, agrarian parties, and "prehistoric parties," such as the feudal clans active in Arab politics.

The concept of party membership is surprisingly ambiguous. Most political parties are complex organizations; they do not have a single membership position common to all members. The primary distinction is between the party's voters and its cardholders. Among the cardholders, there are further distinctions between peripheral and militant, temporary and permanent, members. In a totalitarian party the obligations of membership are very extensive. There is a cadre of "devotees," for whom the party's interests take precedence over all other claims. In a conventional party, activity is seasonal and intermittent, and the party is intended to serve the interests of its members.

All parties, it appears, are autocratic, although some are more autocratic than others.[35] The differences lie in the way the inner circle of leaders is selected, the degree to which power is personalized, and the extent to which control is exercised over members who occupy positions in the government. Control may range from the

[34] Maurice Duverger, *Les Partis Politiques* (Paris: Armand Colin, 1951); trans. as *Political Parties* (London: Methuen, 1954). See also his *Introduction à la Politique* (Paris: Gallimand, 1964). For a wide-ranging summary of other work in this field, see Seymour M. Lipset, "Party Systems and the Representation of Social Groups," *European Journal of Sociology*, Vol. I, No. 1 (1960).

[35] The classic statement of this point, of course, is Robert Michels, *Political Parties* (New York: Collier Books, 1963), originally published in 1911.

loose responsibility of parliamentary representatives in center parties to the rigid discipline of Communist representatives who are regarded simply as party agents and required to remit their official salaries to the party treasury.

The most important feature of a party *system* is the number of parties. The major types are the two-party, the multiparty, and the single-party systems. In a two-party system, one of the parties will have a majority of the votes in any election, but some alternation of majority control from one party to the other is anticipated. Duverger is able to show that this expectation is usually justified and that there are theoretical reasons why the power of either party tends to increase when it is in the minority. In multiparty systems, there is usually no single party with a majority, and governments are formed by coalitions. The single party is associated with dictatorship, although there are some exceptions. In the single-party system, significant political conflicts are displaced from the parliamentary chamber to the committees of the party.

Fundamentally, the political party is a group organized for the purpose of gaining power. Under a parliamentary democracy its purpose is to win elections. Only in this way can a party claim a share of governmental power, place its leaders in political offices, and advance the interests of its members. These objectives are pursued simultaneously by contending parties and therefore are inherently opposed; the same means for winning elections are employed by organizations whose goals are mutually incompatible. What succeeds for one must fail for the other. An election is a zero-sum game.

The maintenance of parliamentary legality is always an impressive achievement; it raises a fundamental question: What keeps the parties from destroying each other and the electoral system? The data suggest a number of general propositions about episodic conflict:

1. *Any system of episodic conflict must include devices for the quantitative measurement of organizational strength.* The outcome of an electoral contest is directly and unequivocally measured by the offices won. The result of any parliamentary episode is accurately reflected by counting votes. The quantification of strength in episodic conflict supports the rationality of organizational activity. Even individuals do not usually enter contests without estimating their chances of success. Organizations are enormously more variable than individuals in strength. It requires no complicated strategical analysis to explain why coastal freighters never attack enemy battle-

ships or why chiropractors do not form a political party of their own. The disparities of strength among organizations are often so great as to leave no conceivable doubt about what the result of a hypothetical conflict would be. Such conflicts are ordinarily avoided.

It is equally important, when an episode of conflict has been terminated, that the result be unequivocally ascertained. Otherwise, aggrandizement effects and simple self-interest lead to disagreement about the result, and the situation is readily transformed into continuous or terminal conflict. This often occurs in sandlot baseball games and South American elections.

The acceptance of scoring procedures is so universal that we are likely to forget its importance. For example, in any electoral system the procedure for assigning seats to the candidate or list of candidates with the most votes is absolutely fundamental and seldom questioned. Certainly, elections are rigged, votes are bought and sold and counterfeited, voters are coerced or intimidated; but none of these abuses ever brings into question the basic assumption that votes should be counted, district by district, and public offices assigned to the candidates who receive more votes. There is a similar lack of ambiguity with respect to the principle that the baseball team which scores the most runs wins the game, or that whoever controls a majority of the voting shares in a corporation is entitled to elect its directors.

There is another aspect of quantification that appears in high relief in the study of political parties. Different *methods* of counting not only lead to different outcomes but also modify the structure of the organizational set in which the episodes of conflict occur. It has long been known, for example, that the introduction of proportional representation in a two-party system will transform it into a multiparty system. Lipset supposes that much finer correlations can be worked out between electoral and party systems:

> If enough cases existed for analysis, the following rank-order correlation might be found between electoral system and the number of political parties: presidential system with single-member districts and one plurality election, tendency to two parties; parliamentary system with single-member districts and alternative ballot or run-off (second) election, tendency to many parties; proportional representation, many parties.[36]

[36] Lipset, *op. cit.*, pp. 14–15.

In sum, the organizational strength measured at the end of episodes of conflict is not an independent attribute but is always at least partly dependent on a particular mode of quantifying outcome.[37]

2. *The procedures appropriate for episodic conflict are peculiarly subject to the principle of limited possibilities. Similar procedures will appear in many different situations.* Murdock and others have proposed that similar social forms often recur in many independent settings because there may be only a few ways that a given human activity can be structured.[38] Descent, for example, may be reckoned through the father, the mother, or both; it is hard to visualize any other alternatives. The electoral process is an excellent example of the principle of limited possibilities. There are only a limited number of ways in which the rulers of a state can be appointed. The methods are subject to the additional qualification that the designation must be unequivocal, rapid enough to ensure continuity, and conformable to the existing class structure. The possibilities are still those outlined by Aristotle—monarchy, tyranny, aristocracy, oligarchy, and democracy. In a modern society without castes and without a dominant religious creed, it becomes difficult to justify the inheritance of office, and electoral consent comes to be as much a requisite for tyranny and oligarchy as for democracy.

It is particularly interesting to look at the three types of party system as examples of limited possibilities. The multiparty system corresponds to the possibility that no party can achieve a majority by itself. When any one party threatens to obtain a majority, the inducement for all other parties to form a coalition becomes very great. If this occurs, a temporary or permanent two-party system has been established.

---

[37] In the Robbers' Cave study, the experimenters were forced to manipulate the results of a series of episodic conflicts (team games, treasure hunts, and so forth) to prevent the subjugation of one team and the destruction of the experimental conditions. Sherif et al., *op cit.*

[38] "Where there are no practical limits to the variety of responses which people can make in particular situations, cultural forms can vary endlessly with little comparability between those of unrelated societies, with the result that satisfactory interpretation must depend very heavily upon historical investigation of local and regional influences. . . . The situation is quite different where there are practical limitations to the variety of responses which people can make. Under such conditions, cultural similarities will appear in many places irrespective of historical contacts, and the influences they exert on other aspects of culture can be treated as comparable." George P. Murdock, *Social Structure* (New York: Macmillan, 1949), p. 115.

The two-party system represents the possibility that political strength is divided in such a way that each party has a realistic chance of obtaining a majority in any election without being strong enough to obtain permanent control of the government or to destroy the other. If these conditions break down, because one of the parties has obtained a permanent advantage, a one-party system appears, corresponding to the possibility that the conflict for power by electoral means has been permanently resolved. Electoral choice is then rendered meaningless, and the arena of political conflict is transferred to the inner councils of the surviving party.

Similar limitations of possibilities can be traced out for athletic contests and other forms of episodic conflict. For example, basketball among the ancient Maya was remarkably similar in its details to the game played by modern high school teams.

3. *Any system of episodic conflict is based upon the overlapping polarization of interests.* What this means is that although organization A opposes organization B with respect to goal X during an episode of conflict, some members of A are allied with some members of B with respect to another goal, Y, and some members of A are allied with other outsiders in opposition to their fellow members of A, with respect to still another goal, Z. Duverger points out, as many others have done, the tendency for any conflict to become dichotomous so that ". . . the centre does not exist in politics: there may well be a Centre party, but there is no centre tendency, no centre doctrine." [39]

He maintains the paradox that the natural movement of societies is toward a two-party system, although multiparty systems are far more common. Where two-party systems exist, as in the United States, each party includes a wide range of inconsistent attitudes and interests. The overlapping of polarizations accounts for both of these phenomena. Divisions of opinion on one issue do not correspond with divisions of opinion on other issues. The polarizations of opinion in American politics overlap to such an extent that it is very difficult to find *any* issue on which all Democrats agree while disagreeing with all Republicans. The polarization on any single major issue never follows party lines exactly, but at the same time the distributions of opinion within the two parties are never identical. In a multiparty system in which a number of major issues divide

[39] Duverger, *op. cit.*, p. 215.

the electorate, but each issue divides them differently, these discrepancies become the basis of party identification.

> The multi-party system in France is a result of the non-coincidence of the main cleavages in opinion . . . If all Frenchmen were in agreement in holding that the antagonism East vs. West took precedence over all others, then there would be only two parties: Communists and Anti-Communists . . . If on the other hand they thought that the Clerical vs. Anti-Clerical issue was basic, as is still held in some corners of France, then there would be only two parties: Catholics and Freethinkers (there was a trend towards this at the beginning of the century). It is on the contrary the very fact that some emphasize the Freedom vs. Planning issue, others the Clerical vs. Anti-Clerical, and yet others the East vs. West that maintains multi-partism.[40]

There is always the lively possibility, of course, that crosscutting will go too far and undermine the party system by providing alternative ideological positions for party leaders on every issue. There would then be a sharp decline of reciprocal commitment between each party's leaders and its electors,[41] and the parties would begin to disintegrate.

Whenever one of the opposing parties in a system of episodic conflict finds itself opposed to another on all possible issues, there is no reason why it should not attempt the destruction of the other and it can be expected to do so.[42] As soon as the divisions cease to correspond with the polarization of interests on *any* important issue, however, neither party can destroy the other without jeopardizing some of the interests of its own members. The growth of nationalism permitted the evolution of parliamentary democracy in the first place by giving all the factions in the state the common interest of opposition to other states. This balance was threatened—in theory but not in practice—by nineteenth-century socialist parties, which were internationalist rather than nationalist in principle, and much more seriously by the emergence of Communist parties with foreign allegiances.

---

[40] *Ibid.*, pp. 231, 233. Note that these comments refer to the Fourth Republic, which broke down when one issue—the Algerian war—took precedence over all others.

[41] This too occurred under the Fourth Republic. See Nathan Leites, *On the Game of Politics in France* (Stanford, Calif.: Stanford University Press, 1959).

[42] The case is not unusual. Lipset cites the first Austrian republic, postwar Italy, and South Africa as examples of political lines following lines of general social cleavage. Lipset, *op. cit.*, p. 30.

Totalitarian regimes generally refuse to recognize any polarization of interests and thereby convert their parliamentary assemblies into audiences for rites of solidarity.

In the modern Western-style state, conflict between organizations with incompatible goals is held in check by the specificity of each contest and the overlapping of affiliations—what Georg Simmel called the cross-stitching of social lines. Enemies on one issue are allies on another, and members of out-groups are simultaneously members of in-groups. This overlapping polarization of membership is the basis of any society, large or small, but although the biological and cultural requirements of small societies assure an appropriate over-lap (men against women on some questions, but children against parents on others), a large-scale society cannot be sure of prevent-ing that consistent polarization of interests and opinions that pro-duces two parties bent on mutual destruction.

4. *Episodic conflict is carried on under explicit—usually written—rules accepted by all participants.* The rules of episodic conflict are usually followed much more meticulously than the rules promulgated for the internal government of the organizational protagonists. They equalize the strategies of the contestants by limiting the weapons they may employ. It is by observance of the rules that episodic conflict is prevented from changing into continuous or terminal conflict. Conformity to the rules is a steady signal that each party accepts the same limitations on aggressive activity, but a violation of the rules puts the other party on notice that the agreements that limit violence and attrition are breaking down. The rules are also themselves legiti-mate means of conflict. They are interpreted literally, and compliance to the letter may be demanded by an opponent. Manipulation of the rules, knowledge of unfamiliar rules, and unexpected application or exceptions are legitimate tactical weapons on the athletic field, in the law courts, at the bargaining table, or in parliamentary maneuvers.

The rules governing episodic conflict are often promulgated by the larger organization the components of which are involved (as the state controls elections) or by an organization specifically created for the purpose of promulgating rules (such as the rules committee of a legislative chamber). Some enforcement agency is almost indis-pensable if the conflict involves large-scale organizations or continues for a considerable time. However, it is notable that rules of episodic conflict can be accepted and enforced by the parties themselves without any recourse to higher authority. This occurs in private athletic contests and in millions of commercial disputes that are never taken to court.[43] Typically, in these cases, the rules accepted are those that have been promulgated for *other* contestants by an enforcement agency.

5. *The emotional effects of episodic conflict tend to be specific to the episodes.* Conflict is accompanied, as everyone knows, by violent sentiments directed toward the enemy, the neutral, the ally, the traitor, and even inanimate aspects of the environment. It is often associated with transformations of values and perspective, causing information to be interpreted in a special fashion, distinct from the perceptions of everyday life. When these effects occur in episodic conflict, they are usually specific to the episodes. Compartmentalization is normal rather than exceptional.[44] Tremendous enthusiasms are generated in the course of an electoral campaign. On the morning after the results are announced, it is often difficult to find a trace of them. The country is threatened with disaster if the opponent wins, but the threat somehow vanishes at the moment of his victory. Even organizational membership may be specific to the episode itself. Some of the most vigorous partisans in a presidential election are unable to identify themselves as Republicans or Democrats between election years. Insulation between opponents, which has risen very high toward the end of the episode, reverts to its normal level almost immediately after.

6. *There appear to be compensating reactions to victory and defeat in episodic conflict that have the general effect of maintaining the equality of the combatants.* The evidence is plainly inadequate, but it appears from casual observation that in cases of episodic conflict the effect of a victory is to decrease the incentives of the victors and to increase those of the losers with respect to the next episode. The party that has lost an election is likely to approach the next

[43] The procedures used are described by Stewart Macaulay, "Non-contractual Relations in Business," *American Sociological Review,* Vol. XXVIII, No. 1 (February, 1963).

[44] This is certainly related to specificity of goals. More than 90 percent of all strikes, for example, have wages, hours, or working conditions as the ascertainable, principal issue. See Ross Stagner, *The Psychology of Industrial Conflict* (New York: Wiley, 1956), p. 423. Dubin has proposed that concentration on fundamental or conventional issues in a company–union conflict can be predicted from the initial disparity of power between the parties. Robert Dubin, "A Theory of Conflict and Power in Union–Management Relations," *Industrial and Labor Relations Review,* Vol. XIII, No. 4 (July, 1960).

campaign with more vigor than the winning party. The defeated football team may be expected to put in longer hours of practice in preparation for its next game than if it had been successful.

These statements require careful qualification. If the difference in strength between the parties is excessive and the victory is overwhelming, the defeated party may be permanently discouraged. Then, too, the successful party may have won because of its superior methods of preparation for a contest, and these may not be much affected by victory or defeat. However, the differential response of victor and vanquished makes itself felt in most systems of episodic conflict, tending to equalize the strength of the parties and to stabilize their relationship. Note, for example, the more-than-random occurrence of very close elections in the United States. The 1960 presidential election was decided by a margin of less than 1 percent, and the 1962 gubernatorial election in Minnesota was decided by fewer than 100 votes.

7. *Episodic conflict is usually gratifying both to participants and to spectators.* This feature of sports, elections, legislative contests, bargaining sessions, and other episodes of conflict is easily overlooked in analyzing these events, but it is crucial for understanding them. The episodic conflicts that arise in nearly every organizational set are not merely tolerated; they are encouraged and pursued with enthusiasm.[45] The function of organized sports in the urban life of great civilizations has scarcely been investigated except for certain marginal issues, but it is plain that the common forms of episodic conflict are not perceived as social problems. Unlike continuous and terminal conflict, episodic conflict is valued in and for itself. The excitement it produces is pleasurable; its pains are transitory, and it cannot be plausibly explained in terms of frustration and aggression.[46]

8. *In episodic conflict, the success of a given tactic is not predict-*

[45] Needless to say, with more enthusiasm in some cultures than in others. Abundant evidence bearing on the cultural conditioning of episodic conflict may be found in Ruth Benedict, *Patterns of Culture* (Boston: Houghton Mifflin, 1934), David McClelland, *The Achieving Society* (Princeton, N.J.: Van Nostrand, 1961), and Everett E. Hagen, *Social Change* (Homewood, Ill.: Dorsey, 1962).

[46] The frustrated and aggressive delinquents studied by McNeil are not at all interested in episodic conflict, although he finds them to have a whole arsenal of devices for terminal conflict. Elton B. McNeil, "Personal Hostility and International Aggression," *Journal of Conflict Resolution,* Vol. V, No. 3 (September, 1961).

able in advance. Each move by either party involves a prediction of the response the opponent will make. If the move is effectively planned, it will be successful despite the opponent's resistance, *if* the manner of his resistance has been correctly predicted. It therefore becomes part of the opponent's program to act otherwise than anticipated. His ability to do so depends in part upon his success in predicting the prediction that the initiator made concerning his own response. The initiator will want to predict this prediction of his own prediction in order to counter it. With each succeeding term of this series, the margin of error increases.

There is nothing unusual about this sequence. It is taken for granted in an individual contest such as a prize fight or a chess match. The contestant who makes a feint cannot know in advance what the response of his opponent will be unless he knows whether the feint will be identified as such. He cannot know this unless his prediction of the opponent's response is accurate. Whatever methods he uses to make his prediction are ordinarily available to his opponent to replicate the process. If the opponent correctly predicts the prediction, he will modify his own response so as to nullify it. Tactics consist largely of self-defeating prophecies.

It may be argued against this principle of indeterminacy that a political party or a football team often succeeds in predicting the moves of an opponent, and of course this is true. The indeterminacy applies to the prediction at the time it is made. In any given contest, a substantial number of predictions will be correct, but there is no way of distinguishing these from incorrect predictions in advance. *Consistently* reliable predictions can be made only when one party to a conflict has completely subjugated the other.

The practical implication is that there can be no "scientific" solution to a tactical problem. The responses of opponents must necessarily be included in such a solution but are necessarily unknown at the time the solution is proposed. Hence, no determinate probability can be assigned to the outcome. The theory of games is concerned with the logic of conflict,[47] and its elegant mathematical apparatus is used to assign probabilities to the various choices and combinations

[47] The fundamental introduction to game theory is John von Neumann and Oskar Morgenstern, *Theory of Games and Economic Behavior* (Princeton, N.J.: Princeton University Press, 1947). For discussion of its applicability to "real life" episodic conflict, see McDonald, *op. cit.,* Jessie Bernard, "The

of choice presented to the "players" in the course of the "game." A game is any episode of conflict involving two or more parties having opposed interests, a range of choices prescribed by rules, and a method of assigning payoffs to each party under each of several predicted outcomes.

Game theory is most illuminating in zero-sum games [48]—when the interests of the parties are symmetrically opposed, so that A's gains are B's losses, and in games of perfect information, in which all possible moves are known in advance. The object of game theory is to assign determinate probabilities to the various choices and combinations of choices presented to the players in the course of the game. In other words, it may be used to ascertain which of several alternative strategies will enable a side to maximize its probable gain or minimize its probable loss or maximize a sum that represents gain minus loss. However, except for certain explorations in military strategy that are shrouded in secrecy, the theory of games has not yet had much effect upon the actual conduct of episodic conflicts, although it is often theoretically illuminating.

The reason why its practical usefulness is so limited is that certain of its requirements may not be met in the situations we want to analyze. First, it must be possible to assign numerical values (or payoffs) to every possible outcome. Second, the probability of any outcome must be known. Third, the maximization of outcome probabilities times values must be the goal of the strategist. He must not be willing to take risks for the sake of a greater gain.

Early in the discussion of game theory, Bernard,[49] summarizing a paper by Neisser,[50] commented:

Theory of Games of Strategy as a Modern Sociology of Conflict," *American Journal of Sociology,* Vol. LIX, No. 5 (March, 1954), and Anatol Rapoport, "The Use and Misuse of Game Theory," *Scientific American,* December, 1962.

[48] Despite the heroic efforts of Schelling, Jacob Marschak, Harsanyi, and others to focus attention on non-zero-sum games involving bargaining and cooperation. See especially Thomas C. Schelling, "For the Abandonment of Symmetry in Game Theory," *Review of Economics and Statistics,* Vol. XLI (1959) and John C. Harsanyi, "On the Rationality Postulates Underlying the Theory of Cooperative Games," *Journal of Conflict Resolution,* Vol. V, No. 2 (June, 1961).

[49] Bernard, *op. cit.* The quotation is from page 423.

[50] Hans Neisser, "Strategy of Expecting the Worst," *Social Research,* Vol. XIX (September, 1952).

As Neisser has pointed out, the theory of games would not be useful to a player in a game where even the best he could hope for on the minimax or maxmin principle was death. Suppose, for example, that the payoff function were of such a nature that his choice was (a) death by torture or (b) death by euthanasia or (c) escape with no shame attached to it. Suppose the minimax theory came up with an optimal strategy of (b). The best he could safely hope for was a comfortable death. The odds against choice (c) would be great, according to minimax; he could win only if his opponent made a wrong play. In such a payoff situation it would not be rational to settle for the safest bet. The "rational" thing would be to take the slender chance that one's opponent would make a mistake.

Rapoport, in a brief but extraordinarily lucid exploration of the limits of game theory, analyzes the plot of Puccini's opera *Tosca* as a non-zero-sum game to illustrate a fundamental shortcoming of the strategies derived from game theory:

> . . . the chief of police Scarpia has condemned Tosca's lover Cavaradossi to death but offers to save him in exchange for Tosca's favors. Tosca consents, the agreement being that Cavaradossi will go through a pretended execution. Scarpia and Tosca double-cross each other. She stabs him as he is about to embrace her, and he has not given the order to the firing squad to use blank cartridges. . . .
>
> The result is the denouement we know. Though both minimize their losses, *they both lose*. Had they kept trust with each other, they would not have won as much as possible, but *both would have won*.[51]

He concludes that the important contribution of game theory is to show that the "hard-headed" analysis of conflict comes to an impasse unless the situation is reformulated in another context and the players perceive the need to adopt common values, improve their communication, and subject themselves to a set of rules that recognize their overriding common interest and substitute mutual trust for the fierce rationality of the game theorist.

This is in fact the function of systems of episodic conflict and helps to explain why the establishment of such a system is often perceived by the participants as a solution to the problems posed by continuous or terminal conflict. A summary of the common characteristics discovered in successful bargaining relationships, that is, those estab-

[51] Rapoport, *op. cit.*, 1962, p. 113.

lished as episodic, shows vividly the advantages that accrue to both sides.

There is full acceptance by management of the collective bargaining process and of unionism as an institution. The company considers a strong union an asset to management.

The union fully accepts private ownership and operation of the industry; it recognizes that the welfare of its members depends upon the successful operation of the business.

The union is strong, responsible, and democratic.

The company stays out of the union's internal affairs; it does not seek to alienate the workers' allegiance to their union.

Mutual trust and confidence exist between the parties. There have been no serious ideological incompatibilities.

Neither party to bargaining has adopted a legalistic approach to the solution of problems in the relationship.

Negotiations are problem-centered—more time is spent on day-to-day problems than on defining abstract principles.

There is widespread union-management consultation and highly developed information sharing.

Grievances are settled promptly, in the local plant whenever possible. There is flexibility and informality within the procedure.[52]

The essentials of episodic conflict are shown very nicely by this list. Both sides are strong and secure, neither side feels its existence threatened by collective bargaining, moderate insulation is established without espionage or boundary threats, the conflict is centered on differences of interests rather than differences of value, the means of conflict are well defined, and the level of violence is very low.

CONTINUOUS CONFLICT

Continuous conflict, or rivalry, is the most interesting, the most universal, and the least understood form of the conflict situation. In continuous conflict, which usually extends over a considerable period, the timing of aggressive action is relatively unimportant and the means are not specified. The struggle involves realistic goals for each group. Polarization is profound. Strategies are more subtle and complex than in situations of episodic conflict.

[52] Charles A. Myers, "Conclusions and Implications," in Golden and Parker, *op. cit.,* p. 47.

The balance of power. What we have called the situation of continuous conflict is the normal peacetime relationship among sovereign states—the continuation of war by diplomatic means. In the era of large-scale nationalism, playful contests of strength in the medieval manner are out of the question. The choice lies between continuous and terminal conflict, and the path that slopes down to terminal conflict is slippery. As Wright points out in a notable chapter,[53] the assumptions of balance-of-power diplomacy are that every sovereign state tends to impose its will on every other and is not affected by any considerations of law or morality or alliance, that military strength is easily mobilized and precisely measurable, that statesmen pursuing such a policy will measure the factors involved with accuracy and guide their behavior accordingly.

Given these assumptions, Wright sets out the following postulates:

> Stability will increase and the probability of war will decrease in proportion as the number of states in the system increases.
> Stability will increase as the parity in the power of states increases.
> Stability will be promoted by a moderate separation of states from one another.
> Stability will be promoted by certainty as to the states which enter into the equilibrium.[54]

He comments that the tendency to localize relations is equivalent to reducing the number of states and that any grouping into durable coalitions has the same effect, so that policies of either neutrality or permanent alliance make for instability.

The balance of power between two unequal states, he says, is the most precarious. Among a large number of states having approximately equal power, it is virtually unshakeable. Complete isolation, such as might be achieved by impenetrable barriers along every frontier, would lead to complete stability—but in that case there would be no balance of power. Short of isolation extreme separation of states makes for instability because other states are unable to respond quickly to an attack on a weaker state. Minimum separation also contributes to instability because it lowers boundaries and reduces each state's independence of action. If it is not known which states are within the system and which are outside, no accurate cal-

---

[53] *A Study of War, op. cit.,* Vol. II, Chapter 20.
[54] *Ibid.,* pp. 755–56.

culation of strength is possible and the entire situation becomes unstable.

Balances of power tend to be destroyed by disturbing societal changes, such as the rise of conquerors, the invention of new weapons, the propaganda of new creeds, and the intervention of outside states. Wright comments that efforts to assure international stability as well as efforts to organize an international rule of law not dependent on military strength have developed out of the balance of power itself.[55]

Similar principles apply to situations of continuous conflict other than international relations. One can speak meaningfully of the balance of power among competing bureaucratic agencies, between the two houses of the same legislature, among churches in the same town, or among departments of the same faculty. In all of these cases, attrition is minimized and violence is reduced as the number of organizations in the set increases, as they approach parity in power, if they are moderately insulated from each other, and if the intervention of outsiders is minimized.

The essential function of continuous conflict is boundary-maintenance. The rivalry among the organizations in most sets is a normal and perennial condition, not a pathological disturbance. The boundaries of related organizations that remain in continuous contact cannot be successfully maintained without some degree of conflict. Only if each organization constitutes an in-group for its members against the surrounding out-groups can the boundaries be sufficiently defended for the organizational program to be carried out. But this assertion leads to very complicated questions of proportion and degree. How much conflict, it may be asked, is required to maintain a boundary under given conditions? How much boundary-maintenance does an organization of a given type require?

Such calculations are obviously not easy; but they can perhaps be approached from the postulate—related to our previous postulate of resistance to status loss—that *any organization in a set will resist an increase in its subjugation by any other member of the set or a decrease in its subjugation of any other member of the set.*

In the hypothetical situation in which two organizations in the

---

[55] Various ingenious approaches are described in Quincy Wright, William M. Evan, and Morton Deutsch (eds.), *Preventing World War III* (New York: Simon and Schuster, 1962). See also Frederick H. Gareau, *The Balance of Power and Nuclear Deterrence* (Boston: Houghton Mifflin, 1962).

same set could not conceivably modify their relative strength or have their strength modified by outside forces, the amount of attrition required to maintain the boundary between them would be zero, and insulation and violence would be fixed at low levels. As the probability of variation in subjugation increases, the amount of attrition required to maintain the boundary increases correspondingly, until it reaches a point at which either party undertakes to destroy, disable, or annex the other, and the situation changes to terminal conflict. The rate at which this point is approached, and the levels of attrition, insulation, and violence at various points along the curve, are determined by the cost of shifting the affected boundaries, the resources at the disposition of the two organizations, and their internal equilibriums.

An impressive empirical demonstration of the boundary-maintaining effect of continuous conflict is provided by Rose's study of ninety-one voluntary associations, of which twenty-four were in contact with opposing groups in the same community, forty-eight with competitive but not opposing groups, and nineteen had neither opposers nor competitors. The evidence supports his hypotheses that "Groups faced with opposition are more active in pursuit of group goals than are groups faced only with competition, and the latter are more active than groups that are faced with neither opposition nor competition," and that "Groups faced with opposition are more likely to develop a complex structure than are groups faced only with competition, and the latter have more structure than groups that are faced with neither opposition nor competition." [56]

Situations of continuous conflict are marked by the partition of goals. It is usually possible in a situation of continuous conflict to identify at least three sets of goals: those shared by both sides, those which differentiate the two sides, and those disputed between them. In the usual case, goals are related to organizational boundaries. The differing goals are specific to the units in conflict, the disputed goals pertain to a parent organization or an organizational set including both parties, and the shared values are drawn from some other situation of continuous conflict in which they find themselves in the same camp, or at least on the same side of a boundary. For example, the distinctive goal of the "Dixiecrat" movement, as described by Lem-

[56] Arnold M. Rose, "Voluntary Associations Under Conditions of Competition and Conflict," *Social Forces,* Vol. XXXIV, No. 2 (December, 1955), 160.

mon,[57] was segregation, and this differed sharply from the civil-rights platform supported by the majority of the Democratic party. The disputed goals are those of the party tradition, going all the way back to the states' rights principle embodied in the Democratic party platform of 1840. The shared goals imply opposition to southern (but not northern) Republicans.

In the struggle for loyalties, recruits, and resources that is characteristic of continuous conflict, goals are likely to be tossed back and forth in unexpected ways. A number of observers have commented on the tendency for hostile organizations to adopt each other's values. This is readily understandable. Continuous conflict involves both an effort to shift boundaries and a resistance to the shift. Value orientations favorable to the aggressor are likely to have some usefulness for the aggressee also. Some studies of concentration camps report that inmates ". . . adopt[ed] the value system and mode of behavior of their jailors. Callousness towards suffering and death, willingness to mistreat others, exploitation and corruption became, in various degrees, the accepted mode of behavior for well-adapted prisoners." [58]

Aggression and defense. We do not have quite enough evidence to assert that there is always an aggressor in a situation of continuous conflict, but it appears probable. In this respect continuous conflict is in sharp contrast to episodic conflict, in which no aggressor can ordinarily be distinguished, and terminal conflict, in which the initiative changes from side to side. It might perhaps be most accurate to speak of offensive and defensive positions. Here again, the model of boundary maintenance is useful. Continuous conflict involves an attempt to shift boundaries to the advantage of an *initiating* organization. Despite occasional reversals, constellations of strength are often stable enough to make the offensive and defensive positions permanent. Thus, in the concentration camps just mentioned, the guards are perpetually on the offensive, the inmates on the defensive. In balance-of-power situations in the history of modern Europe, it has been possible at almost any moment to distinguish between those

[57] Sarah McCulloh Lemmon, "The Ideology of the 'Dixiecrat' Movement," *Social Forces*, Vol. XXX, No. 2 (December, 1951).

[58] Theodore Abel, "The Sociology of Concentration Camps," *Social Forces*, Vol. XXX, No. 2 (December, 1951), 154. This finding has been disputed, however.

powers interested in the revision of boundaries and those devoted to the maintenance of the status quo.[59] In Dimock's case study of expanding jurisdiction in the War Shipping Administration,[60] it is clear that the agency he describes was on the offensive in all of its interagency relationships. In Morris-Jones' summary [61] of the developing conflict between the two houses of the Indian Parliament, it is the lower house that questions the privileges and discusses the abolition of the upper, while in White's *Citadel*,[62] it appears clearly that the interaction between the two chambers of the American Congress is so arranged as to keep the House of Representatives perpetually on the defensive. Even in a situation where the initiative seems to flicker back and forth, as in the struggle between the Communist party and the Red army after the death of Stalin,[63] a closer examination reveals the army fixed in a defensive role.

Perspective distortions. Those associated with continuous conflict are varied and spectacular. They can be explained in a general way by the extensive communication that is usually maintained in these situations,[64] by the complex pattern of overlapping goals, by the presence of numerous neutrals, intermediaries, and marginal participants whose support is uncertain, and by the somewhat schizoid character that such conflicts have for participants who have internalized both the disputed and the shared goals—for example, the bureaucratic intriguer who is a patriot at the same time. Dimock, in the study just mentioned, avers that "It requires men of considerable breadth and perspicacity, therefore, to draw the discreet line

[59] For a thorough elaboration of this statement see Lewis F. Richardson, *Arms and Insecurity: A Mathematical Study of the Causes and Origin of War*, ed. Nicholas Rashevsky and Ernesto Trucco (Pittsburgh: Boxwood Press, 1960).

[60] Marshall E. Dimock, "Expanding Jurisdictions: A Case Study in Bureaucratic Conflict," in Robert K. Merton et al. (eds.), *Reader in Bureaucracy* (Glencoe, Ill.: Free Press, 1952).

[61] Morris-Jones, *op. cit.*

[62] William S. White, *Citadel* (New York: Harper, 1956).

[63] Leon Goure, "The Army: Russia Five Years After Stalin," *The New Leader*, June 9, 1958.

[64] For an interesting study of communication in a continuous conflict situation, see Norman R. Jackman, "Collective Protest in Relocation Centers," *American Journal of Sociology*, Vol. LXIII, No. 3 (November, 1957), 264–72.

between what is socially useful and what is merely a consequence of vanity and combative instincts." [65]

Arnold, in a classic passage, proposes that "Institutional creeds, such as law, economics, or theology, must be false in order to function effectively. This paradoxical statement means that they must express contradictory ideals, and must authoritatively suppress any facts which interfere with those ideals." [66] Elsewhere in his long essay, which defies summarization, Arnold describes two perspective distortions that occur in continuous conflicts. The first of these is personification—the tendency to think of the opposing organization as if it were a person and as if it had human sentiments and reactions. The extent to which this delusion may go is always astounding when the examples are drawn from conflicts in which we ourselves are not involved. Its mildest form is the assumption, almost unavoidable even by sophisticated antagonists, that all members of the enemy think and respond alike. Personification is often more literal than this and the enemy organization is visualized as an evil giant.

The other distortion of perspective that has important tactical consequences is the imputation of evil motives to all acts of the out-group and of virtuous motives to all acts of the in-group. Rapport provides a nice illustration in an account of conflict between town and gown in a New England college community.

> Some years ago, "the college" was accused of taking no interest in town affairs. When a few members of the faculty interested themselves to the extent of running for office as members of the school board or for other minor offices, the tune changed to one charging an attempt to dominate town affairs.[67]

A whole series of ominous examples can be drawn from Holsti's study of the belief system of John Foster Dulles. The following is typical:

> A year later, when questioned about the Soviet plan to reduce their armed forces by 1,200,000 men, he quickly invoked the theme of the bad faith of the Soviet leadership. After several rounds of

[65] Dimock, *op. cit.*, pp. 290–91.

[66] Thurman Arnold, *The Folklore of Capitalism* (New Haven, Conn.: Yale University Press, 1947), pp. 356–57.

[67] Victor A. Rapport, "Conflict in a New England College Town," in Edgar A. Schuler (ed.), *Outside Readings in Sociology* (New York: Crowell, 1956), p. 734.

questions, in which each reply increasingly depreciated the value of the Soviet move in lowering world tensions, he was asked, "Isn't it a fair conclusion from what you have said this morning that you would prefer to have the Soviet Union keep these men in their armed forces?" He replied, "Well, it's a fair conclusion that I would rather have them standing around doing guard duty than making atomic bombs." [68]

Initially, this double-valued orientation seems to develop partly as a sensible precaution against the maneuvers of the enemy and partly as a device for reinforcing insulation. The ultimate effects go much further by assuring that all out-group acts will be perceived as hostile gestures. Thus, hostility increases with every increase of interaction, nullifying the contrary tendency of rising interaction to lessen hostility and introduce "superordinate goals."

The amelioration of continuous conflict.   This problem appears daily in hundreds of different settings, and especially in the higher reaches of giant organizations, in which the rivalry of component units threatens the over-all program. Industrial enterprises with warring subsidiaries, political parties that cannot hold their right and left wings together, denominations divided by chronic schism, government departments that cannot keep the rivalry of their bureaus out of the newspapers, and bureaus the departments and branches of which lobby against each other—all tend to envisage the problem of amelioration in terms of organizational efficiency. The protagonists, particularly those on the defensive, define the problem in terms of self-defense. Continuous conflict is easily transformed into terminal conflict. An uneasy truce may be the prelude to total war. Competition between two evenly matched enterprises may end with the ruin of both. Techniques of mediation are not nearly as well developed here as in the more spectacular arenas of terminal conflict, and there is a great demand for them.

Some hopeful conclusions about amelioration are, however, drawn by Sherif from his summer camp experiments.

[68] Ole R. Holsti, "The Belief System and National Images: A Case Study," *Journal of Conflict Resolution,* Vol. VI, No. 3 (September, 1962). For a broader description of distorted perspectives in Soviet-American relations see Urie Bronfenbrenner, "The Mirror Image in Soviet-American Relations: A Social Psychologist's Report," *Journal of Social Issues,* XVII (1961).

1. When groups in a state of conflict are brought into contact under conditions embodying superordinate goals, which are compelling but cannot be achieved by the efforts of one group alone, they will tend to co-operate toward the common goals.

2. Co-operation between groups, necessitated by a series of situations embodying superordinate goals, will have a cumulative effect in the direction of reducing existing conflict between groups.

3. It is true that lines of communication between groups must be opened before prevailing hostility can be reduced. But, if contact between hostile groups takes place without superordinate goals, the communication channels serve as media for further accusations and recriminations.[69]

Studies of American race relations provide some further support for the hypothesis that a decrease of insulation between hostile groups, when the environing circumstances remain unchanged, is likely to intensify their conflict, while an increase in interaction in the pursuit of some common goal or the defense of the combined group against a common enemy is likely to lead to a swift diminution of hostility. This appears to have been the basis of the conspicuous success of the army's experiment in desegregating combat units in World War II, compared to the questionable results of previous desegregation efforts in training centers.[70]

Other methods of amelioration that have been proposed in the great debate on the prevention of World War III include disarmament, inspection, disengagement, occupation, nonviolent resistance, the exchange of hostages, exchange of leaders, mass psychotherapy, creation of an armed third force, the development of a common language, and the introduction of random settlement mechanisms. But on the whole, and despite scattered clues, we do not yet have enough knowledge about the amelioration of continuous conflict to discuss the subject intelligently.

[69] Sherif, "Superordinate Goals in the Reduction of Intergroup Conflict," *op. cit.*, pp. 355–56.

[70] David G. Mandelbaum, *Soldier Groups and Negro Soldiers* (Berkeley, Calif.: University of California Press, 1952).

TERMINAL CONFLICT

In terminal conflict the object of each organization is to destroy the other or to render it harmless—needless to say, they do not always succeed. Terminal conflict develops out of prior differences of interest. Each side is perceived by the other as critically threatening. Feelings are intense. There is little agreement about rules and a minimum of communication between the parties. The salient feature of terminal conflict is its tendency to get out of hand. Conflicts that begin as realistic struggles for economic advantages often turn into orgies of rage.[71] Partisanship becomes so intense that vital interests are sacrificed to press the fight. It is never easy to arrest terminal conflict at the exact point at which each party has as much to gain from a settlement as from a continuation of the struggle.

In terms of boundary maintenance, terminal conflict may be described as an attempt to destroy boundaries altogether or to render them ineffective. Unlike continuous conflict, in which there are usually well-marked offensive and defensive positions, each antagonist in terminal conflict normally conceives itself to be in the defensive position with the opponent as aggressor. Under certain conditions this illusion facilitates peace-making because each party sees itself as intolerably threatened and is not easily convinced that it appears threatening to the opposition. On the other hand, the bitterness that develops in the course of combat activities is reinforced by the conviction firmly held on both sides that the enemy gratuitously provoked the conflict. Unlike situations of episodic conflict, in which the feelings aroused in each episode are easily dissipated, or situations of continuous conflict, in which the level of hostility rises and falls with the rate of interaction, the hostilities generated in situations of terminal conflict often outlast the settlement and persist for generations.

The obvious example of terminal conflict is total warfare, but the category is not restricted to fights with deadly weapons. An industrial dispute such as the Kohler strike, in which the goal of each side is to ruin the other, is an excellent example of terminal conflict.

[71] Bouthoul describes war as a "rite of destruction" based on "the desire to kill and be killed." Gaston Bouthoul, "Fonctions sociologiques des guerres," *Revue Francaise de Sociologie,* Vol. II, No. 2 (April–June, 1961).

Most of the "community controversies" enumerated by Coleman [72] may be classified as terminal because of their nonrepetitive character and the attempt of each side to settle the controversy once and for all.

Mobilization. The timing of action is critical in terminal conflicts, which normally consist of a series of crises of increasing intensity leading to a major crisis of very brief duration which settles the issue by victory or stalemate. The strategy of terminal conflict turns on the timing of the decisive crisis. The weaker side can often defeat the stronger by concentrating its resources at the right time and place.

Although episodic and continuous conflicts reinforce organizational structure, they do not usually require mobilization on any notable scale. In terminal conflicts reorganization occurs repeatedly as each side attempts to maximize its combat potential. In community controversies, for example, opposition often begins between loosely organized factions, or even between unorganized groups. The first step in the crystallization of the conflict is the consolidation of these groups into stratified and integrated units. The faction that is unable to manipulate its own structure will probably lose. The tendency for the speed of mobilization to determine the issue is especially marked in terminal conflicts that have a revolutionary character. Coleman notes that many community controversies involve revolts against a local administration, and he outlines the following typical sequence of events. Similar sequences seem to occur in revolts and rebellions on a larger scale.[73]

> The administration in power becomes the defendant in the controversy which ensues.

[72] Including controversies between civic groups over the fluoridation of the water supply, the Norwalk, Connecticut, controversy over the plan of a veterans' organization to report to the F.B.I. the names of persons of whose politics they disapproved, the armed destruction of a political machine in Athens, Tennessee, by a determined group of veterans, the Pasadena controversy over school administration, the abandonment of the city manager plan in four cities, the movement against desegregation in Clinton, Tennessee, and a number of similar incidents. Coleman, *op. cit.*

[73] Goodspeed, *op. cit.* The sociological study of revolutions has been somewhat neglected in recent years, but see Lyford P. Edwards, *The Natural History of Revolution* (Chicago: University of Chicago Press, 1927) and Crane Brinton, *The Anatomy of Revolution* (New York: Norton, 1938).

A few active oppositionists, men who are continually in opposition, oppose the administration. These men are sometimes motivated by the hope of power, but often they are ideologically committed to a "cause."

A large group exists—often the majority of the people—who are ordinarily inactive, acquiescent to the administration, but not actively supporting it.

An active group exists, usually a minority of the population, who continually support administration policies, and who were responsible for putting the administration in office in the first place.

The large passive group, or a part of it, becomes active in one of two ways: (a) a change in the general climate of opinion, reinforced by national mass media and by current events, mobilizes certain basic values and dispositions (e.g., patriotism and resulting fear of subversion) which the passive majority has held continuously, but which have been dormant or (b) the ideologically-committed, active oppositionist is not able to use this new hostile atmosphere to gain his ends.[74]

Polarization.   There is a strong pressure in terminal conflict for the reduction of cross-cleavages, the abandonment of inconsistent affiliations, and so far as possible within the limits of the situation, the complete polarization of valences. Coleman quotes a mining camp jingle the theme of which is replicated in every terminal conflict.

> Down in Harlan County, there are no neutrals there
> You either are a union man or a thug, for H. H. Blair
> Which side are you on, man?
> Which side are you on?

During the wars of the eighteenth century, communication between scientists, correspondence among friends and relatives, commercial relations, and even tourist travel between the hostile countries continued. Modern warfare is conceived as terminal, not as episodic, and the state will go to any length in insisting on polarization. Perry [75] analyzes the subordination of family, professional, and occupational roles to the "role of the national" in wartime. He cites the case of the American relatives of an escaped prisoner of war who were

[74] Coleman, *op. cit.,* p. 8.
[75] Stewart E. Perry, "Notes on the Roles of the National: A Socio-psychological Concept for the Study of International Relations," *Journal of Conflict Resolution,* Vol. I, No. 4 (December, 1947).

sentenced to long prison terms for offering the fugitive the shelter of the family home and of the Philadelphia psychiatrists studied by Little and Strecker,[76] who said they would report a patient who violated a rule of the national code to the authorities despite the confidentiality of the doctor–patient relationship. (The proportion who would report ordinary felonies revealed by their patients was very much smaller.)

Ideological invention. The absence of common goals is a conspicuous feature of terminal conflict. Polarization often proceeds to the point at which any interest in common with the enemy is denied. The denial of common goals is most salient when the members of the antagonistic organizations have many shared experiences and affiliations. The rejection of identification must then be proportionately violent. Civil war, Simmel and Clausewitz agree, is more likely to be marked by atrocities and hatred than is war between traditional enemies. The same pattern may be observed in the terminal conflicts of politics, in which antagonism between former associates has a special bitterness.

The organization's need to differentiate its goals from those of the enemy leads to the development of marvelous ideologies, supporting an exclusive claim to symbols that otherwise might be disputed. The hysterical accusations, the wild misconstructions of fact, the queer logics of fanaticism that appear in the pamphlets of segregationists during a southern school crisis or in the speeches of eminent scholars during an international war reflect the attempt to polarize *all* valences in favor of the embattled organization.

Despotism. Among other changes in structure, the level of internal stratification may be expected to increase as a terminal conflict develops. Most democratic states develop traces of dictatorship in a major war. Indeed, the name and concept of dictatorship derives from a custom of the Roman republic whereby absolute power was invested in a magistrate when an enemy force approached the city and divested at the close of hostilities.

The purposes of raising stratification, of "tightening up discipline" as the organization moves into combat, are to raise the level of in-

---

[76] Ralph B. Little and Edward H. Strecker, "Moot Questions in Psychiatric Ethics." *American Journal of Psychiatry,* Vol. CXIII (1956).

ternal activity, to maintain insulation from the enemy, and above all to increase the *speed* of decision-making. On closer view, the effect of terminal conflict on the internal stratification of combatant organizations becomes a little more complicated. There is certainly no one-to-one correlation between stratification and any of the conflict variables. Mobilization usually involves an increase in stratification, but thereafter a number of other effects come into play.

1. An effective combat organization is composed of highly integrated primary groups that, with the passage of time, become increasingly autonomous and resistant to authority.

2. The increase in attrition during a terminal conflict tends to reduce the stratification of the organizations involved. The organizational structure is itself a consumable resource, often used up in the course of battle. A number of wartime studies suggest that continued exposure to the threat of combat ultimately leads to the structural disintegration of a combat unit, even if its resources in personnel and material are undiminished.[77]

3. The concentration of authority in a single powerful leader may seem at first to increase the total amount of stratification in the system, but its ultimate effect may well be in the other direction. The overwhelming authority of the tyrant nullifies status differences among his subordinates.[78] Even without a dictator, something similar occurs as authority is concentrated in a few active leadership positions.

Under the combined effect of these influences, the stratification of a combatant organization follows an uneven, and so far unpredictable, trend as the conflict proceeds. The case is different with respect to the exercise of power over neutrals, outsiders, and accessible components of the enemy (such as captured units). This tends to rise in the course of a conflict, so that the treatment of enemies and neutrals is almost always harsher at the end than at the beginning.

[77] "At some point continued exposure of any military group to stress begins to produce a weakening of primary group solidarity, and an undermining of organizational effectiveness." Janowitz, *op. cit.*, p. 73.

[78] This phenomenon is analyzed in Stanislaw Andrzejewski, *Military Organization and Society* (London: Routledge & Kegan Paul, 1954). See also J. A. A. van Doorn, *Een Sociologische Benadering van het Organisatieverschijnsel* (Leyden: Stenfert Kroese, 1956).

The spiral of ferocity. Dehumanization of the enemy is merely an aspect of other sociological processes in terminal conflict. The polarization of valences and the subordination of all affiliations that are not congruent with the disputed boundary drastically reduce the valences between individuals on opposite sides. With sufficient insulation, the motives of each side become unintelligible to the other while the increase of voluntarism helps to falsify each side's perceptions of its own motives. The enemy's threat to each individual separately, and to the organization as a whole, provokes and seems to justify violent reactions.

> The most common first reaction to threat is an unfortunate one— communication with the enemy ceases. The immediate effect of this withdrawal from direct contact with the opponent is to render the determinants of action as much a consequence of fantasy and fear as of an appraisal of reality. . . . Preparations for defense are always misinterpreted by the antagonist as preparation for attack and a vicious circle is closed.[79]

There appears a kind of interactive spiral in which the seriousness of the threat experienced by A induces him to extend somewhat the ferocity of the conflict by using means that were formerly prohibited or by disregarding rules previously accepted by both sides. If the disrupted agreement is not supported by outside authority but rests only on mutual advantage, its reason for existence disappears when either side ceases to accept it. The increase in A's ferocity is matched by B at the first opportunity. However, A's initiative will ordinarily have benefited its cause. Some time must elapse before the new weapons or the new rules can be countered by B. B is thus placed at a disadvantage. It can be conveniently overcome by a further increase in ferocity, for example by the abandonment of remaining restraints or by the introduction of newer weapons or strategems. And so on.

Coleman [80] describes the spiral of increasing ferocity in cases of community controversy as differences of opinion are converted into general quarrels.

> A third change in the nature of issues as a controversy develops is the shift from disagreement to antagonism. A dispute which

[79] McNeil, "Personal Hostility and International Aggression," *op. cit.,* p. 284.

[80] Coleman, *op. cit.,* pp. 10–11.

began dispassionately, in a disagreement over issues, is characterized suddenly by personal slander, by rumor, by the focusing of direct hostility. This is one of the most important aspects in the self-generation of conflict: once set in motion, hostility can sustain conflict unaided by disagreement about particular issues. The original issues may be settled, yet the controversy continues unabated. The antagonistic relationship has become direct: it no longer draws sustenance from an outside element—an issue. As in an argument between friends, a discussion which begins with *disagreement* on a point in question often ends with each disliking the other . . . [W]e associate with every person we know certain beliefs, interests, traits, attributes, etc. So long as we disagree with only one or a few of his beliefs, we are "divided" in our feelings toward him. He is not wholly black or white in our eyes. But when we quarrel, the process of argument itself generates new issues; we disagree with more and more of our opponent's beliefs. Since these beliefs constitute *him* in our eyes, rather than isolated aspects of him, his image grows blacker. Our hostility is directed toward him personally. Thus the two processes—the first leading from a single issue to new and different ones, and the second leading from disagreement to direct antagonism—fit together perfectly and help carry the controversy along its course.

Another example of the spiral is described by Kirkpatrick:

> The bombing of Germans was cruel and inhuman; our own bombing on a far vaster scale, resulting in casualties to women and children higher than we care to think about, we regard as justified because the Germans started it and because it seemed a means to end the war more quickly. The Germans could and did use the latter argument with the naive assumption that a war should end in a German victory. We, too, like a war to end, but with a victory of our own in-group. There are plenty of Americans who worried lest the destruction of German cities was not great enough to punish an enemy out-group. Had our own cities suffered comparable destruction we would develop, as did the Germans, an accentuated interest in a distinction between military and non-military objectives.[81]

When coupled with an advanced technology the spiral of ferocity makes conflict increasingly dangerous for the participants and ulti-

[81] Clifford Kirkpatrick, "Sociological Principles and Occupied Germany," *American Sociological Review,* Vol. XI, No. 1 (February, 1946), 69.

mately irrational. It is difficult to see what notion of self-interest justified the great expenditure of lives on the Western Front in 1916 and 1917 after the fundamental strategies of both the Allies and the Central Powers had been frustrated and all hope of an easy victory for either side was gone. Modern large-scale wars continue to the loser's point of exhaustion and even somewhat beyond that point, in a spirit of pure rage and hatred. The fear that humanity itself may be destroyed in a world war using fusion weapons is grounded on the empirical observation that the ferocity of war has increased steadily in this century. The German bombing that leveled the center of Rotterdam in 1940 was profoundly shocking to neutral public opinion. By the time of the Hiroshima bombing, five years later, the destruction of an entire city together with its population was widely regarded as a normal act of war. This sort of progression erodes whatever safeguards are available to contain terminal conflict. After the spiral of ferocity has run its course for a time, war is necessarily irrational in that attrition clearly exceeds any foreseeable gain, even for the victors.

Each succeeding conflict, of course, begins with those weapons and under those rules reached in previous conflicts between the same or related protagonists. Had there been no World War II, it might be supposed that the world would enjoy a safeguard—to the extent of the time required for the spiral—against the threat of general urban demolition. The extension of weapons is apparently irreversible. As soon as the first city had been destroyed by saturation bombing, saturation bombing became an accepted and expected method of war.

Continuous reorganization. All terminal conflicts are "total." When the future existence of the organization is at stake, none of the resources that could be useful in the struggle are spared. Existing organizational structures are part of these resources, and since they are available for expenditure, they are always subject to reorganization. There is usually some lapse of time between the moment when the need for reorganization appears and when it is undertaken. Perhaps the common trait of great strategical leaders is their speed in effecting reorganizations—both transitory, such as the relocation of a battle perimeter, and permanent, such as the simplification of a status order to increase the effectiveness of communication.

A terminal conflict always includes one or more crises that change the variables of the situation. Even if there is only one crisis, as in a war decided by a single battle, there will be at least two general reorganizations on each side: that which precedes the battle, and that which follows it. In a more extended struggle, reorganization becomes almost continuous.[82]

The most significant reorganization often occurs after the first crisis, when the issues have been selected and the initial values of the conflict variables can be estimated by the participants. The entire machinery of conflict seems to vanish on the morrow of peace. Violence gives way to fraternization; the integrated structures of the combatants explode into divergent fragments; dormant connections between the victorious and the vanquished reappear overnight. The issues of the conflict are suddenly incapable of arousing purposive activity. The change of perspective is often so radical as to drastically modify the outcome. After the defeats imposed on the South in 1865, the Central Powers in 1918, and the Axis in 1945, the settlements did not last longer than the wars themselves, some of the principal terms being abandoned in each instance within half a dozen years.

The organizational residues left in the wake of a terminal conflict often serve as nuclei for future conflicts of the same kind. The process is imperfectly understood, but it appears that the termination of conflict shatters the structure of the defeated organization and a different structure develops. It is usual for a cadre of diehards to resist the final settlement, whatever it is, and devote themselves to the goal of revising the outcome when they have regathered their forces. The history of the South since 1865 consists largely of such movements—from the first Ku Klux Klan of the 1870's to the White Citizens' Councils of the 1950's. The German general staff after 1918, the Bonapartists after 1815, and the Jacobites after 1688 are familiar examples, and history is crowded with others. There has hardly ever been a major political or economic or ideological conflict that did not leave embattled splinter groups of the defeated side, vowed to renew the struggle at some future time. There is hardly any heretical sect in the whole history of the Roman church, beginning with Arians, that is not represented by a cult in the modern

[82] For example, in the civil rights struggle of 1962–64.

world. The successive schisms of modern socialism have left a myriad of defeated sects all the way across the political spectrum. Diehard groups tend to be tough and resilient. The defensive measures necessary to ensure their survival in the first place protect them in milder times. They are generally conservative and their orientation to the past protects them against adaptation to the present. Surprisingly often, the diehards achieve their program and return to battle at the head of a mass movement.

No comparable ideology develops on the winning side. A number of factors tend to diminish the integration of the victors and their interest in protecting the terms of settlement. Except in those rare instances in which the defeated organization totally disappears, the victors are forced to abandon the violent attitudes toward the enemy developed in the course of the conflict, in order to resume normal relations. Moreover, the submergence of internal dissension during the conflict hastens the resumption of old feuds immediately afterward. The postwar politics of victor countries are intensely partisan.

Social change is often accelerated by victory, for example in the exploitation of newly acquired resources or by the discovery of new possibilities in the organizational structure. Conditions change more rapidly on the winning side than on the losing—organizational time, so to speak, moves faster—and the conflict is sooner left behind and forgotten. Finally, although the defeated side is usually neutralized for a while, the victorious organization readily becomes involved in new conflicts because its enhanced strength creates a danger for others or an opportunity for itself. It is likely to be mobilized for another struggle before the settlement of the original conflict has been worked out in detail.

Unless the victory has been unusually drastic these factors all work in the same direction. They increase the probability that the terms of settlement will be upset and that the defeated side, or some of its elements, will rise again over similar issues. Terminal conflicts, in any system, lead to other terminal conflicts. War breeds war, strikes cause strikes, feuds end in new feuds. The cycle continues until the underlying conditions are changed, either by the transformation of the conflict to episodic form, the disappearance of the parties, or their submission to a common authority.

Name Index

Subject Index